The Adventures of Ibn Battuta

The Adventures of Ibn Battuta

A Muslim Traveler of the 14th Century

UPDATED WITH A 2012 PREFACE

ROSS E. DUNN

UNIVERSITY OF CALIFORNIA PRESS
Berkeley · Los Angeles · London

Ibn Battuta Street in Tangier.
The sign is in French, Spanish, and Arabic.
Photo by the Author.

University of California Press
Berkeley and Los Angeles, California
© 1986, 2005, 2012 by Ross E. Dunn
First Paperback Printing 1989

Library of Congress Cataloging-in-Publication Data

Dunn, Ross E.
   The adventures of Ibn Battuta, a Muslim traveler
of the fourteenth century / Ross Dunn.—Rev. ed.
with a new pref.
      p.   cm.
   Includes bibliographical references and index (p.   ).
   ISBN 978-0-520-27292-7 (pbk. : alk. paper)
   1. Ibn Batuta, 1304–1377.   2. Travelers—Islamic
Empire—Biography.   3. Travel, Medieval. I. Title.
G93.I24D86 2005
910'.917'67—dc22

                                        2004005791

Printed in the United States of America

20   19   18   17   16
12   11   10   9   8   7   6   5   4   3

For Jordan and Jocelyn

And to the Memory of C. F. Beckingham

I met in [Brusa] the pious *shaykh* 'Abdallah al-Misri, the traveler, and a man of saintly life. He journeyed through the earth, but he never went into China nor the island of Ceylon, nor the Maghrib, nor al-Andalus, nor the Negrolands, so that I have outdone him by visiting these regions.

Ibn Battuta

Contents

Maps

Preface to the 2012 Edition

In the seven years since the revised edition of this book appeared, the academic and popular media have continued to polish the reputation of Ibn Battuta, the fourteenth-century Moroccan traveler. Scholars have been writing about him and his extraordinary globetrotting career since the nineteenth century. But in the last couple of decades, he has become something of an icon of globalization. For one thing, his *Book of Travels,* or *Rihla,* completed in 1355, demonstrates that economic and cultural interrelations among societies even thousands of miles from one another were much more complex seven hundred years ago than we used to think. And they have become progressively more complex ever since. Ibn Battuta's narrative also offers a glimpse of the origins of the planet-girdling flow of information that characterizes the human community today. This is because the *Rihla* shows the remarkable world-mindedness of educated Muslims in the fourteenth century, perhaps the first group of people in history capable of thinking of the entire Eastern Hemisphere as a single geographical space within which scholars, merchants, missionaries, and diplomats interacted with one another and shared knowledge. Today, students in schools and universities are being asked to study more world history. When they explore premodern centuries, they almost inevitably meet Ibn Battuta because he witnessed events and described ways of life in so many different places. Here is this same guy, students discover, turning up in Iraq, Russia, India, China, Mali, and Spain. Classroom encounters with Ibn Battuta, a man who walked, rode, and sailed (and at a few points staggered) thousands of miles, might even inspire some young people to find out more about the wider, profoundly intermeshed world around them—and to do some serious traveling.

Apart from dozens of textbooks on world, regional, and Islamic history, where has Ibn Battuta been making a name for himself in the last seven years? Two scholars in Britain have published insightful commentaries on his travels.[1] A portion of the *Rihla* translated from Arabic to English by Samuel Lee back in 1829 has appeared in a new edition.[2] A professor of Arabic in Uzbekistan has published an English edition of Ibn Battuta's journeys through Central Asia along with learned commentary.[3] Googling "Ibn Battuta" pulls up several educational and cultural web sites that describe his career and sing his praises. The great journeyer also continues to gain at least modest notoriety as a world pop-culture figure. In 2005, Dubai, one of the seven United Arab Emirates, opened the Ibn Battuta Mall, a shopping playground organized around six courts. Each one has an architectural and decorative theme evoking places that the Moroccan visited—Tunisia, Egypt, Persia, India, China, and Andalusia. In 2008, Tim Mackintosh-Smith, an Arabic scholar and travel writer, hosted *The Man Who Walked across the World,* a series of films for BBC Four that traced Ibn Battuta's travels. The following year Cosmic Pictures and SK Films premiered *Journey to Mecca,* a dramatic and documentary feature that tells the story—on giant Imax screens—of Ibn Battuta's overland trip to the holy city of Mecca. The film also gives viewers spectacular images of the Islamic pilgrimage, the object of the young Moroccan's first journey in 1324–26. In 2011, *Time* magazine published a special issue that explored ways in which the Muslim world has changed since the era when Ibn Battuta traveled.[4] Finally, his adventures will be dramatized in a full-length feature film that, as of this writing, is in preproduction.

As all scholars of the *Rihla* know, Ibn Battuta himself, along with the Muslim gentleman from Andalusia (southern Spain) who helped him write his story, tells us almost everything we know about his life and personality. Independent sources dating from his own era that attest to his existence are few and brief. When I published the first edition of *The Adventures of Ibn Battuta* in 1987, I assumed that additional evidence of his career was unlikely ever to turn up. In 2010, however, Tim Mackintosh-Smith completed his scholarly and marvelously entertaining three-volume narrative of his several years spent visiting dozens of Ibn Battuta's old haunts from China to West Africa.[5] In the final volume, Mackintosh-Smith reports on three additional documents in which the traveler comes to life independently of the *Rihla.*

One bit of evidence is a letter that the eminent Andalusian scholar Ibn al-Khatib wrote to Ibn Battuta in the early 1360s, that is, several years after the traveler had definitively returned home, on the mundane subject of a land purchase. From this testimony (which I also noted in the preface to the revised edition), we learn that the aging Ibn Battuta served as a judge in Tamasna, an old place name associated with the region around modern Casablanca. This letter is the only source that reveals anything concrete about Ibn Battuta's later life. Mackintosh-Smith learned about the letter from Abdelhadi Tazi, Morocco's most eminent Ibn Battuta scholar.

The second revelation is a set of two manuscripts, the second and third volumes of a work on Islamic law housed in the library of Cairo's Al-Azhar University. As Mackintosh-Smith writes, Professor Tazi showed him two photocopied pages from these documents. These were colophons, or descriptions placed at the end of the manuscripts indicating when, where, and by whom the work was copied. Ibn Battuta, definitely our journeyer, is the author of both colophons. They tell us that he copied the manuscripts in Damascus. Each colophon has a different date in 1326, a year when Ibn Battuta was by his own account in Syria. The two colophons together demonstrate first that Ibn Battuta visited the city when he says he did. The two dates, which are independent of the *Rihla,* also open up new questions and solve a puzzle or two about the complicated chronology of his peregrinations in Syria and Palestine.

The third piece of evidence is arresting, though speculative. Ibn al-Khatib's letter to Ibn Battuta suggests that the two men became friends in Morocco for a few years. Mackintosh-Smith reports that he found and read a book that Ibn al-Khatib published on topographical subjects. In it, he describes in rhyming prose a fictionalized encounter at a caravan stop with a gray-headed old traveler. This man boasts of his journeys to many countries but laments that his life is ending in poverty and friendlessness. In Ibn al-Khatib's story, the old man reveals personality traits that are also evident in the *Rihla*—an attraction to Sufi mysticism, an ability to charm, a tendency to pontificate, and a love of money. Mackintosh-Smith is sure that Ibn Battuta inspired Ibn al-Khatib's fictional portrait.

We do not know that the real traveler, as opposed to the old-timer in the story, ended his life in such a forlorn state. But the tale suggests that his return home left him not at ease and satisfied, but malcontent, restless, and regretful, still yearning for the road. The story adds a poignant touch to the portrait of Ibn Battuta we get in the *Rihla,* not only the descriptions of his thrilling adventures but also his opinions and feelings—his likes, dislikes, pious prejudices, physical courage, sexual appetites, and cravings for friendship with powerful people. An epic movie about him is a good idea, and it could be done without inventing a single scene not taken directly from his own amazing narrative.

November 2011

Notes

1. L. P. Harvey, *Ibn Battuta* (London: I.B.Tauris in association with the Oxford Center for Islamic Studies, 2007); David Waines, *The Odyssey of Ibn Battuta: Uncommon Tales of a Medieval Adventurer* (Chicago: University of Chicago Press, 2010).

2. Ibn Battuta, *The Travels of Ibn Battuta in the Near East, Asia and Africa, 1325–1354* (Mineola, NY: Dover, 2004).

3. Ibrahimov Nematulla Ibrahimovich, *The Travels of Ibn Battuta to Central Asia* (Princeton, NJ: Markus Wiener, 2010).

4. "Summer Journey 2011," *Time Specials,* July 2011.

5. Tim Mackintosh-Smith, *Travels with a Tangerine: A Journey in the Footnotes of Ibn Battutah* (London: John Murray, 2001); *The Hall of a Thousand Columns: Hindustan to Malabar with Ibn Battutah* (London: John Murray, 2005); *Landfalls: On the Edge of Islam with Ibn Battutah* (London: John Murray, 2010).

Preface to the Revised Edition

The year 2004 marks the seven hundredth anniversary of the birth of Abu 'Abdallah ibn Battuta, the Muslim lawyer who crisscrossed the Eastern Hemisphere in the second quarter of the fourteenth century and, with the help of a literary collaborator, wrote a lengthy account of what he saw and did. The world should take note of the septicentenary of this pious and educated Moroccan traveler. Not only did he give us a precious description of places, people, politics, and lifeways in nearly all the urbanized lands of Eurasia and Africa in the later medieval era, he also exposed the premodern roots of globalization. His tale reveals that by the fourteenth century the formation of dense networks of communication and exchange had linked in one way or another nearly everyone in the hemisphere with nearly everyone else. From Ibn Battuta's *Rihla,* or *Book of Travels,* we discover the webs of interconnection that stretched from Spain to China and from Kazakhstan to Tanzania, and we can see that already in the Moroccan's time an event occurring in one part of Eurasia or Africa might reverberate, in its effects, thousands of miles away.

Sailing the Arabian Sea in a two-masted dhow or leading his horse over a snow-covered pass in the Hindu Kush, Ibn Battuta could not have dreamed of the speed and intensity of human interchange today. Even since 1987, when the first edition of this book appeared, humankind has made astonishing advances in electronic technology and communication. One small irony of this "information revolution" is that Ibn Battuta himself has journeyed deeper into the popular imagination. He is today a more familiar historical figure among both Muslims and non-Muslims than he was twenty-five years ago. This has happened, I think, partly because of the increasing intensity of political and cultural relations between Muslim and Western countries and partly because of the broadening of international curriculums in schools and universities, notably in the United States, to embrace Asian and African societies, including famous men and women of the Muslim past.

In the United States, virtually all high school and college world history textbooks introduce Ibn Battuta, and in the past several years I have had numerous invitations to talk about his adventures with middle and high school teachers and students. In 1994, the Hakluyt Society published the fourth and final volume of the English translation of the *Rihla*, bringing to conclusion a project that began in 1929![1] Other publications of recent years include a travel writer's account of journeys tracing Ibn Battuta's path across the Eastern Hemisphere, an abridged edition of the Hakluyt Society translation, a new edition of an English translation of the Moroccan's East and West African trips, and an attractively illustrated commentary in Danish.[2]

Several popular magazines have featured Ibn Battuta, including *National Geographic*.[3] A Spanish-Moroccan production team made a documentary film about him in the mid-1990s, and currently at least two film projects are in the works. In 1993, Moroccan scholars organized an international conference on their native son in Tangier, his birthplace. In 1999, the Islamic Museum of Kuwait produced an enchanting one-man act and multimedia show called "The Travels of Ibn Battuta." Several publications for young people have appeared in English, including a teaching unit for high school students, an issue of the world history magazine *Calliope*, and a fantasy of the "Indiana Jones" variety titled *Ibn Battuta in the Valley of Doom*.[4] In San Francisco a middle school teacher has developed a detailed Ibn Battuta website.[5] Finally, I must mention that in 1976, the International Astronomical Union honored the traveler by naming a lunar crater after him. It is eleven kilometers wide and on the near side of the moon.

I was pleased indeed when the University of California Press agreed to publish this new edition, a seven-hundredth-birthday present to Ibn Battuta. I have made limited changes. I have taken account of the scholarly literature in Western languages that has appeared since 1987, as well as the insights and corrections published in reviews of the first edition. With the exception of an essay by Amikam Elad, who demonstrates that much of Ibn Battuta's description of Syria and Palestine is copied from the travel account of the thirteenth-century traveler Muhammad al-'Abdari, I have seen no new research that significantly alters what we know about the *Rihla* or Ibn Battuta's life.[6] Some new work, however, has offered insights on the *Rihla*'s chronology, itinerary, and reliability. My references to new work are mainly in the chapter endnotes.

The only change I have made to the bibliography is the addition of a new section, "Supplemental Sources for the 2004 Edition." I have also retained the same sources of translations from the *Rihla,* which mainly means that I have not quoted from volume four of the Hakluyt Society edition. I have made certain spelling changes— for example, "Qur'an" instead of "Koran"—and I have replaced the Wade-Giles with the pinyin system for romanizing Chinese place names.

I am indebted to reviewers who pointed out mistakes and interpretive flaws in the first edition, and I would like to thank Tim Macintosh-Smith for meticulously rereading the book and sending me valuable comments. I greatly appreciate the efforts of Mari Coates, my University of California Press editor, whose enthusiasm for the new edition helped me meet her timetable for revisions. Finally, I thank Laura Ryan for research assistance.

Ross E. Dunn
March 2004

Notes

1. See the bibliography for the complete citation. The Hakluyt Society has also published an index to the *Rihla* in a fifth volume. C. F. Beckingham intended to produce a sixth volume, an extended commentary on IB's itinerary and chronology. Sadly, Prof. Beckingham passed away in 1998.

2. Tim Mackintosh-Smith, *Travels with a Tangerine: A Journey in the Footnotes of Ibn Battutah* (London, 2001); Tim Mackintosh-Smith, ed. *The Travels of Ibn Battutah* (London, 2003); Said Hamdun and Noel King, *Ibn Battuta in Black Africa* (Princeton, NJ, 1994); and Thyge C. Bro, *Ibn Battuta: En arabisk rejsende fra det 14. århundrede* (Oslo, 2001).

3. Thomas J. Abercrombie and James L. Stanfield, "Ibn Battuta: Prince of Travelers," *National Geographic* 180 (Dec. 1991): 4–49. Also, Douglas Bullis, "The Longest Hajj: The Journeys of Ibn Battuta," *Saudi Aramco World* 51 (July/Aug. 2000), 2–39.

4. Joan Arno and Helen Grady, *Ibn Battuta: A View of the Fourteenth-Century World* (National Center for History in the Schools, University of California, Los Angeles, 1998); "Ibn Battuta: Muslim Scholar and Traveler," *Calliope* 9 (April 1999); Abd al-Rahman Azzam, *Ibn Battuta in the Valley of Doom* (London, 1996).

5. Nick Bartel, "The Travels of Ibn Battuta: A Virtual Tour with the 14th Century Traveler," http://www.sfusd.k12.ca.us/schwww/sch618/Ibn_Battuta/Ibn_Battuta_Rihla .html.

6. Amikam Elad, "The Description of the Travels of Ibn Battuta in Palestine: Is It Original?," *Journal of the Royal Asiatic Society* (1987), 256–272. Also, Dr. Abdelhadi Tazi, the leading Moroccan authority on IB, has found documentary evidence suggesting that he died in the town of Anfa, not Tangier, where his putative tomb is located.

Preface to the First Edition

Staring at the wall of my windowless office one day in 1976, I suddenly got the idea to write this book. I was teaching world history to undergraduates and trying to give them an idea of Islam in the medieval age as a civilization whose cultural dominance extended far beyond the Middle East or the lands inhabited by Arabs. It occurred to me that the life of Abu 'Abdallah ibn Battuta, the famous Moroccan traveler of the fourteenth century, wonderfully illustrated the internationalist scope of Islamic civilization. He toured not only the central regions of Islam but also its far frontiers in India, Indonesia, Central Asia, East Africa, and the West African Sudan. The travel book he produced at the end of his career is both a tale of high adventure and an expansive portrait of the eminently cosmopolitan world of Muslim princes, merchants, scholars, and theologians within which he moved during 29 years on the road.

Since the mid nineteenth century, when translations of his Arabic narrative began to appear in Western languages, Ibn Battuta has been well known among specialists in Islamic and medieval history. But no scholar had attempted to retell his remarkable story to a general audience. For the non-specialist interested in medieval Islam and the attitudes and preoccupations of its intellectual class the narrative can be absorbing. But the modern reader is also likely to find it puzzlingly organized, archaic, and to some degree unintelligible. My idea, therefore, has been to bring Ibn Battuta's adventure to general readers and to interpret it within the rich, trans-hemispheric cultural setting of medieval Islam. My hope is not only that the Moroccan journeyer will become as well known in the Western world as Marco Polo is but that readers will also gain a sharper and more panoramic view of the forces that made the history of Eurasia and Africa in the fourteenth century an interconnected whole. Ibn Battuta, we shall see, was a kind of citizen of the Eastern Hemisphere. The global interdependence of the late twentieth century would be less startling to him than we might suppose.

Almost everything we know about Ibn Battuta the man is to be found in his own work, called the *Rihla*, which is readily available in printed Arabic editions, as well as translations in English and several other languages. I have not rummaged about ancient manuscript collections in Fez, Damascus, or Delhi to piece his life together since, in so far as anyone knows, no such manuscripts exist. Indeed, this book, part biography and part cultural history of the second quarter of the fourteenth century, is a work of synthesis. In tracing Ibn Battuta's footsteps through the equivalent of some 44 modern countries, I have relied on a wide range of published literature.

I first became interested in Ibn Battuta when I spent the better part of a year translating portions of the narrative in a graduate school Arabic class. I have come to this project, however, with a modest training in that beautiful and intractable language. I have used printed Arabic editions of the *Rihla* to clarify various problems of nomenclature and textual meaning, but I have largely depended on the major English or French translations in relating and interpreting Ibn Battuta's career.

The *Rihla* is not a daily diary or a collection of notes that Ibn Battuta jotted in the course of his travels. Rather it is a work of literature, part autobiography and part descriptive compendium, that was written at the end of his career. In composing the book, Ibn Battuta (and Ibn Juzayy, the literary scholar who collaborated with him) took far less care with details of itinerary, dates, and the sequence of events than the modern "scientific" mind would consider acceptable practice for a travel writer. Consequently, the historian attempting to reconstruct the chronology of Ibn Battuta's journeys must confront numerous gaps, inconsistencies, and puzzles, some of them baffling. Fortunately, the textual problems of the *Rihla* have sustained the attention of historians, linguists, philologists, and geographers for more than a century. In trying to untangle Ibn Battuta's movements from one end of the Eastern Hemisphere to the other, I have therefore relied heavily on the existing corpus of textual commentary. Given the scope and purpose of this book, I could not do otherwise, since any further progress in solving remaining problems of chronology, itinerary, authenticity, and place name identification would require laborious research in fourteenth-century documentary sources. I have, however, tried to address the major difficulties in using the *Rihla* as a biographical record of events. Most of this discussion has been confined to footnotes in order to avoid digressions into technicalities that would break annoyingly into the story or tax the interest of some general readers.

In this age of the "docu-drama" and the "non-fiction novel," I should also state explicitly that I have in no deliberate way fictionalized Ibn Battuta's life story. The words that he speaks, the attitudes that he holds, the actions that he takes are either drawn directly from the *Rihla* or can be reasonably inferred from it or other historical sources.

This book is my interpretation of Ibn Battuta's life and times and not a picture of the fourteenth century "through his eyes." It is not a commentary on his encyclopedic observations, not, in other words, a book about his book. Its subject matter does, however, largely reflect his social experience and cultural perceptions. He was a literate, urbane gentleman interested for the most part in the affairs of other literate, urbane gentlemen. Though as a pious Muslim he by no means despised the poor, he did not often associate with peasants, herdsmen, or city working folk. Nor does he have much to say about them in the *Rihla*. Moreover, he traveled in the circles of world-minded people for whom the universalist values and cosmopolitan institutions of Islam — the mosques, the colleges, the palaces — were more important than the parochial customs and loyalties that constricted the cultural vision of the great majority. Some readers, therefore, will not fail to notice two conceptual biases. One is that political and cultural elites dominate the story at the expense of "the masses," even though the social history of ordinary Muslim folk is no less worthy of the historian's attention. The other is that the cosmopolitan tendencies within Islamic civilization are our primary theme rather than the admittedly great cultural diversity among Muslim peoples, even though one of the strengths of an expanding Islam was its successful adaptability to local patterns of culture.

A few technical matters need to be mentioned. In order to simplify the footnote apparatus, I have not for the most part given page citations for direct quotes from English translations of the *Rihla*. Unless otherwise noted, quotations are taken from the published translations as follows: Chapters 1–8 and 14, H. A. R. Gibb, *The Travels of Ibn Battuta A.D. 1325–1354*, 3 vols.; Chapters 9–11, Agha Mahdi Husain, *The Rehla of Ibn Battuta*; and Chapter 13, N. Levtzion and J. F. P. Hopkins (eds.), *Corpus of Early Arabic Sources for West African History*. For the sake of uniformity I have made a few orthographic changes in quotations from the *Rihla* translations. I have "americanized" the spelling of a number of English words (e.g., "favor" rather than "favour"), and I have changed the spelling of a few Arabic terms (e.g., "Koran" rather than "Qur'an" and "vizier" rather than "vizir" or "wazir"). In transliterating Arabic terms, I have eliminated all diacritical marks, excepting "'" to indicate the two Arabic letters "hamza" and "'ayn."

Acknowledgements

Ibn Battuta has led me so far and wide in the Eastern Hemisphere that in the course of writing this book I have asked for advice and criticism from an unusually large number of scholars and colleagues. I cannot mention them all, but I would like to thank the following individuals for reading and criticizing, sometimes in great detail, all or part of the manuscript: Jere Bacharach, Edmund Burke, P. C. Chu, Julia Clancy-Smith, Michael Dols, Jeanne Dunn, Richard Eaton, G. S. P. Freeman-Grenville, Kathryn Green, David Hart, James Kirkman, Howard Kushner, Ira Lapidus, Michael Meeker, David Morgan, William Phillips, Charles Smith, Ray Smith, Peter von Sivers, and Robert Wilson. I am especially grateful for the enduring support of Professor C. F. Beckingham, a man of learning and urbanity with whom Ibn Battuta would have found much in common. If I failed to understand or heed good advice these individuals gave me, I alone bear the responsibility.

I am grateful to the National Endowment for the Humanities for awarding me a fellowship that funded research and writing in 1980–81. During that year I enjoyed the privilege of affiliation with the Middle East Centre at Cambridge University, thanks to Professor R. B. Serjeant and Dr Robin Bidwell. I am also indebted to the Fellows of Clare Hall for extending me membership in the college as a Visiting Associate. San Diego State University generously supported this project with a sabbatical leave and several small grants. For research assistance or typing services I would like to express my appreciation to Lorin Birch, Veronica King, Richard Knight, Helen Lavey, and Jill Swalling Harrington. Finally, I want to thank Barbara Aguado for making the maps.

The Muslim Calendar

Ibn Battuta reports the dates of his travels according to the Muslim calendar, which is based on the cycles of the moon. The Muslim year is divided into twelve lunar months of 29 or 30 days each. The year is approximately 354 days long, that is, ten or eleven days shorter than a solar year. Consequently, dates of the Muslim calendar have no fixed relationship either to dates of the Gregorian (Western) calendar or to seasons of the year. For example, Christmas is always celebrated in winter in Europe and the United States. By contrast, a Muslim religious holiday will, over time, occur in all four seasons of the year. The base-year of the Muslim calendar is 622 A.D., when the Prophet Muhammad and his followers made the *hijra*, or "migration," from Mecca to Medina. The abbreviation A.H., for *anno Hejirae*, denotes years of the Muslim calendar. In this book I have given key dates according to both calendars. Converting precise dates from one system to the other requires the use of a formula and a series of tables. These may be found in G. S. P. Freeman-Grenville, *The Muslim and Christian Calendars* (London, 1963).

The Muslim lunar months are as follows:

Muharram	Rajab
Safar	Sha'ban
Rabi' al-awwal (Rabi' I)	Ramadan
Rabi' al-thani (Rabi' II)	Shawwal
Jumada l-ula (Jumada I)	Dhu l-Qa'da
Jumada l-akhira (Jumada II)	Dhu l-Hijja

A Note on Money

In the course of his career Ibn Battuta received numerous gifts and salary payments in gold or silver coins. He usually refers to these coins as dinars, though sometimes distinguishing between "gold dinars" and "silver dinars." In the early Islamic centuries the weight of a gold dinar was set at 4.25 grams. In Ibn Battuta's time, however, the weight and fineness of both gold and silver coins, as well as the exchange rate between them, varied greatly from one period or country to the next. It would be futile, therefore, to express the value of money he received in terms of modern dollars or pounds sterling. In fourteenth-century India, where he was paid large sums from the public treasury, a "silver dinar" (or silver *tanka*) was valued at about one-tenth of a gold dinar.

Abbreviations Used in Footnotes

D&S   C. Défrémery and B. R. Sanguinetti (trans. and eds.), *Voyages d'Ibn Battuta*, 4 vols. (Paris 1853–58; reprint edn., Vincent Monteil (ed.), Paris, 1979)

EI₁   *Encyclopaedia of Islam*, 1st edn., 4 vols. (Leiden, 1913–38)

EI₂   *Encyclopaedia of Islam*, 2nd edn., 5 vols. (Leiden, 1954; London, 1956–)

Gb   H. A. R. Gibb (trans. and ed.), *The Travels of Ibn Battuta A.D. 1325–1354. Translated with Revisions and Notes from the Arabic Text Edited by C. Défrémery and B. R. Sanguinetti*, 3 vols. (Cambridge for the Hakluyt Society, 1958, 1961, 1971)

H&K   Said Hamdun and Noel King (trans. and eds.), *Ibn Battuta in Black Africa* (London, 1975)

Hr   Ivan Hrbek, "The Chronology of Ibn Battuta's Travels," *Archiv Orientalni* 30 (1962): 409–86

IB   Ibn Battuta

L&H   N. Levtzion and J. F. P. Hopkins (trans. and eds.), *Corpus of Early Arabic Sources for West African History* (New York, 1981)

MH   Agha Mahdi Husain (trans. and ed.), *The Rehla of Ibn Battuta* (Baroda, India, 1976)

Introduction

> Westerners have singularly narrowed the history of the
> world in grouping the little that they knew about the
> expansion of the human race around the peoples of Israel,
> Greece and Rome. Thus have they ignored all those
> travellers and explorers who in their ships ploughed the
> China Sea and the Indian Ocean, or rode across the
> immensities of Central Asia to the Persian Gulf. In truth
> the larger part of the globe, containing cultures different
> from those of the ancient Greeks and Romans but no less
> civilized, has remained unknown to those who wrote the
> history of their little world under the impression that they
> were writing world history.[1]
>
> Henri Cordier

Abu 'Abdallah ibn Battuta has been rightly celebrated as the
greatest traveler of premodern times. He was born into a family of
Muslim legal scholars in Tangier, Morocco, in 1304 during the era
of the Marinid dynasty. He studied law as a young man and in 1325
left his native town to make the pilgrimage, or *hajj*, to the sacred
city of Mecca in Arabia. He took a year and a half to reach his
destination, visiting North Africa, Egypt, Palestine, and Syria
along the way. After completing his first *hajj* in 1326, he toured
Iraq and Persia, then returned to Mecca. In 1328 (or 1330) he
embarked upon a sea voyage that took him down the eastern coast
of Africa as far south as the region of modern Tanzania. On his
return voyage he visited Oman and the Persian Gulf and returned
to Mecca again by the overland route across central Arabia.

In 1330 (or 1332) he ventured to go to India to seek employment
in the government of the Sultanate of Delhi. Rather than taking
the normal ocean route across the Arabian Sea to the western
coast of India, he traveled north through Egypt and Syria to Asia
Minor. After touring that region, he crossed the Black Sea to the
plains of West Central Asia. He then, owing to fortuitous circumstances, made a westward detour to visit Constantinople, capital of

1

Map 1: Cities of Eurasia and Africa in the Fourteenth Century

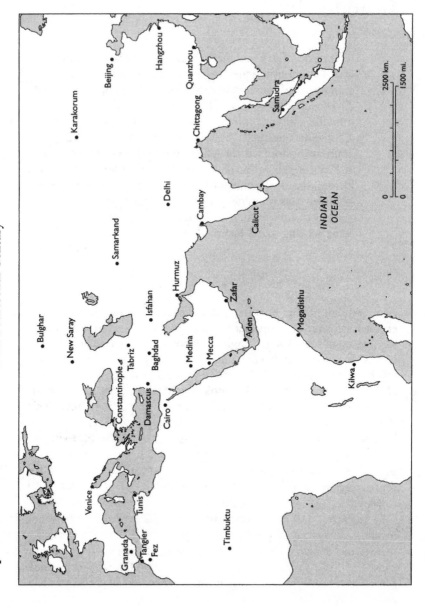

the Byzantine Empire, in the company of a Turkish princess. Returning to the Asian steppes, he traveled eastward through Transoxiana, Khurasan, and Afghanistan, arriving at the banks of the Indus River in September 1333 (or 1335). He spent eight years in India, most of that time occupying a post as a *qadi*, or judge, in the government of Muhammad Tughluq, Sultan of Delhi. In 1341 the king appointed him to lead a diplomatic mission to the court of the Mongol emperor of China. The expedition ended disastrously in shipwreck off the southwestern coast of India, leaving Ibn Battuta without employment or resources. For a little more than two years he traveled about southern India, Ceylon, and the Maldive Islands, where he served for about eight months as a *qadi* under the local Muslim dynasty. Then, despite the failure of his ambassadorial mission, he resolved in 1345 to go to China on his own. Traveling by sea, he visited Bengal, the coast of Burma, and the island of Sumatra, then continued on to Guangzhou. The extent of his visit to China is uncertain but was probably limited to the southern coastal region.

In 1346–47 he returned to Mecca by way of South India, the Persian Gulf, Syria, and Egypt. After performing the ceremonies of the *hajj* one last time, he set a course for home. Traveling by both land and sea, he arrived in Fez, the capital of Morocco, late in 1349. The following year he made a brief trip across the Strait of Gibraltar to the Muslim kingdom of Granada. Then, in 1353, he undertook his final adventure, a journey by camel caravan across the Sahara Desert to the Kingdom of Mali in the West African Sudan. In 1355 he returned to Morocco to stay. In the course of a career on the road spanning almost thirty years, he crossed the breadth of the Eastern Hemisphere, visited territories equivalent to about 40 modern countries, and put behind him a total distance of approximately 73,000 miles.[2]

Early in 1356 Sultan Abu 'Inan, the Marinid ruler of Morocco, commissioned Ibn Juzayy, a young literary scholar of Andalusian origin, to record Ibn Battuta's experiences, as well as his observations about the Islamic world of his day, in the form of a *rihla*, or book of travels. As a type of Arabic literature, the *rihla* attained something of a flowering in North Africa between the twelfth and fourteenth centuries. The best known examples of the genre recounted a journey from the Maghrib to Mecca, informing and entertaining readers with rich descriptions of the pious institutions, public monuments, and religious personalities of the great cities of Islam.[3] Ibn Battuta and Ibn Juzayy collaborated for about two years to compose their work, the longest and in terms of its subject matter the most complex *rihla* to come out of North Africa in the medieval age. His royal charge completed, Ibn Battuta retired to a judicial post in a Moroccan provincial town. He died in 1368.

Written in the conventional literary style of the time, Ibn Battuta's *Rihla* is a comprehensive survey of the personalities, places, governments, customs, and curiosities of the Muslim world in the second quarter of the fourteenth century. It is also the record of a dramatic personal adventure. In the four centuries after Ibn Battuta's death, the *Rihla* circulated, mostly in copied manuscript abridgments of Ibn Juzayy's original text, among people of learning in North Africa, West Africa, Egypt, and perhaps other Muslim lands where Arabic was read.

The book was unknown outside Islamic countries until the early nineteenth century, when two German scholars published separately translations of portions of the *Rihla* from manuscripts obtained in the Middle East. In 1829 Samuel Lee, a British orientalist, published an English translation based on abridgments of the narrative that John Burckhardt, the famous Swiss explorer, had acquired in Egypt.[4] Around the middle of the century five manuscripts of the *Rihla* were found in Algeria following the French occupation of that country. These documents were subsequently transferred to the Bibliothèque Nationale in Paris. Two of them represent the most complete versions of the narrative that have ever come to light. The others are partial transcriptions, one of which carries the autograph of Ibn Juzayy, Ibn Battuta's editor. Working with these five documents, two French scholars, C. Défrémery and B.R. Sanguinetti, published between 1853 and 1858 a printed edition of the Arabic text, together with a translation in French and an apparatus of notes and variant textual readings.[5]

Since then, translations of the work, prepared in every case from Défrémery and Sanguinetti's printed text, have been published in many languages, including Spanish, Italian, German, Russian, Polish, Hungarian, Persian, and Japanese. In 1929 Sir Hamilton Gibb produced an abridged English translation and began work on a complete edition of the work under the auspices of the Hakluyt Society.[6] The last of the four volumes in this series appeared in 1994, and an index came out in 2001.[7] However, English translations of various portions of the *Rihla* have appeared in the past century as books or as articles in anthologies and scholarly journals.

The numerous translations of the *Rihla*, together with the extensive corpus of encyclopedia articles, popular summaries, and critical commentaries on Ibn Battuta and his career that have accumulated since the eighteenth century, are a tribute to the extraordinary value of the narrative as a historical source on much of the inhabited Eastern Hemisphere in the second quarter of the fourteenth century. The book has been cited and quoted in hundreds of historical works, not only those relating to Islamic countries but to China and the Byzantine empire as well. For the history of certain regions, Sudanic West Africa, Asia Minor, or the Malabar coast of India, for example, the *Rihla* stands as the only eye-witness report on political events, human geography, and social or economic conditions for a period of a century or more. Ibn Battuta had no professional background or experience as a writer of geography, history, or ethnography, but he was, as Gibb declares, "the supreme example of *le géographe malgré lui*," the "geographer in spite of himself."[8]

The Western world has conventionally celebrated Marco Polo, who died the year before Ibn Battuta first left home, as the "Greatest Traveler in History." Ibn Battuta has inevitably been compared with him and has usually taken second prize as "the Marco Polo of the Muslim world" or "the Marco Polo of the tropics."[9] Keeping in mind that neither man actually composed his own book (Marco's record was dictated to the French romance writer Rusticello in a Genoese prison), there is no doubt that the Venetian's work is the superior one in terms of the accurate, precise, practical information it contributes on medieval China and other Asian lands in the latter part of the thirteenth century, information of profound value to historians ever since. Yet Ibn Battuta traveled to, and reports on, a great many more places than Marco did, and his narrative offers details, sometimes in incidental bits, sometimes in long disquisitions, on almost every conceivable aspect of human life in that age, from the royal ceremonial of the Sultan of Delhi to the sexual customs of women in the Maldive Islands to the harvesting of coconuts in South Arabia. Moreover his story is far more personal and humanely engaging than Marco's. Some Western writers, especially in an earlier time when the conviction of Europe's superiority over Islamic civilization was a presumption of historical scholarship, have criticized Ibn Battuta for being excessively eager to tell about the lives and pious accomplishments of religious savants and Sufi mystics when he might have written more about practical politics and prices. The *Rihla*, however, was directed to Muslim men of learning of the fourteenth century for whom such reportage, so recondite to the modern Western reader, was pertinent and interesting.

As in Marco's case, we know almost nothing about the life of Ibn Battuta apart from what the autobiographical dimension of his own book reveals. Aside from three minor references in Muslim scholarly works of the fourteenth or fifteenth century that attest independently to the Moroccan's existence and to his achievements as a traveler, no document has ever come to light from his own age that mentions him.[10] To understand his character, his aspirations, his social attitudes and prejudices, his personal relations with other people and, finally, the way he "fits" into fourteenth-century Muslim society and culture, we must rely almost exclusively on the *Rihla* itself. Fortunately, by expressing here and there in its pages his reactions to events, his annoyances, his animosities, and the details of his personal intrigues, he reveals something of his own character.

Western writers have sometimes characterized Ibn Battuta as a brave explorer like Marco Polo, risking his life to discover *terra incognita* and bring knowledge of it to public attention. In fact Ibn Battuta's experience was drastically different from that of the Venetian. Marco traveled as an alien visitor into lands few Europeans had ever seen and whose people knew little, and cared to know little, about Europe. He was an oddity, a "stranger in a strange land," who was given the opportunity to visit China only because of the very special political circumstances that prevailed for a short time in the thirteenth and early fourteenth centuries: the existence of the great Mongol states of Asia and their policy of permitting merchants of all origins and religions to travel and conduct business in their domains. Marco does indeed herald the age of European discovery, not because the peoples of Asia somehow needed discovering to set themselves on a course into the future, but because his book made an extraordinary and almost immediate intellectual impact on a young Western civilization that until that time had a cramped and faulty vision of what the wider world of the Eastern Hemisphere was all about.

Ibn Battuta, by contrast, spent most of his traveling career within the cultural boundaries of what Muslims called the Dar al-Islam, or Abode of Islam. This expression embraced the lands where Muslims predominated in the population, or at least where

Muslim kings or princes ruled over non-Muslim majorities and where in consequence the *shari'a*, or Sacred Law, of Islam was presumably the foundation of the social order. In that sense Islamic civilization extended from the Atlantic coast of West Africa to Southeast Asia. Moreover, important minority communities of Muslims inhabited cities and towns in regions such as China, Spain, and tropical West Africa that were beyond the frontiers of the Dar al-Islam. Therefore almost everywhere Ibn Battuta went he lived in the company of other Muslims, men and women who shared not merely his doctrinal beliefs and religious rituals, but his moral values, his social ideals, his everyday manners. Although he was introduced in the course of his travels to a great many Muslim peoples whose local languages, customs, and aesthetic values were unfamiliar in his own homeland at the far western edge of the hemisphere, he never strayed far from the social world of individuals who shared his tastes and sensibilities and among whom he could always find hospitality, security, and friendship.

Today, we characterize the cosmopolitan individual in several ways: the advocate of international cooperation or world government, the sophisticated city-dweller, the jet-setter. The Muslim cosmopolite of the fourteenth century was likewise urbane, well traveled, and free of the grosser varieties of parochial bigotry. But, above all, he possessed a consciousness, more or less acutely formed, of the entire Dar al-Islam as a social reality. He also believed, at least implicitly, in the Sacred Law as the proper and eminently workable foundation of a global community.

To understand the intellectual basis of Ibn Battuta's cosmopolitanism, we must re-orient ourselves away from the conventional view of history as primarily the study of individual nations or discrete "cultures." In their writings more than twenty years ago the world historians Marshall Hodgson and William McNeill introduced and developed the "global" concept of the Eurasian, or preferably Afro-Eurasian, Ecumene, that is, the belt of agrarian lands extending west to east from the Mediterranean basin to China.[11] It was within this region that the major sedentary civilizations of the Eastern Hemisphere arose, where most cities sprang up, and where most important cultural and technological innovations were made.

Beginning in ancient times, according to McNeill, the Ecumene went through a series of "closures" which involved increasingly complex interrelations among the civilizations of the hemisphere. Thus there evolved a continuous region of intercommunication, or, as we will call it in this book, the intercommunicating zone, which joined the sedentary and urbanizing peoples of the Mediterranean rim, the Middle East, Greater India, and China into a single field of historical interaction and change. Important innovations occurring in one part of the zone tended to spread to the other parts of it through trade, military conquest, human migration, or gradual diffusion. Moreover, the intercommunicating zone "grew" over the course of time by incorporating peoples in peripheral areas — sub-Saharan Africa, Southeast Asia, Central Asia, Europe north of the Alps — into the web of interrelations. Thus, the history of Africa and Eurasia in premodern times becomes more than the stories of individual, geographically bounded nations, cultures, or empires. It is also the history of the "unconsciously inter-regional developments," to quote Hodgson, which "converge in their effects to alter *the general disposition of the Hemisphere.*"[12]

One of the most important dimensions of this "hemispheric history" was the role of pastoral populations who inhabited the great arid belt which ran diagonally from southwest to northeast across the intercommunicating zone, that is the chain of steppes and deserts extending from the Sahara through the Middle East and Central Asia to the Gobi. Contact between the herding peoples of the arid zone and sedentary societies tended in normal times to be mostly beneficial to both, involving the exchange of goods and elements of culture. However, the pastoralists, owing to their mobility and ethos of martial strength, were always a potential threat to the far richer settled civilizations. At periodic intervals beginning in the eighteenth century B.C. or earlier, nomadic invaders poured into neighboring agrarian lands, pillaging cities, terminating dynasties, and generally upsetting prevailing cultural and social patterns over wide areas of Eurasia and Africa. The last great nomadic movement occurred in the thirteenth century, when the Mongols and their Turkish-speaking allies erupted out of Central Asia and conquered China, Russia, and most of the Middle East, creating the largest territorial empire the world has ever known.

Islam had come upon the world scene in the seventh century in connection with the explosion of Arabic-speaking, horse-mounted warriors out of the Arabian desert under the leadership of the

Prophet Muhammad and his successors. Western historical writing has given a great deal of attention to the early evolution of Islamic civilization, that is, the "classical" age of the Abbasid Caliphate (or High Caliphate) centered on Baghdad between the eighth and tenth centuries. For this period the astonishing contributions of Muslims to world history in art, science, medicine, philosophy, and international commerce have been recognized, especially in so far as they were a major formative influence on the rise of Christian European civilization in the early Middle Ages. But precisely because historians of the West have been interested in Islam mainly in terms of its effects on the development of European institutions, the subsequent periods of Islamic history up to modern times have been given less heed. Indeed, the conventional perspective in European and American textbook writing has been that Islamic civilization reached its "peak" during the Abbasid age and thereafter went into a gradual but inexorable "decline." This notion that Islam somehow atrophied after the tenth or eleventh century has largely turned on the Western perception (considerably exaggerated) that Muslims rejected the intellectual heritage of Hellenistic rationalism about the same time that Europeans "rediscovered" it. Consequently, so the argument runs, the West, having adopted a "scientific" and "rational" view of the natural world, was able to "progress" in the direction of world dominance, while "traditional" civilizations such as Islam languished and fell further and further behind.

In fact, the period of hemispheric history from 1000 to 1500 A.D., what we will call the Islamic Middle Period, witnessed a steady and remarkable expansion of Islam, not simply as a religious faith but as a coherent, universalist model of civilized life. To be sure, the intense, concentrated, innovative brilliance of the Abbasid Caliphate was not to be repeated in the subsequent half millennium of Islamic history. Yet if many Muslims did turn intellectually conservative by the standard of modern scientific rationalism, the religion nonetheless pushed outward from its Middle Eastern core as an attractive, satisfying, cohesive system for explaining the cosmos and for ordering collective life among everlarger numbers of people, both sedentary and pastoral, both urban and rural, all across the intercommunicating zone.

The spread of Islam into new areas of the hemisphere during the Middle Period was given impetus by two major forces. One of these was the advance of Turkish-speaking Muslim herding peoples from Central Asia into the Middle East, a movement that began on a large scale with the conquests of the Seljuk Turks in the eleventh century. In the ensuing 300 years Turkish cavalry armies pushed westward into Asia Minor and southern Russia and eastward into India. The second force was the gradual but persistent movement of Muslim merchants into the lands rimming the Indian Ocean, that is, East Africa, India, Southeast Asia, and China, as well as into Central Asia and West Africa south of the Sahara. Yet the principal contribution of both warriors and merchants, establishing in some places Muslim military dominance and in other places only communities of believers under non-Muslim authority, was to prepare the ground for influxes of Muslim religious and intellectual cadres. It was they, over the longer term, who founded the basic institutions of Islamic civilization in these new areas and who carried on the work of cultural conversion among non-Muslim peoples.

A close look at the patterns of travel and migration in the post-Abbasid centuries reveals a quiet but persistent dispersion of legal scholars, theologians, Sufi divines, belle-lettrists, scribes, architects, and craftsmen outward from the older centers of Islam to these new frontiers of Muslim military and commercial activity. At the same time, the members of this cultural elite who were living and traveling in the further regions consistently maintained close ties with the great cities of the central Islamic lands, thereby creating not merely a scattering of literate and skilled Muslims across the hemisphere, but an integrated, growing, self-replenishing network of cultural communication.

Moreover, the most fundamental values of Islam tended to encourage a higher degree of social mobility and freer movement of individuals from one city and region to another than was the case in the other civilizations of that time. Islamic culture put great stress on egalitarian behavior in social relations based on the ideal of a community of believers (the *umma*) having a common allegiance to one God and his Sacred Law. To be sure, a great gulf separated the rich and powerful from the poor and weak, as was the case in all civilized societies until very recent times. But Islam mightily resisted the institutionalizing of ascribed statuses, ethnic exclusivities, or purely territorial loyalties. The dynamics of social life centered, not on relations among fixed, rigidly defined groups as was the case in Hindu India or even, to a lesser degree, the medieval West, but on what Hodgson calls "egalitarian contractualism," the relatively free play of relations among individuals who tended to size one another up mainly in terms of personal conformity to Islamic moral standards.[13] Consequently, wherever in the Dar al-Islam an individual traveled, pursued a career, or bought and sold goods, the same social and moral rules of conduct largely applied, rules founded on the *shari'a*.

The Islamic world in Ibn Battuta's time was divided politically into numerous kingdoms and principalities. Rulers insisted that their administrative and penal codes be obeyed, but they made no claims to divine authority. For the most part, Muslims on the move — merchants, scholars, and skilled, literate individuals of all kinds — regarded the jurisdictions of states as a necessary imposition and gave them as little attention as possible. Their primary allegiance was to the Dar al-Islam as a whole. The focal points of their public lives were not countries but cities, where world-minded Muslims carried on their inter-personal affairs mainly with reference to the universalist and uniform standards of the Law.

The terrible Mongol conquests of Persia and Syria that occurred between 1219 and 1258 appeared to Muslims to threaten the very existence of Islamic civilization. Yet by the time Ibn Battuta began his traveling career Mongol political dominance over the greater part of Eurasia was proving conducive to the further expansion of Islam and its institutions. The powerful Mongol *khans* of Persia and Central Asia converted to the faith, and the conditions of order and security that attended the Pax Mongolica of the later thirteenth and early fourteenth centuries gave freer play than ever to the movement of Muslims back and forth across Eurasia.

It was in the late decades of the Pax Mongolica that Ibn Battuta made his remarkable journeys. In a sense he participated, sometimes simultaneously, in four different streams of travel and migration. First, he was a pilgrim, joining the march of pious believers to the spiritual shrines of Mecca and Medina at least four times in his career. Second, he was a devotee of Sufism, or mystical Islam, traveling, as thousands did, to the hermitages and lodges of venerable individuals to receive their blessing and wisdom. Third, he was a juridical scholar, seeking knowledge and erudite company in the great cities of the Islamic heartland. And finally, he was a member of the literate, mobile, world-minded elite, an educated adventurer as it were, looking for hospitality, honors, and profitable employment in the more newly established centers of Islamic civilization in the further regions of Asia and Africa. In any of these traveling roles, however, he regarded himself as a citizen, not of a country called Morocco, but of the Dar al-Islam, to whose universalist spiritual, moral, and social values he was loyal above any other allegiance. His life and career exemplify a remarkable fact of Afro–Eurasian history in the later Middle Period, that, as Marshall Hodgson writes, Islam "came closer than any other medieval society to establishing a common world order of social and even cultural standards."[14]

Notes

1. Henri Cordier, quoted in Joseph Needham, *Science and Civilization in China,* vol. 4, part 3: *Civil Engineering and Nautics* (Cambridge, 1971), p. 486.
2. Approximate. Henry Yule estimates that IB traveled more than 75,000 miles during his career, not counting journeys while living in India. *Cathay and the Way Thither,* 4 vols. (London, 1913–16), vol. 4, p. 40. Mahdi Husain (MH, p. liii) suggests 77,640 miles.
3. On *rihla* literature in North Africa see M. B. A. Benchekroun, *La Vie intellectuelle marocaine sous les Merinides et les Wattasides* (Rabat, 1974), pp. 9–11, 251–57; André Michel, "Ibn Battuta, trente années de voyages de Pekin au Niger," *Les Africains* 1 (1977): 134–36; A. L. de Prémare, *Maghreb et Andalousie au XIVe siècle* (Lyon, 1981), pp. 34, 92–93.
4. Samuel Lee, *The Travels of Ibn Battuta* (London, 1929). See also D&S, vol. 1, pp. xiii–xxvi.
5. C. Défrémery and B. R. Sanguinetti (trans. and eds.). *Voyages d'Ibn Battuta,* 4 vols. (Paris, 1853–58; reprint edn., Vincent Monteil [ed.], Paris, 1979).
6. H. A. R. Gibb, *The Travels of Ibn Battuta A.D. 1325–1354, Translated with Notes from the Arabic Text Edited by C. Defremery and B. R. Sanguinetti,* 5 vols. Vols. 1–3: Cambridge University Press for the Hakluyt Society, 1958, 1961, and 1971. Vol. 4: Translation Completed with Annotations by C. F. Beckingham. London: Hakluyt Society, 1994. Vol. 5: Index, A. D. H. Bivar, Compiler, Aldershot, England: Ashgate Publishing, 2001.
7. The final volume was translated by C. F. Beckingham, Gibb's former student.
8. Gibb, *Travels in Asia and Africa,* p. 12.
9. A. G. Hopkins, *An Economic History of West Africa* (New York, 1973), p. 78.
10. On the medieval sources that mention IB see Chapter 14.
11. Marshall G. S. Hodgson, *The Venture of Islam: Conscience and History in World Civilization,* 3 vols. (Chicago, 1974); William H. McNeill, *The Rise of the West: A History of the Human Community* (Chicago, 1963). The concept of trans-regional "intercommunicating zones" is also important in the writings of Philip D. Curtin, notably *Cross-Cultural Trade in World History* (Cambridge, England, 1984).
12. Marshall G. S. Hodgson, "Hemispheric Inter-regional History as an Approach to World History," *Journal of World History* 1 (1954): 717.
13. Marshall G. S. Hodgson, "The Role of Islam in World History," *International Journal of Middle East Studies* 1 (1970): 116.
14. Marshall G. S. Hodgson, "The Unity of Later Islamic History," *Journal of World History* 5 (1960): 884.

1   Tangier

The learned man is esteemed in whatever place or
condition he may be, always meeting people who are
favorably disposed to him, who draw near to him and seek
his company, gratified in being close to him.[1]

                                'Abd al-Latif al-Baghdadi

The white and windy city of Tangier lies on the coast of Morocco
at the southwestern end of the Strait of Gibraltar where the cold
surface current of the Atlantic flows into the channel, forming a
river to the Mediterranean 45 miles away. According to legend,
Hercules founded the city in honor of his wife, after he split the
continents and built his pillars, the mountain known as Jebel Musa
on the African shore, the Rock of Gibraltar on the European. For
travelers sailing between Morocco and the Iberian Peninsula the
strait was indeed a river, only 16 miles across at its narrowest point
and traversed in as little as three hours in fair weather. To sail east
or west from one sea to the other was a more dangerous and
exacting feat than the crossing, owing to capricious winds and
currents as well as reefs and sandbars along the shores. Yet
merchant ships were making the passage with more and more
frequency in medieval times, and Tangier was growing along with
the other ports of the strait as an entrepôt between the commercial
networks of the Mediterranean and the North Atlantic. Tangier
was a converging point of four geographical worlds — African and
European, Atlantic and Mediterranean. It was an international
town whose character was determined by the shifting flow of
maritime traffic in the strait — merchants and warriors, craftsmen
and scholars shuttling back and forth between the pillars or gliding
under them between the ocean and the sea.

We have only a faint idea of the local history of Tangier (Tanja)
in the first quarter of the fourteenth century when Ibn Battuta was
growing up there, being educated, and moving in the secure circles
of parents, kinsmen, teachers and friends.[2] But there is no doubt
that life in the town was shaped by the patterns of history in the

Map 2: Region of the Strait of Gibraltar

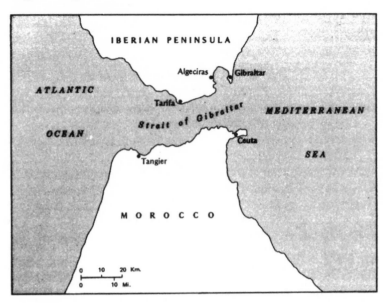

wider world of the strait. If the young Ibn Battuta, preoccupied
with his Koranic lessons, was indifferent to the momentous com-
ings and goings in the region of the channel, these must have had,
nonetheless, a pervading influence on the daily affairs of the city
and its people.

The early fourteenth century was a time of transition for all the
towns bordering the strait, as prevailing relationships between
Africa and Europe on the one hand and the Atlantic and
Mediterranean on the other were being altered, in some ways
drastically. Most conspicuous was the retreat of Muslim power
from Europe in the face of the Christian *reconquista*. During the
half millennium between the eighth and thirteenth centuries, all of
the Maghrib (North Africa from Morocco to western Libya) and
most of Iberia were under Muslim rule. On both sides of the strait
there developed a sophisticated urban civilization, founded on the
rich irrigated agriculture of Andalusia (al-Andalus), as Muslim
Iberia was called, and flourishing amid complex cultural and commercial interchange among cities all around the rim of the far
western Mediterranean. The unity of this civilization reached its
apogee in the twelfth century when the Almohads, a dynasty of

Marinid Mosque at Mansura near Tlemcen
Photo by the Author

The Old City of Tangier.
Photo by the Author.

Moroccan Berbers impelled by a militant ideology of religious reform, created a vast Mediterranean empire, whose lands spanned the strait and stretched from the Atlantic coast to Libya. The Almohad sultans, however, proved incapable of managing such an enormous territory for long. Early in the thirteenth century the political edifice began to come apart amid economic decline, religious quarrels, and countryside rebellions. In northern Iberia Christian kingdoms, which until then had existed in the shadow of Muslim civilization, took the offensive. The victory of the combined forces of Aragon, Castile, and Portugal over an Almohad army at the Battle of Las Navas de Tolosa in 1212 was the first of a succession of spectacular Christian advances against Muslim territory. One by one the great Muslim cities fell, Cordova in 1236, Valencia in 1238, Seville in 1248. By mid century the Almohads were all but driven from Iberia, and all that remained of Muslim power on the northern side of the strait was the mountainous kingdom of Granada. In North Africa the Almohad state split into three smaller kingdoms, one in the Ifriqiya (the eastern Maghrib, today Tunisia and eastern Algeria) ruled by the Hafsid dynasty; a second in the Central Maghrib governed by the 'Abd al-Wadids; and a third in Morocco under a nomadic warrior tribe of Berber nomads known as the Banu Marin, or the Marinids.

Rough and ready cavalrymen with no guiding ideology, the Marinids overthrew the last of the Almohad rulers, established a new dynastic capital at Fez, and restored a measure of political stability to Morocco in the last quarter of the thirteenth century. From the start the new sultans harbored dreams of resurrecting the Mediterranean empire of their predecessors, and with this in mind repeatedly waged war against the 'Abd al-Wadids and the Hafsids, their neighbors to the east. Some of the Marinid kings mounted seaborne campaigns against the Iberian coast, but none of these invasions seriously threatened the Christian hold on the interior of the peninsula. In any event the Moroccans were obliged to pursue an active policy in the region of the strait, which was far too important strategically to be given up to the Christian states without a struggle.

The contest, however, was no simple matter of Islam versus Christianity. The battle of faiths that had dominated the decades of the Almohad retreat was losing some of its emotional ferocity, and a relatively stable balance of power was emerging among six successor states. Four of them were Muslim — the Marinids, the

'Abd al-Wadids, the Hafsids, and the Nasrids, who ruled Granada after 1230. The other two were Christian — Castile and Aragon–Catalonia. From the later thirteenth through the following century these six kingdoms competed in peace and war with little regard to matters of religion, which served mainly as ideological cover for utterly pragmatic political or military undertakings.

War and peace in the Strait of Gibraltar converged on the five principal towns which faced it — Tarifa, Algeciras, and Gibraltar on the European side, Ceuta and Tangier on the African. These ports were the entrepôts of trade between the continents, the embarkation points for warriors on crusade, and the bases for galleys which patrolled the channel. In the later thirteenth and the fourteenth centuries they were the objects of incessant military rivalry among the kings of the region. Algeciras, for example, was ceded by Granada to the Marinids in 1275, returned to Granada in 1294, taken again by Morocco in 1333, and finally seized by Castile in 1344. Indeed, Tangier was the only one of the ports to retain the same political masters throughout this period, following the Marinid occupation in 1275. Part of the reason was that in the politics of the strait, Tangier was, relatively speaking, the least important of the five cities. The others all fronted the narrow easterly end of the channel and were vital to the trade and communication of the western Mediterranean. But Tangier, lying far off to the southwest and almost facing the Atlantic, was a prize of lesser magnitude. It would be the fortune of Portugal, an Atlantic power, to wrest the city from Moroccan control, but not until 1471.

Still, Tangier was of considerable strategic value. The lovely bay, whose white beaches curve off to the northeast of the city, was the only natural indentation of any size on the entire coast of Morocco, and it could easily shelter a fleet of warships. Along with Ceuta (Sabta) and some lesser towns on the strait, Tangier had for several centuries served as a point of embarkation for naval and cargo vessels bound for Iberia. In 1279 Sultan Abu Yusuf, founder of the Marinid dynasty, supervised the massing of a fleet of 72 galleys in the bay in order to send troops to relieve a Castilian siege of Algeciras.[3] Aside from the recurrent movement of Marinid troops, horses, and matériel through the port, the city also played host to numerous bands of Muslim pirates, who harassed shipping in the strait and made raids on the Spanish

Coast.[4] The hazardous and uncertain condition of interstate affairs no doubt stimulated the Tangierian economy and gave the population ample employment building ships, running cargos, hiring out as soldiers and seamen, and trafficking in arms and supplies. Short of a Christian attack, the city had little to lose and much to gain from the prevailing conditions of war and diplomacy in the region.

If the continuing prosperity of the city in the aftermath of the Almohad collapse resulted partly from the vigorous efforts of the Marinids to check the *reconquista*, even more important were developments in trade and seaborne technology. In the course of the Christian crusades to Palestine between the eleventh and the end of the thirteenth centuries, European long-distance shipping took almost full command of the Mediterranean. This was the first great age of Europe's economic development, and although trade between Christian and Muslim states grew by leaps, virtually all of it was carried in Latin vessels. In the western sea the Genoese took the lead, signing a commercial treaty with the Almohads in 1137–38 and thereafter opening up trade with a number of Maghribi ports, including Ceuta, and possibly Tangier, in the 1160s.[5] Merchants of Catalonia, operating principally from Barcelona and protected by the rising power of the kings of Aragon, extended their commercial operations to North Africa by the early 1200s. Traders from Marseille, Majorca, Venice, and Pisa also joined in the competition, offering grain, wine, hardware, spices, and weaponry, plus cotton, woolen, and linen textiles in return for the wool, hides, leather, wax, alum, grain, and oil of North Africa and the gold, ivory, and slaves of the lands beyond the Sahara.

With commercial traffic in the western Mediterranean growing continually in the twelfth and thirteenth centuries, it was only a matter of time before it would spill through the strait into the Atlantic. The Genoese, Catalans, Provençals, and Venetians were all established in the towns of the strait in the 1300s. But there were strong incentives to go further. To the south lay the Atlantic ports of Morocco and the prospect not only of expanding the Maghribi trade but of diverting some of the gold brought up from West Africa before it reached the Mediterranean outlets. By the later twelfth century Genoese vessels were already sailing beyond Tangier, round the northwestern tip of Africa, and down the coast to Salé, Safi, and other Moroccan ports. In 1291 the intrepid

Vivaldi brothers of Genoa vanished into *terra incognita* after setting sail down the coast of Morocco, bound for India two centuries too soon.[6]

It was also after 1275 that Genoese merchants began sailing northwestward from the strait around the great bulge of Iberia and into the waters of the North Atlantic. By 1300 both Genoese and Venetian galleys were making regular trips to ports in England and Flanders, carrying goods from all the Mediterranean lands and returning with woolens, timber, and other products of northern Europe. Here was occurring the great maritime link-up between the ocean and the sea that would weigh so much in the transformation of Europe in the later Middle Ages.

The invasion of the Atlantic by Mediterranean shipping made the Strait of Gibraltar of even greater strategic importance than it had been earlier and gave the cities along its shore a new surge of commercial vitality. Ceuta was the busiest and most prosperous of the towns on either side of the channel in the early fourteenth century.[7] But Tangier, which lay along the southwesterly route from the strait to the ports of Atlantic Morocco, had its share of the new shipping traffic.[8] In fair weather months vessels from Genoa, Catalonia, Pisa, Marseille, and Majorca might all be seen in Tangier bay — slender galleys which sat low on the surface of the water and maneuvered close to shore under the power of their oarsmen; high-sided round ships with their great triangular sails; and, perhaps occasionally after 1300, tubby-looking, square-rigged cogs from some port on the Atlantic coast of Portugal or Spain. And in addition to these, a swarm of Muslim vessels put out from the harbor to "tramp" the Maghribi coast, shuttle cargo to Iberian ports, or fish the waters of the strait. The movement of Christian merchants and sailors in and out of the town must have been a matter of regular occurrence. And in normal times these visitors mixed freely with the local Muslim population to exchange news and haggle over prices.

Tangier was indeed a frontier town in the early fourteenth century. With rough Berber soldiers tramping through the steep streets to their warships, Christian and Muslim traders jostling one another on the wharves and in the warehouses, pirates disposing of their plunder in the bazaar, the city imaged the roisterous frontier excitement of the times. Perched on the western edge of the Muslim world and caught up in the changing patterns of trade and power in the Mediterranean basin, it was a more restless and cosmopolitan city than it had ever been before. It was the sort of place where a young man might grow up and develop an urge to travel.

In the narrative of his world adventures Ibn Battuta tells us virtually nothing of his early life in Tangier. From Ibn Juzayy, the Andalusian scholar who composed and edited the *Rihla*, or from Ibn Battuta himself in the most off-hand way, we learn that he was named Abu 'Abdallah Muhammad ibn 'Abdallah ibn Muhammad ibn Ibrahim al-Lawati ibn Battuta on 25 February 1304; that his family was descended from the Berber tribe known as the Lawata; that his mother and father were still alive when he left Morocco in 1325; and that some members of his extended family besides himself were schooled in Islamic law and had pursued careers as legal scholars (*faqihs*) or judges (*qadis*). Beyond these skimpy facts, we know only what the *Rihla* reveals to us by implication: that he received the best education in law and the other Islamic sciences that Tangier could provide and that during his adolescent years he acquired an educated man's values and sensibilities.

His family obviously enjoyed respectable standing as members of the city's scholarly elite. Tangier was not a chief center of learning in fourteenth-century North Africa; it was not a Fez, a Tlemcen, or a Tunis. When Ibn Battuta was growing up, it did not yet possess one of the *madrasas*, or colleges of higher learning, which the new Marinid rulers had begun founding in their capital.[9] But Tangier, like any city of commerce in the Islamic world, required literate families who specialized in providing a variety of skills and services: the officers of mosques and other pious foundations, administrative and customs officials, scribes, accountants, notaries, legal counsellors, and judges, as well as teachers and professors for the sons of the affluent families of merchants and landowners.

The education Ibn Battuta received was one worthy of a member of a legal family. It is easy enough to imagine the young boy, eager and affable as he would be in adult life, marching off to Qur'anic school in the neighborhood mosque to have the teacher beat the Sacred Book into him until, by the age of twelve at least, he had it all committed to memory. The education of most boys would go no further than this Qur'anic training, plus perhaps a smattering of caligraphy, grammar, and arithmetic. But a lad of Ibn Battuta's family status would be encouraged to move on to advanced study of the religious sciences: Qur'anic exegesis, the traditions of the Prophet Muhammad (*hadith*), grammar, rhetoric, theology, logic, and law. The foremost scholar-teachers of the city offered courses in mosques or their own homes. Students might normally attend the lectures of a number of different men, sitting in a semi-circle at the master's feet as he read from learned texts and discoursed on their meaning. The pupil's task was not simply to grasp the substance of a text but to learn it by heart. The memorization of standard and classical texts comprising the corpus of Islamic knowledge was central to all advanced education. The most respected masters in any field of learning were the people who had not only committed to memory and thoroughly understood the greatest number of books, but who could recall and recite passages from them with ease in scholarly discourse and debate. According to Ibn Khaldun, the great philosopher and historian of the later fourteenth century, memory training was even more rigorously pursued in Moroccan education than in other parts of the Muslim world.[10] The purpose of education in the Islamic Middle Period, it should be understood, was not to teach students to think critically about their human or natural environment or to push the frontiers of knowledge beyond the limits of their elders. Rather it was to transmit to the coming generation the spiritual truths, moral values, and social rules of the past which, after all, Muslims had found valid by the astonishing success of their faith and civilization. Education was in every sense conservative.

Although the narrow discipline of memorization occupied much of a student's time, an Islamic education nonetheless addressed the whole man. In the course of his advanced studies a boy was expected to acquire the values and manners of a gentleman. This included his everyday conversation in Arabic. Despite the Berber-speaking heritage of North Africa, including Tangier and its environs, Arabic was the language of civilized speech in every Maghribi city. A man of learning, unlike the ordinary citizen, was expected to know the subtle complexities of formal Arabic grammar, syntax, and poetics and to decorate his conversation with Qur'anic quotations, classical allusions, and rhymed phrases.[11] Ibn Battuta's family was of Berber origin, but we may suppose that he grew up speaking Arabic in his own household as well as in the company of other educated men and boys. The *Rihla* gives no evidence that he could speak the Berber language of northern Morocco.

The narrative of his life experience reveals that in his youth he mastered the qualities of social polish expected of the urbane scholar and gentleman.

Politeness, discretion, propriety, decency, cleanliness, ways of cooking, table manners and rules of dress all formed part of that extremely refined code of *savoir vivre* which occupied so predominant a place in social relations and moral judgements. Whatever caused shame and could irritate or inconvenience someone was considered impolite. A courteous and refined man . . . evinced in his behavior a combination of attitudes, gestures and words which made his relations with others harmonious, amiable and so natural that they seemed spontaneous.[12]

This description pertains to learned Moroccans in the nineteenth century, but it could easily apply to Ibn Battuta and to the well-bred men of his time. If in the course of his world travels he would display some less fortunate traits — impatience, profligacy, impetuousness, pious self-righteousness, and an inclination to be unctuous in the presence of wealth or power — he was nonetheless an eminently civilized individual. As he grew into adulthood his speech, his manners, his conduct would identify him as an *'alim*, a man of learning, and as a member of the social category of educated men called the *'ulama*.

As his education advanced, he began to specialize in the law, as other members of his family had done. The study of law (in Arabic *fiqh*) was one of the fundamental religious sciences. In Islam the Sacred Law, or *shari'a*, was founded principally on the revealed Koran and the words and actions of the Prophet. Ideally it was the basis not merely of religious practice but of the social order in its broadest expression. Although Muslim kings and princes promulgated administrative and penal ordinances as occasion demanded (and increasingly so in the Middle Period of Islam), the *shari'a* addressed the full spectrum of social relations — marriage, inheritance, slavery, taxation, market relations, moral behavior, and so on. Unlike the situation in the Christian world, no formal distinction was made between canon and secular legal systems. Therefore, Ibn Battuta's juridical training was entirely integrated with his theological and literary education.

In Sunni Islam, that is, mainstream or, perhaps less appropriately, orthodox Islam, the legal systems embraced four major "schools" of law, called *madhhabs*. They were the Hanafi, the Shafi'i, the Maliki, and the Hanbali. The four schools differed in matters of juristic detail, not in fundamental legal principles. The school to which an individual adhered depended largely on where he happened to have been born, since the *madhhabs* evolved during the early centuries of Islam along territorial lines. The Maliki school, named after its eighth-century founder Malik ibn 'Anas, has been historically dominant throughout North Africa. The Almohad rulers of the twelfth and thirteenth centuries possessed a distinctive approach to jurisprudence which set them and the minority of scholars who served them apart from the four schools and involved vigorous suppression of the Maliki doctors. The rude Marinid war captains who replaced the Almohads had no thoughts on the subject of law at all. They were, however, quick to distance themselves from the ideology of their predecessors by championing the re-establishment of Malikism. In this way they gained status and legitimacy in the eyes of Morocco's educated majority and enlisted their help in consolidating the new political order. Therefore, Ibn Battuta grew up and went to school during a time of renaissance in Maliki legal studies. And partly because Malikism had been temporarily out of favor and was now back in, legal education in fourteenth century Morocco tended to stress uncritical, doctrinaire acceptance of the interpretations of law contained in the major Maliki texts.[13] The law classes he attended in Tangier would have involved mainly the presentation and memorizing of sections of the corpus of Maliki *fiqh*, the professors using summaries and abridgments of major legal texts of that school.

As his introductory legal studies proceeded, he was also assimilating the specific cultural style of a Muslim lawyer. The education, as well as the speech and manners, of the juridical class was largely the same everywhere in the Muslim world. Therefore, Ibn Battuta's particular socialization was equipping him to move easily among men of learning anywhere in the Dar al-Islam. If he aspired to be a jurisprudent one day, then he was expected to exemplify the prized qualities of members of his profession — erudition, dignified comportment, moderation in speech and conduct, and absolute incorruptibility. He also adopted the distinctive dress of the legal scholar: a more or less voluminous turban; a *taylasan*, or shawl-like garment draped over the head and shoulders; and a long, wide-sleeved, immaculately clean gown of fine material. Most educated men wore beards. In one passage in the *Rihla* Ibn Battuta makes an incidental reference to his own.[14] (That reference, it might be added, is the only clue he offers anywhere in the narrative as to his own physical appearance. Since the ancestors of a Tangierian might include dark-eyed, olive-skinned Arabs, blue-eyed, fair-haired Berbers, and even black West Africans, nothing can be assumed about the traveler's physiognomy.)

Another important dimension of his education was his introduction to Sufism, the mystical dimension of Islam. Throughout the Muslim world in the thirteenth and fourteenth centuries, Sufism was addressing popular desires for an Islamic faith of warmth, emotion, and personal hope, needs that outward performance of Qur'anic duties could not alone supply. Indeed it was during the later Middle Period that Sunni orthodoxy embraced Sufism wholeheartedly and transformed it into a powerful force for the further expansion of Islam.

Two ideas were at the heart of the Sufi movement. One was that the individual Muslim is capable of achieving direct and personal communion with God. The other was that the path to God could be found through the intermediary of a saintly master or *shaykh*. Such an individual was thought to be a *wali*, a "friend of God," who radiated the quality of divine grace (*baraka*) and could transmit it to others. With the help of his master, the Sufi initiate immersed himself in mystical teachings, rituals, and special prayers and strove to inculcate high spiritual qualities in everyday life. Sufism was also a social movement because it involved the formation of congregations of seekers who gathered round a particular master to hear his teachings and join with him in devotional exercises. All across the Islamic world in Ibn Battuta's time these groups were just beginning to become institutionalized as religious orders, each one organized around common devotion to the spiritual teachings, or "path," of the founder of the order and his successors. These brotherhoods and sisterhoods were also developing as civic organizations and mutual aid societies and, by the fifteenth century in some areas, as loci of considerable political power.

Sufism had a special appeal for rural folk, whose arduous lives demanded a concrete faith of hope and salvation and who were isolated to a greater or lesser extent from the literate, juridically minded Islam of the cities. Sufi lodges, called *zawiyas*, organized as centers for worship, mystical education, and charity, were springing up all across North Africa in Ibn Battuta's time, especially among rural Berber populations to whom they offered a richer, more accessible religion and a new kind of communal experience. In Morocco Sufi preachers were notably active and successful among the Berber-speaking populations of the Rif Mountains, the region south and east of Tangier.[15] Yet mystical ideas were also penetrating the towns in the thirteenth and fourteenth centuries, perhaps rather early in Tangier because of its nearness to the Rif. Moreover, Tangier, for all its intellectual respectability, was not one of the great bastions of scriptural orthodoxy like Fez, where the leading Maliki doctors were still inclined to be suspicious of Sufism, or any other religious idea not documented in their law books or theological treatises.

Although we have no idea what Ibn Battuta's early experience with Sufism may have been, his behavior during his travels is itself evidence that he grew up in a social climate rich in mystical beliefs and that these ideas were tightly interwoven with his formal, scriptural education. By the time he left Tangier, he was so deeply influenced by Sufi ideas, especially belief in personal *baraka* and the value of ascetic devotionalism, that his traveling career turned out to be, in a sense, a grand world tour of the lodges and tombs of famous Sufi mystics and saints. He was never, to be sure, a committed Sufi disciple. He remained throughout his life a "lay" Sufi, attending mystical gatherings, seeking the blessing and wisdom of spiritual luminaries, and retreating on occasion into brief periods of ascetic contemplation. But he never gave up the worldly life. He was, rather, a living example of that moral reconciliation between popular Sufism and public orthodoxy that was working itself out in the Islamic world of his time. Consequently, he embarked on his travels prepared to show as much equanimity in the company of holy hermits in mountain caves as in the presence of the august professors of urban colleges.

Aside from the local teachers and divines of his youth, he is likely to have had contact with men of letters who passed through Tangier at one time or another. The scholarly class of the Islamic world was an extraordinarily mobile group. In the Maghrib of the later Middle Period the learned, like modern conference-hopping academics, circulated incessantly from one city and country to another, studying with renowned professors, leading diplomatic missions, taking up posts in mosques and royal chanceries.

Scholars routinely shuttled back and forth across the Strait of Gibraltar between the cities of Morocco and the Nasrid Sultanate. Indeed, Ibn Battuta had a cousin (the *Rihla* tells us) who served as a *qadi* in the Andalusian city of Ronda.

Apart from this normal circulation, there was over the long run of time a pattern of one-way migration of educated people from Andalusia to North Africa, a kind of Iberian brain drain which accelerated in response to each new surge of Christian power and concomitant loss of security and opportunity for Muslims on the northern side of the strait.[16] Iberia's loss, however, was North Africa's gain, since Andalusian scholars and craftsmen, arriving in sporadic streams between the thirteenth and fifteenth centuries, did much to enliven the cultural life of Maghribi towns. If Tangier took in few immigrants compared with Fez or other premier cities, the legacy of the great Andalusian intellectual tradition must have rubbed off on the city's educated class to a significant extent.

No young scholar, however well connected his family might be, could expect to pursue a religious or public vocation until he had undertaken advanced studies with at least a few eminent teachers. The local masters and "visiting scholars" of Tangier could give a boy a solid foundation in the major disciplines. But any lad with a large intellectual appetite and personal ambition to match was obliged to take to the road along with the rest of the scholarly community. Fez lay only a few days traveling time to the south, and its colleges, just being built under Marinid sponsorship, were attracting students from all Morocco's provincial towns. But though Fez was fast gaining a reputation as the most important seat of learning west of Tunis, it lacked the shining prestige of the great cultural centers of the Middle East, notably Cairo and Damascus. In those cities were to be found the most illustrious teachers, the most varied curricula, the biggest colleges, the rarest libraries, and, for a young man with a career ahead of him, the most respected credentials.

Notes

1. Quoted in George Makdisi, *The Rise of Colleges* (Edinburgh, 1981), p. 91.

2. The limited literary sources on Tangier in the Almohad age and later have been brought together in Edouard Michaux-Bellaire, *Villes et tribus du Maroc: Tanger et sa zone*, vol. 7 (Paris, 1921).

3. Derek Latham, "The Later 'Azafids," *Revue de l'Occident Musulman et de la Méditerranée* 15–16 (1973): 112–13.

4. Charles-Emmanuel Dufourcq, *L'Espagne catalane et le Maghrib aux XIIIe et XIVe siècles* (Paris, 1966), p. 575. Dufourcq notes an upsurge of piracy emanating from Moroccan ports in the early fourteenth century.

5. Hilmar C. Krueger, "Genoese Trade with Northwest Africa in the Twelfth Century," *Speculum* 8 (1933): 377–82. Krueger does not mention Tangier specifically, but there is no doubt that Europeans were sailing there about this time since they were also beginning to put in at Atlantic ports southwest of Tangier.

6. J.H. Parry, *The Discovery of the Sea* (New York, 1974), p. 75.

7. Charles-Emmanuel Dufourcq, "La Question de Ceuta au XIIIe siècle," *Hespéris* 42 (1955): 67–127; Derek Latham, "The Strategic Position and Defence of Ceuta in the Later Muslim Period," *Islamic Quarterly* 15 (1971): 189–204; Anna Mascarello, "Quelques aspects des activités italiennes dans le Maghreb médiéval," *Revue d'Histoire et de Civilisation du Maghreb* 5 (1968): 74–75.

8. Dufourcq, *L'Espagne catalane*, p. 159.

9. A *madrasa* was founded in Tangier some time during the reign of Abu l'Hasan (1331–51). Henri Terrasse, *Histoire du Maroc*, 2 vols. (Casablanca, 1949–50), vol. 2, p. 53.

10. Ibn Khaldun, *The Muqaddimah*, 2nd edn., trans. F. Rosenthal, 3 vols. (Princeton, N.J., 1967), vol. 2, pp. 430–31.

11. On the culture of men of traditional learning in nineteenth- and twentieth-century Morocco, see Dale F. Eickelman, *Knowledge and Power in Morocco: The Education of a Twentieth Century Notable* (Princeton, N.J., 1985).

12. Kenneth Brown, *People of Salé: Tradition and Change in a Moroccan City, 1830–1930* (Cambridge, Mass., 1976), p. 103.

13. Alfred Bel, *La Religion musulmane en Berbérie* (Paris, 1938), pp. 320–22, 327.

14. On the dress of legal scholars in both Granada and Morocco see Rachel Arié, *L'Espagne musulmane au temps des Nasrides* (Paris, 1973), pp. 382–91.

15. Bel, *La Religion musulmane*, pp. 352–53; Terrasse, *Histoire de Maroc*, vol. 1, p. 81.

16. Mohamed Talbi speaks of Muslim emigration from Spain as a "fuite des cerveaux" in "Les contacts culturels entre l'Ifriqiya hafside (1230–1569) et le sultanat nasride d'Espagne (1232–1492)" in *Actas del II Coloquis hispano-tunecino de estudios historicos* (Madrid, 1973), pp. 63–90.

2 The Maghrib

A scholar's education is greatly improved by traveling in
quest of knowledge and meeting the authoritative
teachers (of his time).[1]

Ibn Khaldun

Tangier would have counted among its inhabitants many individuals who had traveled to the Middle East, most of them with
the main purpose of carrying out the *hajj*, or pilgrimage to the
Holy Places of Mecca and Medina in the Hijaz region of Western.
Arabia. Islam obliged every Muslim who was not impoverished,
enslaved, insane, or endangered by war or epidemic to go to
Mecca at least once in his lifetime and to perform there the set of
collective ceremonies prescribed by the *shari'a*. Each year
hundreds and often thousands of North Africans fulfilled their
duty, joining in a great ritual migration that brought together
believers from the far corners of the Afro–Eurasian world. A
traveler bound for the Middle East might have any number of
mundane or purely personal goals in mind — trade, study,
diplomacy, or simply adventure, but the *hajj* was almost always the
expressed and over-riding motive. The high aim of reaching Mecca
in time for the pilgrimage season in the month of Dhu l-Hijja gave
shape to the traveler's itinerary and lent a spirit of jubilation to
what was a long, exhausting, and sometimes dangerous journey.

In the fourteenth century an aspiring pilgrim of Tangier had the
choice of traveling by land or sea, or a combination of the two.
European vessels which put in at Maghribi ports, as well as Muslim
coasting ships, commonly took passengers on board and delivered
them to some port further east along the Mediterranean shore.[2]

Until the age of the steamship and the charter flight, however,
most pilgrims chose the overland route across the Maghrib, Libya,
and Egypt. This route was in fact part of a network of tracks
linking the towns and cities of northern Africa with one another. A
traveler from Morocco might follow a number of slightly varying
itineraries, passing part of the way along the Mediterranean coast

Map 3: Ibn Battuta's Itinerary from Tangier to the Nile Delta, 1325–36

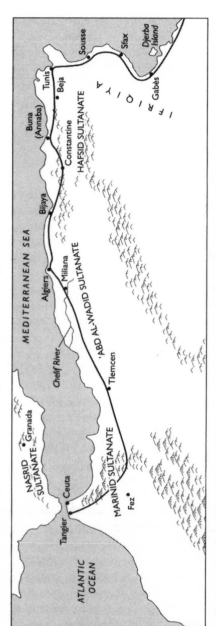

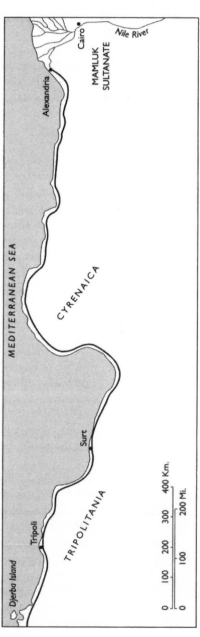

and part of the way across the high steppes which ran west to east between the coastal mountains and the Atlas ranges of the deep interior. Or, pilgrims starting out in southern Morocco could go by way of the oases and river valleys which were strung out at comfortable intervals along the northern fringe of the Sahara. Northern and southern routes alike converged in Ifriqiya. From there to Egypt pilgrims took the coast road, the lifeline between the Maghrib and the Middle East, which ran along the narrow ribbon of settled territory between the Mediterranean and the Libyan desert.

Whether by land or sea, getting to Mecca was a risky affair. If seafarers had to brave storms, pirates, and hostile navies, overland travelers confronted bandits, nomad marauders, or the possibility of stumbling into a war between one North African state and another. Consequently, most pilgrims going overland kept, for the sake of security, to the company of others, often the small caravans that shuttled routinely between the towns and rural markets. Travelers who had little money to start with frequently traded a stock of wares of their own along the way — leather goods or precious stones for example — or offered their labor here and there, sometimes taking several months or even years to finally work or chaffer their way as far as Egypt.

Quite apart from these little bands of pilgrims in the company of merchants and wayfarers was the great *hajj* caravan, which ideally went every year from Morocco to Cairo, and from there to the Hijaz with the pilgrims from Egypt. Starting usually in Fez or Tlemcen, the procession picked up groups of pilgrims along the way like a rolling snowball, some of them walking, others riding horses, mules, donkeys, or camels. By the time the company reached Cairo, it might in some years number several thousand.

The flow of pilgrims across the nearly 3,000 miles of steppe, desert, and mountain separating Morocco from Mecca was one of the most conspicuous expressions of the extraordinary mobility and cosmopolitanism within the Dar al-Islam in the Middle Period. Although North Africa was known as the Island of the West (Jazirat al-Maghrib), a mountainous realm separated from the heartland of Islam by sea and desert, the intercommunciation across the barren gap of Libya, whether by *hajj* caravan or otherwise, was nonetheless continuous — barring times of unusual political instability on one side or the other. And while the commercial aspect of the link was important, its cultural dimension was even more so. If few educated Egyptians, Syrians, or Persians found reason to travel west in the fourteenth century (and tended to think of the Maghrib as Islam's back country, its Wild West), the learned classes of North Africa and Granada were always setting off on tours to the East in order to draw spiritual and intellectual sustenance from their scholarly counterparts in Cairo, Damascus, and the Holy Cities of the Hijaz. For scholarly North Africans the *hajj* was almost always more than a journey to Mecca and home again. Rather it was a *rihla*, a grand study tour of the great mosques and *madrasas* of the heartland, an opportunity to acquire books and diplomas, deepen one's knowledge of theology and law, and commune with refined and civilized men.

Literate Moroccans of the fourteenth century owed their greatest intellectual debt not to the Middle East but to the learned establishment of Muslim Iberia. Yet Andalusia's time was fast running out, and beleaguered little Granada, despite a brave showing of artistic energy in its latter days, could no longer provide much cultural leadership. The Middle East, however, having somehow survived the dark catastrophes of the Mongol century, was experiencing a cultural florescence, notably in the Mamluk-ruled lands of Egypt and Syria. Gentlemen scholars of far western cities like Tangier could readily look there for civilized models, higher knowledge, and learned companionship. And though the road to Mecca was long and perilous, the internationalism of Islamic culture, continuously reaffirmed, held men of learning in a bond of unity and shrank the miles between them.

On 14 June 1325 (2 Rajab 725 A.H.) Ibn Battuta rode out of Tangier and headed southeastward through the highlands of the Eastern Rif to join the main caravan road that ran from Fez to Tlemcen. He was 21 years old and eager for more learning, and more adventure, than his native city could hope to give him. The parting was bittersweet:

My departure from Tangier, my birthplace, took place . . . with the object of making the Pilgrimage to the Holy House [at Mecca] and of visiting the tomb of the Prophet, God's richest blessing and peace be on him [at Medina]. I set out alone, having neither fellow-traveler in whose companionship I might find cheer, nor caravan whose party I might join, but swayed by an overmastering impulse within me and a desire long-cherished in my bosom to visit these illustrious sanctuaries. So I braced my resolution to quit all my dear ones, female and male, and forsook my home as birds forsake their nests. My parents being yet in the bonds of life, it weighed sorely upon me to part from them, and both they and I were afflicted with sorrow at this separation.

He did not, it seems, set out from Tangier with any plan to join the *hajj* caravan, if there was one that year. It was not, in any event, a bad year for a young man to launch forth entirely on his own, for political conditions in the Western Maghrib were untypically calm. Abu Sa'id (1310–31), the reigning Marinid Sultan of Morocco, was a pious and relatively unenterprising ruler and, unlike many of the kings of his line, not much interested in pursuing military adventures either in Iberia or North Africa. Around the end of the thirteenth century the pilgrimage caravans from Morocco had had to be suspended for several years owing to Marinid wars against their eastern neighbor, the 'Abd al-Wadid kingdom.[3] But less intrigued than his predecessors with visions of a neo-Almohad empire, Abu Sa'id permitted a de facto peace to prevail on his eastern frontier during most of his reign. Consequently, merchants and pilgrims could expect to pass between the two realms in relative security.

Riding eastward through Morocco's mountainous interior and then onto the high plains that stretched into the Central Maghrib, Ibn Battuta reached Tlemcen, capital of the 'Abd al-Wadid state, in the space of a few weeks. Although Tlemcen was a busy commercial transit center and intellectually the liveliest city anywhere between Fez and Tunis, he did not linger there. For upon arriving he learned that two envoys from the Hafsid Sultanate of Ifriqiya had been in the city on a diplomatic mission and had just left to return home. The 'Abd al-Wadids, enjoying an unusual break in their wars with the Marinids, had turned their full attention to their eastern marches where they were engaged in a protracted struggle with the Hafsids, notably over control of Bijaya (Bougie), a key Mediterranean port 450 miles west of Tunis. At the time Ibn Battuta arrived in Tlemcen, Abu Tashfin, the 'Abd al-Wadid sultan, was conspiring with a number of Ifriqiyan rebels and pretenders to unseat his Hafsid neighbor and satisfy his own expansionist ambitions.[4] It may be that the two envoys had come to

Tlemcen to try to negotiate peace with Abu Tashfin and were now going home, albeit empty-handed.[5] In any case, someone advised Ibn Battuta to catch up with them and their entourage and proceed on to Tunis in the safety of their company.

The busiest commercial routes out of Tlemcen led northward to the ports of Oran and Honein. But Ibn Battuta took the lonelier pilgrimage trail running northeastward through a series of river valleys and arid plains flanked on one side or the other by the low, fragmented mountain chains that broke up the Mediterranean hinterland. This part of the Maghrib was sparsely populated in the fourteenth century. He might have ridden for several days at a time without encountering any towns, only Berber hamlets and bands of Arabic-speaking camel herders who ranged over the broad, green-brown valleys and depressions.

After what must have been two or three weeks on the road, he caught up with the Ifriqiyans at Miliana, a small commercial center in the Zaccar hills overlooking the plain of the Chelif River. Eager scholar that he was, he could hardly have made better choices of his first traveling companions. One of them was Abu 'Abdallah al-Zubaydi, a prominent theologian, the other Abu 'Abdallah al-Nafzawi, a *qadi* of Tunis. Unfortunately, tragedy struck as soon as Ibn Battuta arrived. Both envoys fell ill owing to the hot weather (it was mid summer) and were forced to remain in Miliana for ten days. On the eleventh the little caravan resumed its journey, but just four miles from the town the *qadi* grew worse and died. Al-Zubaydi, in the company of the dead man's son, whose name was Abu al-Tayyib, returned to Miliana for mourning and burial, leaving Ibn Battuta to continue on ahead with a party of Ifriqiyan merchants.

Descending the steep slopes of the Zaccar, the travelers arrived at the port of Algiers, and Ibn Battuta and his first sight of the sea since leaving Tangier. Algiers was a place of minor importance in the fourteenth century, not the maritime capital it would come to be in another two hundred years. It had little to recommend it to a member of the educated class. Abu Muhammad al-'Abdari, an Andalusian scholar who had traveled from Morocco to Arabia 36 years earlier and had subsequently returned home to write a *rihla* of his experiences, sized up the city's literate establishment and quickly wrote the place off:

> In setting foot in this town, I wondered whether one would be able to meet any enlightened people or any persons whose erudition

would offer some attraction; but I had the feeling of one looking for a horse that wasn't hungry or the eggs of a camel.[6]

Ibn Battuta likely shared al-'Abdari's opinion since he says nothing in his narrative about what Algiers was like. In any case, he and his merchant companions camped outside the walls of the city for several days, waiting for al-Zubaydi and Abu al-Tayyib to catch up.

As soon as they did, the party set out for the port of Bijaya, the western frontier city of the Hafsid kingdom. The journey took them directly eastward through the heart of the Grand Kabylie Mountains, a region of immense oak and cedar forests, spectacular gorges, and summits reaching higher than 6,500 feet, rougher country than Ibn Battuta had seen since leaving home. Bijaya lay up against the slopes of the mountains near the mouth of the Souman River, which separates the Grand Kabylie range from the Little Kabylie to the east. It was a busy international port and the principal maritime outlet for the dense communities of Berber farmers who inhabited the highland valleys behind it.

Bijaya was the first real city Ibn Battuta had the opportunity to explore since leaving Tlemcen. Nonetheless, he was determined to push on quickly, and this in spite of an attack of fever that left him badly weakened. Al-Zubaydi advised him to stay in Bijaya until he recovered, but the young man was adamant: "If God decrees my death, then my death shall be on the road, with my face set towards the land of the Hijaz." Relenting before this high sentiment, al-Zubaydi offered to lend him an ass and a tent if he would agree to sell his own donkey and heavy baggage so that they might all travel at a quicker pace. Ibn Battuta agreed, thanked God for His beneficence, and prepared for the departure for Constantine, the next major city on the main pilgrimage route.

Al-Zubaydi's insistence on traveling fast and light had less to do with his young friend's illness than with the dangers that lay on the road ahead. Ibn Battuta had had the good fortune to cross Morocco and the 'Abd al-Wadid lands during a period of relative peace. But the Eastern Maghrib in 1325 was in the midst of one of the recurring cycles of political and military crisis that characterized the Hafsid age. Sultan Abu Yahya Abu Bakr, who had acceded to the Hafsid throne in 1318, was yet striving to gain a reasonable measure of control over his domains in the face of a Pandora's box of plots, betrayals, revolts, and invasions. On one side were rival members of the Hafsid royal family, who from provincial bases in various parts of the country were organizing movements either to seize the capital city of Tunis or to set up petty kingdoms of their own. On the other side were the 'Abd al-Wadids, who repeatedly invaded Abu Bakr's western territories and tried almost every year, though never successfully, to force the walls of Bijaya.

As if these enemies were not enough, the sultan had to contend with the turbulent and unpredictable Arab warrior tribes who for more than two centuries had been the dominant political force over large areas of rural Ifriqiya. These nomads were descendants of the great wave of Arabic-speaking, camel-herding migrants, known collectively as the Banu Hilal, who had trekked from Egypt in the eleventh century and then gone on to penetrate the steppes and coastal lowlands of the Maghrib as far west as the Atlantic plains. If over the long run the relationship between these companies of herdsmen and the indigenous Berbers of the towns and villages was described far less by hostility than by mutual commercial and cultural dependence, the migrations were nonetheless a source of persistent trouble for North African rulers, who tried time and again to harness the military power of the Arabs to their own ends, only to find their erstwhile allies putting in with rebels and pretenders. In 1325 Arab bands were politically teamed up with at least two Hafsid rebels as well as with Abu Tashfin, the 'Abd al-Wadid. At the same time that Ibn Battuta was making his way across the Central Maghrib, an 'Abd al-Wadid army was laying siege to Constantine and had Sultan Abu Bakr himself bottled up inside the city. In the meantime, a Hafsid pretender and his Arab cohorts took advantage of the sultan's helplessness to occupy Tunis. The kingdom was in a state of civil confusion, the roads were unsafe, and roving bands of Arab cavalry plagued the countryside.

Ignoring the tumult, Ibn Battuta and his companions struck out from Bijaya across the Little Kabylie Mountains and arrived at Constantine without encountering trouble. By this time (it must have been August) the approaches to the city were clear. The 'Abd al-Wadid army had precipitously given up its siege some weeks earlier and returned to Tlemcen in failure, leaving Abu Bakr free to restore a degree of order in the region and lead his loyal forces back to Tunis to eject the rebels.[7]

Although Constantine was the largest city in the interior of the

Eastern Maghrib, Ibn Battuta did not tarry there long. Consequently he has little to recall about it in the *Rihla* — except the one notable fact that he was privileged to make the acquaintance of the governor, a son of Abu Bakr, who came out to the edge of town to welcome al-Zubaydi. The meeting was a memorable one for the young pilgrim because the governor presented him with a gift of alms, the first of many presents he would receive from kings and governors during the course of his travels. In this instance it was two gold dinars and a fine woolen mantle to replace his old one, which by this stage of the journey was in rags. Almsgiving was one of the five sacred pillars of Islam, the duty of princes and peasants alike to share one's material wealth with others and thus remit it to God. The obligation included voluntary giving (*sadaqa*) to specific classes of people: the poor, orphans, prisoners, slaves (for ransoming), fighters in the holy war, and wayfarers. Falling eminently into this last category, Ibn Battuta would during the next several years see his welfare assured, to one degree or another, by an array of pious individuals who were moved to perform acts of kindness, the more readily so since the recipient was himself an educated gentleman well worthy of such tokens of God's beneficence.

Leaving Constantine better dressed and richer, he and his friends headed northeast across more mountainous country, reaching the Mediterranean again at the port of Buna (Bone, today Annaba). After resting here for several days in the security of the city walls, he bade farewell to the merchants who had accompanied him half way across the Central Maghrib and continued on toward Tunis with al-Zubaydi and Abu al-Tayyib. Now the little party "traveled light with the utmost speed, pushing on night and day without stopping" for fear of attack by Arab marauders. Ibn Battuta was once again struck by fever and had to tie himself to his saddle with a turban cloth to keep from falling off, since they dared not stop for long. Their route took them parallel to the coast through high cork and oak forests, then gradually downward into the open plain and the expansive wheat lands of central Ifriqiya. From there they had a level road along the fertile Medjerda River valley to the western environs of Tunis.

Of all the North African cities where art and intellect flourished, Tunis was premier during most of the thirteenth and fourteenth centuries. The Almohads had made it their provincial capital in the Eastern Maghrib, and it was under their patronage that it took on the physical and demographic dimensions of a major city, attaining a population of about 100,000 during peak periods of prosperity.[8] The Hafsids, who started out as Almohad governors over Ifriqiya and subsequently represented themselves as the legitimate dynastic heirs of the empire, continued to rule from Tunis and to cultivate the city's corps of scholars and craftsmen, much as the Marinids, equally driven to identify themselves with the Almohad model of civilized taste, were doing in Fez.

Like other Maghribi cities of that age, Tunis under the Hafsids built its splendid mosques and palaces, laid out its public gardens, and founded its colleges with wealth that came in large measure from long-distance trade. In the early fourteenth century Tunis was the busiest of the ports which lay along the economic frontier between the European seaborne trade of the Mediterranean and the Muslim caravan network of the African interior. The Ifriqiyan hinterland plain was narrow but rich enough to export a wide range of Maghribi products — wool, leather, hides, cloth, wax, olive oil, and grain. Tunis was also a consumer and transit market for goods from sub-Saharan Africa — gold, ivory, slaves, ostrich feathers. What gave the city its special prominence was its strategic position on the southern rim of the Sicilian Channel, which joined (and divided) the maritime complexes of the Western and Eastern Mediterranean. Tunis maintained close commercial ties with Egypt by way of Muslim coastal and overland trade and was well placed to serve as a major emporium for Christian merchants of the Western Mediterranean who found it a convenient place to buy exotic goods of the East without themselves venturing on the voyage to Egypt or the Levant.

What Ibn Battuta recalls about his feelings upon arriving in Tunis is not the elation of a pilgrim who has reached one of the great centers of religious learning along the *hajj* route, but the forlornness of a young man in a strange city:

> The townsfolk came out to welcome the *shaykh* Abu 'Abdallah al-Zubaydi and to welcome Abu al-Tayyib, the son of the *qadi* Abu 'Abdallah al-Nafzawi. On all sides they came forward with greetings and questions to one another, but not a soul said a word of greeting to me, since there was none of them that I knew. I felt so sad at heart on account of my loneliness that I could not restrain the tears that started to my eyes, and wept bitterly.

In no time at all, however things were looking up:

> One of the pilgrims, realizing the cause of my distress, came up
> to me with a greeting and friendly welcome, and continued to
> comfort me with friendly talk until I entered the city, where I
> lodged in the college of the Booksellers.

After dodging tribal marauders all along the road from Bijaya,
Ibn Battuta managed to arrive in Tunis during a period of relative
political calm. The harried Abu Bakr, who had found himself shut
out of the citadel of Tunis by rebels three different times since
1321, returned from Constantine and recaptured the city perhaps
only a few days ahead of Ibn Battuta's arrival there.[9] Indeed Abu
Bakr probably resumed authority just in time for the 'Id al-Fitr,
the feast celebrating the end of Ramadan, the Muslim month of
fasting during daylight hours. Ibn Battuta was on hand to witness
the sultan fulfill his customary duty of leading "a magnificent
procession" of officials, courtiers, and soldiers from the citadel to
a special outdoor praying ground (*musalla*) that accommodated
the crowds gathered for the prayers marking the Breaking of the
Fast.[10]

Ibn Battuta spent about two months in Tunis, arriving some
days before 10 September 1325 and leaving in early November. It
was common for educated travelers or pilgrims to take lodging
temporarily in a college, even though they were not regularly
attending lectures. The *madrasa* of the Booksellers where he
stayed was one of three colleges in existence in Tunis at that
time.[11] His recollections of his first visit to the city are slight, but
we might be sure that he spent most of his time in the company of
the gentlemen-scholars of the city. He may indeed have had exposure to some of the eminent Maliki *'ulama* of the century. Since
the demise of the Almohads, the Maliki school was enjoying as
much of a resurgence in Ifriqiya as it was in Morocco. The Hafsid
rulers were appointing Maliki scholars to high positions of state
and patronizing the *madrasas*, where Maliki juridical texts were
the heart of the curriculum.

If the Tunis elite held out an estimable model of erudition, they
were also masters of refined taste and that union of piety and
restrained wordliness that Ibn Battuta would exemplify in adulthood. During the previous century Tunis had been a distant refuge
for successive waves of Muslims emigrating from Andalusia in the

wake of the *reconquista*. Of all the North African cities with populations of Iberian descent, Tunis had the liveliest and most productive. The Andalusians, coming from a civilized tradition that was more polished than that of North Africa, were leaders in the fields of architecture, craftsmanship, horticulture, music, belle-lettres, and the niceties of diplomatic and courtly protocol. An Andalusian strain seems evident in Ibn Battuta's own mannerly character, and we can wonder what seasoning effect two months in Tunis among such people may have had.

That he was already showing promise as an intelligent Maliki scholar was evident in the circumstances of his departure from Tunis in November 1325. He had left home a lonely journeyer eager to join up with whoever might tolerate his company. He left Tunis as the appointed *qadi* of a caravan of pilgrims. This was his first official post as an aspiring jurist. Perhaps the honor went to him because no better qualified lawyer was present in the group or because, as he tells us in the narrative, most of the people in the company were Moroccan Berbers. In any case, a *hajj* caravan was a sort of community and required formal leadership: a chief (*amir*) who had all the powers of the captain of a ship, and a *qadi*, who adjudicated disputes and thereby kept peace and order among the travelers.

The main caravan route led southward along Tunisia's rich littoral of olive and fruit groves and through a succession of busy maritime cities — Sousse, Sfax, Gabès. Some miles south of Gabès the road turned abruptly eastward with the coast, running between the island of Djerba on one side, the fringe of the Sahara on the other. The next major stop was Tripoli, the last urban outpost of the Hafsid domain.

The province of Tripolitania, today part of Libya, marked geographically the eastern extremity of the island Maghrib. From here the coastline ran southeastward for more than 400 miles, cutting further and further into the climatic zone of the Sahara until desert and water came together, obliterating entirely the narrow coastal band of fertility. Further on the land juts suddenly northward again into latitudes of higher rainfall. Here was the well-populated region of Cyrenaica with its forests and pasturelands and fallen Roman towns. If Tripolitania was historically and culturally the end of the Maghrib, Cyrenaica was the beginning of the Middle East, the two halves of Libya divided one from the other by several hundred miles of sand and sea.

Across the breadth of the coastal Libyan countryside Arab herding tribes ruled supreme, and once again Ibn Battuta and his companions courted trouble. Between Gabès and Tripoli a company of archers, no doubt provided by the Hafsid sultan to protect the *hajj* caravan, kept rovers at bay. In Tripoli, however, Ibn Battuta decided to leave the main group, which lingered in the city because of rain and cold, and push on ahead with a small troop of Moroccans, presumably leaving his judgeship, at least temporarily, in the hands of a subordinate. Somewhere near the port town of Surt (Sirte) a band of cameleers tried to attack the little party. But according to the *Rihla*, "the Divine Will diverted them and prevented them from doing us harm that they had intended." After reaching Cyrenaica in safety, the travelers waited for the rest of the caravan to catch up, then continued, presumably without further incident, toward the Nile.

Crossing Libya, Ibn Battuta had greater reason than ever to be wary of trouble since he no longer had only himself to consider. While the caravan was in Sfax, he entered into a contract of marriage with the daughter of a Tunisian official in the pilgrim company. When they reached Tripoli, the woman was presented to him. The arrangement ended in failure, however, for Ibn Battuta fell into a dispute with his prospective father-in-law while traveling through Cyrenaica and ended up returning the girl. Undaunted, he then wedded the daughter of another pilgrim, this time a scholar from Fez. Apparently with income from his judicial office he put on a marriage feast "at which I detained the caravan for a whole day, and entertained them all." The *Rihla* tells us nothing whatsoever about the character of either of these women or Ibn Battuta's relationship with them. Indeed he would marry several times in the course of his travels, yet neither his wives, nor the slave concubines who were frequently in his train during later periods of his travels, would receive anything other than the scantest mention here and there in the *Rihla*. Wives vanish as casually and as inexplicably from the narrative as they enter it. In the Islamic society of that age a man's intimate family relations were regarded as no one's business but his own, and married Muslim women, at least in the Arabic-speaking lands, lived out their lives largely in seclusion. Ibn Battuta's domestic affairs were not a proper subject for a *rihla*, nor would they be for the biography or autobiography of any public man of that time. Consequently we learn much less than we would like about a significant dimension of Ibn Battuta's traveling life.

Sometime in the late winter or spring of 1326 the caravan reached Alexandria at the western end of the Nile Delta.[12] As treks across northern Africa went, Ibn Battuta managed it in less time than many travelers did, covering the more than 2,000 miles in the space of eight or nine months. If at this point he had been in a hurry to get to the Hijaz, he could have continued across the delta and the Sinai Peninsula, picking up the Egyptian caravan route to Mecca. But the next pilgrimage season was still eight months away, affording him plenty of time to explore the Nile Valley and, and as any serious scholar-pilgrim did, pay his respects to Cairo, which in the first half of the fourteenth century was the reigning intellectual capital of the Arabic-speaking world and the largest city in the hemisphere anywhere west of China.

Notes

1. Ibn Khaldun, *The Muqaddimah*, 2nd edn., trans. F. Rosenthal, 3 vols. (Princeton, N.J., 1967), vol. 3, p. 307.
2. Robert Brunschvig, *La Berbérie orientale sous les Hafsides des origines à la fin du XVe siècle*, 2 vols. (Paris, 1940, 1947), vol. 2, p. 97.
3. M. Canard, "Les relations entre les Merinides et les Mamelouks au XIVe siècle," *Annales de l'Institut d'Études Orientales* 5 (1939): 43.
4. Ibn Khaldun, *Histoire des Berbères et des dynasties musulmanes de l'Afrique septentrionale*, trans. Baron de Slane, 4 vols. (Paris, 1925–56), vol. 2, pp. 462–66, vol. 3, pp. 403–05.
5. Brunschvig (*Berbérie orientale*, vol. 1, p. 148n) suggests this hypothesis.
6. A. Cherbonneau, "Notice et extraits du voyage d'El-Abdary à travers l'Afrique septentrionale, au VIIe siècle de l'Hegire," *Journal Asiatique*, 5th ser., 4 (1854): 158. My translation from the French.
7. The events of this period are described in Ibn Khaldun, *Histoire des Berberes,* vol. 2, pp. 457–66; and Brunschvig, *Berbérie orientale*, vol. 1, pp. 144–50.
8. Brunschvig, *Berbérie orientale*, vol. 1, pp. 356–57.
9. Ibid., vol. 1, p. 146n.
10. Ibid., vol. 2, pp. 301–02; Gb, vol. 1, p. 13n.
11. Robert Brunschvig, "Quelques remarques historiques sur les medersas de Tunisie," *Revue Tunisienne* 6 (1931): 261–85. The college of the Booksellers was known in Arabic as the Ma'ridiyya.
12. In the *Rihla* IB remembers arriving in Alexandria on 5 April 1326 (1 Jumada I 726). Hrbek (Hr, pp. 417–18) argues that the date was more likely mid February (Rabi' I 726) on the grounds that the trip from Tripoli to Alexandria should not have taken the three months Ibn Battuta allots to it, considering that no major delays are noted. Hrbek suggests that the journey probably took 40 to 45 days and that acceptance of an earlier arrival date in Alexandria helps to solve chronological problems that arise later on.

3 The Mamluks

As for the dynasties of our time, the greatest of them is
that of the Turks in Egypt.[1]

Ibn Khaldun

Of the dozens of international ports Ibn Battuta visited in the
course of his travels, Alexandria impressed him as among the five
most magnificent. There was not one harbor but two, the eastern
reserved for Christian ships, the western for Muslim. They were
divided by Pharos Island and the colossal lighthouse which loomed
over the port and could be seen several miles out to sea.
Alexandria handled a great variety of Egyptian products, including the woven silk, cotton, and linen from its own thriving
textile shops. But more important, it was the most westerly situated of the arc of Middle Eastern cities which funneled trade
between the Indian Ocean and the Mediterranean.

From the beginning of the Islamic age the flow of goods across
the Middle East had followed a number of different routes, the
relative importance of each depending on the prevailing con-
figurations of political power and social stability. Ibn Battuta had
the good fortune to make his first and lengthiest visit to Egypt at a
time of high prosperity on the spice route running from the Indian
Ocean to the Red Sea and hence down the Nile to the ports of the
delta.

Contributing to Egypt's affluence was the firm rule of the Bahri
Mamluks, the Turkish-speaking warrior caste who had governed
that country and Syria as a united kingdom since 1260. Over the
second half of the thirteenth century the Mamluks had been
obliged to go to war several times to prevent the Mongol armies of
Persia from overruning Syria and advancing to the Nile. It is to the
credit of Mamluk cavalry that they stopped the Tatars and saved
Egypt from catastrophe by the skin of its teeth. Thus the cities of
the Nile were spared the fate of Baghdad, which the Mongols laid
waste in 1258 and reduced to the status of a provincial market
town.

Map 4: Ibn Battuta's Itinerary in Egypt, Syria, and Arabia, 1326

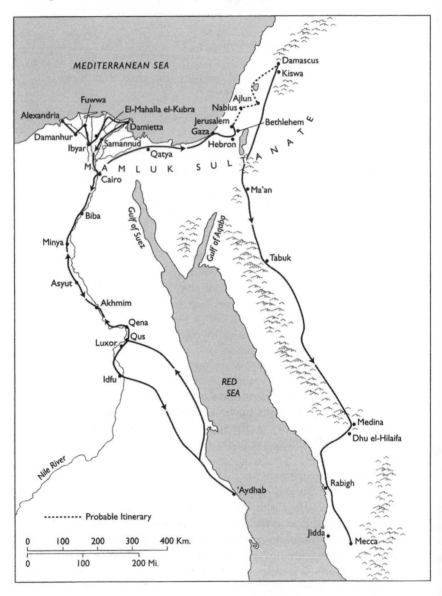

Although the Mongol threat to Syria did not end until about 1315, Egypt entered the fourteenth century with a firm government, a generally stable social order, and bright opportunities to exploit the commercial potential of its geographical position. Under the meticulous supervision of Mamluk soldiers and customs officers, the products of Asia were unloaded at the port of 'Aydhab half way up the Red Sea, moved overland by camel train to the Nile, then carried down the river on lateen-rigged vessels to Alexandria and the warehouses of Italian, French, and Catalan traders. Symon Semeonis, an Irish cleric who visited Alexandria in 1323 on his way to the Holy land, experienced the Mamluk customs bureaucracy at work:

> On our arrival in the port, the [European] vessel, as is the custom, was immediately boarded by a number of Saracen [Muslim] harbor officials, who hauled down the sail, and wrote down the names of everybody on board. Having examined all the merchandise and goods in the ship, and having made a careful list of everything, they returned to the city taking the passengers with them . . . They quartered us within the first and second gates, and went off to report what they had done to the Admiral of the city, without whose presence and permission no foreigner is allowed either to enter or leave the city, and no goods can be imported.[2]

Ibn Battuta spent several weeks in the busy port, seeing the sights (including the Pharos lighthouse and the third-century marble column known as Pompey's Pillar) and fraternizing with the men of letters in the mosques and colleges. In Egypt the Maliki school of law was not nearly so widedly used as the Shafi'i code, but Malikism was dominant in Alexandria owing to the large representation of North Africans and Andalusian refugees among the educated population.[3] In the *Rihla* Ibn Battuta recounts the achievements and miracles of several scholars and mystics of the city, most of them of Maghribi origin.

At one point during these weeks he spent a few days as the guest of one Burhan al-Din the Lame, a locally venerated Sufi ascetic. Among the special talents of more enlightened Muslim divines was the gift of foretelling the future. It was in the company of Burhan al-Din that the young pilgrim got a first inkling of his destiny. The holy man, perceiving that Ibn Battuta had in his heart a passion f' travel, suggested that he visit three of his fellow Sufis, two of them in India, the third in China. Ibn Battuta recalls the incident: "I was amazed at his prediction, and the idea of going to these countries having been cast into my mind, my wanderings never ceased until I had met these three that he named and conveyed his greeting to them."

For the moment, however, Ibn Battuta was content to wander in the valley of the Nile. Alexandria was not located on the river but linked to it by a canal, constructed a few years before his arrival, which ran eastward to the Rosetta Branch at the town of Fuwwa. Most commercial traffic to the interior went by river vessel through the canal and from there upstream to Cairo, which lay about 140 miles inland at the apex of the delta, a journey of five to seven days with the usual favorable northerly winds.

Ibn Battuta was in no particular hurry at this point, however, since the next season of the *hajj* was still about seven months off. Where most young scholars might have made a beeline for Cairo, the great metropolis, this pilgrim, already displaying his characteristic zeal to see everything, spent about three weeks, probably during April 1326, wandering through the rich commercial and textile-producing towns of the delta — Damanhur, Fuwwa, Ibyar, Damietta, Samannud, and others.[4] Along the way he sought out and lodged in the houses of numerous judges, savants, and Sufi *shaykhs*, including a celebrated saint of Fuwwa who also prophesied that the young man would one day wind up in India. He continued to support himself with the gifts and hospitality of the pious, not the least of his benefactors being the Mamluk governor of Damietta, who befriended him and sent him several coins. It might be presumed that Ibn Battuta was traveling in the Delta in the company of the woman he had married in Libya, except that she is never mentioned in the *Rihla* again.

At Samannud on the Damietta branch of the river he boarded one of the high-masted ships which thronged the river and sailed directly upstream toward Cairo. Numerous Christian and Jewish travelers — merchants, ambassadors, Holy Land pilgrims — sailed the Nile between the coast and Cairo during the fourteenth and fifteenth centuries, and few of them (in the narratives they later wrote) failed to marvel at the crowded, colorful, ever-blooming life of the river. Symon Semeonis extolled its natural wonders:

> This river is most pleasant for navigating, most beautiful in aspect, most productive in fishes, abounding in birds, and its

water is most wholesome and pleasant to drink, never harmful or offensive, but well suited to man's needs. Many other excellent things might be said about it were it not the retreat of a highly noxious animal, resembling the dragon, which devours both horses and men if it catches them in the water or on the banks.[5]

Ibn Battuta, a minority among travelers in his failure to mention the crocodiles, was impressed by the sheer crush of humanity along the banks, a density of habitation in startling contrast to what he had seen crossing North Africa:

> There is no need for a traveler on the Nile to take any provision with him, because whenever he wishes to descend on the bank he may do so, for ablutions, prayers, purchasing provisions, or any other purpose. There is a continuous series of bazaars from the city of Alexandria to Cairo . . . Cities and villages succeed one another along its banks without interruption and have no equal in the inhabited world, nor is any river known whose basin is so intensively cultivated as that of the Nile. There is no river on earth but it which is called a sea.

For all their teeming life, the market towns lining the lower Nile were but petty reflections of what the wayfarer beheld on reaching Cairo, the greatest bazaar of them all. Travelers of the time, whatever their origin, stood bedazzled at the city's overpowering size. "This city of Cairo has a population greater than that of all Tuscany," wrote the Italian gentleman Frescobaldi of his visit in 1384, "and there is a street which has by itself more people than all of Florence."[6]

Modern scholars suggest the population of Cairo in the first half of the fourteenth century may have been between 500,000 and 600,000, or six times larger than Tunis and fifteen times larger than London at the same period.[7] A convergence of historical factors explains the phenomenal growth of the city from the later thirteenth to the mid fourteenth century. One was its status as capital of the Mamluk kingdom and chief residence of virtually the entire Turkish ruling class, around whom Egyptian political and economic life turned. Another was its position as the intersecting point of the prosperous Red Sea-to-Nile spice route and the trade and pilgrimage roads from the Maghrib and sub-Saharan West

Africa. A third was the happy fact that its rulers had repulsed the Mongol horde and probably saved the population from being massacred. Indeed Cairo became a permanent refuge in the later thirteenth century for thousands of people from Iraq and Syria who fled the approach of the Tatars in panic.

Although Cairo was spreading physically in several directions in the early fourteenth century, the majority of the population, including foreign visitors and refugees, lived packed inside the walled city, which lay about a mile and a half east of the river. This was Cairo properly termed, al-Qahirah (The Victorious). It was founded by the Fatimid dynasty in the tenth century as a royal residence and garrison and thereafter evolved as the center of commercial and intellectual life for the greater urban region, eventually superseding in this respect the older Islamic city, known as Fustat or Misr, which was located some distance to the south.

Habitation within walled Cairo was so dense and the surge of humanity so frantic that the city had the appearance of being drastically overpopulated. The crush of people, camels, and donkeys in the central commercial district was so great that Ibn Battuta might have found a tourist's stroll down the Bayn al-Qasrayn, the main avenue, a thoroughly nerve-rending experience. There were thousands of shops in the vicinity of the avenue, as well as more than thirty markets, each one a concentration of a particular craft or trade — butchers, goldsmiths, gem dealers, candlemakers, carpenters, ironsmiths, slave merchants. Armies of peddlers and food vendors also jammed the streets, hawking victuals to the Cairene citizens, almost none of whom had the facilities to cook at home. The centers of international trade in the city were the caravansaries, called *funduqs* or *khans*. These were sometimes huge and splendidly decorated structures built around a central courtyard and containing rooms on the ground floor for storing goods and upstairs for lodging merchants. Some *khans* were constructed for particular groups of foreign traders, such as Maghribis, Persians, or Europeans. A caravansary for Syrian merchants built in the twelfth century had 360 lodgings above the storerooms and enough space for 4,000 guests at a time.[8]

The affluence of Cairo in the 1320s was a reflection of the competence of the Mamluk government, indeed of a system of political and social organization that was working in the early fourteenth century about as well as it ever would. When Ibn

Battuta entered the Mamluk domain, he fell under a political authority whose relationship to the general population was quite unlike what he had known at home. Whereas the Marinids of Morocco were of Berber stock, ethnically undifferentiated from most of the local population, the Mamluks were, in their Central Asian origins, Turkish language, and military ethos, utterly alien to their native Egyptian subjects. At the heart of the Mamluk government was the practice of recruiting the members of the ruling military and administrative elite from among young men of Turkish tribes in the steppe lands north of the Black and Caspian Seas. These youths entered Syria and Egypt as slaves, or in Arabic "mamluks." They were then converted to Islam, educated in the fundamentals of religion, taught the arts of mounted warfare, and finally given their legal freedom and position of service in the Mamluk state. It was from among the ranks of these alien-born cavalrymen that the top government commanders (*amirs*) were chosen.

Though the day to day management of the realm required constant contact and intertwining of interests between Mamluks and native Eyptians, the ruling minority nonetheless stood as a caste apart in its monopoly of political power and physical force. Ordinary folk were not even permitted to ride horses. Indeed, the purpose of the Mamluk system of recruitment and social insulation was not only to build and perpetuate an army of rugged Asian soldiers, unequivocally loyal to the state, but also to preserve the integrity and esprit de corps of the whole governing establishment by locking the subject peoples, even the locally born sons of Mamluks, out of it entirely. The ever-looming symbol of Mamluk dominance and exclusivity was the Citadel, an awesome complex of palace, mosques, offices, living quarters, and stables that stood on a rocky prominence 250 feet above Cairo. Here the sultan resided with an elaborate court and several regiments of mounted troops, cut off, to whatever degree he wished, from the commoners thronging the streets below.

The origins of this "oligarchy of lost children," as one historian has characterized the Mamluks,[9] are linked to the tumultuous events of the eleventh century, when Turkish steppe warriors swarmed over the Middle East, seized power almost everywhere, and filled the political void left by the collapse of the classical Abbasid empire centered on Baghdad. Although by the twelfth century the unity of the Middle East was shattered, Turkish warlords made accommodations with local Arab and Persian populations and, with the aid of their comrades-in-arms and a continuing flow of slave recruits from Central Asia, succeeded in restoring law and order over fairly extensive areas of the Middle East and Asia Minor and founding a series of military dynasties. The Age of the Turk descended on Egypt in 1250 when a corps of slave-soldiers in the service of the Ayyubid dynasty staged a *coup d'état* and took power. In the course of the following half century the Bahri Mamluks, so named for the fact that they were originally quartered on an island in the Nile (Bahr al-Nil), consolidated their rule over Egypt, conquered greater Syria, expelled the Latin Crusaders, and repeatedly beat back Mongol assaults from Persia. By the time Ibn Battuta arrived in Cairo the Mamluk empire had expanded to embrace not only Egypt, Syria, and Palestine, but also southeastern Asia Minor and the Red Sea rim.

Although the Mamluks often lived up to their barbarian origins in their treatment of the native population (crucifixion and the severing of limbs were common punishments for crimes against the state), they nevertheless worked out a routine standard of cooperation with the '*ulama* and notability, who embodied Arab civilization. It was, after all, only through the educated elite, as literate spokesmen for the lower orders of society and as interpreters of the Sacred Law, that the Turks were able to make the social accommodations necessary to ensure the steady and tranquil flow of tax revenues from agricultural land and commerce. In turn, the scholarly class not only accepted the fact of Mamluk power as the only alternative to chronic instability but willingly stepped forward to make the government work, serving under Turkish commanders as judges, scribes, tax-collectors, market inspectors, chiefs of city quarters, hospital administrators, as well as preachers, teachers, and Sufi *shaykhs*.

The rise of the Mamluks was also the achievement of the intelligent, ruthless, and surprisingly civilized men who wore the black satin robe of the sultanate during the first century of the empire. Ibn Battuta had the luck to arrive in Cairo at the triumphant mid point of the reign of al-Nasir Muhammad ibn Qala'un, who ruled (with some brief interruptions) from 1293 to 1341, longer than any sultan in the 267 years of the Mamluk regime. Such longevity was in fact a remarkable achievement, since the Turkish elite, appearing cohesive and fiercely fraternal from without, were quarrelsome and faction-ridden within. Power

The Dome of the Rock, Jerusalem.
Photo by the Author.

**The Mausoleum of the Mamluk sultan al-Mansur Qala'un
(1279–1290), Cairo.**
Photo by the Author.

and position in the hierarchy depended largely on personal ability and pluck, obliging any officer with ambition to compete viciously against his fellows for the high offices (including the sultanate itself) and the stupendous personal grants of agricultural land revenues that went with them.

The reign of al-Nasir Muhammad was the age of Cairo at its most resplendent, when the city blossomed into maturity as the world capital of Arab art and letters. While the Mongol horde ransacked its way through the Middle East, devastating Baghdad and plundering Damascus (1299–1300), Cairo offered a secure haven for scholars, craftsmen, and rich merchants who were nimble enough to escape across the Sinai Peninsula, taking with them the knowledge, artistic skills, and wealth that helped make Cairo the most cosmopolitan center of civilized culture anywhere in the Dar al-Islam.

Mamluk officers were not granted agricultural estates outright but only rights to revenue from the land's productivity. They did not normally live on their rural holdings and chose, if they could, to live in Cairo. Consequently, rents and taxes from thousands of peasant villages poured into the city and were lavishly expended on religious endowments, as well as on palaces, *khans*, racetracks, canals, and mausoleums, producing in all the most energetic surge of building that Cairo had ever known. Moreover, Mamluk architects chose increasingly to build in stone rather than the brick and plaster of earlier generations, and so their monuments have endured. The skyline of domes and minarets which impresses the eye of the modern tourist in Old Cairo is for the most part the skyline of the fourteenth and fifteenth centuries.

During his stay of about a month in the city,[10] Ibn Battuta toured the monuments of the Bahri Mamluks, as well as the mosques and mausoleums of earlier dynasties. Since a disastrous earthquake in 1303 had destroyed many public buildings,[11] he must have seen numerous construction projects going on while he was there. Sultan al-Nasir was not only a generous patron of religious institutions, building some thirty mosques in the course of his reign, he also sponsored numerous civic enterprises, including a canal which ran between the walled city and the river and opened an extensive new area to urban settlement.

Among the structures which most impressed Ibn Battuta was the Maristan, or hospital, built by Qala'un, the father and predecessor of al-Nasir. Today a sad shell of crumbling walls, it was one of the finest architectural creations of the age. "As for the Maristan," Ibn Battuta reports, "no description is adequate to its beauties." A modern historian describes its operation, showing that however brawling and unhealthy life in the narrow streets of the city might be, Cairo's charitable institutions were sanctuaries of civilized calm:

> Cubicles for patients were ranged round two courts, and at the sides of another quadrangle were wards, lecture rooms, library, baths, dispensary, and every necessary appliance of those days of surgical science. There was even music to cheer the sufferers; while readers of the Koran afforded the consolations of the faith. Rich and poor were treated alike, without fees, and sixty orphans were supported and educated in the neighboring school.[12]

If the credit for such enlightened philanthropy went to the sultans and *amirs* who paid for it, the inspiration and management were the achievement of the educated community of Cairo, among whom Ibn Battuta would have spent most of his time. He offers in the *Rihla* a brief Who's Who of the city's leading lights, but he gives no indication that he pursued systematic study with any of them, as in fact he would do in Damascus later that same year. It seems likely, though, that he attended lectures in some of the *madrasas*.

The colleges were the vital centers of intellectual and civic life wherein the religious, social, and cultural norms governing Egyptian society were taught and exemplified. A *madrasa* was in fact a mosque, though one designed primarily for teaching rather than for congregational prayer. It was Saladin who brought the *madrasa* idea from Iraq to Cairo in the twelfth century with the specific intention of founding Sunni schools to combat and suppress the Shi'i doctrines of the preceding Fatimid dynasty. As the city grew and prospered new colleges sprang up one after another, enough of them by the fourteenth century to elicit Ibn Battuta's comment that "as for the *madrasas* in Cairo, they are too many for anyone to count." The colleges of the Mamluk age were designed on a cruciform plan with a relatively small open courtyard, in contrast to the vast spaces within the chief congregational, or Friday, mosques. Opening onto the court were four vaulted halls, or *liwans*, where classes were normally held.

This was the classic *madrasa* form of Ibn Battuta's time, providing in fact the model for Marinid college building in Morocco.

The college curriculum offered in Cairo would have been perfectly familiar to Ibn Battuta, as it was largely identical to what was presented in North African schools, except that the Shafi'i system of law was dominant rather than the Maliki. As in Tunis, Fez, or Tangier, education turned on the revealed and linguistic sciences, especially law. Studies in medicine, astronomy, mathematics, and philosophy were also available, though the teaching was usually conducted privately rather than in the *madrasas*. Cairo in the Mamluk age did not nurture people of creative originality (with the notable exception of Ibn Khaldun, who was a Tunisian but moved permanently to Egypt in 1383), but it did produce theologians, jurisprudents, historians, encyclopedists, and biographers of spectacular erudition and nimbleness of mind. It was these luminaries that Ibn Battuta, and hundreds of scholars like him from throughout the Arabic-, Persian-, and Turkish-speaking Islamic world, came to the great city to see and hear.[13]

Ibn Battuta might well have remained in Cairo much longer than a month, since at the end of that time (mid May 1326) there still remained more than five months before the start of the *hajj* rituals in Mecca. The official Egyptian caravan, which traveled to the Hijaz across Sinai under the protection of the Mamluks, did not normally leave Cairo until the middle of the month of Shawwal, in that year mid September.[14] But Ibn Battuta had an impetuousness about him (as he had already demonstrated in his journey across North Africa), and he was not inclined to wait for caravans or fellow travelers for very long. In fact he decided to proceed to Mecca on his own, not by the Sinai route at all, but by way of Upper Egypt to the Red Sea port of 'Aydhab and from there by ship to Jidda on the Hijaz coast.

Pilgrims traveled both the northern and southern routes out of Cairo in the first half of the fourteenth century. The Sinai road was the shorter of the two, and it was relatively more secure because the sultans sponsored annual caravans and dispatched army units to maintain and police the route. The southerly track to 'Aydhab and Jidda was longer and there was no officially organized caravan. But this was the route of the spices, in Ibn Battuta's time one of the busiest and strategically most important lanes of international trade in the Afro–Eurasian world. The commercial infrastructure of trails, river transport, cameleers, *khans*, and markets was extensively developed and elaborately organized, affording the wayfarer a normally safe journey from Cairo to 'Aydhab. Moreover, a pilgrim could normally expect to travel all the way to that town, located near the modern Sudanese border, without passing beyond the reach of Mamluk law and order. The sultan posted garrisons in Qus, Idfu, Aswan, and other important towns on the river and, when the situation called for it, dispatched punitive expeditions against the Arab or Beja tribes of the desert and Red Sea Hills. These unruly herdsmen, in normal times collaborators in the transit trade as guides and camel drivers, were quick to despoil caravans or defy Mamluk authority whenever the opportunity was too tempting to resist — a fact of Egyptian politics not, as we shall see, to be lost on Ibn Battuta.

The young pilgrim's two- to three-week journey up the Nile valley to the town of Idfu was accomplished without much adventure. He traveled by land rather than on the river, and at several points along the way he lodged in the homes, colleges, or lodges of scholars and Sufis.[15] While passing through the town of Minya, he became embroiled in a minor incident, interesting for what it reveals of his high sense of civilized propriety — as well as a less appealing inclination to sanctimonious meddling:

> One day I entered the bath-house in this township, and found men in it wearing no covering. This appeared a shocking thing to me, and I went to the governor and informed him of it. He told me not to leave and ordered the lessees of (all) the bath-houses to be brought before him. Articles were formally drawn up (then and there) making them subject to penalties if any person should enter a bath without a waist-wrapper, and the governor behaved to them with the greatest severity, after which I took leave of him.

A grateful governor and an annoyed corps of bath operators behind him, he continued on to Idfu, one of the principal transshipment centers for the overland haul to the coast. Here he crossed to the east bank of the river, hired camels, and set out for 'Aydhab in the company of a party of bedouin Arabs. Their trek southeastward through the desert and then over the bare and smouldering Red Sea Hills took 15 days, about the normal time for the trip.[16]

Although Ibn Battuta's brief description of 'Aydhab — its mosque, its men of learning, some customs of the inhabitants — is factual and detached, a traveler coming out of the desert would be likely to react to the town with a discomfiting ambivalence. On the one hand it was a flourishing port, its warehouses crammed with pepper, cloves, ivory, pearls, textiles, Chinese procelain, and all manner of exotic goods from Asia and tropical Africa, as well as the linen, silk, coral, sugar, and precious metals of Egypt and the Mediterranean. On the other hand, the fiery climate, the barren surroundings, and the country crudeness of the local hill folk made 'Aydhab one of the most uninviting transit stops anywhere from the Mediterranean to China. Thousands passed through, but no one stayed a moment longer than required. Ibn Jubayr, the celebrated Andalusian pilgrim and *rihla* writer of the twelfth century, despised the place. After noting in his book that the town was rich and of great commercial importance, he fervently advised pilgrims to get to Mecca by some other way if they possibly could:

It is enough for you of a place where everything is imported, even water; and this (because of its bitterness) is less agreeable than thirst. We had lived between air that melts the body and water that turns the stomach from appetite for food. He did no injustice to this town who sang, "Brackish of water and flaming of air."[17]

Ibn Jubayr also took pains to warn travelers against the avarice of the ship captains, who loaded their vessels with pilgrims "until they sit one on top of the other so that they are like chickens crammed in a coop."[18] Somehow enduring these indignities, not to mention delays and storms, Ibn Jubayr had managed to reach Jidda after a week under sail and so continued on to Mecca. Ibn Battuta, as it happened, was not so lucky. When earlier he had passed through the town of Hiw (Hu) on the Nile, he paid a visit to a saintly *sharif* (descendant of the Prophet), one Abu Muhammad 'Abdallah al-Hasani. Upon hearing of the young man's intention to go to Mecca, the *sharif* warned him to return to Cairo, prophesying that he would not make his first pilgrimage except by the road through Syria. Ignoring the omen, Ibn Battuta had continued on his way southward. Reaching 'Aydhab, he discovered much to his chagrin that the local ruling family, a clan of the Beja people who inhabited the hills behind the city, were in revolt against the Mamluk governor.[19] The rebels had sunk some ships in the harbor, driven out the Egyptian garrison, and in this climate of violence no one was hoisting sail for Jidda. If he were to be assured of reaching the Hijaz before the start of the *hajj*, Ibn Battuta had no real choice but to retrace his steps to Cairo and continue from there by one of the northern routes. Fortunately, the trip back did not take long. The Nile was reaching summer flood stage, and so after crossing the desert again and rejoining the river at Qus, he boarded a ship and returned to the capital in eight short days, arriving there, he recalls, in mid July.

Perhaps during his voyage down the river, where he had the leisure to think out his plans, he came to the conclusion that if he did not linger in Cairo he could reach Syria in time to catch the *hajj* caravan which normally left Damascus on or about 10 Shawwal (10 September of that year), or about two weeks earlier than the departure of the pilgrims from Cairo.[20] It may have been his rather happy-go-lucky impetuosity that was driving him, or perhaps he thought it prudent to heed the word of the *sharif* of Hiw that he was destined to reach Mecca by way of Syria. In any case he stayed in Cairo, astonishingly enough, only one night before setting out for Syria, the Asian half of the Mamluk empire.

The main route from Cairo to Damascus was the royal road of the kingdom, since Damascus was a kind of second capital, responsible for the military governance of Greater Syria and for the defense of the eastern marches against the Mongols of Persia. The sultan himself frequently traveled to Damascus, usually in the company of an army. Moreover, Damascus was as great a city as Cairo in the production of luxury goods. The military lords of Egypt depended heavily on the caravans from Syria for their fine silks and brocades, their ceramics and glassware, their magnificent tents and horse-trappings, all of these articles traded mainly for Egyptian textiles and grain. Damascene artisans, such as masons, marble workers, and plasterers, frequently accompanied the caravans to Cairo to work in the construction of palaces, mausoleums, and mosques. For both commercial and political reasons, then, the Mamluks were assiduous in protecting and provisioning the Cairo–Damascus artery, hemming it with garrison posts and building bridges and caravansaries to facilitate the passage of people and goods.

If Ibn Battuta had gone to Mecca with the Egyptian *hajj* caravan, he would have traveled due east across the peninsula to Aqaba, then southward into the Hijaz. Instead, he set a northeastward course through the farming towns of the eastern delta and from there along the sandy Mediterranean plain to Gaza, the desert portal to Palestine. We have no idea with whom he may have been traveling, though he refers vaguely in the *Rihla* to "those who were with me" on this stretch of his journey. All along this trail the government provided public caravansaries where, according to the *Rihla*, "travelers alight with their beasts, and outside each *khan* is a public wateringplace and a shop at which the traveler may buy what he requires for himself and his beast." At Qatya, a station located several miles east of the modern day Suez Canal, the state maintained a customs house where officials examined passports and merchandise and collected a bonanza in duties from the mercantile caravans moving between Syria and Egypt. Symon Semeonis, who passed through Qatya in 1323, describes Mamluk police techniques:

The village . . . is entirely surrounded by the desert and is furnished with neither fortifications nor natural obstacles of any kind that might impede the passage of travelers. Every evening after sunset a straw-mat or carpet is drawn at the tail of a horse, sometimes near the village, sometimes far from it, now in one place, now in another, transversely to the route, for a distance of six or eight miles, more or less, according to the Admiral's orders. This renders the sand so smooth that it is impossible for either man or beast to pass without leaving traces to expose their passage. Every morning before sunrise the plain is scoured in all directions by specially appointed horsemen, and whenever any traces of pedestrians or of horsemen are discovered, the guards hasten in pursuit and those who have passed are arrested as transgressors of the Sultan's regulations and are severely punished.[21]

At Gaza Ibn Battuta turned off the heavily traveled road leading to the Levantine ports and headed eastward into the high country of Judaea, having in mind to visit the sacred cities of Hebron (al-Khalil) and Jerusalem before continuing to Damascus.[22] The trail along the hilly backbone of Palestine, from Hebron to the Galilee, was not an important commercial road, but it was a route of pilgrimage for all three monotheistic faiths. After the wars of the

Crusades ended in the 1290s, increasing numbers of Latin pilgrims traveled to the Holy Land in small groups, by way of either Egypt or the Levant. Although they were frequently harassed and invariably overcharged, usually by local Muslims of the meaner sort, the Mamluk authorities, particularly in the fourteenth century, generally saw to it that they were protected from bodily harm.

Hebron was special to Muslim, Christian, and Jew alike because it was the burial place of the fathers of monotheism: Abraham, Isaac, and Jacob, as well as their wives and Jacob's son Joseph. In Mamluk times only Muslims were permitted to enter the mosque, built originally as a Crusader church, that stood over the tomb cave containing cenotaphs of the three Patriarchs. In the *Rihla* Ibn Battuta describes the mosque, a massive stone structure "of striking beauty and imposing height," as well as the cenotaphs standing inside, as a traveler of any faith might see them today. He also offers learned testimony to the truth of the tradition that the three graves do indeed lie beneath the mosque, a tradition verified by Frankish knights, who opened the cave in 1119 and discovered what were presumably the holy bones.[23]

The distance from Hebron to Jerusalem through the terraced Judaean hills was only 17 miles, and Ibn Battuta probably made the trip, including a brief look around Bethlehem, in a day or two. Jerusalem plays so solemn a part in the religious and cultural heritage of Western peoples and commands so much attention in contemporary world politics that we are inclined to assume it was always one of the great urban centers of the Middle East. In fact the Jerusalem of the fourteenth century was a rather sleepy town of no great commercial or administrative importance. Its population was only about 10,000,[24] and it was ruled as a sub-unit of the Province of Damascus. Its defensive walls were in ruins, part of its water supply had to be carried in from the surrounding countryside, and it was located on none of the important trade routes running through Greater Syria. From the point of view of a Mamluk official or an international merchant, it was a city of eminently provincial mediocrity. What kept it alive and sustained its permanent population of scholars, clerics, shopkeepers, and guides was the endless stream of pilgrims that passed through its gates. Jerusalem was a place of countless shrines and sanctuaries. For Christians the spiritual focus of the city was the Church of the Holy Sepulchre, for Jews it was the Western Wall of the temple (the Wailing Wall), and for Muslims it was the Haram al-Sharif, the Noble Sanctuary, revered as the third most blessed spot in the Dar al-Islam, after the Ka'ba in Mecca and the tomb of the Prophet in Medina.

During his stay in the city of perhaps a week, Ibn Battuta probably spent a good deal of his time in the Haram, an expansive trapezoid-shaped area bounded by buildings and city walls and dominating the southeastern quarter of the city. The entire Haram was itself an enormous mosque open to the sky, though within it stood several sanctuaries having specific religious significance for Muslims. The most venerated of these was the Kubbat al-Skhra, the Dome of the Rock, a wondrously beautiful building set in the center of the Haram on the site of the ancient Temple of Solomon. This shrine, dating from the seventh century, is in the shape of a regular octagon, sumptuously ornamented with interwoven Arabic scriptural quotations and geometric designs and surmounted by a massive dome. Inside the sanctuary and directly beneath the dome lies embedded in the earth the blessed Rock of Zion. It was from here, it is told, that the Prophet Muhammad, transported at lightning speed from Mecca to Jerusalem in the company of the Angel Gabriel, was carried on the back of a great winged steed up to the Seventh Heaven of Paradise, where he stood in the presence of God. It is in commemoration of Muhammad's Night Journey that Muslims enter the Dome, make a circuit of the Rock, and descend to the little grotto beneath it.

Ibn Battuta mentions in the *Rihla* a number of the scholars and divines resident in Jerusalem. One of these, a Sufi master of the Rifa'i brotherhood named 'Abd al-Rahman ibn Mustafa, took a special interest in the young man and was apparently impressed enough by his sincerity and learning to give him a *khirqa*, the woolen, patch-covered cloak worn by Sufi disciples as a sign of their allegiance to a life of God-searching and self-denial. In the few days that Ibn Battuta stayed in Jerusalem he obviously could not have gone through any of the rigorous spiritual training required of initiates prior to receiving their *khirqas*. A master could, however, bestow a lower form of investiture upon a person whom he wished to encourage in the mystical path.[25] The incident seems to be one more bit of evidence that Ibn Battuta's piety and knowledge of Sufism were conspicuous enough, even in his youth, to place him on occasion in the graces of the most august saints and wise men, even though he had no plans to give himself wholeheartedly to the mystical life.

In his time Sufism was becoming intricately melded into the everyday religious life of Muslims. Although there were those who adopted asceticism or celibacy as methods personally suitable for drawing closer to God, Sufism was in no general way "monkish" or confined to a spiritually militant minority. Rather it was the intimate, inward-turning, God-adoring dimension of Muslim faith, complementing outward, public conformity to the ritual and moral duties of the Sacred Law. It could take expression, depending on the individual's personal inclination, in everything from a life of mendicant wandering to occasional attendance at brotherhood meetings where mystical litanies were recited. Sufi masters, such as Ibn Battuta's friend in Jerusalem, rarely limited their patronage to their formal disciples, but rather gave freely of their spiritual guidance and *baraka* to ordinary men and women who needed the solace or healing that only a surer feeling of God's presence could provide. Although Ibn Battuta's life of worldly adventure had little in common with that of a cloistered dervish, he associated with mystics whenever he could, as if to fortify himself with a deeper calming grace before taking to the road again.

Jerusalem, however, was not to be the place for a devotional retreat, for the *hajj* season was drawing nearer and Damascus beckoned. Ibn Battuta's exact route northward is uncertain, but he very likely traveled through Nablus, Ajlun, and the Galilee and from there across the Golan Heights to the Syrian capital.[26] This journey was probably accomplished in a few days' time since the entire trip from Cairo to Damascus, if the dates he gives us are correct, took no more than 23 days. By his own reckoning he arrived in Damascus on 9 August 1326 (9 Ramadan 726).

[Damascus] stands on the place where Cain killed his brother Abel, and is an exceeding noble, glorious, and beauteous city, rich in all manner of merchandise, and everywhere delightful, . . . abounding in foods, spices, precious stones, silk, pearls, cloth-of-gold, perfumes from India, Tartary, Egypt, Syria, and places on our side of the Mediterranean, and in all precious things that the heart of man can conceive. It is begirt with gardens and orchards, is watered both within and without by waters, rivers, brooks, and fountains, cunningly arranged, to minister to men's luxury, and is incredibly populous, being inhabited by divers trades of most cunning and noble workmen, mechanics, and merchants, while within the walls it is adorned beyond belief by baths, by birds that sing all the year round, and by pleasures, refreshments, and amusements of all kinds.

Thus wrote Ludolph von Suchem,[27] a German priest who visited the city on his way home from the Holy Land in 1340–41. Muslims honored Damascus as the earthly equivalent of Paradise, and so it must have seemed to any haggard pilgrim tramping out of the Syrian waste. Quite unlike Jerusalem, bone dry on its craggy hill, Damascus lay in an oasis of extravagant greenness, a garden, in the gushy phrases of Ibn Jubayr, "bedecked in the brocaded vestments of flowers."[28] Although bordered by desert on three sides and by the Mountains of Lebanon on the west, which all but blocked rain-bearing clouds from the Mediterranean, the city drew life from the river that flowed down the slopes of the Anti-Lebanon and onto the plain, where Damascene farmers distributed its waters to the channels that fed thousands of orchards and gardens. Because the mountains prevented easy communication with the coast, Damascus was not in a choice geographical position to handle long-distance trade between East and West. But it prospered as an international emporium in spite of this, owing to the profuse fertility of its oasis (al-Ghuta), which supported a population of about 100,000.[29]

Indeed Ibn Battuta saw Damascus in the flush of a new prosperity. During most of the preceding half century, hostilities between the Mamluks and the Mongol Ilkhans of Persia had weakened Syrian trade links to India. But the Mongol threat had dissipated by 1315. Diplomatic relations between the two states improved and trade routes from Damascus to Iraq and the Persian Gulf were opened once again. Furthermore, the city had developed a thriving trade with Asia Minor and the Black Sea region, specially in horses, furs, metals, and slaves, including, of course, Mamluk recruits.

The visible splendor of Damascus, however, was a reflection not so much of international trade as of the city's status as the Mamluk capital-in-Asia with its enormous garrison and the magnificent households of the high commanders. The royal armies, passing continually in and out of the city, required the production of huge quantities of provisions and weapons, while the ruling elite, together with their counterparts in Cairo, kept Damascene craftsmen busy day and night turning out exquisite wares and finery.

Saif al-Din Tankiz, viceroy of Damascus from 1313 to 1340, was not only a man of exceptional administrative ability (Ibn Battuta refers to him as "a governor of the good and upright kind"), but a builder and city planner whose imagination and energy rivalled that of his sovereign lord al-Nasir Muhammad. Mirroring the sultan's work in Cairo, Saif al-Din undertook a vast program to beautify and improve his city, endowing numerous mosques, *madrasas*, and other pious institutions, widening streets and squares, directing the expansion of residential areas outside the walls, and even waging an obsessive war against the surplus population of stray dogs.[30] The Damascus that Ibn Battuta saw in 1326 was, like Cairo, a city in the process of transforming itself under the stimulus of a political regime that, at least for the time being, had struck a congenial balance between harsh, swaggering authoritarianism and a love of civilized taste and comfort.

The guardians of Damascene high culture were of course the Arabic-speaking scholars, who, like their colleagues in Cairo, affiliated with numerous religious, educational, and philanthropic foundations scattered throughout the city. Whereas Cairo had no pre-eminent center of learning in the fourteenth century, Damascus had its Great Mosque, called the Mosque of the Umayyads after its eighth-century builders. Around it all the other pious institutions revolved as satellites.

During part of his stay in the city, Ibn Battuta boarded in one of the three Maliki *madrasas* there. (Malikism was the least important of the four legal schools in Syria and was represented by fewer colleges than the others.) But he may have fairly well lived in the Great Mosque, sitting beneath the marble columns of the golden-domed sanctuary, all around him the murmuring voices of lecturers and Qur'anic readers and children in circles reciting their sacred lessons. The prayer hall, a three-aisled nave more than 400 feet long, was open on its northern side and joined to a spacious court rimmed by arcades where, according to the *Rihla*, "the people of the city gather . . . in the evenings, some reading, some conversing, and some walking up and down." The staff of officials attached to the mosque was huge, including, Ibn Battuta tells us, 70 *muezzins* (prayer callers), 13 *imams* (prayer leaders), and about 600 Qur'anic reciters. He describes the sanctuary as a place of continuous religious and educational activity, a never-ending celebration of God's glory and beneficence:

The townspeople assemble in it daily, immediately after the dawn prayer, to read a seventh part of the Qur'an . . . In this mosque also there are a great many "sojourners" who never leave it, occupying themselves unremittingly in prayer and recitation of the Qur'an and liturgies . . . The townsfolk supply their needs of food and clothing, although sojourners never beg for anything of the kind from them.

Ibn Battuta was one among this throng of wandering seekers, and it was during his 24 days in Damascus waiting for the *hajj* caravan to depart that he undertook his first formal studies abroad. Next to Cairo, Damascus possessed the greatest concentration of eminent theologians and jurists in the Arabic-speaking world, many of them refugees from Baghdad and other Mesopotamian or Persian cities who had fled the Mongol tide. So the young scholar had before him a galaxy of luminaries from which he might choose his teachers.

In the advanced curriculum the professor usually read and offered commentary on a classical book, then tested his students' ability to recite it as well as understand its meaning. He awarded those who performed competently an *ijaza*, or certificate, which entitled them to teach the same text to others. In the *Rihla* Ibn Battuta claims to have taken instruction and received *ijazas* from no less than 14 different teachers. He mentions in particular his "hearing" one of the most venerated texts in Islam, the Book of Sound Tradition of the Prophet (the *Sahih*) by the great ninth-century scholar al-Bukhari. He also details the essential information written on his *ijaza*: the chain of pedagogical authority linking his own teacher through numerous generations of sages back to al-Bukhari himself. This particular course of study, he tells us, took place in the Great Mosque and was completed in 14 daily sessions.

Nothwithstanding the young man's appetite for knowledge, it strains the imagination to see how he could have carried to completion 14 different courses in the space of 24 days.[31] He could not have devoted his every waking moment to his studies since he was by no means free of more mundane concerns. For one thing, his entire stay in Damascus took place during the month of Ramadan, when Muslims are required to fast during daylight hours, a strenuous obligation that upset the normal routines of daily life. He also admits in the *Rihla* that he was down with fever during a good part of his stay and living as a house guest of one of the Maliki professors, who put him under a physician's care. On top of that, he found time during this fleeting three and a half weeks to get married again, this time to the daughter of a Moroccan residing in Damascus. Given these preoccupations, we can surmise that he exaggerated the extent of his studies, that he undertook them during subsequent visits to Damascus without making that fact clear in the narrative,[32] or that some of the *ijazas* were awarded him, as was often done, in recognition of the piety and scholarly potential he demonstrated rather than as diplomas for books mastered.[33] But there is still no reason to doubt that despite illness and nuptial cares, he spent long August hours in the cool of the ancient mosque, absorbing as much learning as he could and gathering credentials that would contribute several years later to his appointment as a *qadi* to the Sultan of India.

Notes

1. Ibn Khaldun, *The Muqaddimah*, 2nd edn., trans. F. Rosenthal, 3 vols. (Princeton, N.J., 1967), vol. 1, p. 366.
2. Symon Semeonis, *The Journey of Symon Semeonis from Ireland to the Holy Land*, trans. and ed. Mario Esposito (Dublin, 1960), p. 67.
3. "Al-Iskandariyya," EI$_2$, vol. 4, p. 134.
4. Gibb (Gb, vol. 1, p. 33n) states that IB probably did not visit all the towns of the Nile Delta that he claims to have seen during his first trip through the area. Although he passed through the delta at least three more times over the course of his travels, the *Rihla* bunches descriptions of places and persons into the narrative of the first visit and presents almost no new details in connection with subsequent trips. This method of organizing the story was in fact a literary device used in a number of points in the *Rihla*. It makes for several knotty problems of itinerary and chronology at various stages of the narrative. In the case at hand, Gibb's argument rests on the fact that IB mentions a date (29 Sha'ban, 31 July 1326) in association with his visit to the town of Ibyar (Abyar) that cannot possibly be correct, since by the end of July he was presumably on his way to Damascus. Hrbek (Hr, pp. 418–20) disagrees, pointing out that despite the discrepancy of the date pertaining to Ibyar, other evidence (dates connected with named personages in various delta towns) tends to confirm IB's statement that he visited the places he says he did during his first journey. Gibb and Hrbek do agree that he could not have been in the delta on 31 July.
5. Symon Semeonis, *Journey*, p. 67.
6. P. H. Dopp, "Le Caire vu par les voyageurs occidentaux du Moyen Âge," *Bulletin de la Société Royal de Géographie d'Égypte* 23 (1950): 135.
7. Several scholars have suggested this general estimate of the population, though more recently André Raymond argues for a much lower fourteenth-century (pre-Black Death) population of about 250,000. "La population du Caire, de Maqrizi à la *Description de l'Égypte*," *Bulletin d'Études Orientales* 28 (1975): 214.
8. Stanley Lane-Poole, *The Story of Cairo* (London, 1902), p. 270.

9. Gaston Wiet, *Cairo: City of Art and Commerce* (Norman, Okla., 1964), p. 68.

10. An estimate in accord with Hrbek's overall chronological reconstruction of IB's first visit to Egypt. Hr, pp. 420–21.

11. K. A. C. Creswell, *The Muslim Architecture of Egypt*, 2 vols. (Oxford, 1952, 1959), vol. 1, pp. 66, 78, vol. 2, p. 195.

12. Lane-Poole, *Story of Cairo* p. 212.

13. On the cosmopolitanism of the leading colleges of Cairo in the fifteenth century, see Carl F. Petry, *The Civilian Elite of Cairo in the Later Middle Ages* (Princeton, N.J., 1981).

14. 'Abdullah 'Ankawi, "The Pilgrimage to Mecca in Mamluk Times," *Arabian Studies* 1 (1974): 147.

15. In his travels on the Nile Ibn Battuta has very little to say about the ruins of ancient Egypt (called in Arabic *barbas*). His brief description of the Pyramids, located just across the river from Cairo, is vague and partially inaccurate, leading Gibb to the conclusion that he never bothered to visit them personally (Gb, vol. 1, p. 51n). It must be remembered that the purpose of the *Rihla* was to edify literate Muslims on the places, personalities, and marvels of the Islamic world of their day and not on the architecture of pagan temples.

16. Hr, p. 421.

17. Ibn Jubayr, *The Travels of Ibn Jubayr*, trans. R. J. C. Broadhurst (London, 1952), p. 67.

18. Ibn Jubayr, *Travels*, p. 65.

19. The Mamluk government had a policy of sharing the commercial duties of the port with the local powers-that-be out of strategic necessity, but it frequently fell into altercations with them over the just distributions of the revenue. See Yusuf Fadl Hasan, *The Arabs and the Sudan from the Seventh to the Early Sixteenth Centuries* (Edinburgh, 1967), pp. 73–79.

20. 'Ankawi, "Pilgrimage to Mecca," p. 149.

21. Symon Semeonis, *Journey*, p. 103.

22. He may have traveled from Gaza to Asqalon, a ruined port several more miles up the coast, before turning inland to Hebron. Hr, p. 425.

23. Guy Le Strange, *Palestine under the Moslems* (Beirut, 1965), pp. 316–17.

24. Nicola A. Ziadeh, *Urban Life in Syria under the Early Mamluks* (Beirut, 1953), p. 97.

25. "Khirka," EI$_2$, vol. 5, pp. 17–18; Gb, vol. 1, p. 80n.

26. It is at this point in the narrative that the reader encounters the first major discrepancy between itinerary and chronology. According to the *Rihla*, IB traveled extensively in Greater Syria following his departure from Jerusalem, visiting more than twenty towns and cities before reaching Damascus. Since he could not possibly have made such a complicated trip within the 23 days he allots for the entire journey from Cairo to Damascus, both Gibb and Hrbek have concluded that the itinerary after Jerusalem is largely artificial. Hrbek offers various bits of internal evidence to show that visits to particular places in Syria must have taken place during subsequent trips. He further suggests (and Gibb agrees) that IB took a direct route northward from Jerusalem to Damascus (Hr, pp. 421–25; Gb, vol. 1, p. 81n). I have accepted the probable route Hrbek suggests, though it is conjectural. And I have reconstructed IB's Syrian itinerary on the premise that he did not travel extensively in the region in 1326.

Gibb and other scholars have shown that the *Rihla*'s descriptions of several cities in Greater Syria reproduce passages from the text of Ibn Jubayr, who traveled in the 1180s. In an article published in 1987, Amikam Elad demonstrated that most of IB's descriptions of places in Palestine are copied from *al-Rihla al-Maghribiyya*, the travel account of Muhammad al-'Abdari, another Andalusian journeyer of the late thirteenth century. "The Description of the Travels of Ibn Battuta in Palestine: Is It Original?"

Journal of the Royal Asiatic Society, 1987, pp. 256–272. As Elad points out, it is fruit-less to attempt to resolve the serious chronological problems with the Syria–Palestine itinerary if the authenticity of IB's visits to particular cities is in question. Elad does not argue, on the other hand, that IB never traveled to that region.

27. Ludolph von Suchem, *Ludolph von Suchem's Description of the Holy Land, and of the Way Thither,* trans. Aubrey Stewart (London, 1895), p. 129.

28. Ibn Jubayr, *Travels,* p. 271. Large blocks of IB's description of Damascus were taken from the *rihla* of Ibn Jubayr, who was there in 1184. However IB updates the material and adds various observations of his own.

29. Ziadeh, *Urban Life in Syria,* p. 97.

30. Ira Lapidus, *Muslim Cities in the Later Middle Ages* (Cambridge, Mass., 1967), pp. 22, 70, 72, 75.

31. He may have stayed 34 days, depending on whether the *hajj* caravan left Damascus on the 1st or the 10th of Shawwal. See Chapter 4, note 3.

32. Though IB makes no explicit mention of it, some evidence suggests that he spent time in Damascus in the late months of 1330. If so, his marriage and some of his studies might have occurred then. On this chronological problem see Chapter 6, note 2.

33. See Marshall G. S. Hodgson, *The Venture of Islam,* 3 vols. (Chicago, 1974), vol. 2, p. 444.

4 Mecca

The first House established for the people was that at
[Mecca], a place holy, and a guidance to all beings. Therein
are clear signs — the station of Abraham, and whosoever
enters it is in security. It is the duty of all men towards God
to come to the House a pilgrim, if he is able to make his way
there.[1]

The Qur'an, Sura III

Ibn Battuta gives no indication of how many people like himself were
gathering in Damascus in 1326 to join the *hajj* caravan to Mecca, but it
was very likely several thousand. Frescobaldi, the Florentine
nobleman who was in Damascus in 1384 at the start of the pilgrimage,
estimated the company at 20,000.[2] In fact the size of the caravan varied
greatly from year to year depending on a whole range of factors
affecting individual decisions whether to attempt the trip — political
and economic conditions at home, weather, prospects for trouble
along the route. For most pilgrims the journey was a spiritually
gladdening adventure, but it was also an extremely arduous one,
requiring a sound body and careful advance preparations. Every
participant was obliged to secure provisions for the round trip, as well
as a mount, though Mamluk authorities did set up charitable funds to
provide food and animals for the poorest among the travelers. Unless
a pilgrim carried most of his supplies along with him, the journey could
turn out to be extremely expensive, especially since the citizens of
Medina and Mecca, desert-bound as they were and heavily dependent
on the *hajj* trade for their survival, cheerfully exacted the highest
prices they could get for food, lodging, and various services. Ibn
Battuta himself was in bad financial straits toward the end of his stay in
Damascus and might not have been able to set out that year had it not
been for the generosity of the Maliki jurist with whom he stayed while
he was sick. This gentleman, he tells us in the *Rihla*, "hired camels for
me and gave me traveling provisions, etc., and money in addition,
saying to me, 'It will come in useful for anything of importance that
you may be in need of' — may God reward him."

The gathering of the pilgrims at Damascus was a decidedly political event. Both the Cairo and Damascus caravans set forth under the flag of the Mamluk state. Their safety en route and their timely arrival in Mecca in advance of the dates of the appointed rituals reflected on the capacity of the regime to maintain law and order in the realm. Moreover, in the latter half of the thirteenth century the Mamluks had imposed their political suzerainty over the rulers of Mecca and Medina. The former were a dynasty of Arabian Hasanid *sharifs*, that is, descendants of Hasan, son of 'Ali and grandson of the Prophet. The latter were also *sharifs* but the progeny of Husayn, 'Ali's other son. The annual arrival of the *hajj* caravans at Mecca was an occasion for the ruling Sharif, called the Amir, to reaffirm, through an exchange of gifts and tribute, his fealty to the sultan and his recognition of Mamluk protectorship of the Holy Places, a responsibility carrying great prestige in the Muslim world.

In the political pecking order of *hajj* groups, the Cairo caravan was pre-eminent. Each year the sultan appointed an *amir al-hajj* from among his favorite officers to lead the caravan and to act as his representative in Mecca. At the head of the procession went the *mahmal*, a green, richly decorated palenquin, which symbolized the sultan's formal authority, though no one rode inside it. The *amir al-hajj* was also placed in charge of the *kiswa*, the huge black cloth that was woven and inscribed each year in Cairo and carried to Mecca to be draped over the Ka'ba. Though the Syrian caravan also had its *amir al-hajj* appointed either by the sultan or his viceroy, he stood down from the Cairene leader during ceremonies at the Holy Places. He was expected either to remain neutral or to follow the lead of his Egyptian colleague in negotiations or disputes with the *sharifs* or with the caravans from Iraq or the Yemen.

A number of other officials accompanied the Cairo and Damascus caravans to keep order among the pilgrims and see to their special needs. Some of these principals were Mamluks, others were educated Arabs. They included a *qadi*, an *imam*, a *muezzin*, an intendant of intestate affairs (to take charge of and record the property of pilgrims who died along the route), a secretary to the *amir al-hajj*, medical officers, Arab guides, and a *muhtasib*, who policed business transactions and public morality.

On 1 September 1326 (or it may have been the 10th)[3] Ibn Battuta set out, now for the second time in four months, to fulfill that "desire long-cherished" in his heart. (As later events would show, he left behind, and presumably divorced, the woman he had married in Damascus a short time earlier.) The staging ground for the caravan was the village of al-Kiswa a few miles south of the city. Here the main body of pilgrims from the city waited a few days for stragglers to catch up, while the *amir al-hajj* completed the job of organizing the various groups of travelers in a fixed order of march.

The distance from Damascus to Medina was about 820 miles, and the caravan normally covered it in 45 to 50 days. The itinerary varied somewhat from year to year, but it coincided generally with the route of the now abandoned Hijaz Railway, which the Ottoman Turks built as far as Medina before World War I. From Damascus the trail ran southward along the fringe of the Syrian Desert to the oasis of Ma'an, located on about the same latitude as Cairo. From there the route turned slightly southeastward, veering away from the Gulf of Aqaba and running through the interior highlands along the eastern flank of the Hijaz mountains. At Tabuk, the northern gateway to Arabia, the caravan stopped for a few days while the pilgrims rested and watered their camels before venturing into the fierce land of nude mountains and vast, black lava fields that lay between there and Medina.

Ibn Battuta thought the northern Hijaz a "fearsome wilderness," and indeed it was at any season of the year. The trek through it was a physical trial for the stoutest of pilgrims, and the odds against calamity in one devilish form or another were not encouraging. Some pilgrims invariably perished along the way every year from exposure, thirst, flash flood, epidemic, or even attack by local nomads, who seldom hesitated to disrupt the Sacred Journey for what it might bring them in plunder. In 1361 100 Syrian pilgrims died of extreme winter cold; in 1430 3,000 Egyptians perished of heat and thirst.[4] Ibn Battuta recounts in the *Rihla* that a certain year the pilgrims were overcome south of Tabuk by the violent desert wind known as the *samum*: "Their water suplies dried up, and the price of a drink of water rose to a thousand dinars, but both buyer and seller perished."

He does not report that any unusual tragedies befell his own caravan, and we may suppose that the company kept to the normal schedule. He traveled, he tells us, in the company of a corps of Syrian Arab tribesmen, who may have been serving as guides. He also made the acquaintance of a number of educated travelers like himself, among them a Maliki jurist from Damascus and a Sufi from Granada whom he would meet again several years later in India. He also struck up a friendship with a gentleman of Medina, who made him his guest during the caravan's four-day visit to that city.

Medina, where the Prophet Muhammad preached, founded the first Muslim state, and died in 632, was the most bountiful of the little islands of fertility scattered along the slopes of the Hijaz mountains, a green spot of habitation existing in uneasy symbiosis with the bedouin of the desert. Before Islam, it was but one of several commercial stopovers on the camel route linking the Yemen with the Middle East. In 622 A.D. Muhammad and his tiny band of converts, retreating from a histile and uncomprehending Mecca, moved north to Medina, which in the ensuing 34 years enjoyed its brief moment of political glory as the capital of the rapidly expanding Arab empire. After the center of Muslim power shifted to Damascus, Medina lost its political and military importance and would have been relegated once again to the back ridges of history were it not that the grave of the Prophet became an object of veneration.

The Mosque of the Prophet, which sheltered the sacred tomb as well as those of his daughter Fatima and the Caliphs Abu Bakr and 'Umar, became "al-Haram," a place of inviolability. In the Middle Period Medina was as much a city of pilgrims as Mecca was; even the native townsmen were largely of non-Arabian origin. A journey to the Mosque of the Prophet was not obligatory for Muslims as part of the *hajj* duties. Nonetheless, few pilgrims failed to visit Medina, even though they may have reached the Hijaz from the west or south and would not pass through the city except as a special diversion from Mecca.

On the evening of the same day that the caravan made camp outside the walls of the city, Ibn Battuta and his companions went to the mosque, "rejoicing at this most signal favor, . . . praising God Most High for our safe arrival at the sacred abodes of His Apostle." The sanctuary was in the form of an open court, surrounded on all sides by colonnades. At the southeast corner amidst rows of marble pillars stood the pentagonal tomb of Muhammad, and here Ibn Battuta repaired to pray and give thanks. During the following four days, he tells us in the *Rihla*,

we spent each night in the holy mosque, where everyone [engaged in pious exercises]; some, having formed circles in the court and lit a quantity of candles, and with book-rests in their midst [on which

were placed volumes] of the Holy Qur'an were reciting from it;
some were intoning hymns of praise to God; others were
occupied in contemplation of the Immaculate Tomb (God increase it in sweetness); while on every side were singers
chanting in eulogy of the Apostle of God.

During the days, he undoubtedly found time to visit other
mosques and venerated sites in and around the city, including the
cemetery (al-Baqi') east of the walls that contained the graves of
numerous kinsmen and Companions of the Prophet. He is also
likely to have made a point of seeing the little domed tomb of
Malik ibn 'Anas, the great eighth-century jurist and founder of the
Maliki school of law.

In the modern age charter buses whisk pilgrims along the paved
highway connecting Medina with Mecca, but Ibn Battuta and his
fellows faced 200 more miles of fiery desolation before reaching
the goal of their hopes. Yet this final stage of the journey was
different: haggard wayfarers became celebrants, uplifted and ren-
ewed, and the whole dusty company was transformed into a
joyous, white-robed procession. The change took place at Dhu l-
Hulaifa, a tiny settlement just five miles along the southbound
road out of Medina. This was one of the five stations (*mikats*) on
the five principal trails leading to Mecca where pilgrims were
required to enter into the state of consecration, called *ihram*.
Here male pilgrims took off their traveling clothes, washed themselves, prayed, and finally donned the special garment, also called
ihram, which they would continue to wear until after they entered
the Holy City and, if it were the time of the Greater Pilgrimage,
performed the rites of *hajj*. The garment consisted of two large,
plain, unstitched sheets of white cloth, one of which was wrapped
around the waist, reaching to the ankles, the other gathered
around the upper part of the body and draped over the left
shoulder. Nothing was worn over or beneath the *ihram*, and feet
were left bare or shod only in sandals without heels. Women did
not put on these garments, but dressed modestly and plainly,
covering their heads but leaving their faces unveiled. Once the
pilgrim assumed the *ihram*, symbolizing the equality of all men
before God, he was required to behave in a manner consistent
with the state of sanctity into which he had voluntarily entered.
The Prophet warned: "The Pilgrimage is in months well-known;
whoso undertakes the duty of Pilgrimage in them shall not go in to

his womenfolk nor indulge in ungodliness and disputing in the Pilgrimage. Whatsoever good you do, God knows it."[5]

After fulfilling the ceremonies of *ihram*, the caravan set forth once again, the pilgrims walking straighter now and shouting God's praises into the great Arabian void. The route followed a southwesterly course across low ridges of the Hijaz hills and then down to the plain bordering the Red Sea. The company reached the coast at Rabigh, a station about 95 miles north of Jidda, where the routes from Syria and Egypt finally converged and where the Egyptian pilgrims took the *ihram*. From here the caravan turned into the desert again, marching now southwestward along the coastal plain. Probably seven days after leaving Rabigh[6] they arrived in the morning hours at the gates of Mecca, the Mother of Cities.

It was mid October 1326. Twenty-two years old and a year and four months the pilgrim-adventurer, Ibn Battuta rode triumphantly into Mecca's narrow, brown valley and proceeded at once to the "illustrious Holy House," reciting with his companions the prayer of submission to the Divine will.

What is Thy Command? I am here, O God!
What is Thy Command? I am here!
What is Thy Command? I am here!
Thou art without companion!
What is Thy Command? I am here![7]

Among the cosmopolitan cities of Ibn Battuta's time, Mecca was in one sense pre-eminent. From the end of Ramadan and throughout the months of Shawwal and Dhu l-Qa'da, pilgrims from every Islamic land gathered in the city to pray in the Sacred Mosque, and, on the ninth day of the month Dhu l-Hijja, to stand in fellowship on the plain of 'Arafat before the Mount of Mercy. As Islam expanded into more distant parts of Asia and Africa during the Middle Period, the call to the *hajj* embraced an ever-larger and more diverse range of peoples. In the rites of the perambulations around the Ka'ba, the great stone cube that stood in the center of the mosque, Turks of Azerbaijan walked with Malinke of the Western Sudan, Berbers of the Atlas with Indians of Gujerat. The grand mosque, called the Haram, or Sanctuary, was the one place in the world where the adherents of the four main legal schools, plus Shi'is, Zaydis, 'Ibadis, and other sectarians, prayed together in one place according to their slightly varying ritual forms. Though there was a fixed order of prayer in the mosque for the four schools, reports Ibn Battuta,

> at the sunset prayer they pray all at the same time, each imam leading his own congregation. In consequence of this the people are invaded by some wandering of attention and confusion; the Malikite [worshipper] often bows in time with the bowing of the Shafi'ite, and the Hanafite prostrates himself at the prostration of the Hanbalite, and you see them listening attentively each one to the voice of the *muezzin* who is chanting to the congregation of his rite, so that he does not fall victim to his inattention.

Black Muslims and white Muslims, Sunnis and Shi'is all came to Mecca with the single declared purpose to fulfill a holy duty and to worship the One God. But they also came, incidentally, to trade. Pilgrims almost always brought goods with them to sell, sometimes whole caravan loads. The bedouin and oasis-dwellers of the Hijaz and the Yemen hauled in huge quantities of foodstuffs to feed the multitude. Ibn Jubayr wrote of his visit in 1183:

> Although there is no commerce save in the pilgrim period, nevertheless, since people gather in it from east and west, there will be sold in one day . . . precious objects such as pearls, sapphires, and other stones, various kinds of perfume such as musk, camphor, amber and aloes, Indian drugs and other articles brought from India and Ethiopia, the products of the industries of Iraq and the Yemen, as well as the merchandise of Khurasan, the goods of the Maghrib, and other wares such as it is impossible to enumerate or correctly assess.[8]

Though Mecca's own hinterland was a stony desert, Ibn Jubayr found the market street "overflowing" with "figs, grapes, pomegranates, quinces, peaches, lemons, walnuts, palm-fruit, water-melons, cucumbers and all the vegetables."[9]

If Mecca at the season of the *hajj* was a microcosm of all the peoples and all the wares of a good part of Africa and Eurasia, its cosmopolitanism was in other respects shallow. It was a cosmopolitanism derived from a unique annual event and not from the existence of mighty, urbane educational or philanthropic institutions as was the case with Cairo or Damascus. When the pilgrims rolled up their prayer mats and headed back to their homelands in the latter part of Dhu l-Hijja, the city reverted to the more prosaic activities of a dusty western Arabian town. Though foreign traders, scholars, and stranded poor folk were to be seen in the city all through the year, the population dwindled quickly when the feast days were over. Mecca had no substantial agricultural base of its own and was almost completely dependent on neighboring oases and countries for its sustenance. In those conditions Mecca could never have grown into a metropolis or supported majestic colleges, *khans*, and palaces of the sort that distinguished the mature urban centers of Islam. Though the city had its colleges, most of them were modest, and teaching was largely conducted in the Haram.[10]

If privation and remoteness finally doomed Mecca to second-rate city-hood, those very conditions suited it perfectly as a place for spiritual retreat and ascetic exercise. Simply to live there for a short time was an act of self-denial — at least it was before the age of automobiles, public toilets, and air conditioners. The city lies, not like Medina, in the midst of an oasis, but at the bottom of an arid depression surrounded by a double range of treeless mountains. From the north, the south, and the southwest, three ravines lead the visitor down into "this breathless pit enclosed by walls of rock,"[11] where summer temperatures soar to 126 degrees Fahrenheit. Before modern technology revolutionized the logistical aspects of the *hajj*, water and housing ran chronically short, epidemics broke out among the pilgrims, and flash floods raged suddenly down the central streets of the town, on several occasions flooding the Haram and severely damaging the Ka'ba. Yet like all deserts, the Meccan wilderness possessed a pure and terrifying beauty, an immensity of light and shadow that hinted at the workings of the Infinite. And though the land was unyieldingly grim, it inflicted its dangers and discomforts on all equally, reducing to triviality differences of race and class and driving the pilgrims together in the knowledge that only God is great.

Whatever a pilgrim may have suffered on the road to Mecca, his personal cares were quickly enough forgotten as he entered the court of the Haram and stood before the great granite block enveloped in its black veil. "The contemplation of . . . the venerable House," wrote Ibn Jubayr, "is an awful sight which

The Haram and the Ka'ba, Mecca
Library of Congress

distracts the senses in amazement, and ravishes the heart and mind."[12] Even the infidel Englishman Richard Burton, who visited the mosque in disguise in 1853, declared that "the view was strange, unique" and "that of all the worshippers who clung weeping to the curtain, or who pressed their beating hearts to the stone, none felt for the moment a deeper emotion than did [I]."[13]

Generations of rulers have made numerous alterations to the Haram and the Ka'ba, so that the structures look substantially different today from the way they did when Ibn Battuta saw them. In its modern form the Ka'ba is in the shape of a slightly irregular cube, set almost in the center of the court and rising to a height of 50 feet. The walls of blue-grey Meccan stone are draped year round with the *kiswa*, made of black brocade and embellished with an encircling band of Koranic inscription in gold. A single door, set about seven feet above the ground and concealed by its own richly decorated covering, gives entry to the windowless interior of the sanctuary. There are no relics inside, simply three wooden pillars supporting the roof, ornamental drapes along the walls, lamps of silver and gold hanging from the ceiling, and a copy of the Koran. At the eastern corner of the exterior of the Ka'ba is embedded the revered Black Stone, which measures about twelve inches across and is set in a rim of silver. The surface of the stone is worn smooth and no one can be certain of its composition. In Koranic tradition Abraham built the Ka'ba, a wooden structure as it originally stood, to commemorate the One God. Though in pre-Islamic times the sanctuary was a home of idols and its precinct a place of pagan rites, Muhammad restored it to its original purpose as a temple consecrated to the primordial monotheism of Abraham.

When a visitor arrives in Mecca, whether or not he intends to undertake the *hajj*, he must as his very first act perform the *tawaf*, the circumambulation. He walks around the Ka'ba seven times counterclockwise, stepping quickly the first three times, then walking more slowly, all the while reciting prayers special to the occasion. Each time he passes the eastern corner he strives to kiss or touch the Black Stone, not because some wondrous power is invested in it but because the Prophet kissed it. During the less congested months of the year, the pious visitor may perform the *tawaf* and kiss the stone at his leisure several times a day. But in the *hajj* season the mosque becomes a revolving mass of humanity, giving the illusion that the very floor of the courtyard is turning round the Ka'ba.

Facing the northeast façade of the shrine is a small structure (today in the shape of a little cage surmounted with a golden dome) called the

Maqam Ibrahim. Inside lies the stone said to bear the footprints of the Patriarch, who used the rock as a platform when he constructed the upper portions of the House. When the pilgrim has completed his *tawaf*, he goes to the Maqam where he prays a prayer of two prostrations. Near the Maqam is the blessed well of Zamzam. Here the Angel Gabriel (according to one tradition) miraculously brought forth a spring to quench the thirst of Hagar and her little son Isma'il after her husband Abraham had gone off into the desert. From the Maqam the pilgrim moves to the well to drink, which in Ibn Battuta's time was enclosed in a building of beautiful marble. The sacred water is sold in the cloisters of the mosque and in the streets of the city. During their sojourn the pilgrims perform their ritual ablutions with it and some, despite the heavily saline taste, drink profuse amounts for its reputed healing qualities.

When the pilgrim has drunk from the well, he may leave the mosque by the southeastern gate and proceed several yards to a little elevation, called al-Safa, which lies at one end of a Meccan street. From the steps of al-Safa he walks or jogs about a quarter of a mile along the street to another small eminence called al-Marwa. He repeats this promenade seven times, reciting prayers along the way, to commemorate Hagar's frantic search for water along the ground lying between the two hills. This rite is called the *sa'y*, that is, the Running. With the performing of it the pilgrim has completed the preliminary rites of the *hajj* and may at last find his lodgings and begin to introduce himself to the city.

The Syrian caravan of the year 1326 (726 A.H.) arrived at the western gate of Mecca sometime before dawn. Though probably exhausted from a night's march, Ibn Battuta and his companions made their way at once to the center of the city and entered the Haram by the gate called al-Salam. Praising God who "hath rejoiced our eyes by the vision of the illustrious Ka'ba," they performed the *tawaf* of arrival:

> We kissed the holy Stone; we performed a prayer of two bowings at the Maqam Ibrahim and clung to the curtains of the Ka'ba at the Multazam between the door and the black Stone, where prayer is answered; we drank of the water of Zamzam . . .; then, having run between al-Safa and al-Marwa, we took up our lodging there in a house near the Gate of Ibrahim.

The "house" Ibn Battuta repaired to was in fact a Sufi hospice (he uses the term *ribat*) called al-Muwaffaq, located near the southwestern side of the mosque. In his usual fashion he quickly struck up acquaintances with the pious residents of the lodge, some of them Maghribis. We may suppose that he put to good advantage the three weeks he had to himself before the start of the *hajj* festival, exploring the secondary shrines and historic sites of the Prophet's birthplace, rummaging through the wares in the market street, and perhaps climbing to the top of one of the holy mountains whose barren slopes roughed out the contours of the town. He also formed an opinion of the local citizenry, judging them generous, kindly, and proper.

> The Meccans are elegant and clean in their dress, and as they mostly wear white their garments always appear spotless and snowy. They use perfume freely, paint their eyes with kuhl, and are constantly picking their teeth with slips of green arak-wood. The Meccan women are of rare and surpassing beauty, pious and chaste.

The use of perfumes, oils, and makeup would of course have been out of fashion for everyone during the days preceding the *hajj*, when personal frippery was forbidden. Ibn Battuta himself, keeping to his ritual declaration of intention to complete the rites of the pilgrimage in a state of consecration, continued to wear his white *ihram* garb from the time he assumed it on the road from Medina until his *hajj* was fulfilled a month later. He also, we may presume, obeyed with precision the special taboos that attended the state of *ihram*. In all certainty he did not get into arguments or fights, kill plants or animals, engage in sexual relations, cut his hair or nails, wear sewn garments, or adorn himself with jewelry.[14]

We can also be sure that during these three weeks he spent the better part of his days and probably some of his nights in the Haram, where he performed additional *tawafs* (always meritorious in the sight of God), drank from the well, and made conversation with new acquaintances. The great mosque was indeed the center of all public life in Mecca. The streets of the town, winding through the canyons and down the slopes of the encircling hills, all converged on the Haram, whose court formed the very bottom of the alluvial depression. The mosque was in the shape of an irregular parallelogram, the roofed-over portion of the structure between the outer walls and the court being suported by a forest of marble columns (471 of them by Ibn Jubayr's count). Nineteen gates on all four sides gave access to the colonnades and court, and five minarets surmounted the mosque, four of them at the corners.[15] The Haram was not only the place of the pilgrim stations but also the center for daily prayers, Qur'anic reading, and education. In the shade of the cloisters, or in the court when the sun was low, sat rings of learners and listeners, while copyists, Qur'an readers, and even tailors occupied benches set up beneath the arches of the colonnades.[16] When prayers were not in session or the crush of pilgrims not too great, Meccan children played in the court, and the people of the city streamed back and forth through the gates, routinely using the sacred precinct as a short cut between one part of town and another. For poorer pilgrims the mosque was home. "Here," wrote John Burckhardt, another nineteenth-century Christian who penetrated the Haram incognito, "many poor Indians, or negroes, spread their mats, and passed the whole period of their residence at Mecca. Here they both eat and sleep; but cooking is not allowed."[17] There was not a single moment day or night throughout the year, so says the tradition, when at least a few of the faithful were not circling the Ka'ba. In the evening the square was lighted with dozens of torches and candles, bathing the worshippers and the great cube in a flickering orange glow.

When a pilgrim reached Mecca and circuited the Ka'ba, he still had, in an important religious sense, twelve miles to go before he would terminate his sacred journey. No Muslim was privileged to claim the title "al-Hajj" until he had traveled through the desert ravines east of the city to the plain of 'Arafat and, on the ninth day of Dhu l-Hijja, stood before the Mount of Mercy, the place where Adam prayed and where in 632 Muhammad preached his farewell sermon to his pristine congregation of believers. This annual retreat into the Meccan wilderness embraces the complex of ceremonies that makes up the *hajj* proper, or Greater Pilgrimage, which Muslims regard as separate from (though also including) the rituals of the *tawaf* and the *sa'y*. The Meccan rites, performed alone and at any time of the year, are called the *'umra*, that is, the Visit or Lesser Pilgrimage.

Before Islam, Mecca was the center for a yearly pilgrimage of Arabian tribes that was purely pagan. The Prophet retained some of those rites but utterly transformed their purpose into a

celebration of Abraham's unyielding monotheism. The ceremonies rested on the authority of the Qur'an and on the traditionally accepted practices of the Prophet. Although minor
details of the procedures vary according to the different juridical
schools (such as that male Shafi'is have their heads shaved at a
different point in the sequence of rites than do members of the
other *madhhabs*), the *hajj* is the supreme expression of the unity of
all believers. Indeed, when on the tenth of Dhu l-Hijja each
pilgrim kills a goat or sheep in remembrance of God's last-minute
instruction to Abraham to sacrifice a ram rather than his own son,
Muslims the world over do the same, thus uniting themselves
symbolically with their brothers and sisters in the Arabian desert.

Today, more than two million Muslims commonly arrive in
Mecca each year and set out for 'Arafat in a white-robed horde on
the eighth and ninth days of the sacred month. Many walk, but
others travel in buses and cars along the multilane highway which
winds out from the city. Saudi government helicopters circle
overhead and crowd control experts monitor the proceedings from
closed circuit television centers. First aid stations line the route,
cropdusters spray the plain against disease, and an army of
vendors greets the tired pilgrims at their destination with soft
drinks and barbecued chicken. In Ibn Battuta's time the journey
was of course far less agreeable, even dangerous if the local
bedouin took the occasion to plunder the procession. Those who
could afford the price rode in enclosed camel-litters. But most of
the pilgrims walked the hot stony trail; the pious did it barefoot.

By tradition the pilgrims spend the night of the eighth day at
Mina, a settlement in a narrow valley four miles east of the city.
On the following morning they go on to the 'Arafat plain and
range themselves in a great circle around the jagged little hill
called the Mount of Mercy. A city of tents and prayer mats is
quickly unfurled. At noon begins the Standing, the central and
absolutely essential event of the *hajj*. Throughout the afternoon
and until the sun sets the pilgrims keep vigil round the Mount, or
on its slopes if they can find room, reciting the prayer of obeisance
to God ("What is Thy Command? I am Here!") and hearing
sermons preached from the summit.

Precisely at sunset the Standing formally concludes and the
throng immediately packs up and starts back in the direction of
Mecca. By tradition the pilgrim must not perform his sunset prayer
at 'Arafat but at Muzdalifah, a point three miles back along the

road to Mina. And equally by tradition everyone who is physically able races to get there as fast as he can. In Ibn Battuta's time the "rushing" to Muzdalifah might have brought to mind the millennial charge of some gigantic army of white-clad dervishes. Today it has more the character of a titanic California commuter rush, meticulously orchestrated by the Saudi authorities to prevent hopeless traffic jams. Once arrived at Muzdalifah most of the pilgrims bed down for the night, though women, children, and the infirm may continue immediately on to Mina ahead of the crowd.

On the morning of the tenth the pilgrims assemble at Mina for the start of the Feast of the Sacrifice ('Id al-Adha), four days of celebration and desacralizing rites that bring the *hajj* to conclusion. Mina's sacred landmarks are three modest stone pillars, which stand at intervals from the eastern to the western end of the valley. As his first act the pilgrim must take a handful of pebbles (which he usually picks up along the road from 'Arafat) and cast seven of them at the western pillar. Just as the faithful Abraham threw stones at the devil to repulse his mesmeric suggestions that the little Isma'il need not after all be sacrificed, so the pilgrim must take aim at the devil-pillar as witness to his personal war against evil in general. When he has completed the lapidation, he buys a sheep or goat (or even a camel if he is rich) from any of the vendors who have collected thousands of animals for the occasion. He sets the face of the creature in the direction of the Ka'ba and kills it by cutting its throat as Abraham did after God mercifully reprieved his son. This act brings to an end the period of *ihram*. The pilgrim must find a barber (dozens are on hand) and have his head shaved, or at least some locks cut, and then he is free to exchange his ritual garb for his everyday clothing. As soon as the rites of Mina are accomplished he returns to Mecca to perform the *tawaf* once again, now released from all prohibitions save for sexual intercourse.

From the tenth to the thirteenth the solemnities of the Standing give way to jubilation and fellowship. The pilgrims return to Mina for two or sometimes three nights. They throw pebbles at all three of the devil-pillars each day, sacrifice additional animals, and socialize with countrymen and new-found friends. On the twelfth the first groups of *hajjis* begin leaving for home, taking care to perform the *tawaf* of farewell as their final ritual act.

From the fourteenth century to today the fundamental ceremonies of the *hajj* have been altered only in the merest details. Ibn

Battuta's own brief and matter-of-fact recounting of these events in the *Rihla* might be startlingly familiar to some young civil servant of Tangier, making the sacred journey by Royal Air Maroc.

The great majority of pilgrims who streamed out through the Meccan gullies in mid November 1326 were heading back to the prosaic lives they had temporarily abandoned to make the holy journey. Some of them would take many months to reach home, working their way along, getting stranded here or there, or taking time to see the great mosque and college cities of the Middle East. Ibn Battuta does not tell us in the *Rihla* just when he decided that he would not, for the time being, return to Morocco. When he left Tangier his only purpose had been to reach the Holy House. Once there, did the Meccan bazaar, the exotic faces, the stories of strange sights and customs set his mind to some master plan for exploring the hemisphere? Was it there that he made his impossible vow to roam the world without ever retracing his steps? Had he begun to realize the possibilities of traveling thousands of miles in every direction from Mecca without ever going beyond the limits of the familiar society of men who shared his values, his habits, and his language? Whatever soul-stirring effects his first *hajj* may have had on him, he was certainly no longer the boy who stood forlornly in the center of Tunis with nowhere to go and no one to talk to. After a year and a half away from home, he had already seen more of the world than most people ever would, he was cultivating a circle of learned and internationally minded friends, and he had won the title of "al-Hajj," itself an entrée to respect among influential and well-traveled people. When he set off for Baghdad with the Iraqi pilgrims on 20 Dhu l-Hijja, one fact was apparent. He was no longer traveling to fulfill a religious mission or even to reach a particular destination. He was going to Iraq simply for the adventure of it. It is at this point that his globetrotting career really began.

Notes

1. Arthur J. Arberry, *The Koran Interpreted* (New York, 1955), p. 86.
2. Theophilus Bellorini and Eugene Hoade, eds. and trans., *Visit to the Holy Places of Egypt, Sinai, Palestine and Syria in 1384 by Frescobaldi, Gucci and Sigoli* (Jerusalem, 1948), p. 23.

3. The Syrian caravan normally left Damascus on 10 Shawwal, or 10 September in 1326. 'Abdullah 'Ankawi, "The Pilgrimage to Mecca in Mamluk Times," *Arabian Studies* 1 (1974): 149. Since the *Rihla* is sometimes given to rounding off significant dates at the first day of the month, Ibn Battuta may well have left on or about 10 Shawwal rather than the 1st.

4. 'Ankawi, "The Pilgrimage to Mecca," pp. 160–61.

5. Arberry, *Koran*, pp. 54–55.

6. IB gives the traveling time from Rabigh to Khulais (a palm grove on the route) as three nights. Ibn Jubayr made the trip from Mecca to Khulais in four days. *The Travels of Ibn Jubayr*, trans. R. J. C. Broadhurst (London, 1952), pp. 188–91.

7. A pilgrimage prayer translated in Ahmad Kamal, *The Sacred Journey* (London, 1961), p. 35.

8. Ibn Jubayr, *Travels*, pp. 116–17.

9. Ibid., p. 117.

10. C. Snouk Hurgronje, *Mecca in the Latter Part of the Nineteenth Century* (Leiden, 1931), pp. 171–72.

11. Eldon Rutter, *The Holy Cities of Arabia*, 2 vols. (London, 1928), vol. 1, p. 117.

12. Ibn Jubayr, *Travels*, p. 80.

13. Richard Burton, *Personal Narrative of a Pilgrimage to El-Medinah and Meccah*, 2 vols. (New York, 1964), vol. 2, p. 161.

14. IB states in the *Rihla* that when he assumed the *ihram* garments he declared his intention of performing the rites of the Greater Pilgrimage (*hajj*) without the Lesser Pilgrimage ('*umra*, or visit). The latter, comprised essentially of the *tawaf* and the *sa'y*, could be performed at any time of the year. When a Muslim entered Mecca at a time other than the *hajj* season, he could deconsecrate himself following the *tawaf* and the *sa'y* of arrival. He would then be in a state called *tamattu'*, meaning that he could enjoy a normal life and wear everyday clothes until the start of the *hajj*, if in fact he planned to remain in the town until then. IB, however, vowed to perform the *hajj*, which included the *tawaf* and *sa'y* plus the rites of the walk to Arafat, without interrupting the state of *ihram*. Therefore, he was required to wear his white clothes and obey the attendant prohibitions until his *hajj* was completed. See "Hadjdj," EI₂, vol. 3, p. 35.

15. Gb, vol. 1, p. 203 n. IB counts five minarets, but Ibn Jubayr (*Travels*, p. 87) says there were seven, which agrees with nineteenth-century observers. There are seven today, though the precise locations of the towers have varied over the centuries.

16. Ibn Jubayr, *Travels*, p. 86.

17. Burckhardt, *Travels*, vol. 1, p. 273.

5 Persia and Iraq

He also said: "After us the descendants of our clan will
wear gold embroidered garments, eat rich and sweet food,
ride fine horses, and embrace beautiful women but they
will not say that they owe all this to their fathers and elder
brothers, and they will forget us and those great times."[1]

The Yasa of Chinggis Khan

When Ibn Battuta made his first excursion to Iraq and western
Persia, more than a century had passed since the birth of the
Mongol world empire. For a Moroccan lad born in 1304 the story
of Chinggis Khan and the holocaust he brought down on civilized
Eurasia was something to be read about in the Arabic version of
Rashid al-Din's *History of the Mongols*. The Tatar storm blew
closer to England than it did to Morocco and had no repercussions
on life in the Islamic Far West that Ibn Battuta's great grandfather
was likely to have noticed. For the inhabitants of Egypt and the
Levant the Mongol explosion had been a brush with catastrophe,
mercifully averted by Mamluk victories but imagined in the dark
tales told by fugitives from the dead and flattened cities that were
once Bukhara, Merv, and Nishapur. For the Arab and Persian
peoples of the lands east of the Euphrates the terrible events of
1220–60 had been a nightmare of violence from which they were
still struggling to recover in the fourteenth century.

"With one stroke," wrote the Persian historian Juvaini of the
Mongol invasion of Khurasan, "a world which billowed with
fertility was laid desolate, and the regions thereof became a desert,
and the greater part of the living dead, and their skin and bones
crumbling dust; and the mighty were humbled and immersed in
the calamities of perdition."[2] The Mongols wreaked death and
devastation wherever they rode from China to the plains of
Hungary but nowhere more so than in Persia, where most of the
great cities of the northern region of Khurasan were demolished
and their inhabitants annihilated. A modern historian estimates
that the total population of Khurasan, Iraq, and Azerbaijan may

81

Map 5: Ibn Battuta's Itinerary in Persia and Iraq, 1326–27

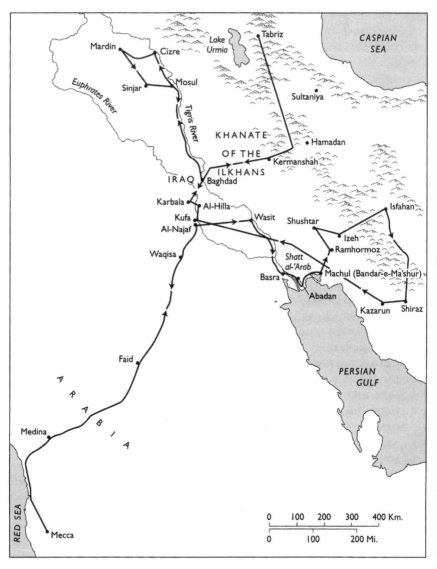

have dropped temporarily from 2,500,000 to 250,000 as a result of mass extermination and famine.[3] The thirteenth-century chronicler Ibn al-Athir estimated that the Mongols killed 700,000 people in Merv alone.[4] That figure is probably a wild exaggeration, but it suggests the contemporary perception of those calamitous events. The Mongol terror did not proceed from some Nazi-like ideological design to perpetrate genocide. Nor was it a spontaneous barbarian rampage. Rather it was one of the cooly devised elements of the greater Chinggis Khanid strategy for world conquest, a fiendishly efficient combination of military field tactics and psychological warfare designed to crush even the possibility of resistance to Mongol rule and to demoralize whole cities into surrendering without a fight. Once the armies had overrun Persia and set up garrison governments, wholesale carnage on the whole came to an end. Even the most rapacious Tatar general understood that the country could not be systematically bled over the long term if there were no more people left. After about 1260, and in some regions much earlier, trade resumed, fields were planted, towns dug themselves out, and remnants of the educated and artisan classes plodded back to their homes. Some cities, such as Tabriz, opened their gates to the invaders, and so were spared destruction. Others, Kerman and Shiraz for example, were in regions far enough to the south to be out of the path of the storm; they later acquiesced to Mongol overlordship while preserving a degree of political autonomy.

And yet for the mass of Arabic- or Persian-speaking farmers, on whose productive labor the civilization of Mesopotamia and the Iranian plateau had always rested, the disaster was chronic. Over the long run the military crisis was not so much an invasion of Mongol armies at it was the last great trek of Turkish steppe nomads from Central Asia into the Islamic heartland, a re-enactment and indeed a continuation of the eleventh-century migrations that had populated parts of the Middle East with Turkish tribes and put their captains in political control of almost all of it. Chinggis Khan could never have done more than found some unremarkable tribal state in Inner Asia were it not for his success at incorporating into his war machine numerous Turkish clans inhabiting the grasslands between Mongolia and the Caspian Sea. Turkish warriors trooped to the flag of Genghis by the tens of thousands, partly because the Mongols had defeated them, partly for the military adventure, partly because rain fell more often and grass grew taller progressively as one moved west and south. Turks far outnumbered ethnic Mongols in the mounted armies that attacked Persia, and they brought with them their wagons, their families, and their enormous herds of horses and sheep, which fed their way through Khurasan and westward along the flanks of the Alburz Mountains to the thick pastures of Azerbaijan.

Although many of the Turkish invaders had themselves been converted to Sunni Islam in the preceding centuries as a result of contact with urban merchants and missionaries from Khurasan, they joined eagerly in the violent dismembering of Persian society, ridding the land of the farms, crops, irrigation works, and cities that obstructed the free movement of their herds. Over several decades thousands of Iranian peasants were killed, enslaved, and chased off their land. To make matters worse, the early Mongol rulers, beginning with Genghis Khan's grandson Hulegu in 1256, could not quite make up their minds whether to carry through policies designed to reconstruct the country and revive agriculture or to treat the land as permanent enemy territory by taxing the peasants unbearably and permitting commanders, tribal chiefs, and state "messengers" to devour the countryside at the slightest sign of agrarian health.

Ghazan (1295–1304), the seventh Ilkhan (or "deputy" of the Great Khan, as the Mongol rulers of Persia were called), made a determined effort to improve the administrative and fiscal system in ways that would lighten the peasants' tax load, relieve them of indiscriminate extortion on the part of state officials, and restore their will to produce. The reforms had modest success, but they did not drive the economy decisively upward, owing to the petulant resistance of officials and war lords and the failure of Ghazan's successors to persevere with sufficient energy. The strength and well-being of any civilized society depended on the prosperity of its agriculture, and in this respect Persia and Iraq entered the fourteenth century still dragging the chains of the Mongol invasion. "There can be no doubt," wrote the Persian historian Mustawfi in 1340, "that even if for a thousand years to come no evil befalls the country, yet will it not be possible completely to repair the damage, and bring back the land to the state in which it was formerly."[5]

Yet if the understructure of the Persian economy was weak, the Mongols succeeded remarkably well at paving over their own work of mass contamination with a new urban culture shiny enough to make an educated visitor forget all about the horrors of Merv. Like the Marinids, the Mamluks, and other crude conquerors fresh from the steppe, the Ilkhans were quick to surrender to the sophisticated civilization that enveloped them. Indeed the mind of the Mongol warrior was so culturally deprived that it presented a vast blank on which all sorts of refined and humane influences could be written. In the earlier phase of the conquest the Tatar leaders turned for guidance to their Turkish subordinates, some of whom were Muslims with literate skills gained as a result of two or three centuries of contact with the cities of Khurasan on the fringe of the steppe. These allies supplied the Mongol language with a written script (Uigur Turkish) and a corps of clerks and officials who did much of the initial work of installing Tatar government throughout the Genghis Khanid empire. Even as the invasion of Persia was still going forward, the people of distinctly Mongol origin in the forces, a minority group almost from the beginning, were intermarrying with Turks, taking up their language and ways, and rapidly disappearing into the great migrating crowd. By the end of the thirteenth century, purely Mongol cultural influences on Persia, excepting in matters of warfare and military pomp, had all but vanished.

The Turkish model, however, was only half-way civilized and in the end no match for the Persian one at the elevated levels of literate culture. The Mongol invaders inherited proprietorship of an edifice of civilization far more complex and luxurious than anything they had ever experienced. The cultural Persianization of the Ilkhanid regime was getting under way even while the smoke still hung over Baghdad. Hulegu (1256–65) was in theory subordinate to the Great Khan of the Mongols (Kublai Khan in China after 1260), but in fact he was the founder of an Iraqo–Persian kingdom, one of the four major successor states to the monolithic empire of Genghis. Orderly government and efficient taxation of the population in a realm that extended from the Oxus to Anatolia absolutely required, as in Mongol China, the help of the native elite. Though thousands of educated people had been killed in the invasions, the remnants soon emerged from the wreckage and presented themselves for public service. Even the early Ilkhans, who favored Buddhism or Christianity rather than Islam, had no choice but to put administration and finance in the hands of the same families of native Muslim scribes and officials who had been running Persia before the invasion.

In fact the Mongol leaders were transformed into Persians, or at least Turco–Persians, to a degree that the Mamluks never were in their relation to literate Egypt. The explanation is that the Mongol governing class was not a permanently alien elite continuously recruited fresh from the steppe. And it did not maintain itself by erecting a political system that depended on the maintenance of sharp cultural separations between rulers and subjects. Rather, the Turco–Mongol soldiery came to Persia to stay and became progressively identified with Persian ways. The dynasty, moreover, was founded on conventional principles of hereditary kingship over the Persian and Iraqi people, a relationship which gradually splintered the connections of sentiment and culture between the Ilkhans and their kinsmen of Inner Asia.[6]

The Mongols' accommodation to the native Irano–Muslim bureaucracy spurred their conversion to Islam, itself an inevitable step in their Persianization. Chinggis had set a policy of toleration for all religions within the empire, and ultimately the formless tribal shamanism to which he remained loyal withered under a barrage of divine truths which missionaries of all the world-universalist faiths fired at his various successors. In Persia the proselytizers of several varieties of Buddhism, Christianity, and Islam competed for the attention of the Ilkhans like so many peddlers determined to make a sale. The Mongols at first swung erratically from one religious preference to another, depending upon which rite could muster the most influence at court.

Ghazan was the first ruler to proclaim Islam the state religion. He required the entire court to convert, put up mosques throughout the country, and endowed numerous pious institutions in the cities. With Mongol military power and Persian popular sentiment behind him, he wiped out Buddhism in that land. He also pulled down Nestorian Christian churches and put an end once and for all to naive European hopes that the Tatars could be brought over to Rome. Oljeitu (1304–16), Ghazan's successor and the most spiritually erratic of all the Ilkhans, was born a Nestorian, took up Buddhism, then converted to Islam. He first adopted Hanafi Sunnism, then Shafi'i; in 1310 he became a militant Shi'i and started a violent campaign to persecute Sunnis in general. His young son Abu Sa'id (1316–35), however, brought the court quickly back to Sunnism. What is more, he kept it that way. Most of his subjects were relieved and satisfied. Though Shi'ism has been the state religion of Iran since the sixteenth century, the great majority of Persians and Iraqis were still Sunnis (mostly Hanafi or

Shafi'i) in the fourteenth. Ibn Battuta, dyed-in-the-wool Sunni that he was, could not have picked a more felicitous time to visit the Ilkhanid state than in the reign of Abu Sa'id. When the Mongols converted to Islam, they also became both the disciples and the patrons of Persian art and culture. The decades of the holocaust had snuffed out intellectual and artistic life over much of the land, but it came to life so quicky after 1260 that the brief eighty years of the Ilkhanid age turned out to be an era of impressive cultural achievement, especially near the end when Ibn Battuta was there to bear witness to it. Like their steppe cousins in Cairo, the Mongol rulers did not hesitate to commit unspeakable barbarisms with one hand while with the other paying out large sums to promote refined craft and learning. Just a year after setting fire to Baghdad and a fair part of the stored up knowledge of the Abbasid Caliphate, Hulegu founded an observatory at Maragheh in which Persian and Chinese scholars collaborated to work out astronomical tables that would be of immense importance to later generations. Ghazan executed his enemies by having them cloven in half, but he took an avid personal interest in the natural sciences and medicine.

It was notably under Ghazan and his two successors that urban culture in Persia got back much of its old energy. To be sure, no single Persian city rivaled Cairo. But in Tabriz, the premier Mongol center, a great deal of monumental building was undertaken, even the construction of whole new suburbs. Oljeitu Khan founded a new capital at Sultaniya. The world of letters throve again too. The Mongols never had much time for love poetry or advanced theology, but they did appreciate practical science, geography, and history. The master historian of the age was Rashid al-Din, a Jewish convert to Islam who served as minister of state (vizier) under three Ilkhans. During the reign of Oljeitu, he completed his massive *Collection of Histories*, the first truly universal history of humankind ever written, or even imagined. The work embraced not only the whole of the Islamic world but also China, Byzantium, and even the recently civilized kingdoms of western Europe.[7]

Rashid al-Din's global vision was a reflection of an internationalist spirit at the Mongol court that reached even beyond the Dar al-Islam. Taking a remarkably large-minded view of the boundaries of civilization, the monarchs reigned over an astonishing transmigration of ideas and technology that made

Ilkhanid culture an eclectic synthesis of Persian, Arabic, Turkish, Chinese, and even Tibetan elements. Over the political bridge that Genghis threw across the Asian grassland-sea marched hundreds of Chinese engineers, scientists, doctors, artists, and propagators of Buddhism seeking service and opportunity in Persia. A smaller number of Persians visited China. Though direct communciation between the two regions died down in the late thirteenth century when the Ilkhans converted to Islam and their diplomatic relations with the Peking Mongols deteriorated, Chinese cultural influences left enduring marks on Persian miniature painting, calligraphy, and textile and pottery design. In 1294 Gaykhatu Khan (1291–95) even introduced block-printed paper money on Chinese inspiration, though the Persians rejected this newfangled idea out of hand, resulting in a temporary collapse of the commercial economy.[8]

The cosmopolitanism of the Ilkhanids, coupled with their enthusiastic adoption of everything Persian, also did much to restore circulation on the routes of scholarship and craft linking Persian and Iraqi cities with the rest of the Islamic world. Indeed the Mongol period witnessed an important expansion of the Persian language as well as Irano –Islamic styles in art and humane letters into both Turkish Anatolia and India, where they increasingly set the standard of what polished culture should be.

When the Mongol–Mamluk military struggle for Syria finally ended about 1315, intellectual links were quicky restored between Cairo, the new capital of Arab letters, and both the Arabic-speaking towns of Iraq and the Persian cities of the Iranian plateau. In the central Islamic lands Arabic and Persian continued to share the status of intellectual *linguae francae*. Many important writers, such as the historian Rashid al-Din, saw to it that their works were made available in both languages.[9] Thus, when Ibn Battuta entered Iran, his first excursion beyond the Arabic-speaking world, his inability to speak the native tongue was no particular disadvantage as long as he kept to the network of the learned, where bilingualism was common and where, at the very least, the symbolic language of religious observance, civilized manners, and Sunni erudition could always see him through. Indeed, for an educated Muslim traveler with good urban connections, it was almost as if the assault of the pagan Mongols had never even happened.

Ibn Battuta left Mecca on 17 November 1326 (20 Dhu l'Hijja 726) in the company of the pilgrims returning to Iraq and the wider region of eastern Islam. This was the official caravan of the Ilkhanid state, similar in organization to the Mamluk caravans sent from Damascus and Cairo. He had the good fortune to travel under the formal protection of the *amir al-hajj*, one Pehlewan Muhammad al-Hawih, who paid out of his own purse the cost of hiring half a double camel litter for the young man. Why should the *amir*, a favored official at the court of the Ilkhan of Persia, take an interest in this 22-year-old nonentity from Morocco? Part of the reason is that the caravan commander commonly patronized scholarly personages in the pilgrim company, especially if they were needy. Beyond that, Ibn Battuta did develop something of a personal acquaintanceship with the *amir*, as would be demonstrated in the following year. There may be a further hint here of the lad's natural flair for disarming important people with his earnest piety and gregarious personality. In any case the enclosed camel litter was a godsend of comfort, far preferable to crossing the Arabian Peninsula on foot.

By Ibn Battuta's reckoning the pilgrim train was enormous: "Anyone who left the caravan for a natural want and had no mark by which to guide himself to his place could not find it again for the vast number of people." But the enterprise was also as efficiently organized as the Mamluk caravan from Syria had been. "Great supplies of luxuries" were readily available, and the poorer *hajjis* were entitled to free food, water, and medicine. "They used to march during the night and light torches in front of the file of camels and litters," Ibn Battuta recalls, "so that you saw the countryside gleaming with light and the darkness turned into radiant day."

The route north was more or less the one that pilgrims had followed ever since the early days of the Caliphate, when Zubayda, wife of the illustrious Harun al-Rashid, endowed the construction of a chain of water tanks and wells along the trail to keep the caravans safely supplied. From Medina, where the company laid over for six days, the track ran northeastward across the Nejd plateau, through the oasis of Faid, then along the eastern edge of the great Nafud sand desert. At a place called Waqisa on the desert edge of the Mesopotamian basin, greeting parties from the Iraqi city of Kufa met the caravan with fresh provisions of flour, bread, dates, and fruit. About six days later the column reached the Kufa region, halting at al-Najaf (Mashhad 'Ali) just a few miles south of the Euphrates. The entire journey from Mecca to Mesopotamia took approximately 44 days.[10]

Ibn Battuta rested at al-Najaf for a few days since it was the burial place of 'Ali ibn Abi Talib, the fourth Caliph and son-in-law of the Prophet. 'Ali's grand mausoleum in the heart of the town was a place venerated by all Muslims, but for the Twelver Shi'a, the largest of the Shi'i sects in Islam, it was a center of holy pilgrimage second only to Mecca. Though most of the population of greater Iraq and Persia were still Sunni in the fourteenth century, important Shi'i communities were scattered throughout the Ilkhanid realm, with the largest concentrations in lower Mesopotamia.[11]

The theological breach between the two groups centered on the Shi'i doctrine of the Imam, the leader-messiah descended from 'Ali, who would one day reveal himself and fill the earth with truth and righteousness until the time appointed for the Last Judgement. Twelve Imams in the hereditary line of 'Ali through his sons Hasan and Husayn had ruled the early Shi'i community, which started out as a dissident political "party" (the general meaning of the term Shi'a) opposed to the majority leadership. The 'Alid Imams were regarded by their followers as possessing infallible and esoteric knowledge of the prophetic Revelation and as divine-right rulers whose temporal supremacy had been usurped by the Umayyad and Abbasid Caliphs. The twelfth Imam in the line, according to the teachings of the "Twelver" variety of Shi'ism, disappeared in the ninth century but did not die. One day he would return. Sunnis, by contrast, believed that the meaning of the Qur'anic revelation in relation to all aspects of both spiritual and mundane experience was to be interpreted by the consensus of the community of believers, a unity collectively described in the four schools of jurisprudence. Sunnis gave 'Ali a hallowed place in Islamic history, but as a Caliph and a Companion of the Prophet, not as the progenitor of a dynasty of theocrats. Shi'i law was not in most respects significantly different from Sunni, and most of the time the two groups managed to live in peace. Except during surges of fanaticism on one side or the other, they treated one another with simple suspicion and the common varieties of religious prejudice.

Ibn Battuta makes it abundantly clear that he had little time for Shi'is, Twelver or otherwise. At several points in the *Rihla* he takes righteous potshots at their beliefs or recounts disparaging little anecdotes about their fanatical and misguided observances. He invariably refers to them as "Rafidis," or "Turncoats," a term of deprecation Sunnis commonly used. His intolerance may have been stiffened by the fact that the Maliki intellectual class in Morocco was inclined to juristic and theological dogmatism, largely in reaction to the anti-Maliki policies of the Almohads. In any case he did not mix much with Shi'i scholars and deliberately avoided visiting certain towns having predominantly Shi'i populations. He probably spent only a few days in al-Najaf (just where he does not say), though in the *Rihla* he gives a thorough and objective description of Ali's beautiful domed mausoleum.[12]

From al-Najaf the pilgrim caravan continued on northward to Baghdad, its terminus. But Ibn Battuta, apparently not in the mood to see that city just yet, decided to make for Basra at the far southern end of the Tigris–Euphrates delta. A troop of local Arabs was going that way, so he hired a camel and joined them. Rather than taking a direct route to Basra by following the course of the Euphrates, the party first traveled due east along the northern fringe of the Great Swamp, a region of marshland, creeks, and lakes that covered the delta from the latitude of Kufa almost to the Persian Gulf.[13]

In five days the caravan reached the city of Wasit. Ibn Battuta's companions remained there for three days in order to trade, so he took the opportunity to make an overnight excursion to the village of Umm 'Ubaida to visit the tomb of Shaykh Ahmad ibn al-Rifa'i, the twelfth-century founder of the Sufi order with which he had become affiliated during his stay in Jerusalem. At the *zawiya* of Umm 'Ubaida he had the luck to meet one of the Shaykh's descendants, who was also visiting, and to be treated to a display of ecstatic exercises for which the Rifa'i disciples were well known:

When the afternoon prayers had been said, drums and kettle-drums were beaten and the [Sufi] brethren began to dance. After this they prayed the sunset prayer and brought in the repast, consisting of rice-bread, fish, milk, and dates. When all had eaten and prayed the first night prayer, they began to recite their *dhikr* [mystical litany] . . . They had prepared loads of firewood which they kindled into flame, and went into the midst of it dancing; some of them rolled in the fire, and others ate it in their mouths, until finally they extinguished it entirely . . . Some of them will take a large snake and bite its head with their teeth until they bite it clean through.[14]

Ibn Battuta was too much the sober urban scholar to go in for that sort of religious frenzy, so a one-night sojourn at the lodge may have been quite enough for him. In any case he returned to Wasit to find that his caravan had already departed. He set off on his own in pursuit, perhaps a foolish thing to do in the Great Swamp, since a group of Sufi brethren who had straggled behind the caravan on its way to Wasit had been attacked and robbed by a band of Shi'i marsh-dwellers. In a day or two, however, he safely caught up with his party, which was now moving southward along a route generally parallel to the Tigris. Some time in the latter part of January 1327 the caravan reached Basra.[15]

It is easy enough to understand why Ibn Battuta made a point of seeing Basra. Any literate young man, even from the Far West, would have known what this city had been six centuries earlier: the veritable Athens of Islam where the classical civilization of the Arabs had first been conceived and cast. It had been the home of numerous early Muslim luminaries: theologians, philosophers, poets, scientists, and historians. It had also been the laboratory where the rules of classical Arabic grammar were worked out, the rules by which educated men conversed and wrote and distinguished themselves from common folk. Though Baghdad superseded it in the ninth century as the intellectual capital of the Arabs, Basra continued to prosper for several hundred years owing to its status as chief port of the Caliphate on the Persian Gulf.

The Mongols left the city alone when they conquered Lower Iraq, but their assault on Baghdad and other Mesopotamian towns, which produced a severe decline in agricultural and industrial productivity, afflicted the economy of Basra as well. By the time Ibn Battuta visited the town, it had shrunk to such an extent that its beautiful grand mosque stood alone two miles outside the inhabited area. For a scholar who knew his history there was an even sadder testimony to decline than the deterioration of the architecture. When he attended Friday worship in the mosque, he was appalled to hear the preacher committing dreadful errors of grammar in his sermon. "I was astonished at his conduct," he recalls, "and spoke of it to the *qadi* Hujjat al-Din, who said to me 'In this town there is not a man left who knows anything of the science of grammar.'"

Except for its thick forests of date-palms, the city had little to recommend it that was not past and gone. Ibn Battuta must have devoted most of his time there to visiting the mosque and the graves of several of the early immortals of Arab letters, as well as some of the Companions of the Prophet. As usual the local Sunni worthies, a small and undistinguished group, favored him with money, clothes, and food. The Ilkhanid governor also received him and gave him presents. He probably stayed not more than a week or two.[16]

From Basra he took passage on a *sambuq*, a small, lateen-rigged boat common in the Mesopotamian river trade, and sailed for ten miles along the Ubulla canal, passing "through an uninterrupted succession of fruit gardens and overshadowing palmgroves both to right and left, with traders sitting in the shade of the trees, selling bread, fish, dates, milk, and fruit." The canal emptied into the Tigris estuary, called the Shatt al-'Arab, which linked the region of Basra with the gulf.[17] Here, he transferred to a second vessel and sailed overnight to Abadan, which in that century was a few miles from the coast, though today it is more than twenty miles owing to the gradual build-up of the alluvial delta.[18]

While stopping at a small hospice in Abadan, he learned of a local Sufi anchorite, who lived year round in the marsh and sustained himself entirely on fish. He immediately went looking for this hermit and found him seated in the shell of a ruined mosque. The *shaykh* gave the young man the blessing he sought and even offered him a large fish for his supper. Ibn Battuta recalls in the *Rihla* that he was deeply moved by this meeting, to the point that "for a moment I entertained the idea of spending the rest of my life in the service of this *shaykh*." Indeed, he seems to have had a recurring fascination for this sort of uncompromising asceticism, probably a tug of the heart that many gregarious, worldly men feel from time to time. At a number of junctures in his career he experienced little crises of the soul, when he thought of throwing up his life of adventure for the self-denying and rapturous existence of a true Sufi disciple. In the end, however, what he calls "the pertinacity of my spirit" won out, and he was back on the road and into the world of affairs.

In this case he was back on the road in no time. Under the urging of an acquaintance from Basra, he contrived to get to Baghdad, not by turning around and heading back up the Tigris, but by making for the mountains of Persian Luristan, which was decidedly in the wrong direction. His plan was to make a long looping tour east of Mesopotamia through the Persian region of Jibal, or what he calls Iraq al-Ajami. Indeed it is at this point in the narrative that he speaks of his "habit" of shunning any road he had already traveled by.

As it worked out, his next important destination was to be the city of Isfahan in the Jibal province on the far side of the lofty Zagros

Mountains. Apparently in the company of his Basran friend, he went by ship from Abadan eastward along the delta coastline to the port of Machul, now Bandar-e-Ma'shur, in the Iranian part of Mesopotamia. There he hired a horse from some merchants and headed northward across the plain of Khuzistan, a province of marshes and sugar-cane fields. He followed a generally northward route through the agricultural towns of Ramhormoz (Ramiz) and Shushtar (Tustar), then turned westward to meet the Zagros, which rose suddenly as a barricade of rock along the eastern rim of the plain.

The mountain crags and pinnacles, which formed the natural frontier between Mesopotamia and the Iranian plateau, were inhabited by fierce herding peoples called the Lurs. The Mongols had subdued this country perfunctorily in Hulegu's time, but owing to its wild isolation from the centers of administration, they left law and order in the hands of a client dynasty of tribal barons, called *atabegs*. Ibn Battuta regarded some of the Lurs customs that came to his attention as thoroughly brutish and heterodox, but the *atabeg* and the little groups of literate men of the villages and hospices treated him well and gave him the usual presents owing to wayfarers.[19] From Idhaj (or Malamir, and now Izeh), the mountain capital of the *atabegs*, he advanced northeastward through the frigid high passes of the Zagros (it was probably March) and thence to the orchard city of Isfahan, which lay at the western edge of the central plateau at an altitude of 4,690 feet. He was now in the heart of Persia.

He found lodging in what seems to have been a Sufi center of abundant proportions, possessing not only a mosque, a kitchen, and rooms for disciples and travelers, but also a fine marble-paved *hammam*, or bath. The local head of the *zawiya*, a Persian named Qutb al-Din Husain, was also a *shaykh* of the Suhrawardiyya, one of the largest mystical orders of the later Middle Period with widespread affiliations in the eastern Islamic lands, including India. One day the young visitor was looking out the window of his room in the lodge and noticed a white *khirqa*, or patched Sufi's robe, spread out in the garden to dry. He recalls thinking to himself that he would like to have one of them, just as he had collected one from the Rifa'i *shaykh* in Jerusalem, as a symbol of honorific connection with the Suhrawardiyya. In the next moment Qutb al-Din abruptly entered his room and ordered a servant to bring the robe, which he threw over his guest's shoulders. Astonished, Ibn Battuta fell to kissing the *shaykh*'s feet, then, in his impetuous way, begged if he might not have his blessed skull cap as well. The request was granted forthwith. In the *Rihla* Ibn Battuta takes pains to list the chain of authority (*isnad*) linking him by virtue of this investiture with the twelfth-century founder of the brotherhood. But as in the Jerusalem episode, he assumed no obligation to pursue the Sufi way simply by accepting the *shaykh*'s casual blessing on a God-fearing traveler.

He spent two weeks with Qutb al-Din in Isfahan, enjoying the preserved watermelon and other fruits of the Isfahan plain laid out at the *zawiya*'s table. At this point in history the city was not the noble capital it had been under the Seljuk Turks and would be again three centuries later under the Shi'i Safavids. Because of a sad inclination among the inhabitants to engage in violent factional rows, coupled with the turmoil of the early Mongol years, the city was only beginning to recover some of its earlier vigor.[20] Perhaps dissatisfied with what the town had to show him of Persian culture, Ibn Battuta decided to travel another 300 miles south to Shiraz, chief city of the province of Fars.

This journey, accomplished in ten days, took him along one of the historic trade routes of central Iran and through the central region of the ancient Persian empire. Since it was probably about mid April,[21] he followd the so-called summer road through the Zagros foothills rather than the winter road which ran nearer the high desert to the east.[22] During the final days of the trip he climbed through a series of blooming mountain valleys and thence into the fertile, mile-high basin that sheltered Shiraz, the "Garden City."

The luck of Shiraz in the Middle Period was that the Mongol monster had not been inclined to devour Fars province, the region being too hot for steppe herdsmen and too far away from the main Tatar centers in Azerbaijan. The city not only survived but opened its gates to refugees from the north, and so, as with Cairo, its intellectual life received a fillip from the arrival of well-educated fugitives. Ibn Battuta was attracted to Shiraz partly because of its reputation as the greatest center of Persian letters and partly because it was a city where, according to his contemporary Mustawfi, "most of the people strive after good works, and in piety and obedience to the Almighty have attained a high degree of godliness."[23] The city was sometimes called the Tower of Saints (Burj-i-Awliya) because of the profusion of holy tombs. It was also

one of the loveliest towns in Persia, and still is. Ibn Battuta remembers that "its inhabitants are handsome in figure and clean in
their dress. In the whole there is no city except Shiraz which
approached Damascus in the beauty of its bazaars, fruit-gardens
and rivers."

The young jurist wanted above all to meet the chief *qadi* of the
city, Majd al-Din, a famous Persian scholar especially admired
among Sunnis for having brilliantly defied the Shi'i Ilkhan Oljeitu.
When this ruler converted to Shi'ism, according to the version of
the story recounted in the *Rihla*, he ordered that the *khutba*, the
praise formulas recited at the beginning of the Friday mosque
sermon, be changed throughout the land to exalt the name of 'Ali.
When the people of Shiraz refused to cooperate, he commanded
that Majd al-Din be executed by being thrown to a pack of
ferocious dogs trained to eat humans. But when the dogs were let
loose, Ibn Battuta relates, "they fawned on him and wagged their
tails before him without attacking him in any way." The Ilkhan
was so astounded at the deliverance of this Muslim Daniel that he
played out the Darius role perfectly, prostrating himself at the
qadi's feet, showering him with honors, and renouncing his errant
doctrine for the Sunni faith. Ibn Battuta's ending to the story is a
bit artful, since we know from other sources that the most Oljeitu
did was to call off persecutions of Sunnis while remaining a loyal
Twelver until his death in 1316. Majd al-Din meanwhile held his
post throughout the reign of Abu Sa'id and for twenty years after
the collapse of the Mongol state.[24]

Soon after arriving in Shiraz in the company of three unnamed
traveling companions, Ibn Battuta went to salute Majd al-Din, who
questioned him about his homeland and his travels. The *shaykh*
also offered him a small room in his college. Ibn Battuta does not
say how long he stayed in the city, but the general chronological
framework of the Persian tour would suggest that he remained
something less than two weeks, visiting the mosques and the tombs
of numerous Shirazi lights, including Abu 'Abdallah ibn Khafif,
one of the forefathers of Persian Sufism, and the renowned poet
Sa'di, who was buried in a lovely garden outside the city.[25]

Since there were no more specially interesting towns to visit
between Shiraz and the seaports of the gulf, Ibn Battuta resolved
to turn west and head once again in the general direction of
Baghdad. His route took him through two high passes of the
southern Zagros and the little town of Kazarun, then northwest-

ward into the Khuzistan plain. Somewhere north of the port of Machul he crossed his outbound trail of some three months earlier. Advancing once again into the Mesopotamian marshlands, he forded the Tigris at an unidentified point perhaps about midway between Wasit and Basra. He finally arrived at Kufa on the Euphrates five or six weeks after leaving Shiraz.[26] He was now back on the main pilgrimage road. From Kufa, he continued upriver past the ruins of ancient Babylon and the Shi'i towns of al-Hilla and Karbala. About the first week of June 1327 he reached the Tigris and the city of the Caliphs.[27]

He gives the definite impression in the *Rihla* that he was traveling to Iraq primarily to see Baghdad. But he was under no illusions about the sad state of the city in his own time. He went there to honor its past and perhaps to walk among the ruins along the west bank of the river, imagining the ghosts of the divines and jurisprudents who had lived there five centuries earlier, founding the moral and intellectual code of civilization by which his own generation still lived. In the *Rihla* he introduces his description of the city with a set of perfunctory praise formulas ("of illustrious rank and supreme pre-eminence") but then goes on to reiterate the mournful admission of his twelfth-century predecessor Ibn Jubayr that "her outward lineaments have departed and nothing remains of her but the name . . . There is no beauty in her that arrests the eye, or summons the busy passer-by to forget his business and to gaze."

It was not in fact as bad as all that. As with the buildup of silt in the irrigation canals, the city's waning had been gradual, in most periods almost imperceptible. Despite Turkish military *coups*, sectarian violence, urban gang warfare, and the menace of floods pouring over neglected dykes, Baghdad retained a good share of both its international commercial prosperity and its residual pre-stige as capital of the Caliphs long after the glorious eighth and ninth centuries. Even the rampaging Mongols left many of its public buildings standing and quite a few of its people alive. In fact Hulegu's army had barely finished the sacking when he ordered, in typical fashion, that a vigorous restoration program should begin. Under an administration of local Arab and Persian officials, the city quickly pulled itself up to the status of provincial capital of Mesopotamia.

Baghdad was no longer an important stop on a Middle Eastern study tour and Ibn Battuta found most of its numerous colleges in ruins. But teaching continued, notably in the Nizamiya, the eleventh-century prototype of the four-sided *madrasa*, and in the Mustansiriya, a college built in 1234 to provide professorial chairs and lecture rooms for all four of the major juridical schools.[28] The Mosque of the Caliphs, one of the great congregational mosques located on the east bank of the river, had been burned down in the Mongol assault, but Ibn Battuta found it fully rebuilt and offering advanced studies. Although he stayed only two or three weeks in the city, he found time to go to the mosque to hear a set of lectures on one of the important compilations of Prophetic Traditions.

If Baghdad's intellectual life had had more to offer, he might have been content to remain there throughout the summer, awaiting the departure of the *hajj* caravan in mid-September. Any traveler less obdurate than he would probably have been thankful for a long rest at this point before starting another trek across the Arabian waste. But unexpectedly, a new adventure suddenly came his way, and it would have been entirely out of character for him to pass it up.

He arrived in Baghdad to learn that the Ilkhan himself was currently in residence, perhaps having wintered there as the rulers sometimes did to escape the cold of Azerbaijan. Abu Sa'id was then making preparations to return to the north, most likely to Sultaniya, the capital founded by his father Oljeitu. The Ilkhan always traveled in the company of a huge retinue, called in Arabic the *mahalla*, or "camp," which was in effect the entire royal court in motion: several *amirs* and their mounted troops, myriad religious and administrative personnel, and a small army of servants and slaves. In addition, the ruler's wives and favorites, called the *khatuns*, all had their own suites of bodyguards and functionaries. Ibn Battuta jumped at the chance to tag along with the royal procession, "on purpose," he explains, "to see the ceremonial observed by the king of al-'Iraq in his journeying and encamping, and the manner of his transportation and travel." Either before leaving Baghdad or *en route* with the *mahalla*, he managed to secure the patronage of 'Ala al-Din Muhammad, one of the Ilkhan's leading generals.

Abu Sa'id, the last of the Mongols of Persia, ascended the throne in 1316 at the age of twelve. He was in fact about a year younger than Ibn Battuta, who describes him as being "the most beautiful of God's creatures in features, and without any growth on his cheeks." The traveler also admired him for his civilized qualities. He was not only a committed Sunni, but a generous, pious, and tolerant one. According to the fifteenth-century Egyptian writer Taghribirdi, he was "an illustrious and brave prince, with an imposing aspect, generous and gay."[29] He wrote both Arabic and Persian with a beautiful hand, played the lute, composed songs and poems, and, in the latter part of his reign, even lightened some of the tax load on the peasantry. Whereas several of his Mongol predecessors were confirmed alcholics and some of them died of the consequences, he prohibited the use of spirits in the kingdom in accord with the Sacred Law — though with what success we do not know. There seems to have been little in his character that recalled his ancestor Chinggis Khan. He represents rather the definitive conversion of the Ilkhanid state to polished Persian culture. Perhaps if he had reigned longer, he would have been a great builder like his contemporary al-Nasir Muhammad of Egypt. As it was, the political foundations he laid during his last eight years were not strong enough to ensure the survival of the regime, which utterly collapsed at his death in 1335, leaving Persia to face the remainder of the century in fragmentation and war.[30]

In the summer of 1327, however, the dynasty looked vigorous enough to the Moroccan traveler, when he witnessed the nosiy, fearsome extravaganza of a Mongol Khan on the march:

Each of the *amirs* comes up with his troops, his drums, and his standards, and halts in a position that has been assigned to him, not a step further, either on the right wing or on the left wing. When they have all taken up their positions and their ranks are set in perfect order, the king mounts, and the drums, trumpets and fifes are sounded for the departure. Each of the *amirs* advances, salutes the king, and returns to his place; then the chamberlains and the marshals move forward ahead of the king, and are followed by the musicians. These number about a hundred men, wearing handsome robes, and behind them comes the sultan's cavalcade. Ahead of the musicians there are ten horsemen, with ten drums carried on slings round their necks, and five [other] horsemen carrying five reed-pipes . . . On the sultan's right and left during his march are the great *amirs*, who number about fifty.

Ibn Battuta may have had only a general notion of where he might be going when he left Baghdad with this *mahalla* in the latter part of June.[31] In his description of the journey, he does not name any of the stations but states only that he traveled in the company of the Ilkhan for ten days. The king was almost certainly heading for the new capital of Sultaniya (172 miles northwest of Tehran), probably following the trans-Persian "Khurasan Road" by way of Kermanshah, the central Zagros, and Hamadan.[32] Somewhere near Hamadan the *amir* 'Ala al-Din Muhammad, Ibn Battuta's patron, was suddenly ordered to leave the *mahalla* and proceed northward to Tabriz, apparently on urgent business of state.[33] He almost certainly traveled with a lean, fast-riding detachment, and Ibn Battuta was given leave to go along. Again, his route to Tabriz is a mystery, but the party may have taken the old Abbasid high road from Hamadan northwestward through the mountains, passing east of Lake Urmiya.[34] Meanwhile, Abu Sa'id and his suite lumbered on toward Sultaniya.

Ibn Battuta could count it a stroke of good fortune to have this unexpected visit to Tabriz, for it was the premier city of the Persian Mongols and, at just this moment in history, one of the key commercial centers of the Eurasian world. Located in a grassy plain dominated to the south by the 12,000 foot pinnacle of Mount Sahand, Tabriz had been nothing more than the main town of the region until the Turco–Mongol herdsmen flooded into Azerbaijan. This migration produced a dramatic shift of both military power and population growth away from Mesopotamia to the high northwestern rim of Persia. The local notability had been wise enough to greet the Mongol invaders with the keys to the city, thus offering the Ilkhans the convenience of establishing their first capital in a town that their fellow Tatars had not first demolished.

The anchoring of the Mongol state and the revival of trade found Tabriz rather than Baghdad the main junction of trans-Persian routes linking the Mediterranean, Central Asia, and the Indian Ocean. The city also attracted colonies of Genoese, Venetians, and other south Europeans, who responded fast to Mongol tolerance and internationalism by advancing in from their bases on the Eastern Mediterranean and Black Sea coasts. Even the Ilkhans who had converted to Islam observed the Pax Mongolica tradition of open trade and travel. Abu Sa'id, for example, signed a commercial treaty with Venice in 1320, and though Ibn Battuta does not mention the presence of Europeans in Tabriz in connection with his visit, we know some were there.[35]

The Ilkhan Ghazan made Tabriz worthy of the cultivated

Persian gentlemen who staffed his secretariat by beautifying the town and ordering the construction of an entirely new suburb of grand buildings, including a mosque, a *madrasa*, a hospice, a library, a hospital, a residence for religious and state officials, and his own mausoleum — none of which has survived to the present.[36] Around the end of the fourteenth century Tabriz had a population of 200,000 to 300,000 people.[37] Oljeitu established his own new capital at Sultaniya, and Abu Sa'id honored the change. But Sultaniya was the Ilkhanids' Brazilia. The court and bureaucratic elite resisted mightily the notion of leaving comfortable Tabriz, which remained the far greater city of the two.[38]

Ibn Battuta, unfortunately, had little time to take in the sights of the town. On the very morning after he arrived there with the Mongol envoys, 'Ala al-Din received orders to rejoin the Ilkhan's *mahalla*. The Moroccan apparently decided there was nothing for it but to stick with his benefactor if he were to be assured of getting back to Baghdad in time for the *hajj* departure. And so off he went after a single night and without meeting any of the city's scholars. He did, however, manage to squeeze in a look around. He lodged in a magnificent hospice, where he dined, he tells us, on meat, bread, rice, and sweets. In the morning he toured the great bazaar ("One of the finest bazaars I have seen the world over") where the international merchantry displayed the wares of all Eurasia.

He undoubtedly chafed at having to leave Tabriz so precipitately. Yet he was to be unexpectedly compensated soon enough. For when he returned to the *mahalla* several days later, 'Ala al-Din arranged for him to meet the Ilkhan himself. The audience in the royal tent was probably brief, but Abu Sa'id questioned the visitor about his country, gave him a robe and a horse, and even ordered that a letter of introduction be sent to the governor of Baghdad with instructions to supply the young *faqih* with camels and provisions for the journey to the Hijaz. There was nothing very special about a pious ruler giving charity to a scholar on his way to the *hajj*. And Ibn Battuta, for his part, has relatively little to say in the *Rihla* about Abu Sa'id and his court compared, for example, to the dozens of pages he devotes to the sultan of Delhi. But, at the time, the experience was significant if only as more evidence of those combined qualities of good breeding, piety, and charm which smoothed the young traveler's way into the presence of the high and powerful.

The *Rihla* is silent on the itinerary and schedule back to

Baghdad, including his traveling companions. The entire round trip could have taken as little as 35 days, since he journeyed a good part of the way with a fast-moving royal envoy. He might then have been back in Baghdad as early as about mid-July.[39] He still had two months to wait for the *hajj* caravan, which traditionally left Baghdad on 1 Dhu l-Qa'da, or in that year 18 September. Since he had come back from his Tabriz expedition so quickly he "thought it a good plan" to squeeze in a tour, a rather uneventful one as it turned out, of the upper Mesopotamian region, known as the Jazira. He traveled northward along the Tigris to the important Kurdish city of Mosul, then on to Cizre (Jazirat ibn 'Umar) in modern Turkey near the Iraqi border. This stretch generally replicated the route taken by Marco Polo 55 years earlier on his outbound journey from the Levant to China and by Ibn Jubayr in 1184, from whose book the *Rihla* lifts most of its descriptive material on the Tigris towns. From Cizre, Ibn Battuta made a loop of about 360 miles through the plateau country west of the river. He got as far as the fortress city of Mardin (which is in modern Turkey), then doubled back by way of Sinjar (and a corner of modern Syria) to Mosul. His hosts along the way included the Ilkhanid governor at Mosul (who lodged him and footed his expenses), the chief *qadi* at Mardin, and a Kurdish mystic whom he met in a mountain-top hermitage near Sinjar and who gave him some silver coins which he kept in his possession until he lost them to bandits in India several years later.

When he returned to Mosul he found one of the regional "feeder" caravans ready to depart for Baghdad to join the main assembly of pilgrims. He also had the fortune to meet an aged holy woman named Sitt Zahida, whom he describes as a descendant of the Caliphs. She had made the *hajj* numerous times and had in her service a group of Sufi disciples. Ibn Battuta joined her little company and enjoyed her protection while traveling back along the Tigris. The acquaintance was sadly brief, for she died later during the Arabian journey and was buried in the desert.

In Baghdad again, Ibn Battuta sought out the governor and received from him, as ordered by Abu Sa'id, a camel litter and sufficient food and water for four people. Luckily, the *amir al-hajj* was the same Pehlewan Muhammad al-Hawih who had looked after him on the previous year's journey. "Our friendship was strengthened by this," he recalls, "and I remained under his protection and favored by his bounty, for he gave me even more than had been ordered for me." Ibn Battuta might then have expected to return to Mecca in style except that at Kufa he fell sick with diarrhea, the illness persisting until after he reached his destination. During the long journey he had to be dismounted from his litter many times a day, though the *amir* gave instructions that he be cared for as well as possible. By the time he arrived in Mecca he was so weak that he had to make the *tawaf* and the *sa'y* mounted on one of the *amir*'s horses. On the tenth of Dhu l-Hijja, however, while camped at Mina for the sacrifice, he began to feel better.

Perhaps after this punishing experience he deduced that he needed a rest. In a year's time he had traveled more than 4,000 miles, crossed the Zagros Mountains four times and the Arabian desert twice, visited most of the great cities of Iraq and western Persia, and met scholars, saints, *qadis*, governors, an *atabeg*, and even a Mongol king. At this point he might have sat against a pillar of the Haram and written a respectable *rihla* about nothing more than his travels of 1325–27. The trip to Persia, however, would appear in retrospect as little more than a trial run for the heroic marches that were to follow. What he needed in the fall of 1327 was an interval for rest, prayer, and study. Then, spiritually refreshed, he would be off again.

Notes

1. V. A. Riasonovsky, *Fundamental Principles of Mongol Law* (Tientsin, 1937), p. 88.

2. Juvaini, *The History of the World Conqueror*, trans. J. A. Boyle, 2 vols. (Cambridge, Mass., 1958), vol. 1, p. 152.

3. John M. Smith, "Mongol Manpower and Persian Population," *Journal of the Economic and Social History of the Orient* (1975): 291.

4. Edward G. Browne, *A Literary History of Persia*, 4 vols. (Cambridge, England, 1929–30), vol. 2, p. 439.

5. Hamd-Allah Mustawfi, *The Geographical Part of the Nuzhat al-Qulub*, trans. G. Le Strange (Leiden, 1919), p. 34.

6. D. O. Morgan argues that by the early fourteenth century a significant number of Turco–Mongols were giving up nomadism for proprietorship of agricultural estates acquired in the form of revenue grants *(iqtas)* from the Ilkhan, thereby planting their social roots in Persian soil. "The Mongol Armies in Persia," *Der Islam* 56 (1979): 81–96.

7. See Rashid al-Din, *The Successors of Genghis Khan*, trans. John A. Boyle (New York, 1971); and John A. Boyle, "Rashid al-Din: The First World Historian," in *The Mongol World Empire 1206–1370* (London, 1977), pp. 19–26.

8. E. Ashtor, *A Social and Economic History of the Near East in the Middle Ages* (Berkeley, 1976), p. 257.

9. Rashid al-Din, *Successors of Genghis Khan*, p. 6.

10. Since IB gives all the stations on his trip from Mecca to al-Najaf, no apparent problems arise with Hrbek's estimate of 44 days (Hr, p. 427). For this section of the narrative IB once again draws heavily on Ibn Jubayr's descriptions of the route and halting places.

11. A. Bausani, "Religion under the Mongols," in J. A. Boyle (ed.), *The Cambridge History of Iran* (Cambridge, England, 1968), vol. 5, pp. 538–47.

12. IB does not mention the length of this stay in al-Najaf. Hrbek (Hr, p. 428) suggests three to five days on the speculative grounds that he would not have tarried long in a Shi'i town.

13. G. Le Strange, *The Lands of the Eastern Caliphate* (Cambridge, England, 1905), pp. 24–85. The author describes the complex topography of the Tigris – Euphrates basin in Abbasid times and later, stressing the fact that the course of the rivers and tributary streams and canals have changed repeatedly over the centuries.

14. For clarity of meaning I have changed Gibb's translation of the Arabic *al-fuqara'* (D&S, vol. 2, p. 5) from "poor brethren" (Gb, vol. 2, p. 273) to "Sufi brethren."

15. Hrbek's estimate of the chronology (Hr, pp. 428–29) is based on computations of distances and traveling times from other Islamic sources.

16. This is Hrbek's guess (Hr, p. 429) based on the idea that when IB sojourned in a spot for a substantial length of time, he always noted it.

17. Le Strange (*Lands*, pp. 46–49) describes the canal system as it existed about that time. Also W. Barthold, *An Historical Geography of Iran*, trans. Svat Soucek, ed. with an introduction by C. E. Bosworth (Princeton, N.J., 1984), pp. 203–05.

18. Le Strange, *Lands*, pp. 48–49.

19. IB's description of the trip through the Zagros presents serious chronological difficulties. He passed through this region a second time in 1347 on his way back to North Africa. His remarks on the season, on the identity of the *atabeg*, and on certain events at the princely court make it reasonably clear that almost all of the descriptive information he associates with the 1327 trip actually pertains to the later one. The same is likely true concerning his personal experiences, notably a bout with fever. Both Gibb (Gb, vol. 2, p. 288n, 290n) and Hrbek (Hr, pp. 429–31) agree that in the *Rihla* the two trips are confused.

20. "Isfahan," EI₂, vol. 4, p. 102.

21. Hrbek (Hr, pp. 431–33) rejects the *Rihla*'s statement that IB got his *khirqa* from Qutb al-Din at Shiraz on 7 May 1327, since he could not possibly have reached Baghdad during the month Rajab (23 May–21 June 1327), a period when he himself asserts he was in that city. Hrbek suggests that owing to a lapse of memory or a copyist's mistake, the date of the investiture should perhaps read 14 Jumada I rather that 14 Jumada II, that is, 7 April rather than 7 May. If he left Isfahan in the earlier part of April, he would have had time to reach Baghdad during Rajab.

22. Edward G. Browne, *A Year amongst the Persians* (London, 1893), pp. 220–62; Le Strange, *Lands*, p. 297.

23. Mustawfi, *Nuzhat al-Qulub*, pp. 113–14.

24. Gb, vol. 2, pp. 300n, 304n.

25. IB also visited Majd al-Din in 1347 while *en route* from India to Syria. Hrbek suggests ten days for the visit in 1327, though the *Rihla* presents a good deal of confusion between the first and second stays. Hr, pp. 433–34; Gb, vol. 2, p. 301n.

26. Hrbek's calculations of the Persian chronology are speculative since IB provides only three fixed dates for the entire period of travel from Mecca to Baghdad. The long journey from Shiraz to Baghdad is especially troublesome as routes and stations are extremely vague. Hrbek suggests 35–40 days for this itinerary (Hr, p. 434).

27. Hrbek's estimate (Hr, p. 434), is in accord with IB's statement that he was in the city during the month of Rajab.

28. "Masdjid," EI₁, vol. 3, p. 354.

29. Quoted in Henry M. Howorth, *History of the Mongols*, 3 vols. (London, 1876–88), vol. 3, p. 624.

30. At the time IB was visiting Persia, the young Ilkhan was under the political domination of the Amir Choban, who held a position at court tantamount to mayor of the palace. Shortly after IB left Persia, however, Abu Sa'id abruptly and ruthlessly eliminated Choban and two of the commander's sons and took full charge of his kingdom. IB's account of the fall of the Choban family is one of the few historical sources on these events. See J. A. Boyle, "Dynastic and Political History of the Il-Khans" in Boyle, *Cambridge History of Iran*, vol. 5, pp. 406–13.

31. Hrbek (Hr, p. 437) suggests a June departure.

32. Mustawfi, the fourteenth-century geographer and historian, names the stations on the Baghdad-to-Khurasan high road in Mongol times. Le Strange, *Lands*, pp. 61, 227–28.

33. Gibb (Gb, vol. 2, p. 344n) suggests that 'Ala al-Din probably got the order to go to Tabriz near Hamadan, calculated on the ten days already traveled from Baghdad.

34. Le Strange, *Lands*, pp. 229–30.

35. W. Heyd, *Histoire du commerce du Levant au Moyen-Âge*, 2 vols. (Leipzig, 1936), vol. 2, pp. 124–25.

36. "Tabriz," EI₁, vol. 4, p. 586.

37. I. P. Petrushevskey, "The Socio-Economic Condition of Iran under the Il-Khans" in Boyle, *Cambridge History of Iran*, vol. 5, p. 507.

38. "Tabriz,", EI₁, vol. 4, p. 586.

39. IB states that when he got back to Baghdad he still had more than two months to go before the departure of the *hajj* caravan. If it left at the normal time, about 1 Dhu l-Qa'da (18 September 1327), we can infer in general when the Tabriz excursion ended. Gibb (Gb, vol. 2, p. 346n) suggests it was before the end of June. Hrbek (Hr, pp. 436–37) offers 1 July or later. He also argues for a fast trip to Tabriz and back on the grounds that he was traveling part of the way with a royal official in a hurry.

6 The Arabian Sea

God is He who has subjected to you the sea, that the ships
may run on it at His commandment, and that you may
seek His bounty; haply so you will be thankful.[1]

The Qur'an, Sura XLV

In the *Rihla* Ibn Battuta briefly describes a residence in Mecca of
about three years, from September 1327 to the autumn of 1330. In
fact, the overall chronological pattern of his travels from 1327 to
1333 suggests that he lived in the city only about one year, taking
the road again in 1328.[2] In either case he spent an extended period
in the sacred city, living as a *mujawir*, or scholar-sojourner. "I led
a most agreeable existence," he recalls in the *Rihla*, "giving myself
up to circuits, pious exercises and frequent performances of the
Lesser Pilgrimage." During this period, or at least the first year, he
lodged at the Muzaffariya *madrasa*, an endowment of a late sultan
of the Yemen located near the western corner of the Haram.[3] As a
pilgrim-in-residence he had no trouble making ends meet on the
charity of alms-givers and learned patrons. The *imam* of the
Hanafi community, he reports, was "the most generous of the
jurists of Mecca," running up an annual debt of forty or fifty
thousand dirhams dispensing alms to *mujawirs* and indigent
travelers. The young Moroccan's special benefactor appears to
have been an esteemed North African jurist known as Khalil. This
sage was the Maliki *qadi* of Mecca at the time and the *imam* of the
pilgrimage rites. While Ibn Battuta was living at the Muzaffariya,
the *shaykh* had bread and other comestibles sent to him every day
following the afternoon prayer.

The *Rihla* condenses Ibn Battuta's residence into a few brief
paragraphs and has much less to say about his own experiences
than about the identities of various personages arriving in the *hajj*
caravans. Muslim readers of the narrative would not of course
have to be given an elaborate account of how a sojourner passed
his time in the Holy City. It was taken for granted that a pious man
would lead a placid life of prayer, devotion, fellowship, and

Map 6: Ibn Battuta's Itinerary in Arabia and East Africa, 1328–30 (1330–32)

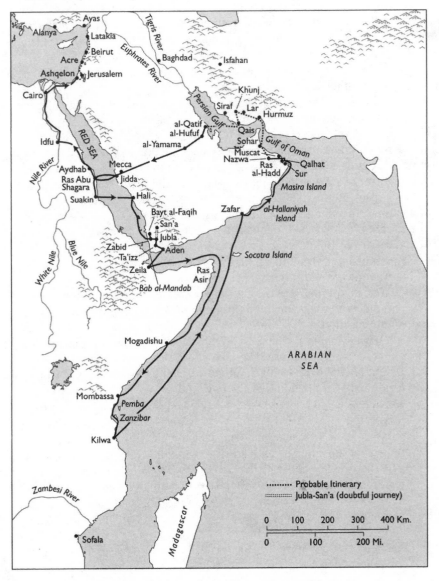

- Ayas
- Alanya
- Latakia
- Beirut
- Baghdad
- Isfahan
- Acre
- Jerusalem
- Ashqelon
- Cairo
- Khunj
- Siraf
- Lar
- Hurmuz
- al-Qatif
- al-Hufuf
- Qais
- Sohar
- Gulf of Oman
- Idfu
- al-Yamama
- Muscat
- Nazwa
- Qalhat
- Mecca
- Ras al-Hadd
- Sur
- Aydhab
- Jidda
- Ras Abu Shagara
- Masira Island
- Suakin
- Hali
- Bayt al-Faqih
- Zafar
- al-Hallaniyah Island
- San'a
- Jubla
- Socotra Island
- Zabid
- Ta'izz
- Aden
- Zeila
- Ras Asir
- Bab al-Mandab
- RED SEA
- Nile River
- Tigris River
- Euphrates River
- Persian Gulf
- White Nile
- Blue Nile
- Mogadishu
- ARABIAN SEA
- Mombassa
- Pemba
- Zanzibar
- Kilwa
- Zambesi River
- Sofala
- Madagascar

Legend:
- .... Probable Itinerary
- :::::::::: Jubla–San'a (doubtful journey)

Scale:
0 100 200 300 400 Km.
0 100 200 Mi.

learning. It is curious nevertheless that Ibn Battuta makes no mention of having undertaken courses of study with any of the important professors. He says nothing of books learned or *ijazas* collected as he does in connection with his earlier and briefer stay in Damascus. But we may assume that he attended lectures on law and other subjects in the Haram or the colleges round about it.[4]

The Haram was the central teaching institution in Mecca, that is to say, the place where the greatest number of classes gathered each day.[5] The leading *'ulama* of the city controlled the right to teach there, preventing any literate stranger from simply walking in and setting up a class. Only after a scholar's knowledge and reputation had been adequately examined could he set down his carpet or cushion in an assigned place in the colonnades, a spot he might then have the right to occupy for the entire teaching year, if not his lifetime. The professor always lectured facing the Ka'ba, the students ranged in a circle around him, those behind sitting in very close so they might catch every word. The size of classes varied considerably, as they do in any modern university, depending on the subject being studied and the master's fame. Anyone was free to listen in, and around the outer fringes of the circle people came and went as they pleased. A class usually lasted about two hours, including reading of a text, commentary on it, and questions.

The teaching day started early, and if Ibn Battuta planned to attend the first lecture of the morning he would be in the Haram right after the prayer of first light when the lesson circles began to assemble. In the hours of the dawn, classes met in the open court around the Ka'ba, but when the Arabian sun loomed over the east wall of the mosque they quickly retreated into the shadow of the colonnades. The most important teaching went on during the cool hours of the morning and late afternoon. But circles might be seen in the mosque at any time of day, applying themselves to the religious sciences or the auxiliary subjects of grammar, elocution, calligraphy, logic, or poetics. Even in the late evening between the sunset and night prayers a professor might squeeze in an additional dictation or commentary. On Fridays most classes recessed, the community devoting itself to prayer and the hearing of the congregational sermon.

Ibn Battuta's serious academic work would have taken place during the first seven months of the year, beginning in mid Muharram when the pilgrim throng had departed. These were the tranquil, slow-paced months in the life of the town, when a young scholar might study in leisure, extending his knowledge of the *shari'a*, learning some fine points of grammar, or perhaps penetrating more deeply the spiritual mysteries of Sufism. In the eighth month (Sha'ban) the curriculum shifted to inspirational and didactic talks on the approaching month of fasting. With the arrival of Ramadan the regular teaching year came to an end. In the tenth and eleventh months (Shawwal and Dhu l'Qa'da) lectures were given on the subject of the *hajj* and how to perform it properly. But as the Day of Standing approached, the influx of pilgrims, chanting and chattering, made public lecturing progressively impractical. Only when the crowds drifted away in the first weeks of the new year would the academic cycle begin once again.

As little as Ibn Battuta reveals about his months of contemplative immobility, there is little doubt that he became better educated, mainly, one supposes, in the corpus of Maliki jurisprudence. The depth of his education should not of course be overstated. He never became a jurist of first rank, and his judgeship in the Sultanate of Delhi was, as we shall see, a type of sinecure. But he also benefited from his sojourn by the fact that any individual who was known to have lived in the Holy City for an extended period commanded a degree of prestige not accorded the ordinary pilgrim who simply came and went. A veteran *mujawir* was credited with exemplary devotion to God and to His House. In a more practical light, a season or more in Mecca gave him the chance to make friends with all sorts of literate and influential people from distant countries, associations on which he might draw for hospitality over the ensuing two decades.

When Ibn Battuta left Mecca after the *hajj* of 1328 (1330), his expressed intention was to visit the Yemen. He says nothing in the *Rihla* about plans to cross the equator into tropical Africa, or climb the mountains of Oman, or visit the pearl fisheries of the Persian Gulf. Yet he was already accustomed to finding himself in places he never intended to go. It is just possible that in Mecca he had heard reports of well-paying opportunities for foreign scholars at the royal court of Delhi and that he was already thinking of making his way to India in order to offer his services. The obvious way to get there was to go to the Yemen first, then take ship for Gujarat on the northwest coast of India. As it turned out, he went no further east than the Gulf of Oman on this adventure, delaying his journey to India another two years.

Whatever his long-range plans may have been in 1328 (1330), he left Mecca and headed west to the coast following the pilgrimage events. He took two days getting to Jidda, the port of Mecca, where a motley fleet of Red Sea craft waited to ferry pilgrims across to 'Aydhab or transport them down to Aden in the Yemen from where they would board bigger ships bound for the Persian Gulf, Africa, and India. Experienced caravaner though he was, this was to be his first real sea voyage. He could hardly have been cheered by that prospect when, reaching Jidda harbor, he found the profit-minded captains loading passengers, to use Ibn Jubayr's phrase, "like chickens crammed in a coop." In fact, a Meccan *sharif*, a brother of the two ruling princes and a man certainly worth knowing, invited the young *faqih* to accompany him to the Yemen. But upon discovering that space on the *sharif*'s vessel would be shared with a number of camels, Ibn Battuta promptly declined the proposal and went looking elsewhere. He finally found passage on a *jalba*, probably a standard two-masted ship of modest proportions used commonly in the Red Sea trade.[6]

Ibn Battuta's refusal to set sail in the company of a small herd of dromedaries was none too cautious. The Red Sea was the most relentlessly dangerous of the waters on which the Mediterranean-to-China connection depended. Coral reefs lined both shores, shoals lay lurking in unknown places, and currents were irregular. Added to these hazards were the perils of the Saharan–Arabian desert which the Red Sea bisected: sandstorms, unendurable heat, and an absence of fresh water along most of the shore. If a ship went aground and the passengers managed to struggle ashore, they then faced the likelihood of perishing of thirst or being robbed and killed by pirate-bedouins, who waited patiently for just such accidents to occur.

The ships that braved this unfriendly sea could not have inspired much confidence in a landlubber like Ibn Battuta. Not only were Red Sea vessels usually small and overcrowded: like all Indian Ocean ships in that age, their hulls were constructed of wooden planks (usually of teak) laid end to end and stitched together with cords of coconut or palm fiber. Iron nails or bolts, which held together ships of the Mediterranean in the fourteenth century, were not used at all, and no ribbing or framework was installed to give the hull additional strength. Though stitched hulls may have proven more pliant in surf or in sudden contact with submerged rocks, Red Sea craft were fair weather vessels. Their pilots cast anchor at night, and when the weather looked bad they ran for port. "Their parts are conformable weak and unsound in structure," remarks Ibn Jubayr on the *jalbas* of 'Aydhab. "Glory to God who contrives them in this fashion and who entrusts men to them."[7] On the other hand, experienced pilots had the measure of their ships, they knew every inch of the coast, and they could smell a storm coming long before it hit. "We observed the art of these captains and the mariners in the handling of their ships through the reefs," continues Ibn Jubayr. "It was truly marvelous. They would enter the narrow channels and manage their way through them as a cavalier manages a horse that is light on the bridle and tractable."[8]

Though Ibn Battuta's pilot, a Yemeni of Ethiopian origin, was probably one of these old salts, no display of good seamanship could reverse the fact that it was the wrong time of year to be sailing south from Jidda with any expectation of making a quick run to a Yemeni port. In the northern half of the Red Sea the winds are northerly or northwesterly the year round, and between May and September they blow as far south as the Strait of Bab al-Mandeb. In those months commercial shippers normally planned to embark from Jidda or 'Aydhab in order to catch a favoring wind all the way to Aden. During the rest of the year, however, the winds were southeasterly from the strait to a latitude not far south of Jidda. If, as we suggest, Ibn Battuta left Mecca shortly after the *hajj* of 1328, the southwesterlies had already blown up south of Jidda. And sure enough: "We traveled on this sea with a favoring wind for two days, but thereafter the wind changed and drove us off the course which we had intended. The waves of the sea entered in amongst us in the vessel, and the passengers fell grievously sick."

Sailing on the tack across the open sea but falling away to leeward, the pilot finally landed at a promontory on the African coast called Ras Abu Shagara (Ras Dawa'ir) whose location is not far south of Jidda.[9] It was a common occurrence for ships crossing the Red Sea to miss their intended port either north or south and be forced to put in at roadsteads along the desert shore. Here, the Beja nomads of the Red Sea Hills made it their business to hire out camels and guides to lead travelers to a port, or, if it suited their fancy, to seize their possessions, plunder their ship, and leave them to die in the wilderness.[10] It seems likely that Ibn Battuta's captain was blown into shore by the storm and could not get out again with any hope of beating southward. In the event, the Beja were right on hand, and fortunately for the Moroccan and his seasick mates their intentions were honorable. Camels were rented and the company proceeded southward along the coast to the small Beja port of Suakin.

There, Ibn Battuta found another ship, which managed to get out of port and make for Arabia. After sailing to windward for six days, he finally reached the coast at a latitude barely south of Suakin's. Leaving his ship behind once again, he traveled 30 miles inland to the agricultural district of Hali (Haly), located in the coastal region known as Asir. He had already made acquaintance with the tribal ruler of Hali when they traveled together to Jidda after the *hajj*. He spent several days as the chieftain's guest, taking time also to visit a noted ascetic and joining the local Sufi brethren in prayers and recitation of litanies.

Back on the coast again, he boarded one of his host's own vessels, which took him southward to a little port along the Yemeni coast.[11] From there he proceeded overland across the arid coastal plain to Zabid, chief city of lowland Yemen.[12]

After enduring the steaming cheerlessness of a Red Sea voyage for several weeks, his journey into the interior of Yemen must have seemed a happy relief, almost a reminder of home. Like Morocco, the Yemen was a land of geographical extremes. Terrain, soil, altitude, and temperature were to be experienced in profuse variety; almost any sort of vegetable or fruit could be grown in one subregion or another. The coastal strip fronting the Red Sea was dry and grim, but the highlands were temperate and green, utterly contradicting the usual stereotype of *Arabia deserta*. The summer monsoon winds, blowing out of Africa and brushing across the southwestern corner of the peninsula, drop their rains on the high mountain valleys, nourishing a dense population of sturdy farmers. These Arabic-speaking hill folk had strong traditions of tribal independence. But the agrarian economy encouraged, as it always did everywhere, the ambitions of statebuilders. As in Morocco in the Middle Period, the politics of the Yemen turned on the persistent tensions between centralizing sultans with their governors and tax-collectors, and the fissiparous tribesmen of the valleys, who much preferred to be left alone.

Ibn Battuta visited the country when the cycle of dynastic centralization was at a peak. The Yemen had not been far enough removed from the Middle East heartland to escape the ubiquitous Turk. Kurdo–Turkish invaders from Egypt had seized the region in the twelfth century and later proclaimed an independent dynasty known as the Rasulid.

The heart of this realm was formed by a triangle of three major cities: Zabid, the lowland winter headquarters of the sultans; San'a, the bastion of the mountains; and Ta'izz, the dynastic capital and highland city of the south. The San'a region was the most difficult to hold, for it was the home of tribes adhering to the Shi'i sect known as the Zaydi, whose doctrines included a preference for choosing their own 'Alid *imams* as rulers. Zaydi imamism was thus an ever-present ideology of potential revolt against the sultans of Ta'izz, who, like the population of the greater part of the country, were Sunni Muslims of the Shafi'i school.

At the time of Ibn Battuta's passage, Malik Mujahid Nur al-Din 'Ali, fifth sultan in the Rasulid line (1321–62), had only just managed to pull the realm more or less together after spending the first six years of his reign squashing myriad plots and rebellions. In 1327 he seized Aden, the great port at the Strait of Bab al-Mandeb. Since Aden was the key transit center for virtually all the trade passing between the Indian Ocean and the Red Sea, the customs revenue was immense. When the sultan had his governors collecting it and pumping it directly into the treasury at Ta'izz, the investment in high urban culture rose accordingly.

Despite the wild mountains and ferocious hill folk, Yemen's cities drew freely on the cosmopolitan influences passing back and forth through the strait of Bab al-Mandab. Indian, Ceylonese, and Chinese ambassadors visited the Rasulid court, and the sultans, vigorous promoters of trade, enjoyed considerable prestige in the mercantile circles of the Indian Ocean.[13] They competed furiously with the Mamluks for domination of the Red Sea and the spice trade, but the two states generally enjoyed peaceful relations. The Rasulids, not surprisingly, looked to Cairo for ideas as to what civilized government should be like. Court ritual and military regalia followed Mamluk models fairly closely, and the sultans had their own corps of slave soldiers in partial imitation of the *mamluk* system.[14]

When Ibn Battuta stepped into this diminutive civilization tucked into the corner of the Arabian waste, he had no trouble connecting with the scholarly establishment. In Zabid, a date-palm city located about 27 miles in from the coast, they gave him lodgings and promenaded him through their cool groves on the outskirts of town. In their company he listened to tales of the life of one of their most famous saints, a thirteenth-century scholar and miracle-worker named Ahmad ibn al-'Ujayl. In the *Rihla* Ibn Battuta could not pass up the opportunity to recount how the *shaykh* had once demolished the rationalist doctrines of the local Zaydi Shi'a. One day, the story goes, a group of Zaydi doctors paid a visit to the master outside his hospice and enjoined him to debate the subject of predestination.

The maintained that there is no predestined decree and that the [creature who is made] responsible for carrying out the ordinances of God creates his own actions, whereupon the *shaykh* said to them, "Well, if the matter is as you say, rise up from this place where you are." They tried to rise up but could not, and the *shaykh* left them as they were and went into the hospice. They remained thus until when the heat afflicted them sorely and the blaze of the sun smote them, they complained loudly of what had befallen them, then the *shaykh*'s associates went in to him and said to him "These men have repented to God and recanted their false doctrine." The *shaykh* then went out to them and, taking them by their hand, he exacted a pledge from them to return to the truth and abandon their evil doctrine.

After probably a brief sojourn in Zabid, Ibn Battuta decided to visit the tomb of this celebrated saint in the village of Bayt al-Faqih (Ghassana) about 25 miles north along the coastal plain. While he was there, he made friends with a son of the *shaykh*, who invited him to travel to the mountain town of Jubla (Jibla) southwest of Zabid to visit another scholar. He remained there for three days, then continued southward in the company of a Sufi brother assigned to lead him along the mountain trails to Ta'izz, the Rasulid capital. If Ibn Battuta remembers his route through the Yemen accurately, he was behaving in his characteristic way of meandering first in one direction, then in another, relying on serendipitous discoveries of good companionship to determine his itinerary.[15]

Ta'izz lay at an altitude of 4,500 feet on the northern slope of the mountain called Jabal Sabir. Ibn Battuta describes the town as having three quarters, one for the sultan's residence and his slave guards, high officials, and courtiers; a second for the *amirs* and soldiers; and a third for the common folk and the main bazaar. Though he does not mention it, he must have prayed in the beautiful three-domed mosque called the Muzaffariya, which still serves as the Friday mosque of the city.[16]

Finding the citizenry of Ta'izz on the whole "overbearing, insolent and rude, as is generally the case in towns where kings have their seats," Ibn Battuta nevertheless got the usual warm welcome from the scholars. He was even given the privilege of meeting the king himself at one of the public audiences held every Thursday. Just as the Ilkhan Abu Sa'id had done, Malik Mujahid questioned the visitor about Morocco, Egypt, and Persia, then gave instructions for his lodging. Ibn Battuta has left in the *Rihla* a precious eye-witness description of the ceremonial of the Rasulid sovereign:

> He takes his seat on a platform carpeted and decorated with silken fabrics; to right and left of him are the men-at-arms, those nearest him holding swords and shields, and next to them the bowmen; in front of them to the right and left are the chamberlain and the officers of government and the private secretary . . . When the sultan takes his seat they cry with one voice *Bismillah*, and when he rises they do the same, so that all those in the audience-hall know the moment of his rising and the moment of his sitting . . . The food is then brought, and it is of two sorts, the food of the commons and the food of the high officers. The superior food is partaken of by the sultan, the grand *qadi*, the principal *sharifs* and jurists and the guests; the common food eaten by the rest of the *sharifs*, jurists and *qadis*, the *shaykhs*, the *amirs* and the officers of the troops. The seat of each person at the meal is fixed; he does not move from it, nor does anyone of them jostle another.

Ibn Battuta left Ta'izz on a horse given him by the sultan, but his immediate destination is none too certain at this point in the narrative. He may have journeyed 130 miles north along the backbone of the Yemeni mountains to San'a, spiritual capital of the Zaydis, and then back to Ta'izz again. But this excursion along treacherous trails through some of the grandest scenery in the world is described with such brevity and nebulous inexactitude as to raise serious doubts about its veracity.[17] It is more likely that he went directly from Ta'izz to Aden on the south coast of Arabia, arriving there sometime around the end of 1328 (1330) or early part of 1329 (1331).[18]

Looking out upon the Arabian Sea, Ibn Battuta was about to enter a world region where the relationship of Islamic cosmopolitanism to society as a whole was significantly different from what he had hitherto experienced. Up to that point he had traveled through the Irano–Semitic heartland of Islam, where the cosmopolitan class set itself apart from the rest of society in terms of its standards — urbane, literate, and committed to the application of the *shari'a* as the legal and moral basis of social relations. This class was the guardian of high culture and the means of its transmission within the Dar al-Islam. But it also shared its religious faith and its broader cultural environment with the less mobile and nearer-sighted peasants and working folk who constituted the vast majority. The lands bordering the Indian Ocean, by contrast, displayed a greater diversity of language and culture than did the Irano–Semitic core, and the majority of people inhabiting these lands adhered to traditions that were neither Irano–Semitic nor Muslim. In this immense territory Islamic cosmopolitanism communicated more than the unity and universality of civilized standards; it also expressed the unity of Islam itself in the midst of cultures that were in most respects alien. In the Middle East an individual's sense of being part of an international social order varied considerably with his education and position in life. But in the Indian Ocean lands where Islam was a minority faith, all Muslims shared acutely this feeling of participation. Simply to be a Muslim in East Africa, southern India, or Malaysia in the fourteenth century was to have a cosmopolitan frame of mind.

This mentality may be partly attributed to the general tendency of minority groups in foreign societies to preserve and strengthen links with the wider cultural world of which they feel themselves members. But more to the point was the fact that Muslim minorities of the Indian Ocean were heavily concentrated in coastal towns, all of whose economies turned on long-distance seaborne trade. The intensity of this trade continuously reinforced the world-awareness of the populations of these towns, and compelled anyone with a personal stake in mercantile ventures to keep himself keenly informed of market conditions throughout the greater maritime world. A measure of the internationalism of Indian Ocean ports, whether in India, Africa, Malaysia, or the Arab and Persian lands, was the degree to which the inhabitants responded more sensitively to one another's economic and political affairs than they did to events in their own deep hinterlands.

In the high age of the Abbasid Caliphate Muslim mariners, mostly Arabs and Persians, penetrated the southern seas, establishing trading colonies as far distant as China. The decline of the Caliphate undercut the dominant role of these merchants, but it had no contrary effect on the prestige of Islam as the religion of trade. In Ibn Battuta's time the western half of the Indian Ocean was every bit a Muslim lake, and the seas east of India were becoming more so with every passing year.

The ascendancy of Muslim trade is partly to be explained by simple Eurasian geography — the central position of the Irano -Semitic region in funneling goods between the Mediterranean and the spice and silk lands. But equally important was the ease with which Muslim merchants set themselves up in alien territories. The *shari'a*, the legal foundation on which they erected their communities and mercantile enterprises, traveled along with them wherever they went, irrespective of any particular political or bureaucratic authority. Moreover a place in the commercial community was open to any young man of brains and ambition, whatever his ethnic identity, as long as he were first willing to declare for God and the Prophet. As the repute of Muslims as the movers and shakers of international trade and the prestige of Islam as the carrier of cosmopolitan culture spread across the southern seas, more and more trading towns voluntarily entered the Islamic orbit, producing what the historian Marshall Hodgson calls a "bandwagon effect" of commercial expansion.[19] Concomitant to this was a great deal of conversion in coastal regions and the rise of scholarly establishments and Sufi orders having their own webs of international affiliation overlaying the mercantile network.

The Muslim communities of these maritime towns kept their faces to the sea, not the interior forest and bush, since the difference between prosperity and survival depended urgently on the arrivals and departures of ships. The development of complex interrelations among urban centers as far distant from one another as Aden and Malacca followed upon a basic natural discovery known among peoples of the ocean rim since ancient times. Across the expanse of the sea the direction of winds follows a regular, alternating pattern. During the winter months, from October to March, the northeast monsoon wind blows from off the Eurasian continent, passing across India and both the eastern and western seas in the direction of East Africa. In the west the wind extends about as far as 17 degrees south latitude, that is, near the mid point of the Mozambique Channel. In summer, from April to September, the southwest monsoon prevails and the pattern is reversed. Centuries before Islam, mariners of the Arabian Sea possessed a rich body of technical information on the monsoons in relation to other climatic and geographic factors, data on whose strength they could plan, and survive, long-distance voyages. By the later Middle Period, Muslim knowledge of the timing and direction of the monsoons had advanced to a state where almanacs were being published with which port officials and wholesale bazaar merchants could predict the approximate time trading ships would arrive from points hundreds or even thousands of miles away.

The seasonal rhythm of the winds gave Indian Ocean trade and travel an element of symmetry and calculability not possible in the Mediterranean. There, the wind patterns were more complicated, and the fury of the winter storms, howling down through the mountain passes of Europe, all but prohibited long-distance shipping for a few months each year. The Indian Ocean, lying astride the equator, was a warmer, calmer, friendlier sea. It was especially so in the months of the northeast monsoon, when, notwithstanding the possibility of hurricanes, waters were placid and skies clear for weeks at a time, and when navigators could depend on a long succession of starry nights to make astronomical calculations of their position. Shipping activity was greater in the winter season than it was in summer, when the rain-bearing southwest monsoon brought stormier conditions. Still, trans-oceanic circulation depended on the full annual cycle of the winds, by which ships sailed to a distant destination during one half of the year and home again in the other.[20]

We may suspect that when Ibn Battuta arrived in Aden, he did not know exactly what his next move would be. If India and a job at the court of Delhi were already in his mind, he may have changed his plans on the strength of the sailing schedules. Presuming he reached Aden about mid January 1329 (1331),[21] the northeast monsoon would have been at its peak, producing strong easterly winds. This was not a normal time for ships to embark from that port on direct voyages to the western coast of India. Nor was it the ideal time to set out for Africa, though some vessels did so. The problem was getting out of the Gulf of Aden against the wind. Once a ship beat eastward far enough to round Ras Asir (Cape Guardafui), the headland of the Horn of Africa, it could run before the northeast wind all the way to Zanzibar and beyond.[22] There is no evidence in the *Rihla* that before reaching Aden Ibn Battuta had a plan to visit tropical Africa. But his past record of impulsive side-tripping suggests that he may have been improvising his itinerary once again. If a ship were embarking for the East African coast, then he would go along too.

In the meantime he rested at Aden for at least several days. Part of the time he stayed as a guest in the home of one of the rich international merchants:

> There used to come to his table every night about twenty of the merchants and he had slaves and servants in still larger numbers. Yet with all this, they are men of piety . . . doing good to the stranger, giving liberally to the poor brother, and paying God's due in tithes as the law commands.

When the young scholar was not sharing in this bounty, he was probably exploring the city and the harbor and perhaps sizing up the reliability of any ships bound for Africa. In the Middle Period the commercial life of Aden was concentrated at the eastern end of a mountainous, balloon-shaped peninsula jutting out from the South Arabian coast. Part of this *presque-isle* was an extinct volcano, Aden town occupying its crater, which on the eastern side was exposed to the sea. The harbor, facing the town, was enclosed within a stone wall with sea-gates, which were kept padlocked at night and opened every morning on the order of the governor.[23]

Like 'Aydhab, Aden was an international transit center whose famed prosperity had little to do with the trade of its local hinterland, whose contribution to the import–export economy was modest. It controlled the narrows of Bab al-Mandeb and skimmed off the tariffs on a continuous flow of low-bulk luxury goods moving predominantly westward: spices, aromatics, medicinal herbs, plants for dyeing and varnishing, iron, steel, brass and bronze containers, Indian silks and cottons, pearls, beads, ambergris, cowrie shells, shoes, Chinese porcelain, Yemeni stoneware,

African ivory, tropical fruits, and timber. In the *Rihla* Ibn Battuta gives a list of ten different Indian ports from which merchants commonly sailed to Aden.

Walking along Aden beach, Ibn Battuta is likely to have seen a crowd of ships moored in the harbor or laid up on the beach, since mid winter was a season for cleaning hulls and refitting. The scene would not have been the same as the one he grew up with in Tangier bay, since Mediterranean and Indian Ocean shipbuilding traditions were as different as the patterns of wind and climate. For one thing, he would probably not have seen any galleys, whose use in the Indian Ocean was confined mainly to pirate gangs and navies. He would certainly not have seen any of the square-rigged round ships, which were just beginning to enter the Mediterranean from Atlantic Europe in his time. To his untrained eye the dhows of Aden might have looked tediously alike, except for variations in size and hull design. All of them would have been double-ended, that is, their hulls would have come to an edge at both ends of the ship, the square, or transom, stern being a sixteenth-century development introduced by the Portuguese. All of them would have been carvel built, that is, the teak or coconut wood planks of the hull laid edge to edge and lashed together with coir cord rather than nails. And most of them would have carried two triangular, or lateen, sails, a big mainsail and a smaller one on a mizzenmast aft. The largest of fourteenth-century trading vessels were as big as the dhows of modern times, having cargo capacities of up to 250 tons and mainmasts reaching 75 feet or more above the deck.[24]

The lack of variety in Indian Ocean shipbuilding was far less a reflection of stolid mariner conservatism than of centuries of experimentation and refinement to solve the technological problems of using the monsoons to full advantage. The key breakthrough was the lateen sail, that gracefully curved, wing-like form that brings to Western minds all the images of Sindbad and the *Arabian Nights*. The lateen was probably first developed in the western Indian Ocean in ancient times, then diffused into the Mediterranean in the wake of seventh-century Muslim expansion. Square sails, such as those being used in northern Europe in the fourteenth century, performed efficiently when the wind was astern. But if the breeze turned too much toward the beam of the ship, the sail was taken aback, that is, it was pushed against the mast. The lateen, on the other hand, was a fore-and-aft sail. The wooden yard to which it was attached sloped downward toward

Dhow under sail off the west coast of India
Ray Smith

Daulatabad, The Deccan, Central India
Ray Smith

the bow and thereby provided a stiff leading edge against the breeze. Consequently the sail could be set much closer to the wind without being taken back. A well-built lateen-rigged craft could sail in almost *any* direction except into the eye of the wind.

The Indian Ocean dhow was not, however, in total harmony with its monsoonal environment. The sewn, unreinforced hull construction, whatever the advantages of its plasticity, could not tolerate more than a modest tonnage of cargo. The size of ships was also limited by the rigging itself, since the mainsail yard was usually about as long as the vessel and extremely heavy. A large crew was required to hoist it (perhaps thirty or more on the biggest ships), and they of course displaced precious space for goods and paying passengers. Moreover the crew had to perform extremely laborious and difficult procedures to maneuver the sail and spar. When wind conditions changed, the sail was never reefed aloft. Rather the yard was hauled down, the sail removed, and a smaller or larger one hoisted in its place, a task that might have to be carried out in a heavy gale. Going about, that is, turning the ship to the opposite tack, was an even trickier operation. It was always done by wearing round (turning tail to wind), and this involved pushing the luff end of the yard up to a position vertical to the mast, swinging it from one side of the mast to the other, then letting it fall again, all the while preventing the loose, sheet end of the enormous sail from flapping wildly out of control. The heavier the weather, the harder it was to control the rigging, all the worse if the crew had to push and stumble its way through a muddle of passengers, cargo, and livestock. Many a ship was lost when it blew too close to a dangerous shore, and the crew could not bring it round in time or lost control of the sail altogether. The danger was especially great during the high season of the southwest monsoon, when only a very brave captain or a fool would dare to approach the western coast of India. The conventional method for survival in violent storms was to haul down the yard, jettison the cargo, and make vows to God.

Although Ibn Battuta logged thousands of miles at sea in the course of his adventures, the *Rihla* is a disappointing record of fourteenth-century shipbuilding and seamanship. Since he presumably had no sailing experience in early life, and his Tangerian upbringing was no doubt remote from the workaday world of the port, he was excusably indifferent to the rudiments of nautical technology. He is far better at recalling the characteristics of port towns and the pious personages inhabiting them than the humdrum details of navigation and life at sea.[25]

Sailing out of Aden, he has nothing whatsoever to say about the size or design of the ship to which he committed his fate, not even a classificatory name.[26] Since it was bound for the distant reaches of the East African coast, it was probably a relatively large vessel. Trading dhows of that age sometimes had cabins of a sort, presumably with roofs that served as decks. But they were probably not completely decked, obliging passengers to endure the voyage in an open hold, settling themselves as best they could amongst shifting bales of cargo.

Dhows making the run from Aden (or Omani and Persian gulf ports) to East Africa carried a wide assortment of goods, some of them destined for the interior trade and some exclusively for the Muslim coastal towns, whose inhabitants depended on manufactured imports to maintain households of reasonable civility and comfort. The staples of the upland trade were cloth (fine, colored stuffs produced mainly in India) and glass beads. The coastal population, especially the well-to-do families of merchants, scholars, and officials, consumed most of the luxury items. No genteel household would have been without its celadon porcelain from China, its "yellow-and-black" pottery from South Arabia, its silk wardrobes, glassware, books, paper, and manufactured tools. In exchange for these goods, the ships returned north with a range of raw, higher-bulk African commodities destined for dispersal throughout the greater Indian Ocean basin: ivory, gold, frankincense, myrrh, animal skins, ambergris, rice, mangrove poles, and slaves.

Embarking from Aden, Ibn Battuta's ship made a southwesterly course for the port of Zeila on the African shore of the gulf. Zeila was a busy town, the main outlet for inland trade extending to the Christian kingdom of Ethiopia, but the ship anchored there for only one night. Ibn Battuta made a quick foray into the bazaar, but his nostrils were assaulted by the unhappy combination of fresh fish and the blood of slaughtered camels. Pronouncing Zeila "the dirtiest, most diasgreeable, and most stinking town in the world," he and his sailing companions beat a fast retreat to the ship.

The following day the vessel made an eastward course out of the gulf. In the winter monsoon season this could be accomplished only by making long tacks, beating to windward until they cleared Ras Asir. Once past the headland, they swung round to the southwest, hoisted the largest mainsail aboard, and ran before the monsoon.[27] Ibn Battuta reckoned a voyage of 15 days from Zeila to the next port-of-call, Mogadishu. The captain almost certainly coasted the whole way. His passengers would never have been out of sight of the great sand dunes heaped along the desolate Somali shore.

Until around the time of Ibn Battuta's visit, Mogadishu was the busiest and richest port of the coast. It was in easy sailing range of the Persian Gulf, even easier than from the Yemen. The winter monsoon had carried the first Muslim settlers there, probably from the Gulf, in the tenth century or even earlier. Within two hundred years the town was booming, owing partly to its landward connections with the Horn and Ethiopia and partly to the transit trade in ivory and gold shipped there from the smaller towns further south.

Like any of the other emporiums of the western ocean, Mogadishu had plenty of employment for the commercial brokers (called *dallals* in South Arabia) who provided the crucial mediation between the arriving sea merchants and the local wholesalers. Their speciality was knowledge of market conditions and working familiarity with both the civilities of the local culture and the relevant languages. In this case Arabic and Persian were the *linguae francae* of the ocean traders. Somali, as well as Swahili, the Bantu tongue that may have just been coming into use along the coast at this time, were the languages of the townsmen and hinterlanders.[28] When Ibn Battuta's ship anchored in Mogadishu harbor, boatloads of young men came out to meet it, each carrying a covered platter of food to present to one of the merchants on board. When the dish was offered, the merchant fell under an obligation to go with the man to his home and accept his services as broker. The Mogadishi then placed the visitor under his "protection," sold his goods for him, collected payment, and helped him find a cargo for the outbound passage — all this at a healthy commission deducted from the profits. Sea merchants already familiar with the town, however, had their own standing business connections and went off to lodge where they pleased.[29]

When the ship's company informed the greeting party that Ibn Battuta was not a merchant but a *faqih*, word was passed to the chief *qadi*, who came down to the beach with some of his students and took the visitor in charge. The party then went immediately to the palace of Mogadishu, as was the custom, to present the learned guest to the ruler, who went by the title of Shaykh. Upon arriving there, the Moroccan recalls,

> one of the serving-boys came out and saluted the *qadi*, who said to him, "Take word to the intendant's office and inform the Shaykh that this man has come from the land of al-Hijaz." So he took the message, then returned bringing a plate on which were some leaves of betel and areca nuts. He gave me ten leaves along with a few of the nuts, the same to the *qadi*, and what was left on the plate to my companions and the *qadi*'s students. He brought also a jug of rose-water of Damascus, which he poured over me and over the *qadi*.

The Shaykh, moreover, commanded that the visitors be entertained in a residence for students of religion. Retiring there and ensconcing themselves on the carpets, the party addressed themselves to a meal of local fare, compliments of the palace: a stew of chicken, meat, fish, and vegetables poured over rice cooked in ghee; unripe bananas in fresh milk; and a dish comprised of sour milk, green ginger, mangoes, and pickled lemons and chilies. The citizens of Mogadishu, Ibn Battuta observed, did justice to such meals as these: "A single person . . . eats as much as a whole company of us would eat, as a matter of habit, and they are corpulent and fat in the extreme."

Dining with these portly notables over the course of the next three days, the young scholar would likely have found them all speaking Arabic. Neither Mogadishu, however, nor any other towns of the coast could be described as alien enclaves of Arabs or Persians, ethnically isolated from the mainland populations. On the contrary, these were African towns, inhabited largely by people of African descent, whether Somali or Bantu-speaking stock. The spread of Islamic culture southward along the coast was not synonymous with the peopling of the region by colonists from the Irano–Semitic heartland. The rulers, scholars, officials, and big merchants, as well as the port workers, farmers, craftsmen, and slaves, were dark-skinned people speaking African tongues in everyday life.

Human migration, however, accompanied trade as one of the enduring consequences of the harnessing of the monsoons. It was seaborne settlers from Arabia and the Persian Gulf who introduced Islam into the little ports and fishing villages along the coast, and it was the continuing trickle of newcomers who, along with the visiting merchants, assured and reinforced the Islamic-mindedness of coastal society. For Arabs and Persians of the arid northern rim of the sea, East Africa was a kind of medieval America, a fertile, well-watered land of economic opportunity and a place of salvation from drought, famine, overpopulation, and war at home. There is even some evidence of a thirteenth-century plantation at Mogadishu of a group of settlers from Tashkent, refugees from a Central Asian war.[30] The great majority of immigrants were males, who quickly married into the local families or took slave concubines, thereby obliterating any tendencies toward racial separatism.

Among new arrivals, the warmest welcome went out to *sharifs* (or *sayyids*), who probably represented a substantial proportion of colonists from South Arabia. A *sharif* was a person recognized as a descendant of the Prophet. As a group, *sharifs* brought to the coastal towns two qualifications in unlimited demand. One was literacy and knowledge of the *shari'a*; the other was that elusive attribute called *baraka*, the aura of divine blessing that was believed to attend sharifian status. Aside from commerce, which everyone seemed to have had a hand in, sharifian families performed multiple functions as town officials, judges, secretaries, political mediators, Sufi teachers, miracle-workers, and general validators of the Islamic status of the community and its government. Above all, the *sharifs*, as well as other literate immigrants, strove to implant the Sacred Law, specifically the Shafi'i school predominant in South Arabia. This was their most significant contribution to East African cosmopolitanism, for the law was the seal of oceanic unity on which the towns thrived.

On the fourth day of his visit Ibn Battuta went out to meet the Shaykh, a *sharif* of distant Yemeni origin whose family had emerged as sultans of the city in the previous century. It was Friday, and following prayer in the central mosque the young guest (outfitted in new robes and turban for the occasion) was formally introduced. Then the ruler (whose name was Abu Bakr) led his retinue back to the palace.

All of the people walked barefoot, and there were raised over his head four canopies of colored silk and on the top of each canopy was the figure of a bird in gold. His clothes that day were a robe of green Jerusalem stuff and underneath it fine loose robes of Egypt. He was dressed with a wrapper of silk and turbaned with a large turban. Before him drums and trumpets and pipes were played, the *amirs* of the soldiers were before and behind him, and the *qadi*, the *faqihs*, the *sharifs* were with him. He entered his council room; in that order, the viziers, *amirs* and the commanders of the soldiers sat down there in the audience chamber . . . They continued in this manner till the afternoon prayer.[31]

Ibn Battuta seems to have witnessed more of these proceedings in subsequent days and may have stayed in Mogadishu for a week or two. But he was soon aboard ship again and continuing southward along the tropical coast known to the Arab geographers as the land of Zanj. Crossing the equator near the modern border between Somalia and Kenya, he saw the dry scrub land of the north gradually giving way to lusher vegetation and dense clusters of mangrove forest around the estuaries of creeks and narrow rivers. The ship anchored for one night off the island-town of Mombasa, a modest commercial center at the time, though it would become one of the leading ports of the coast in the next century. After Mombasa, they passed between the mainland and the islands of Pemba and Zanzibar, finally putting in at Kilwa, an islet just off the coast of what is today Tanzania. This was as far south as the ocean merchants normally went. With fair winds and calm seas, the voyage from Mogadishu to Kilwa should have taken something well short of two weeks, bringing the Moroccan and his shipmates there sometime in March 1329 (1331).[32]

Traveling through the Islamic world in the relatively stable times of the early fourteenth century, Ibn Battuta had the good fortune to intersect with a number of kingdoms and cities just as they were experiencing an eruption of cultural energy. Kilwa was a case in point. Growing up alongside other East African towns as a rustic fishing village awakened to the promise of upland ivory and gold, it was fast surpassing Mogadishu at the start of the century as the richest town on the coast. The rise of Kilwa (Kulwa) seems to have been linked to the sudden and shadowy appearing of a new ruling family, called the Mahdali, who traced their line to a sharifian clan of the Yemen. In all likelihood they came south along with other families of Arabian descent, not directly from the peninsula, but from Mogadishu or other northerly ports. In any case they staged a *coup*, bloodless or not, against the earlier rulers of Kilwa sometime near the end of the thirteenth century.

Before the appearance of the Mahdali, most of the gold trade seems to have been controlled by the merchants of Mogadishu, but about three or four decades before Ibn Battuta's visit, Kilwa seized Sofala and other, smaller ports south of the Zambezi River through which the gold was funneled to the market from the mines of Zimbabwe. Consequently, the Kilwans clamped a near monopoly on the trade, elevating their city to the status of the principal transit center for gold in the western ocean. All this was achieved without marshalling a great navy. Kilwa's goals were limited economic ones, not the creation of a seaborne empire. Indeed the political organization of the coast was more akin to a configuration of city-states on the fourteenth-century Italian model than to the land kingdoms of the Middle East. And though Ibn Battuta speaks of Kilwa's "*jihads*" against the Africans of the mainland, relations with the upcountry people must have been reasonably good most of the time if trade were to flow.

Kilwa's gold rush made its merchants, the Mahdali family among them, extravagantly wealthy by coast standards. Living amongst the laboring and seafaring population in the unwalled and thoroughly unplanned town at the northern end of the island, the well-to-do families enjoyed a style of living that was, in the words of a scholar of coastal archaeology, "competent, comfortable, and satisfying."[33] They lived in stone houses of up to three storeys and entertained guests in spacious sunken courtyards. They wore silk and cotton garments and plenty of gold and silver jewelry. They had indoor plumbing. They ate off imported Chinese porcelain. They attended the Friday sermon in a domed and vaulted mosque of coral rock that had been expanded to four or five times its size in the early part of the century.

When the leading citizens had audience with Sultan al-Hasan ibn Sulayman (Abu l-'Mawahid Hasan), fourth ruler in the Mahdali line (1309–32),[34] they climbed to the highest point of the island overlooking the sea, where the great stone palace of Husuni Kubwa was being constructed. When they had business with him or his factor (for the sultan was probably the richest merchant in the city), they probably appeared at the spacious emporium, resembling the plan of a Middle Eastern *khan*, which took up nearly half the area of the palace. The working folk down in the town enjoyed a reasonable standard of living, but they lived in closely packed little houses of mud-and-wattle and dined off coarser ware than Chinese celadon.[35] Ibn Battuta was used to seeing impressive public monuments and in the *Rihla* he makes no mention whatsoever of the town's distinctive architecture, though he certainly prayed in the central mosque and probably visited Husuni Kubwa.[36] Wherever he traveled, however, he invariably took notice of pious and generous kings, believing as any member of the *'ulama* class did that piety and generosity were the essential qualities of any temporal ruler worthy of his title. He describes al-Hasan ibn Sulayman as "a man of great humility; he sits with poor brethren, and eats with them, and greatly respects men of religion and noble descent."

If Ibn Battuta arrived at Kilwa in March, he is likely to have stayed no more than a few weeks. The recommended seasons for leaving the tropical coast were near the beginning (March and April) or the end (September) of the southwest monsoon. Sailing from Kilwa harbor in April, a captain could expect to reach an Arabian or even Indian destination before high summer, when the winds blasted those coasts with such force that ports had to be closed.[37] The *Rihla* has no comment on the voyage or the ship other than the destination, the port of Zafar (Dhofar) on the South Arabian shore. A month's voyage would have brought Ibn Battuta there sometime in early May.[38]

Governed by an autonomous Rasulid prince, Zafar was one of the chief ports of South Arabia, an entrepôt on the India-to-Africa route and an exporter of frankincense and horses, the latter collected from the interior districts and shipped to India. It was a torrid place (the people bathed several times a day, Ibn Battuta reports), but in contrast to its grim hinterland it was also verdant, owing to monsoon rains along the low shore. It was not a bad town to spend a summer, which the traveler very likely did, since there was little ship traffic until September, when the southwesterly winds broke up. He lodged and boarded with the usual dignitaries, feasting on fish, bananas, and coconuts, and chewing betel leaves, a favored breath sweetener and aid to digestion.

If he was contemplating a voyage to India at this point, he could easily have found a ship to sail him directly there in September. Instead, he took passage on "a small vessel" making for the Gulf of Oman. The ship was probably a coastal tramp, for the pilot was a local fellow. He put in at several anchorages along the way, including an island, perhaps one of the Kuria Muria Islands (where Ibn Battuta met an old Sufi in a hilltop hermitage), the long island of Masira (where the pilot lived), and finally, at the far side of the headland of Ras al-Hadd, the little port of Sur on the Gulf of Oman.[39] It was a scorching, thoroughly disagreeable voyage. Ibn Battuta lived on dates, fish, and some bread and biscuits he bought in Zafar. He might have had meals of roasted sea bird, but when he discovered that the blasphemous sailors were not killing their game by slitting the throat as the Qur'an prescribes, he kept well away from both the crew and their dinners. Somewhere along that desert coast he and his fellow passengers celebrated the Feast of the Sacrifice of the year 729 A.H., or 3 October 1329 (or 731 A.H., 12 September 1331).

Anchored off Sur a few days later, Ibn Battuta saw, or thought he could see, the busy port of Qalhat, which lay 13 miles further up the coast. His ship was to put in there the following day, but he had taken an intense dislike to the impious crew and wanted as little to do with them as he could. And since Qalhat promised to be a more interesting place to spend the night than Sur, he resolved to go there on foot. The intervening coastline was hot, rugged, and completely waterless, but the locals assured him that he could make the distance in a few hours. To be on the safe side, he hired one of the sailors to guide him. A passenger friend, a scholarly Indian by the name of Khidr, decided to go along as well, probably for the lark. Grabbing an extra suit of clothes and leaving the rest of his possessions on board with instructions to rendezvous the next day, he and his companions set off. It promised to be a day's promenade followed no doubt by a good dinner and lodging at the house of the *qadi* of Qalhat.

In fact if things had gone any worse the two gentlemen would never have reached Qalhat at all, and the travels of Ibn Battuta might have ended in the wilds of Oman. Not long after leaving Sur, he became convinced that their guide was plotting to kill them and make off with the bundle of extra clothes, which would probably fetch a good price in the local bazaars. Luckily, Ibn Battuta was carrying a spear, which he promptly brandished when he realized that the villainous guide had in mind to drown his employers as they were crossing a tidal estuary. Cowed for the moment, the sailor led them further up into the rocks, where they found a safe ford and continued on through the desert. Thinking all the time that Qalhat was round the next bend, they tramped on and on, scrambling across an endless succession of treacherous ravines that connected with the shore. They had not brought along nearly enough water, although some horsemen passed by and gave them a drink.

Toward evening, the sailor insisted they work their way back down to the coast, which by that time was about a mile away. But Ibn Battuta refused, thinking the rogue's only plan was to trap them among the rocks and run with the clothes. Then night fell, and though the sailor urged them to push on, Ibn Battuta insisted they leave the trail they were following and go into hiding. He had no idea how far they still had to walk, and, what was worse, he glimpsed a party of strange men lurking nearby. Khidr by this time was sick and utterly overcome with thirst. And so mustering as much strength and will as he could, Ibn Battuta kept watch throughout the night, holding the contested garments under his robe and clutching the spear, while Khidr and the malevolent guide slept.

At dawn they returned to the trail and soon came upon country folk going into Qalhat to market. The sailor agreed to fetch water and after trudging across more ravines and precipitous hills they at last reached the gates of the city. By this time they were exhausted, Ibn Battuta's feet so swollen inside his shoes "that the blood was almost starting under the nails." To add insult to injury, the gatekeeper would not let them pass to find lodgings until they had presented themselves before the governor to explain their business.

As Ibn Battuta might well have expected from previous experience, the governor turned out to be "an excellent man," who invited the two prostrate scholars to be his guests. "I stayed with him for six days," Ibn Battuta recalls, "during which I was powerless to rise to my feet because of the pains that they had sustained." Nothing more is heard of their tormentor, who presumably returned to his ship a disappointed thief, but none the worse for trying.

From the *Rihla*'s description of Qalhat and its environs, Ibn Battuta is likely to have spent at least a few days having a look around, following recovery from his ordeal. Politically a dependency of the Sultanate of Hurmuz, Qalhat, like Muscat, Sohar, and other ports stretched along the coast between Ras al-Hadd and the Strait of Hurmuz, was a monsoon town of the first order.

Cut off from the rest of Arabia by the sea on three sides and the sandy waste of the Empty Quarter on the fourth, the city communicated with western India more easily than with any other shore. Strolling through the bazaar, Ibn Battuta would have seen many Indian traders, selling rice and other foodstuffs to the port and hinterland population, buying horses, and of course dealing in all sorts of Asian luxuries bound ultimately for Tabriz, Cairo, Kilwa, and Venice.

Friend Khidr is mentioned no more after Qalhat. Perhaps he booked passage on a dhow and returned to India. By this time Ibn Battuta seems to have resolved to head for Mecca again. And perhaps he had had his fill, for the time being, of pitching, undecked boats and their rascally crews. Qalhat was in fact to be his last view of the Indian Ocean for twelve years. Turning westward into the grim canyons of the eastern Hajar Mountains in the company of unnamed caravaners, he set a course across the rugged heartland of Oman. The only stage he mentions is Nazwa (Nizwa), the chief town of the interior and capital of a dynasty of tribal kings known as the Banu Nabhan.[40]

His description of his journey from central Oman back to Mecca leaves such a baffling trail of gaps, zigzags, time leaps, and confused information that the route and chronology cannot be explained with any assurance, at least not until he arrives at al-Qatif, a town on the Arabian shore about half way up the Persian Gulf. He claims to have gone directly from Nazwa to Hurmuz, the great emporium guarding the narrow passage into the gulf and, at that time, the principal staging center for the overland caravan trade to Tabriz, Turkey, and the Black Sea. Hurmuz lay at the northern end of a barren little island (Jarun, or Jirun) five miles off the coast of Persia. Ibn Battuta says nothing about how he got there, but of course he would have had to make a short sea voyage across the strait, perhaps from Sohar, an important port on the coast of Oman about 120 aerial miles over the mountains from Nazwa. Nor does he indicate how long he stayed in Hurmuz, and his description of the town and its ruler seems to be associated entirely with a second visit he made there in 1347 on his way home from India and China.[41]

From Hurmuz he crossed to the mainland and made a northwestward excursion by way of Lar through the interior of Fars, or southern Persia, with the aim of visiting a Sufi *shaykh* at a place he calls Khunju Pal, probably the village of Khunj.[42] He then returned to the coast, but he mistakenly remembers the two ports of Siraf and Qais as one and the same place, leaving doubt as to which one he visited, if not both.[43] He describes pearl fisheries off the eastern shore (pearls being the leading export from the gulf to India), but their location remains vague. From Qais (or Siraf) he traveled to Bahrain, meaning to him the Arabian coastal district opposite the island that carries the same name.[44] But once again, he is completely mute on the matter of his return voyage to the western side of the gulf.

After a presumably short stay in al-Qatif, he set off across Arabia, now for the fourth time and from a third new direction. Traveling southward to the oasis of al-Hasa (now al-Hufuf), then southwestward across the al-Dahna sand dunes, he arrived at al-Yamama, today a ruin 58 miles southeast of the modern Saudi capital of Riyadh. Here, he met a tribal chieftain of the Banu Hanifa Arabs and joined his party going to Mecca. The *Rihla* says nothing of the remaining stages nor of the date of arrival in the Holy City. If he left Oman about November, he would probably have reached Mecca some time in the winter of 1330 (1332). In any case, having climbed through the highlands of Yemen, crossed the equator to tropical Africa, endured several wearisome sea voyages through the hottest regions on earth, and almost lost his life for a clean suit of clothes, he was well deserving of another interlude of rest with his Qur'an and his law books in the shade of the Haram.

Notes

1. A. J. Arberry, *The Koran Interpreted* (New York, 1955), p. 211.
2. IB states that he performed the *hajj* four successive times beginning in 1327 (727 A.H.) and that he resided in Mecca for approximately three years. It is possible, however, that he stayed in the city only about one year, leaving for Aden and East Africa following the pilgrimage of 1328 (728 A.H.). The question of the length of his residence in Mecca is bound up with a much bigger chronological problem, which we must introduce here.
   IB tells us that he left Mecca for East Africa following the *hajj* of 1330 (730 A.H.) and that he arrived back in the city some time before the pilgrimage of September 1332 (732 A.H.). He states that he then left Mecca again following the 732 *hajj en route* to Egypt, Syria, Anatolia, Central Asia, and India, and that he arrived at the banks of the Indus River on 12 September 1333 (1 Muharram 734), thus accomplishing that ambitious journey in the space of one year. Yet his own itinerary and chronological clues show that the trans-Asian trip took about three years. Therefore, the two dates are irreconcilable and present the most baffling chronological puzzle in the *Rihla*.
   For the entire complex and roundabout journey from Mecca to India IB offers

not a single absolute date, nor does anything he says in connection with his long sojourn in India absolutely verify the year of his arrival there. Even the day he gives for crossing the Indus, 1 Muharram, that is, the first day of the new year, suggests a literary convention, symbolizing the start of the second major part of his narrative. Yet I am inclined to agree with Gibb (Gb, vol. 2, pp. 529–30) that IB's India arrival date of September 1333 is approximately correct (see Chapter 8, note 26). Working backward through the itinerary from that date, IB's description of traveling times, feast day celebrations, and seasons suggests that he must have left Arabia for Syria, Anatolia, and Central Asia no later than the winter or spring of 1330 (730 A.H.). If that dating is correct, he must have left Mecca for East Africa following the pilgrimage of October 1328 (728 A.H.). Returning from Africa to Arabia, he states that he celebrated the Feast of Sacrifice (that is, the ceremony culminating the *hajj* festival) off the South Arabian coast. He does not mention the year, but if my hypothesis is correct, it would have been 3 October 1329 (10 Dhu l-Hijja 729). From South Arabia he traveled through Oman and the Persian Gulf region, then returned to Mecca. If he stayed in the city a relatively short time (not waiting for the pilgrimage of 730 A.H. to come around) and then started on his India journey, he would have traveled through Egypt and Syria in 1330 (730 A.H.), a chronology which accords with the 1333 India arrival date.

Hrbek, contrary to Gibb, argues that IB's Mecca departure date of 1332 (732 A.H.) is correct and that the India date is wrong (Hr, p. 485). He believes that IB could not have erred or lied in asserting that he attended the pilgrimages of 1329, 1330, and 1332 without the learned and well-traveled Moroccans for whom the *Rihla* was written knowing the truth of the matter. Unfortunately, Hrbek never published the second part of his study of the chronology, so we have no idea how he might have argued that IB arrived in India two years later than he says he did.

Hrbek's argument about the Mecca departure date is in any case weakened by his admission that Gibb is probably correct in asserting that IB traveled in Egypt and Syria in 1330 (730 A.H.). That is, some of the events the *Rihla* groups with IB's travels in Egypt and Syria in 1326 actually occurred in 1330. Most of the evidence that Gibb and Hrbek present centers on known dates of office of governors or religious officials whom IB says he met (Gb, vol. 2, pp. 536–37; Hr, pp. 483–84). Hrbek (Hr, p. 483) also points out IB's statement, linked in the *Rihla* to 1326, that he attended a celebration in Cairo marking Sultan al-Nasir Muhammad's recovery from a fracture of his hand. All independent chronicle sources state that this event occurred in March 1330. Hrbek fits this evidence into his own hypothesis by suggesting, I think rather lamely, that IB sandwiched a trip to Egypt and Syria (utterly unreported in the *Rihla*) between the pilgrimages of 1329 and 1330. I prefer Gibb's argument that IB was already heading in the direction of Anatolia in 1330. Gibb indeed presents some interesting though inconclusive evidence, which Hrbek fails satisfactorily to refute, that IB traveled in Asia Minor in 1331 (Gibb, vol. 2, pp. 531–32; Hr, pp. 485–86).

No evidence I have seen eliminates the possibility that IB left Mecca after the *hajj* of 1328 (728 A.H.) and traveled to East Africa in 1329. Yet why would he state that he stayed in Mecca throughout 1329 and most of 1330 and that he returned for the pilgrimage of 1332 if the truth were otherwise? And how can we challenge him when he describes, though briefly and impersonally, certain events which occurred in Mecca during those periods of time? While I share Gibb's view that the India arrival date is nearly correct, I have no convincing answers to these questions. It must be remembered, however, that the relationship between the entire chronological structure of the *Rihla*, a work of literature, and IB's actual life experience is highly uncertain.

3. Gb, vol. 1, p. 203n.

4. IB mentions only that the Muzaffariya, where he lived, had a classroom and that a Moroccan acquaintance lectured on theology in the building. But he does not report that he attended a course.

5. In basing this description of education in Mecca mainly on the work of the

Dutch orientalist C. Snouck Hurgronje, who lived in the city for a year in the 1880s, I am assuming that the general patterns endured over the centuries. Snouck Hurgronje notes that "from the chronicles of Mecca . . . we may conclude with certainty that a life of learning like that which we have described, has been astir in the town for centuries past." *Mekka in the Latter Part of the Nineteenth Century* (Leiden, 1931), p. 211. Also A. S. Tritton, *Materials on Muslim Education in the Middle Ages* (London, 1957); and "Masdjid," EI₁, vol. 3, pp. 361–67, 368–71.

6. Ibn Jubayr crossed the Red Sea on a *jalba* and describes it. *The Travels of Ibn Jubayr*, trans. R. J. C. Broadhurst (London, 1952), pp. 64–65. Also G. R. Tibbetts, *Arab Navigation in the Indian Ocean before the Coming of the Portuguese* (London, 1971), p. 56; and R. B. Serjeant, *The Portuguese off the South Arabian Coast* (Oxford, 1963), p. 134.

7. Ibn Jubayr, *Travels*, p. 65.

8. Ibid., p. 69.

9. Hr, p. 439; Tibbetts, *Arab Navigation*, p. 413.

10. Ibn Jubayr, *Travels*, pp. 64–65.

11. He landed at a port he calls al-Ahwab. Gibb states that its precise whereabouts is a mystery, but Tim Macintosh-Smith (personal communication) tells me that the location is known locally. (Gb, vol. 2, p. 366).

12. At this point we need to note that the chronology of the journey from Mecca to East Africa, the Persian Gulf, and back to Mecca again is extremely uncertain. Traveling times between stages and length of stays are not often provided, and the internal chronological evidence is more limited than for the earlier journeys. One can be only as precise about the chronology as is warranted by IB's statements and other internal evidence. Hrbek's method of rationalizing a chronology for each segment of the journey in order to make everything fit between the few dates IB provides seems to be excessively conjectural. But his guesses are more often than not plausible.

13. Gaston Wiet, "Les marchands d'Épices sous les sultans mamelouks," *Cahiers d'Histoire Égyptienne*, ser. 7, part 2 (May 1952): 88; "Rasulids," EI₁, vol. 3, pp. 1128–29.

14. Al-Khazrejiyy, *The Pearl Strings: A History of the Resuliyy Dynasty of Yemen*, trans. J. W. Redhouse, 5 vols. (Leiden, 1906–18), vol. 3, part 3, p. 108.

15. Hrbek (Hr, pp. 440–41) suggests that a more rational route would have been Zabid–Ghassana–San'a–Jubla–Ta'izz–Aden and that IB may have failed to remember accurately the succession of stops. But he admits that there is no internal evidence in favor of revising the itinerary.

16. R. B. Lewcock and G. R. Smith, "Three Medieval Mosques in the Yemen," *Oriental Art* 20 (1974): 75–86.

17. The *Rihla*'s description of the journey Ta'izz–San'a–Aden is completely silent on the routes taken, the stages, and the length of stopovers. Moreover, the brief gloss on San'a is a combination of standard descriptive clichés and false information. The several lines devoted to this detour have the air of a purely literary adventure, possibly added by Ibn Juzayy (with or without IB's complicity) on the grounds that readers would expect a traveler to the Yemen to tell them something of San'a, whether he had been there or not. The San'a trip might fall into the same category as the spurious journey to Bulghar described in Chapter 8, note 12, below. Robert Wilson, formerly of the Faculty of Oriental Studies, Cambridge University, has pointed out to me that everything IB says about San'a could have been drawn from the existing body of conventional geographical knowledge on the subject, from, for example, Ibn Rusta (tenth-century geographer), *Kitab al-A'lak al Nafisa*, ed. J. de Goeje (Leiden, 1892), pp. 109–10. Hrbek (Hr, pp. 440–41) doubts that IB went to San'a. So does Joseph Chelhod, a scholar of medieval Yemen. "Ibn Battuta, Ethnologue," *Revue de l'Occident Musulman et de la Méditerranée* 25 (1978): 9.

18. This approximate time of year is suggested by both Gibb (*Travels*, vol. 2, p. 373) and Hrbek ("Chronology," p. 441).

19. Marshall G. S. Hodgson, *The Venture of Islam*, 3 vols. (Chicago, 1974), vol. 2, pp. 542–48.

20. On the economy and organization of monsoon trade in the southern seas see Phillip D. Curtin, *Cross-Cultural Trade in World History* (New York, 1984), pp. 96–135.

21. Gibb (Gb, vol. 2, p. 373) and Hrbek (Hr, p. 441) agree that he was probably in Aden about that time of year.

22. Tibbetts, *Arab Navigation*, pp. 372–73, 378. This book is in part a translation of the nautical works of Ahmad ibn Majid, the famous Arabian mariner-author who died in the early sixteenth century. Aside from the navigational information contained in the translation, Tibbetts has added extensive notes and commentary to produce in all a richly detailed study of Indian Ocean seafaring in the later Middle Period. Alan Villiers, a modern successor to Ibn Majid, sailed from Aden to East Africa in an Arab dhow, leaving in December 1939. *Sons of Sinbad* (London, 1940).

23. R. B. Serjeant, "The Ports of Aden and Shihr," *Recueils de la Société Jean Bodin* 32 (1974): 212; S. D. Goitein, "Letters and Documents on the India Trade in Medieval Times," *Islamic Culture* 37 (1963): 196–97.

24. W. H. Moreland, "The Ships of the Arabian Sea about A.D. 1500," *Journal of the Royal Asiatic Society* 1 (1939): 176; Tibbetts, *Arab Navigation*, pp. 48–49.

25. Tibbets (*Arab Navigation*, p. 3) remarks that "Ibn Battuta is not very observant of nautical affairs." The same point is made by Michel Mollat, "Ibn Batoutah et la Mer," *Travaux et Jours* 18 (1966): 53–70.

26. The design of the hull was the basis for classifying Indian Ocean ships. IB does provide a classificatory name for some of the vessels he traveled on during his career, but this is not necessarily very helpful. The connection between the medieval name of a ship and its precise hull design cannot be ascertained with certainty. See J. Hornell, "Classification of Arab Sea Craft," *Mariner's Mirror* 28 (1942): 11–40; A. H. J. Prins, "The Persian Gulf Dhows: New Notes on the Classification of Mid-Eastern Sea-Craft," *Persica* 6 (1972–74): 157–165; George Hourani, *Arab Seafaring in the Indian Ocean in Ancient and Early Medieval Times* (Princeton, N.J., 1951), pp. 87–89.

27. Alan Villiers (*Sons of Sinbad*, pp. 21–243, *passim*) describes in dramatic detail his voyage from Aden to Mogadishu, Zanzibar, and the Gulf of Oman in 1939–40.

28. Neville Chittick remarks that the "Maqdishi" language IB says he heard in the town was either Somali or an early form of a Swahili dialect, probably the latter. "The East African Coast, Madagascar and the Indian Ocean," *Cambridge History of Africa*, 5 vols. (Cambridge, England, 1977), vol. 3, p. 189.

29. In his research on the *dallals* (brokers) of South Arabia, R. B. Serjeant notes the striking similarity between their functions and practices in modern times and IB's description of the brokers of Mogadishu. "Maritime Customary Law in the Indian Ocean" in *Sociétés et compagnies de commerce en Orient et dans l'Océan Indien, Actes du 8(ème) Colloque International d'Histoire Maritime* (Paris, 1970), pp. 203–204.

30. B. G. Martin, "Arab Migration to East Africa in Medieval Times," *International Journal of African Historical Studies* 7 (1974): 368.

31. I have quoted this passage from Said Hamdun and Noel King's lively translation (H&K, pp. 16–17).

32. Both Gibb (Gb, vol. 2, p. 379n) and Hrbek (Hr, p. 442) suggest that he sailed from Mogadishu in late February or early March. By the end of March the northeast monsoon was dying out (Tibbetts, *Arab Navigation*, p. 378).

33. Peter Garlake, *The Early Islamic Architecture of the East African Coast* (London, 1966), p. 117.

34. On the regnal dates of the Mahdali dynasty see Elias Saad, "Kilwa Dynastic Historiography: A Critical Study," *History in Africa* 6 (1979): 177–207.

35. More is known about life in Kilwa than any other coastal town in that age thanks largely to the excavations of Neville Chittick, *Kilwa: An Islamic Trading City on the East African Coast*, 2 vols. (Nairobi, 1974).

36. IB's description of the East African coast, though brief, is the only eye-witness account of the medieval period, so historians have squeezed the *Rihla* for every tidbit of information. See Neville Chittick, "Ibn Battuta and East Africa," *Journal de la Société des Africanistes* 38 (1968): 239–41.

37. Tibbetts, *Arab Navigation*, pp. 373, 377–78. Alan Villiers (*Sons of Sinbad*, p. 191) left the mouth of the Rufiji River south of Kilwa in late March for his return voyage to Oman.

38. Hamdun and King (H&K, p. 68) have it from East African sailors that the trip would take about four weeks. Gibb (Gb, vol. 2, p. 382n), based on Villiers' journey from Zanzibar to Muscat, says three to four weeks. Hrbek (Hr, p. 444) suggests six to eight weeks, which seems too long.

39. IB reports that he visited the hermit on "the Hill of Lum'an, in the midst of the sea." Gibb (Gb, vol. 2, 391n) thinks this place must be the island of Hallaniyah. Tim Mackintosh-Smith, who traced IB's journey along the southern coast of Arabia, has doubts. Tim Mackintosh-Smith, *Travels with a Tangerine: A Journey in the Footnotes of Ibn Battutah* (London, 2001), pp. 256–58.

40. The veracity of IB's stay in Nazwa is uncertain, so I have not drawn attention to his description of the Banu Nabhan king of Oman, who he claims to have met, nor to his remarks on the religious beliefs of the Omanis. The interior region of Oman was the bastion of the Islamic sect known as the Ibadis. Reversing the Shi'ia doctrine of the supremacy of the House of 'Ali, the Ibadis believed that any member of the community of believers could be chosen as the Imam as long as he displayed the proper moral qualities and a capacity to uphold the Qur'anic law. If he failed, the community was obliged to withdraw its support. The Banu Nabhan (1154–1406), however, were not Imams, and their ascendancy represented a hiatus in the Imamate, which was restored in the fifteenth century. Roberto Rubinacci, "The Ibadis," in A. J. Arberry and C. P. Beckingham (eds.), *Religion in the Middle East,* 2 vols. (Cambridge, England, 1969). vol. 2, pp. 302–17; and Salij ibn Razik, *History of the Imams and Seyyids of Oman,* trans. G. P. Badger (London, 1871).

IB's description of Nazwa is brief and fuzzy, he makes inaccurate or doubtful remarks about Ibadi customs, and his itinerary from Nazwa to Hurmuz on the far side of the Persian Gulf is a complete blank. Neither Gibb nor Hrbek explicitly questions the truthfulness of IB's journey through the interior of Oman. J. C. Wilkinson, a scholar of Omani history, expresses grave doubts and has pointed out to me some of the textual problems with this section of the *Rihla* (personal communication).

41. Hrbek (Hr. pp. 445–48) develops a line of argument suggesting that IB did not visit Hurmuz, Persia, or any point on the eastern shore of the Gulf in 1329 (1331), but rather has inserted into the narrative a description of a journey that actually took place in 1347 when he traveled from India to Hurmuz and thence to Shiraz. Hrbek thinks that in 1331 he went directly from Nazwa to al-Qatif overland along the eastern coast of Arabia. The argument is based heavily on the fact that IB's description of Hurmuz, his meeting with its sultan (Tahamtan Qutb al-Din), and the civil war in which that ruler had been engaged all relate to a situation pertaining in 1347. The other points Hrbek makes to sustain his theory are inferential and speculative. I cannot accept it, partly on the grounds that IB may well have blended his descriptions of *two* trips to Hurmuz, and partly on the fact that in his report of an interview with the King of Ceylon in 1344 he speaks of having discussed with that monarch the pearls he had already seen on the island of Qais off the eastern shore of the Gulf. MH, p. 218.

42. Hr, p. 450; Gb, vol. 2, p. 406n.

43. Ibid., p. 407n. Gibb thinks he visited Qais; Hrbek (Hr, p. 450) believes it was Siraf. In the fourteenth century Qais was a far more important commercial center than Siraf and a likelier place for IB to embark for Arabia.

44. IB refers to Bahrain as a city, but Hrbek (Hr. p. 451) believes his description of such a place refers in fact to al-Qatif, the chief town of the coastal district known in earlier Muslim times as Bahrain. The term later referred solely to the island.

7 Anatolia

> This country called Bilad al-Rum is one of the finest
> regions in the world; in it God has brought together the
> good things dispersed through other lands. Its inhabitants
> are the comeliest of men in form, the cleanest in dress, the
> most delicious in food, and the kindliest of God's
> creatures.[1]
>
> Ibn Battuta

Sometime near the end of 1330 (1332) Ibn Battuta boarded a
Genoese merchant ship at the Syrian port of Latakia (Ladiqiya)
and sailed westward into the Mediterranean, bound for the south
coast of Anatolia. He was on his way to India and once again
headed squarely in the wrong direction.

His intentions had been straightforward enough when he left
Arabia some months earlier. He would go to Jidda, buy passage
on a ship for Aden, and continue from there to India on the winter
monsoon, just as hundreds of returning South Asian pilgrims were
doing at the same time. First, though, he must secure the services
of a *rafiq*, a guide-companion who knew India well, spoke Persian,
and would have contacts of some value in official circles. Although
the illustrious Sultan of Delhi was welcoming scholars from abroad
and offering them prestigious and rewarding public posts, a young
North African could not wander through rural India on his own
and then, if he made it to Delhi at all, simply turn up unannounced
at the royal palace. A *rafiq* was essential, and after several weeks
in Jidda he failed to find one.[2]

At this point he seems to have decided it would be better to
approach India by a more circuitous route and hope to meet up
with persons along the way who could lead him to Delhi and
provide him with the necessary connections. And so boarding a
sambuq he sailed directly to the Egyptian coast, made his way to
'Aydhab, and from there retraced his journey of a few years
earlier across the desert and down the Nile to Cairo. He rested
there a short time, then continued across Sinai, now for the second

137

Map 7: Ibn Battuta's Itinerary in Anatolia and the Black Sea Region, 1330–32 (1332–34)

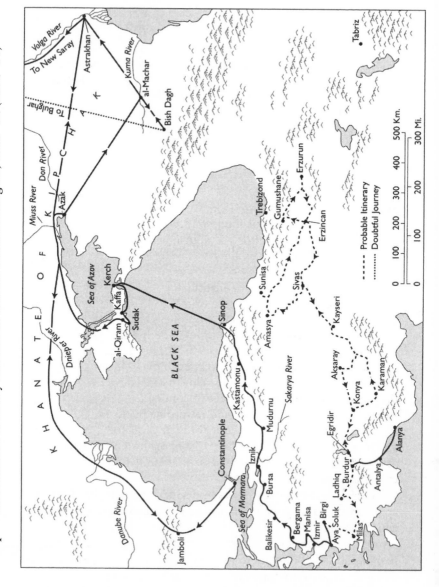

time, to Palestine. From this point his precise itinerary is uncertain, but he is likely to have traveled northward (including a quick inland detour to Jerusalem) through the Levantine coast towns — Ashqelon, Acre (Akko), Beirut, and finally Latakia.[3] Arriving there, he had in his company one al-Hajj 'Abdallah ibn Abu Bakr ibn Al-Farhan al-Tuzari. All we know of this gentleman, whom Ibn Battuta met in Cairo, is that he was an Egyptian legal scholar and that he determined to accompany the Moroccan on his travels. As it came to pass, the two men would remain fast friends and companions for many years.

Sailing from the coast of Syria to Anatolia in order to get to India made some sense, for it is precisely what Marco Polo had done more than sixty years earlier on his way to the Persian Gulf. From the south Anatolian ports of Ayas (Lajazzo), Alanya, and Antalya, trade routes ran northward over the Taurus Mountains to the central plateau where they joined the trans-Anatolian trunk road linking Konya, Sivas, and Erzurum (Arz al-Rum) with Tabriz and thence with Central Asia or the gulf. But since Ibn Battuta would spend about two years in Anatolia and the Black Sea region and finally approach India by way of the Hindu Kush and Afghanistan, a far more difficult and time-consuming passage than the gulf route, we can only conclude that he was playing the tourist again, his Indian career plans sidetracked in favor of more casual adventures.

There was nothing unusual about him and al-Tuzari taking passage out of Latakia on a European vessel. Italians, Catalans, and Provençals had long since eliminated Muslim shipping from the eastern Mediterranean except for coasting trade and the short run between the Levantine coast and Cyprus. Using Famagusta, the chief port of Cyprus, as the hub of their operations in the eastern sea, the Genoese called at both Levantine ports and those along the south Anatolian coast.[4]

Ibn Battuta describes the vessel he boarded as a *qurqura*, which was probably lateen-rigged, two-masted, and fitted with two or even three decks. It may have been much larger than any ship he had seen in the Indian Ocean, since the Italian "round ships" of the time, with their great superstructures over the bow and stern, were known to hold as much as 600 tons dead weight of cargo and as many as 100 crewmen.[5] As usual, Ibn Battuta fails to tell us what sort of lading the ship was carrying, perhaps a load of Syrian cotton or sugar, but he does note that the captain treated his

Muslim passengers "honorably" and did not even charge them for the trip. Making a course northwestward around the tip of Cyprus, the ship approached Alanya, the western Taurus Mountains looming behind it, some time in the last weeks of 1330 (1332).[6]

Except for his brief trip to Tabriz in Azerbaijan, Ibn Battuta was for the first time visiting a land whose Muslim inhabitants were mostly Turkish. Arab travelers to Anatolia in the twelfth and thirteenth centuries, a modern scholar has noted, experienced jarring attacks of culture shock when they confronted the alien ways of the Turks, as if finding themselves in some remote part of equatorial Africa.[7] In the centuries of the Abbasid Caliphate the ridges of the eastern Taurus had effectively protected the Asian territory of Christian Byzantium from the Arab armies of Iraq and Syria. But the high green valleys of eastern Anatolia were a magnet to the hordes of Turkish herdsmen who poured into the Middle East in the eleventh century as part of the conquests of the Great Seljuks. The natural route of this vast sheep and horse migration was westward from Khurasan to Azerbaijan, then on to Anatolia. At Manzikert in 1071 Seljuk cavalry achieved the military triumph over the Byzantine army that had eluded the Abbasids for three centuries. Once the Greek defenses of the eastern mountains collapsed, one nomadic throng after another advanced through the passes and fanned out over the central plateau. Within a century Byzantium had given up all but the western quarter of Anatolia, and a new Muslim society was emerging which had had no more than peripheral contact with the world of the Arabs.

The transformation of Asia Minor from a land of Greek and Armenian Christians to the country we call Turkey was a long and extremely complex process not by any means completed until several centuries after Ibn Battuta made his visit. When the empire of the Great Seljuks broke up in the twelfth century, their dynastic heirs, the Seljuks of Rum (as Anatolia was traditionally known to Muslims, a term harking back to the rule of "Rome") gradually consolidated their authority over the central and eastern regions. While the Seljukid commanders settled down in Konya and other ancient Greek and Armenian towns and took up the ways of the city, Turkish pastoral clans, conventionally called Turcomans (or Turkmens), continued to drift over the Anatolian plateau and into the highland valleys that rimmed it on all sides. In the first half of the thirteenth century, however, the majority of the inhabitants of the region were still neither Muslim nor Turkish. Large Christian populations thrived in the towns and crop-bearing lands of the Seljukid domain. A steady process of conversion to Islam was occurring, sometimes as a result of unfriendly pressures, but it was slow. Moreover, along the perimeters of Anatolia, Christian polities continued to survive: the kingdom of Little Armenia in Cilicia bordering the southeastern coast, the Empire of Trebizond (a Greek state that had broken away from Constantinople) on the Black Sea, and of course the remaining Asian provinces of Byzantium. Moreover, the frontier between Byzantium and the sultanate became relatively stable, and the two governments treated one another much of the time in a spirit of neighborly diplomacy.

This political pattern was radically disrupted in the aftermath of the Mongol invasions. In 1243 the Tatars stormed over the Armenian mountains, flattened the Seljukid army at Kose Dagh, and penetrated deep into the plateau. In 1256 they returned again in a campaign strategically linked to Hulegu's conquest of Iraq. In the following year Konya, the Seljukid capital, was taken, and by 1260 Mongol garrisons occupied most of the important towns of eastern and central Anatolia. The sultanate was not abolished, however, but propped up as a vassal state paying tribute to the Ilkhanate of Persia. Indeed the invasion was carried off without the usual cataclysm of terror and destruction. Only one city, Kayseri, was sacked, and the conquest never seriously threatened Byzantine territory. Trebizond and Little Armenia continued to endure under the Mongol shadow.

Yet if the military record of the invasion seems a vapid sideshow set against the terrifying drama in Persia, it nonetheless jolted Anatolia into an era of profound political and cultural change by laying it open to more migrations of Central Asian nomads. The first thirteenth-century wave of Turcomans arrived in panicky flight from the Mongol war machine, the second came in its ranks. Throughout the Ilkhanid period, more bands continued to press in. The immediate demographic effects of these movements are obscure, but there is no doubt that in the century after 1243 the ethnically Turkish population of Anatolia rose dramatically. Turkish came to be spoken and written more widely, and the situation of Christian communities, especially in rural villages in the path of migrating flocks and herds, became more and more precarious.

In the west of the peninsula the Turco-Mongol irruption confronted Byzantium with unprecedented nomadic pressure. Giving way to the new migrants arriving from Azerbaijan, Turcoman groups long established in central Anatolia pushed westward. Moreover, as the Tatar overlords turned their attention to the business of tax collecting and civil order, many of the newcomers preferred to pass on quickly to the mountain peripheries where Mongol-Seljukid authority was safely nominal. Here great leagues of Turcoman warriors led a wild and wooly existence, raiding back into Seljukid territory and battling one another for choice grazing land.

The very shape of Anatolia, a finger between the seas pointing due westward, directed the surge of pastoral movement into the Byzantine marches and the upper reaches of the valleys that ran down to the Aegean. Ever since the ninth century the Muslim – Byzantine frontier had given employment to mounted fighting men, called *ghazis*, who made a vocation of staging raids into Greek territory and living off the booty. Organized in war bands and often operating just beyond the boundaries of the Muslim government whose military interests they served, these volunteer champions of *jihad* lived by a chivalric code of virtue and loyalty founded on the precepts of the Qur'an and the teachings of the early Sufis. Though not all *ghazis* were of Turkish blood, the tactics and traditions of mounted holy war had been elaborately developed on the Muslim frontiers of Central Asia. Turkish warriors led the conquest of eastern and central Anatolia on behalf of the Seljuks, and though the Mongols were not in the beginning Muslims at all, the *ghazi* spirit was already deeply engrained in the Turkish warrior-herdsmen who preceded and followed them. Frontier warfare died down in the high period of the Seljukid sultanate when relations with Byzantium were relatively calm, but it flared up again in the crowded, turbulent conditions of the western marches in the later thirteenth century.

The withering of the great state structures that governed Anatolia encouraged this new phase of roisterous disorder on the frontier. Behind the lines of Turcoman advance, the sultanate was no longer in a position to control or restrain the nomads to its own ends. The Ilkhanid governors, obliged to take an ever-greater share of responsibility for the affairs of the state they themselves had defeated and repressed, were by 1278 running eastern Anatolia as a distant province of Persia with neither the will nor the soldiery to take charge of the Turcoman peripheries. Just beyond the nomad frontier, the Byzantine defenses proved weaker than expected. In 1204 the Frankish and Venetian leaders of the Fourth Crusade, having decided to capture Constantinople rather than Jerusalem, had forced the Greek emperor to rule in exile from the Anatolian city of Nicaea (Iznik). The traditional capital was restored in 1261, but this Latin interlude seriously weakened Byzantine resources. Preoccupied thereafter with the protection of their European and Aegean territories against Christian rival states, the emperors of the later thirteenth century defended their Asian domain in a spirit of phlegmatic resignation.

As the Seljukid dynasty slid gently into oblivion, several small Turcoman principalities, or amirates, emerged along a mountainous arc extending from the border of Little Armenia in the south to the coasts of the Black Sea. Some of these states were tiny and ephemeral, but by the beginning of the fourteenth century about twelve important centers of power, including the Ilkhanid provinces as one of them, dominated the new political map of Anatolia. The princes, or *amirs*, of these states ruled simply by virtue of their fitness as Turcoman war captains, the biggest of the "big men" who succeeded in gathering a larger following of mounted archers than their rivals with promises of booty and land. As the Byzantines fell back to their ships almost everywhere except the fragment of Asian territory opposite the Bosphorus, the Aegean hinterland was partitioned among five principal amirates extending along the curve of the arc: Menteshe in the south, then Aydin, Sarukhan, Karasi, and in the far north facing the remaining Byzantine strongholds the Osmanlis, or state of Osman.

The Muslim conquest of western Anatolia in the first half of the fourteenth century was in the long view only the beginning of a new age of Turkish power. For under the banner of the descendants of Osman, called by Europeans the Ottomans, Turkish cavalry would cross the Bosphorus and the Dardanelles and swarm into the Balkans. Traveling among the Turkish amirates in 1331, two years before his own Moroccan sovereign was preparing a last and utterly futile attempt to retake Spain for Islam, Ibn Battuta may have gained some comfort from the spectacle in Anatolia, where the situation was quite the reverse. By the time he ended his traveling career, the Ottoman armies were advancing on Greece. Barely more than a century and a half after his death they would be attacking the eastern frontiers of Morocco and marching up the Danube to Central Europe.

Though the Anatolia Ibn Battuta saw was nearing the end of the century of political cracking and straining that marked the transition from the Seljukids and Byzantines to the Ottoman Empire, the continuity of urban and lettered culture was never really broken. Putting up their mosques and palaces in the midst of ancient Greek cities, the Turkish dynasties were naturally profoundly influenced by Byzantine architecture, craftsmanship, and everyday custom. But their model of Muslim civilization was the Persian one they brought with them over the mountains. A literate tradition of their own still in the future, the Turkish rulers and officials who took up residence in the towns encouraged the immigration of Persian scholars, secretaries, and artisans, who helped to make Konya in the twelfth and thirteenth centuries an important international center of belles-lettres, Sufi teaching, and architectural innovation. Then, in the Mongol panics of the 1220s and later, many more educated and affluent Persians arrived in Anatolia, attracted by the prosperous urban culture of the sultanate. Like Cairo and Shiraz, Konya and other Anatolian towns found themselves benefiting unexpectedly from the flight of brains and money from greater Persia. These refugees, as it turned out, did not get far enough away from home by half, but the Mongol invasion was so uncharacteristically mild that city life went on much as before. Indeed, under Ilkhanid sovereignty the high culture of eastern and central Anatolia became more Persianized than ever before.

In the west the hard-riding Turcoman chiefs wasted no time forsaking their tents for the urban Byzantine citadels they captured and assembling around themselves Persian-speaking immigrant scholars who would show them proper civilized behavior. At the time of Ibn Battuta's visit Persianate letters and refinements prevailed in the courtly circles of the amirates. Moreover the Arabic influence at higher levels of society was not entirely missing. Arabic was the accepted language of building and numismatic inscriptions and of legal and fiscal documents. Some Persian scholars could speak the language, and a few notable intellectual figures from Arab lands lived and worked in Asia Minor.[8] Though Ibn Battuta did not know Persian at that point in his travels (by his own admission) and would never learn much Turkish (a fact he was loath to admit), he could expect to have no more trouble making himself understood among the learned fraternity of Anatolia than he had had in Iran.[9]

The spectacular city of Alanya ('Alaya), where Ibn Battuta, al-Tuzari, and apparently other companions stepped onto Anatolian soil in the early winter of 1330 (1332), was one of the chief south coast ports linking the interior beyond the coastal ridges of the western Taurus with the lands of the Arabs and Latins. The harbor and shipyards lay at the eastern foot of a great Gibraltar-like promontory rising 820 feet above the sea and surmounted by a complex of walls and forts.[10] The ruler of this bastion was the *amir* of Karaman, one of the most powerful of the Turcoman states to emerge in the later thirteenth century. In the company of the local *qadi* Ibn Battuta prayed the Friday prayer in the mosque of the citadel and the following day rode out ten miles along the shore to pay respects to the Karamanid governor at his seaside residence. There was the usual interview, and the traveler accepted his first present, money in this instance, from an Anatolian dignitary.

After a presumably short stay in Alanya, Ibn Battuta and his friends continued westward along the coast, probably on the same Genoese ship, to Antalya, the next major port. Like Alanya, it had been a Seljukid town until taken over by a Turcoman war lord who subsequently founded a local dynasty called the Teke. Ibn Battuta spent his first night in the local *madrasa* as the guest of its *shaykh*. But the next day a man dressed in frowzy-looking clothes and wearing a felt cap on his head came to the college and, addressing the visitors in Turkish, invited them to come to dinner. The invitation was translated and Ibn Battuta politely accepted. But after the man had gone away he protested to his host that the fellow was obviously poverty-sticken and should not be imposed upon to provide a meal.

> Whereupon the *shaykh* burst out laughing and said to me "He is one of the *shaykhs* of the . . . Akhis. He is a cobbler, and a man of generous disposition. His associates number about two hundred men of different trades, who have elected him as their leader and have built a hospice to entertain guests in, and all that they earn by day they spend at night."[11]

And so, following the sunset prayer the puzzled visitor and his host went off with the shabby cobbler to his lodge.

> We found it to be a fine building, carpeted with beautiful Rumi rugs, and with a large number of lustres of Iraqi glass . . . Standing in rows in the chamber were a number of young men wearing long cloaks, and with boots on their feet. Each one of

them had a knife about two cubits long attached to a girdle round his waist, and on their heads were white bonnets of wool with a piece of stuff about a cubit long and two fingers broad attached to the peak of each bonnet . . . When we had taken our places among them, they brought in a great banquet, with fruits and sweetmeats, after which they began their singing and dancing.

Thus Ibn Battuta had his introduction to the *fityan* associations of Anatolia, the institution that would subsequently see him through more than 25 different towns and cities with displays of hospitality more lavish and enthusiastic than he would experience anywhere else in the Muslim world.[12] The *fityan* organizations, also called the *akhis* (originally a Turkish word meaning "generous"), were corporations of unmarried young men representing generally the artisan classes of Anatolian towns. Their purpose was essentially the social one of providing a structure of solidarity and mutual aid in the urban environment. The code of conduct and initiation ceremonies of the *fityan* were founded on a set of standards and values that went by the name of *futuwwa*, both words coming from the same Arabic root and referring in concept to the Muslim ideal of the "youth" (*fata*) as the exemplary expression of the qualities of nobility, honesty, loyalty, and courage. The brothers of the *fityan* were expected to lead lives approaching these ideal qualities, which included demonstrations of generous hospitality to visiting strangers. The leaders of the associations were usually prestigious local personages of mature years who held the honorific title of "Akhi."

Known from Abbasid times in varying forms of organization and purpose, the precepts of the *futuwwa* appear to have entered Asia Minor from Iran where *fityan* corporations had long been established (though Ibn Battuta barely mentions them in connection with his travels there). By the thirteenth or fourteenth centuries associations existed in probably every Anatolian town of any size. In the era of political upheaval and fragmentation extending from the Mongol invasion to the rise of the Ottoman Empire, the *fityan* were filling a crucial civic function of helping to maintain urban cohesiveness and defense. Each association had its distinctive costume, which normally included a white cap and special trousers, and the members met regularly in their lodges or the homes of their Akhis for sport, food, and fellowship. Drawing their initiates from young workers and craftsmen, the clubs were organized to some degree along occupational lines, though they were not synonymous with trade guilds, which also existed. Meetings and initiation rites incorporated prayers and mystical observances, the religious dimension reinforcing the secular bonds of common interest and civic idealism.

Coming away from his first *fityan* banquet "greatly astonished at their generosity and innate nobility" and doubtless looking forward to the pleasant evenings that lay on the road ahead, Ibn Battuta turned his back on the Mediterranean and pushed northward through the coastal hills to the lake district of the southwestern interior and the territory of the Amirate of Hamid. At the town of Burdur he and al-Tuzari (and perhaps other companions) stayed in the house of the mosque preacher, but the *fityan* put on a marvelous entertainment, "although," he admits, "they were ignorant of our language and we of theirs, and there was no one to interpret between us." Turning northeastward next day the travelers continued to Egridir (Akkridur), capital of the Hamid dynasty situated at the southern end of a beautiful mountain lake.

From this point in the Anatolian journey Ibn Battuta's reconstruction of his itinerary presents serious and puzzling implausibilities. Though we will never be quite sure which way he went after leaving Egridir, the force of logic would suggest that he continued eastward over the Sultan Daghlari mountains to Konya at the southwestern edge of the central plateau, arriving there sometime early in January 1331 (1333).[13]

Talking with the scholars under the domes of the beautiful Seljukid mosque of 'Ala al-Din or the college of Ince Minare, Ibn Battuta might have felt a bit as though he were back in Iran again, for Konya, whose population was a mix of Turks, Persians, Greeks, Armenians, and Jews, was the most Persianized of Anatolian cities at the level of educated culture.[14] It was not, admittedly, the grand capital it had been in the heyday of the Seljukids. But it was an important trade center, and it glowed with the residual prestige of its great endowments and the memory of Jalal al-Din Rumi, the thirteenth-century Sufi poet whose works are classics of world literature.

During the late winter and spring of 1331 (1333), if our guess at the actual itinerary is correct, Ibn Battuta traveled from Konya across the central plateau to as far east as Erzurum in the

mountains of Armenia, and then back again. If he had at the time
no immediate desire to go to India, some of the merchants and
scholars he met on the trail probably did, for much of the way he
kept to the Mongol-controlled trunk roads connecting both the
eastern Mediterranean and the Black Sea with Tabriz and the
main spice and silk routes beyond it. In 1271 the young Marco
Polo and his father had disembarked at Ayas in Little Armenia
and followed the trans-Anatolian road by way of Sivas, the
principal long-distance emporium of the eastern interior, to the
upper Tigris and thence to China.

In the later twelfth and the thirteenth centuries the Seljukids
had built numerous caravansaries (*khans*) along the main routes
eastwards of Konya. A merchant bound for Persia could not have
found grander or more comfortable road accommodations
anywhere in the Muslim world. Designed to serve both ordinary
travelers and sultans on the march during the long and cold
Anatolian winters, the most elaborate *khans* had, in addition to
the usual sleeping quarters and storerooms grouped around an
open courtyard, a large covered hall, a bath, a small mosque, and
a massive, ornately carved portal. The Mongols built even more
hostelries and placed contingents of mounted police along the
roads to collect tolls and ensure the safety of the merchants. Even
today the ruins of 23 *khans* still stand along the old road between
Konya and Sivas.[15]

In the *Rihla* Ibn Battuta does not, surprisingly enough, mention
staying in any of these caravansaries. But he has much to say about
the hospitality of the Akhis. At all his major stops between Konya
and Sivas (excepting Karaman [Laranda], the capital of the
Karamanid dynasty, where he was entertained by the sultan
himself) he lodged with the local *fityan*. At Sivas he had the happy
experience of being argued over by two different associations for
the honor of regaling him first. One group of brothers representing
the Akhi Bichaqchi met him and his companions at the gate of the
city:

> They were a large company, some riding and some on foot.
> Then after them we were met by the associates of the . . . Akhi
> Chalabi, who was one of the chiefs of the Akhis and whose rank
> was higher than that of Akhi Bichaqchi. These invited us to
> lodge with them, but I could not accept their invitation, owing
> to the priority of the former. We entered the city in the

company of both parties, who were boasting against one another, and those who had met us first showed the liveliest joy at our lodging with them.

Ibn Battuta stayed with one club for three nights, the other for six, and during that time had an interview with the Ilkhanid governor, for he was now once again in the territory of the Mongol king. He gave the usual account of his wanderings, but it was also an occasion where he reveals the aptitude for well-timed unctuousness that would later serve him so well in India. The governor questioned him about the rulers of various countries through which he had traveled:

> His idea was that I would praise those of them who had been generous and find fault with the miserly, but I did nothing of the kind, and, on the contrary, praised them all. He was pleased with this conduct on my part and commended me for it, and then had food served.

From Sivas eastward the sequence of stopovers given in the *Rihla* leaves doubt as to the precise route Ibn Battuta and his companions followed. The high road to Tabriz, the route of the spice merchants, ran from Sivas across the hills of the eastern plateau to Erzincan (Arzanjan), a large Armenian city, and thence to Erzurum, the last important town west of the passes leading into Azerbaijan. Ibn Battuta, however, made two long and arduous side trips. One was to Amasya (Amasiya) and Sunisa (Sunusa), two Ilkhanid towns in the Pontic Mountains (Kuzey Anadolou Daghari), the lofty range that runs parallel to the Black Sea coast. The other was to Gumushane (Kumish), high up in the forests on the main road between Erzurum and the sea.[16] He intended to stay in Erzurum only one night but was obliged to remain for three, at the insistence of an elderly Akhi, who personally catered the visitors' meals, though he was by local accounts more than 130 years old!

As the itinerary in the *Rihla* has it, Ibn Battuta and his friends were suddenly and inexplicably transported as if by jet aircraft from Erzurum to the city of Birgi, which lay almost 700 miles to the west. He says nothing of his return journey from eastern Anatolia, but by his own account he was in Egridir, capital of the Hamid principality, at the beginning of Ramadan, which was 8

June in 1331 (16 May in 1333). Accounting logically for his whereabouts during the previous several months, he may well have been
in Egridir for a second time, returning westward, when Ramadan
arrived.[17] He remained there several days, attending the royal
court and breaking the fast every evening in the company of the
sultan and his *qadi*.

He then rode westward to Ladhiq, prosperous capital of the
little amirate of Denizli, where he celebrated the 'Id al-Fitr, the
Breaking of the Fast, with the local doctors of the law. He was now
approaching the Aegean and passing into the marches where
Turcoman cavalry had only in the previous few decades expelled
the Byzantine armies and landlords and where the majority of the
urban population was still Christian. Ladhiq had a large and
economically vigorous population of Greeks engaged in the production of fine cotton fabrics. "Most of the artisans there are
Greek women," the *Rihla* reports, "for in it there are many
Greeks who are subject to the Muslims and who pay dues to the
sultan . . . The distinctive mark of the Greeks there is their
[wearing of] tall pointed hats, some red and some white, and the
Greek women for their part wear capacious turbans."

The *fityan* associations were there too of course, and this time
their vehement ministrations were almost enough to send Ibn
Battuta and his friends fleeing in panic:

> As we passed through one of the bazaars, some men came down
> from their booths and seized the bridles of our horses. Then
> certain other men quarrelled with them for doing so, and the
> altercation between them grew so hot that some of them drew
> knives. All this time we had no idea what they were saying, and
> we began to be afraid of them . . . At length God sent us a
> man, a pilgrim, who knew Arabic, and I asked what they
> wanted of us. He replied that they belonged to the *fityan*, that
> those who had been the first to reach us were the associates of
> the . . . Akhi Sinan, while the others were the associates of
> the . . . Akhi Tuman, and that each party wanted us to lodge
> with them . . . Finally they came to an agreement to cast lots,
> and that we should lodge first with the one whose lot was
> drawn.

After resting in Ladhiq for some days following the festivities of
'Id al-Fitr, the little party joined a caravan going west. Now their

road wound down along the valleys of the ancient Aegean lands of Phrygia and Caria and past the vineyards and olive groves that signalled the travelers' return to the Mediterranean rim.

Throughout the rest of 1331 (1333) Ibn Battuta continued his tour of Turkish principalities, moving northward through the Aegean hinterland and visiting in succession the courts of Menteshe, Aydin, Sarukhan, Karasi, Balikesir, and finally Osman. These were the front line states of the Muslim advance, which by the time of his arrival in the region had left the hapless Byzantines clinging precariously to a few patches of fortified Asian territory. Moreover, by 1331 Turkish bands were already raiding Aegean islands and the Balkan shore opposite the Dardanelles, preliminary bouts for the invasion of Europe that was soon to come.

The speed with which the Byzantines vacated the Aegean littoral left the Turkish invaders suddenly in possession of a region of tremendous agricultural and commercial wealth and an urban tradition going back more than two millennia. Barely out of the saddle, the upstart *ghazi* chiefs readily transformed themselves into civilized princes. Ibn Battuta was much impressed by his reception at Birgi, capital of the Amir Mehmed of Aydin, where he arrived probably some time in July. Owing to the intense summer heat, he spent several days in the company of the sultan and his retinue at a royal mountain retreat. Then, moving down out of the highlands to the Aegean coast, the travelers turned north again, visiting in succession the ancient cities of Aya Soluk (Ephesus), Izmir (Smyrna), Manisa, Bergama (Pergamom), Balikesir, and finally Bursa and Iznik (Yaznik, Nicaea). Akhis, *shaykhs*, and princes came forward all along the way to host him and ply him with gifts. Everywhere except in Aya Soluk. There he forgot to get off his horse when he saluted the governor, a son of the *amir* of Aydin, thus breaking a fundamental Turkish courtesy. Consequently the governor snubbed him by sending him nothing more valuable than a single robe of gold brocade. The traveler also seems to have had an unsatisfactory time in the mini-amirate of Balikesir, whose sultan he describes as "a worthless person" and its people as "a large population of good-for-nothings" for failing to build a roof on their new congregational mosque and therefore having to conduct the Friday prayer in a grove of walnut trees.

In a completely contrasting tone he reports his introduction to Orkhan, ruler of the principality of Osman: "This sultan is the greatest of the kings of the Turkmens and the richest in wealth, lands and military forces." From the perspective of the mid 1350s when the *Rihla* was composed, such a comparative evaluation would have seemed painfully accurate to all the other western amirates as well as the Christians of Constantinople. For between the time of the Moroccan's visit to Anatolia and the close of his traveling career, the Osmanlis, or Ottomans, elbowed their way into world history.

Osman, the Turcoman chief, who appears in history through a fog of later Ottoman legend, started his military career in the late thirteenth century organizing mounted archers in the Sakarya river region sandwiched between the great amirates of Germiyan and Kastamonu. He achieved fame suddenly in 1301 when he defeated a 2,000-man Byzantine force near Izmit (Nicomedia). As Greek resistance stiffened out of desperation to keep their remaining footholds in Asia, Osman's ranks swelled with Turcoman cavalry from other amirates. In 1326, the year Osman died, the important Greek city of Bursa was taken and became for a time the Ottoman capital. In early 1331 Orkhan, his son and successor, captured Iznik and in the following six years virtually eliminated Byzantine power east of the Bosphorus.

Ibn Battuta passed through the Osmanli kingdom at the historic moment when it was consolidating a rich agricultural and urban base in Anatolia and was on the brink of almost seven decades of military expansion in every direction. Orkhan's talents as a military leader were apparent to the visitor:

> Of fortresses he possesses nearly a hundred, and for most of his time he is continually engaged in making the round of them, staying in each fortress for some days to put it into good order and examine its condition. It is said that he had never stayed for a whole month in any one town. He also fights with the infidels continually and keeps them under siege.

Less than fifteen years after Ibn Battuta observed Orkhan's compulsive war-making, the Ottoman army conquered the neighboring amirate of Karasi and soon thereafter crossed the Dardanelles into Thrace. The Byzantine fortress of Gallipoli fell in 1354, and when Orkhan died in 1360, the Turkish war machine was poised for the conquest of southeastern Europe.[18]

When he was not fighting, Orkhan found time to establish a

madrasa in Iznik in 1331[19] and would undertake a good deal more public building later in his reign, laying the cultural foundations that would transform his still very Greek cities into Turko–Muslim ones. The *fityan* clubs were already active in Bursa. Ibn Battuta lodged in the hospice of one of the Akhis and passed the night of the fast of Ashura (10 Muharram, or 13 October 1331) there in a "truly sublime" state, listening to Qur'anic readings and a homiletic sermon. He also met Orkhan himself during his stay in Bursa (though he has nothing to say about the meeting) and received from him a gift of "a large sum of money." In Iznik he met the Khatun, wife of Orkhan, and remained in that city for some weeks owing to one of his horses being ill.

When he started out again sometime in November,[20] now traveling eastward to his rendezvous with the Black Sea, he had in his company, he tells us, three friends (including al-Tuzari), two slave boys, and a slave girl. This is one of the few occasions in the *Rihla* where he reveals precisely the composition of his entourage. He was also trailing, we may surmise, several horses and a large accumulation of baggage. Heading into the last stage of his journey through Asia Minor, it seems clear that a significant change had occurred in both his material welfare and his own sense of his social status as an *'alim* of moderate fortune. He speaks in the *Rihla* of "the prestige enjoyed by doctors of law among the Turks." Indeed, as a jurist, a pilgrim, and a representative of Arab culture, he was treated with more honor and deference among the Turkish princes, themselves hungry for approval as legitimate and respectable Muslim rulers, than anywhere else in his travels up to that point. In turn he began to assert himself more as a mature and lettered man in the presence of secular power. In Milas at the court of Menteshe he successfully interceded before the sultan on behalf of a jurist who had fallen out of favor owing to a political slip. In Aydin the *amir* Mehmed asked him to write down a number of *hadiths*, or traditions of the Prophet, recalled from memory, then had expositions of them prepared in Turkish. Later, at the palace in Birgi Ibn Battuta loudly denounced a Jewish physician, who had a prominent position at court, for seating himself in a position above the Qur'an readers. The incident was not so much an expression of anti-semitism as a demonstration of his sense of pious propriety and his willingness to stand up for righteous standards as he perceived them, whatever the sultan's reaction.[21]

Visiting about twenty princely courts (including seats of governors) in the space of less than a year, he could well support his claim to status as a gentleman of consequence with a growing store of assets in hospitality gifts, not only clothes, horses, and money, but slaves and concubines. For the first time in his travels he speaks of acquiring bonded servants, anticipating the day in India when he would be accompanied by a large retinue of them. The *amir* of Aydin gave him his first slave, a male Greek captive. In Ephesus he purchased for himself a young Greek girl for forty gold dinars. In Izmir the sultan's son gave him another boy. In Balikesir he bought a second girl. When he left Iznik he had, as he reports, only three slaves (one perhaps having been sold), but he was in any case traveling as a man of substance. The conspicuous evidence of his wealth and prestige would continue to grow during the ensuing journey across Central Asia.

But first he had to get across the Pontic Mountains to the Black Sea in the dead of a bitter Anatolian winter. In stark contrast to his summer promenade through the orchards and vineyards of the lovely Aegean valleys, the final trek out of Asia Minor was a chain of annoyances and near fatal calamities reminiscent of his distastrous march to Qalhat along the South Arabian coast. The trouble began at the Sakarya River several miles east of Iznik when the little party started to follow a Turkish horsewoman and her servant across what they all thought was a ford. Advancing to the middle of the river, the woman suddenly fell from her horse. Reaching out to save her, her servant jumped into the frigid water but both of them were carried away in the swirling current. A group of men on the opposite bank, witnessing the accident, immediately swam into the stream and managed to drag both victims ashore. Half-drowned, the woman eventually revived, but her servant perished. The men then warned Ibn Battuta and his companions that they must go further downstream to cross safely. After heeding this advice, they discovered a primitive wooden raft, loaded themselves and their baggage on it, and were pulled across by rope, their horses swimming behind.

Then at the village of Goynuk (Kainuk), where they lodged in the house of a Greek woman for a night, they encountered heavy snow. A local horseman guided them onward through the drifts as far as a Turcoman village, where another rider was hired to take them to Mudurnu (Muturni), the next important town on the far side of a wooded mountain pass.[22] After leading them deep into the hills, the guide suddenly made signs that he wanted money. When he was refused any compensation until he delivered his employers safely into town, he snatched a bow belonging to one of the travelers and threatened to steal it. Ibn Battuta relented then, but the moment the rogue had money in his hand he fled, leaving the startled little band to find their own road in the deep snow. Eventually they came to a hill where the track was marked by stones, but by this time the sun was setting. If they tried to camp in the forest overnight, they were likely to freeze to death; if they continued on they would only lose their way in the dark.

> I had a good horse, however, a thoroughbred, so I planned a way of escape, saying to myself, "If I reach safety, perhaps I may contrive some means to save my companions," and it happened so. I commended them to God Most High and set out . . . After the hour of the night prayer I came to some houses and said "O God, grant that they be inhabited." I found that they were inhabited, and God Most High guided me to the gate of a certain building. I saw by it an old man and spoke to him in Arabic; he replied to me in Turkish and signed me to enter. I told him about my companions, but he did not understand me.

Then, in a thoroughly improbable stroke of providence, Ibn Battuta found that he was at a Sufi hospice and that one of the brethren was a former "acquaintance" of his, an Arabic-speaking chap (from what corner of the world we are not told) who quickly grasped the situation and sent a party to rescue the stranded companions. After a warm night and a hot meal in the lodge, the group continued on to Mudurnu, arriving just in time for the Friday prayer.

Convinced now that they needed an interpreter, Ibn Battuta engaged a local man (who had made the *hajj* and spoke Arabic) to take them to Kastamonu, the largest town in the region, which lay ten days to the northeast. Though the man was prosperous and reasonably well educated, he quickly revealed himself to be a greedy and unscrupulous character, selling anything he could lay his hands on in the village market places, stealing part of the daily expense funds, and appropriating for himself the money the travelers wished to pay a sister of his who fed them in a village along the way. But they still needed the fellow to get them through the mountains. "The thing went so far that we openly accused him and would say to him at the end of the day 'Well, Hajji, how much of the expense-money have you stolen today?' He would reply 'So much,' and we would laugh at him and make the best of it."

On top of all these miseries Ibn Battuta's slave girl almost drowned crossing another river.

The weary caravaners must have been blessedly relieved to arrive at Kastamonu, capital of the principality of the Jandarids and an island of moderately civilized comfort in the snowy wilderness. Ibn Battuta once again received the sort of treatment to which he was accustomed, feasting with the local scholars, meeting the *amir* in his lofty citadel overlooking the city,[23] and accepting the usual robes, horse, and money. He remained there some weeks, enjoying his last encounter with a generous Anatolian prince and perhaps waiting for the weather to improve. Then, riding northeastward into the Pontic, now apparently with an entourage of nine, he crossed one of the high passes and descended through the dense forests of the northern slopes, the Black Sea and the land of the Golden Horde before him.

Notes

1. Gb, vol. 2, p. 416.

2. IB's reference to a stay of 40 days in Jidda cannot be taken as a precise recollection. As Hrbek points out (Hr, pp. 453, 467) IB repeatedly reports the length of his stopovers in particular places as "forty days" or "about forty days." The use of this number as a conventional rounded figure was common among Middle Eastern and Muslim peoples. It appears frequently in Islamic ideology and ritual in Morocco. See Edward Westermarck, *Ritual and Belief in Morocco*, 2 vols. (London, 1926), vol. 1, p. 143.

3. The *Rihla*'s earliest description of travels through Greater Syria appears to be a compilation of four separate journeys, the second one being in 1330 (1332) (see Chapter 3, note 26 and Chapter 6, note 2). Thus it is difficult to know precisely which cities he visited during each of the four tours. He claims, without adding any descriptive material, to have passed through Hebron, Jerusalem, and Ramla on his way from Gaza to Acre in 1330 (1332). Hrbek (Hr, p. 454) is inclined to believe, for reasons of chronology and logic, that these stopovers are out of place and that he went directly up the coast to Latakia without passing into the interior. However, IB could have fitted in a second visit to the holy places of Hebron and Jerusalem and been back on the coast in a matter of a few days. Moreover, he may have visited several towns and castles in far northern Syria in 1330. He mentions them, however, only in connection with the 1326 itinerary.

4. In the 1330s the Genoese were probably just beginning to frequent Levantine ports after a hiatus of several decades owing to conflict between the Mamluks and the last of the Crusader states. W. Heyd, *Histoire du commerce du Levant au moyen-âge*, 2 vols. (Leipzig, 1936), vol. 1, pp. 547–8, vol. 2, pp. 61–62.

5. Eugene H. Byrne, *Genoese Shipping in the Twelfth and Thirteenth Centuries* (Cambridge, Mass., 1930), pp. 5–9.

6. IB claims to have taken ten nights to get from Latakia to Alanya, but if the wind was favorable, as he says, the trip could have been made in two or three days. Hr, pp. 454–55.

7. Claude Cahen, *Pre-Ottoman Turkey* (London, 1968), p. 153.

8. Ibid., pp. 227, 256, 349–50.

9. IB gives an oblique impression that he learned Turkish at some point in his career, but, as Gibb points out (Gb, vol. 2, p. 420n), there is no evidence that he did.

10. Seton Lloyd and D. S. Rice, *Alanya (Ala'iyya)* (London, 1958).

11. Where Gibb has translated IB's term *al-fata akhi* as "Young Akhi," I have made it simply "Akhi." The leaders of the *fityan* were seldom young.

12. Speros Vryonis, *The Decline of Medieval Hellenism in Asia Minor and the Process of Islamization from the Eleventh through the Fifteenth Century* (Berkeley and Los Angeles, 1971), pp. 396–402. The author lists 26 places where IB speaks of being entertained by a *fityan* club. I count 27 or possibly 28.

13. The main difficulty with the journey through Anatolia is that the trip from Konya to Erzurum is arbitrarily inserted in the narrative between his stops at Milas and Birgi, both cities in the far west of the peninsula. IB says nothing of how he got from Milas to Konya or from Erzurum to Birgi. The journey through eastern Anatolia seems obviously misplaced, but there are no internal clues to help sort out the actual itinerary. Hrbek (Hr, pp. 455–64) suggests that if IB's movements were reasonably logical, he is likely to have gone from Antalya to Egridir, then turned eastward at that point and traveled on to Konya and Erzurum. He would have returned to Egridir by a fairly direct route and arrived there in time for Ramadan (8 June 1331 or 16 May 1333). He states that he was in that city for the start of the fast. Such a pattern of movement would fit in well with the chronology of the Anatolian travels taken as a whole. That is, arriving on the south coast in late 1330 (1332), he would have spent the first five months or so going to Egridir, Konya, Erzurum, and back again. He would then have continued westward to Milas, Birgi, and the Aegean coast, traveling through that region, as he states several times, during the summer. There is at least one annoying snag in this hypothetical reconstruction. IB places himself in Egridir for the start of Ramadan, but during a single visit to that town. Hrbek's speculative solution hangs on the assertion that IB probably visited Egridir twice and that the Ramadan visit in May occurred following his return from the eastern region. There are of course several examples in the *Rihla* of his collapsing descriptions connected with two or more visits to a place into a single, first visit. I believe Hrbek's reconstruction remains plausible for want of anything better. P. Wittek thinks that owing to the chronological and geographical problems of the Konya–Erzurum trip, IB made it up on hearsay. *Das Fürstentum Mentesche* (Amsterdam, 1967), p. 66. However, IB's eastern Anatolian detour presents numerous details of personal experience.

14. "Konya," EI₂, vol. 5, pp. 253–56; J. Bergeret, "Konya," *Archéologia* 96 (July 1976): 30–37.

15. Halil Inalcik, *The Ottoman Empire: The Classical Age, 1300–1600*, trans. Norman Itzkowitz and Colin Imber (London, 1973), pp. 53, 108–09.

16. IB's precise itinerary in eastern Anatolia is impossible to fathom. The *Rihla* has him going directly from Sunisa to Gumushane, but no direct route existed owing to the high mountains. Hrbek speculates on alternative roads he could have taken (Hr, pp. 458–59).

17. See note 13.

18. In contrast to the standard historiography I have not closely identified the early Ottoman conquests with the holy war of *ghazis*. A recent essay convincingly argues that the ideology of tribal solidarity and the shared adventure of "nomad

predation" unified Osman's and Orkhan's military enterprises, not *jihad* against the Greeks. See Rudi Paul Lindner, *Nomads and Ottomans in Medieval Anatolia* (Bloomington, Ind., 1983).

19. Inalcik, *Ottoman Empire*, p. 8.

20. IB states that he was in Bursa for the fast of Ashura (10 Muharram 732 or 13 October 1331). He took two days getting from Bursa to Iznik and remained in the latter city 40 days (probably more or less).

21. D&S, vol. 2, p. xiii. These authors point out that IB demonstrated considerable tolerance toward non-Muslims. In this instance the Jewish physician did something reprehensible in his eyes.

22. Charles Wilson (ed.), *Murray's Handbook for Travellers in Asia Minor* (London, 1895), p. 14.

23. "Kastamuni," EI$_2$, vol. 4, pp. 737–39; Wilson, *Murray's Handbook*, p. 7.

8 The Steppe

We traveled eastward, seeing nothing
but the sky and the earth.[1]

William of Rubruck

If Ibn Battuta had inquired among the merchants of Sinope the
most sensible way to get from the northern coast of Anatolia to
India, they probably would have told him to go to Tabriz by way of
Trebizond, then on to Hurmuz and a ship to the Malabar coast. He
chose, on the contrary, to make for the city of al-Qiram (Solgat, or
today Stary Krim) in the interior of the Crimean Peninsula on the
far side of the Black Sea. Al-Qiram was the seat of the Mongol
lord governing the province of Crimea under the authority of
Ozbeg, Khan of Kipchak, the kingdom known later to Europeans
as the Golden Horde. It was also the chief inland transit center for
goods passing from Kaffa and other Italian colonies on the
Crimean coast to the towns of the populous Volga River basin, the
heart of the khanate.

Ibn Battuta does not explain why he and his companions decided to cross the sea and approach India by the longer, more
difficult route across the Central Asian steppe, but it is easy
enough to guess. For one thing, he had already seen Tabriz,
Hurmuz, and a good bit of Persia, and if he was to honor his
extravagant pledge to shun territory already covered, then the
northern route, the fabulous silk road of Inner Asia, was his
obvious alternative. We may also suspect that by this time he had
devised a grand scheme not only to visit all the great cities of the
central lands of Islam, but to penetrate the outer fringes of the
expanding civilized world as well. He had been to Kilwa, the last
outpost of *qadis* and city comforts in the southern tropics. And
now he had the opportunity to discover the limits of cultured
society in the wilds of the north, where summer nights were so
short that intricate theological problems arose as to the hours of
prayer and the fast of Ramadan. Moreover, the previous year and
a half in Anatolia had taught him all he needed to know about the

159

satisfaction Turkish princes seemed to derive from entertaining and rewarding visiting *faqihs*. He was certainly well aware that the Kipchak state had become officially Islamic only in his lifetime and that New Saray (al-Sara'), its capital on the Volga, was a flower of cosmopolitan industry and culture that had bloomed overnight in the frigid steppe. If the little *amirs* of Asia Minor could treat him so well and contribute so materially to his personal fortune, what might he expect from Ozbeg Khan, whose territories and wealth were so much greater.

In the *Rihla* he proposes a list of "the seven kings who are the great and mighty kings of the world." One of them, naturally enough, was the Sultan of Morocco, who commissioned the writing of the book. Another was the Mamluk ruler of Egypt and a third the Sultan of India. The remaining four were Mongols of the House of Genghis: the Yuan emperor of China, the Ilkhan of Persia, and the khans of Chagatay and Kipchak. Though the Mongol world empire no longer existed in the Moroccan's time except as a political fiction, its four successor kingdoms (plus the White Horde of western Siberia) ruled among them the greater part of the land mass of Eurasia. Admittedly Ibn Battuta did more than justice to Ozbeg and his cousin the Khan of Chagatay to put them on his list at all, for unlike the others (excepting perhaps the Sultan of Morocco, who had to be included anyway) they were not masters of one of the core regions of agrarian civilization. They were heirs rather to the Inner Asian plains, the core of the Turko –Mongol domain where the pastoral way of life still predominated, and where civilization came harder and later owing to the limits of agriculture and to physical distance or isolation from the main Eurasian centers of culture and trade.

But if mighty kings are to be judged by the size of their kingdoms, the khans of Kipchak and Chagatay were among the awesome, for together their territories covered an expanse of grassland, desert, and mountain more than half the size of the continental United States. From the fertile grain-growing valley of the Volga, Ozbeg Khan dispatched his governors to the Crimea, to the northern Caucasus, to the alluvial delta (called Khwarizm) of the Amu Darya (Oxus) River, and to the immense Ukrainian steppe north of the Black Sea. To the forested uplands in the northwest he sent his cavalry to collect annual tribute from the Christian princes of Russia and orchestrated their dynastic affairs to keep them weak and divided. In the Slavic southwest he intervened when it suited him in the affairs of the kingdom of Bulgaria. In his foreign policy he exerted an influence of a special sort over the Mamluk sultanate, because his kingdom supplied Cairo with most of its ruling class, the young male slaves who were captured in frontier wars or were purchased or extracted from poor families of the Kipchak steppe.

Ibn Battuta visited the lands of Kipchak just a century after the Mongols launched their invasion of western Eurasia. In six years of cataclysmic violence (1236–41) the Tatar juggernaut under the generalship of Batu and Subedei had devoured cities and towns of Russia, Poland, and Hungary, leaving the Pope and the kings of the Latin West trembling for the future of Christendom. Though the conquerors withdrew from eastern Europe as precipitately as they had come, Batu, son of Jochi and grandson of Genghis Khan, established a camp near the lower Volga which became as Saray, or later Old Saray, the capital of the Khanate of Kipchak. Ibn Battuta knew the state under that name, the Golden Horde being an appellation bestowed by the Russians two centuries later. The adjective "golden" remains open to different explanations, but "horde" came from the Turkish word "ordu," meaning camp or palace. The name carries a certain irony, for it suggested to the fourteenth century a meaning contrary to the modern image of a throng of wild barbarians riding into battle. The *ordu* of Batu (d. 1256) and his successors was the core of a stable and disciplined government under which, as in Persia, rampant bloodshed and destruction yielded to political conditions favoring revival of agriculture, increased international trade, and the rise of towns, some of them, like Old and New Saray, from the ground up.

Prior to the Mongol invasion Islam was the dominant faith among the settled Bulghar Turks of the middle Volga region but had made little headway in the Crimea or the Ukrainian steppe. The khans of the Golden Horde were for the most part as internationally minded as their cousins in Persia, encouraging the traders of all nations, tolerating confessional diversity, and for the first seventy years of the khanate's history keeping the promoters of both Islam and Christianity guessing as to what religion the royal court would finally accept. In 1313 Ozbeg ascended the throne and, as Ghazan had done in Persia 18 years earlier, proclaimed Islam the religion of state. His decision was a blow to both the Roman and Byzantine churches, which had until then held sanguine hopes of bringing the khans to Christ.

The victory of Islam was in fact almost certainly inevitable. If Mongol internationalism had from the point of view of European history the effect of "opening" western Asia to Latin priests and Italian merchants, it gave in the long run far greater advantage to Muslim traders and preachers, who had already been pressing into the steppe zone for centuries. The Volga had close historic links with the Muslim Irano–Turkish cities of northern Persia and Transoxiana, that is, the regions east of the Caspian. Those cities offered a much handier and weightier model of civilization to the khanate than either Byzantium or Latin Europe could do. As the new political order in western Asia emerged, the caravans from the southeast brought ever-growing numbers of merchants, scholars, craftsmen, and Sufi brethren, seeking fortunes and converts in the burgeoning towns of the khanate. Whether Christian friars and Italian traders were present or not, these towns assumed from the later thirteenth century an increasingly Muslim character.

Ozbeg's Islamic policy was in fact recognition of a cultural conversion of the region that was already taking place. The Russian tributary states of the northern forests remained loyal to their Orthodox church, and the Islamization of the steppe was by no means complete when Ibn Battuta passed through, since he himself bears witness to Turkish Christian communities in the Crimea. For him, however, the important development was not the conversion of the countryside; rather, the establishment of Islam as the "official" religion signified that the *shari'a* was to have a larger role in society, superseding local or Mongol custom in matters of devotion and personal status. If the Sacred Law were to be applied in the realm, then *qadis* and jurists had to be imported from the older centers of literacy. Thus in Ibn Battuta's time the towns of the western steppe were firmly linked to the international network of judges, teachers, and scribes along which he always endeavored to travel.

He remembers spending more than a month and a half in Sinope in the early spring of 1332 (1334), the last eleven days waiting for a favorable wind after he, al-Tuzari, and other companions booked passage on a ship bound for the Crimea. He remarks that the vessel belonged to some "Rumi," probably in this case Genoese rather than Greek.[2] Italian shipping had invaded the Black Sea in force following the fall of Constantinople to Frankish Crusaders in 1204. Both the Genoese and the Venetians held mercantile colonies in the Crimea and along the shore of the Sea of Azov. In Ibn Battuta's time these two powers competed murderously for the trade of the Black Sea, but they had virtually no commercial competition from either Muslims or Greeks.

When captains of the Black Sea were under sail, they usually preferred to hug the coast because of the tempests that might suddenly come blasting off the northern steppe. Though we have no clue whether Ibn Battuta's ship was a big one, his pilot seemed confident enough to launch into the open sea and make a straight course for the Crimea. But three nights out of Sinope a violent storm blew up. In his Indian Ocean travels Ibn Battuta had seen nothing like it.

We were in sore straits and destruction visibly before our eyes. I was in the cabin, along with a man from the Maghrib named Abu Bakr, and I bade him go up on deck to observe the state of the sea. He did so and came back to me in the cabin saying to me "I commend you to God."

The vessel could make no headway against the furious wind and was blown back nearly to Sinope. The storm subsided for a time, then returned as savagely as before, and the ship was again driven back. Finally the wind swung round to the stern and after several days of panic and near-catastrophe the Crimean mountains loomed ahead. The captain made for Kerch on the western bank of the strait leading into the Sea of Azov. But as he approached the port he sighted people on the shore apparently trying to signal him off. Fearing enemy war galleys in the harbor (Venetians? Turkish pirates?), he turned westward along the coast, probably heading for either Kaffa or Sudak.

Then, for reasons unexplained, Ibn Battuta asked the captain to put him and his companions ashore, not in a port but at a roadstead somewhere along the rural Crimean coast. The party disembarked and, after spending the night in a church, negotiated with some local Christian Turks for the hire of horses and a wagon. Within a day or so they reached Kaffa, chief colony of the Genoese merchantry.

Ibn Battuta counted about 200 ships in Kaffa harbor. Some of them would carry away the cloths and other luxury wares that had come along the silk road from Persia or China. Others would load their decks with war captives and the sad children of impoverished steppe folk, consigning some to the slave market of Cairo, others to the sugar plantations of Cyprus or the rich households of Italy. But mainly, ships' holds would be filled with the raw products of the steppe and forest: grain from the Volga, timber from the mountains of southern Crimea, furs from Russia and Siberia, salt, wax, and honey. Though the Franks built their houses and conducted their business in Kaffa at the pleasure of the Khan of the Golden Horde and though good relations between them sometimes broke down, this city was the most profoundly Latinized of all the Black Sea ports. Probably a large minority of the population was Genoese, the rest a heterogeneous crowd of Turkish soldiers and nomads, Russian fur traders, Egyptian slave agents, Greeks, Circassians and Alans, not to mention Florentines, Venetians and Provençals.[3]

Ibn Battuta, in any case, was not to feel at home in Kaffa. When he and his friends arrived there they went to lodge in the mosque. While they were resting inside, the Catholic churches of the town suddenly began ringing their bells. Pious Muslims in general regarded church bells as one of the more odious manifestations of Christian sacrilege. Ibn Battuta for one had never heard such a satanic clamor. Reacting with more bravado than sense, he and his companions bounded to the top of the minaret and began chanting out the Qur'an and the call to prayer. Soon the local *qadi* rushed to the scene, weapon in hand, fearing the visitors would be in danger for provoking the hostility of Europeans. What the Christians in the streets below might have done in response to this comic opera gesture we will never know, but the incident ended with no sectarian violence.

Leaving Kaffa within a day or two, Ibn Battuta and his party continued on by wagon to their immediate destination al-Qiram, the provincial capital and main staging point for the trans-Asian caravans. Traveling now in the company of an officer of state on his way to see the governor, their route presumably took them westward along the coast as far as the port of Sudak (Surdak or Soldaia), then inland over the steep southern scarp of the Crimean mountains.[4] Al-Qiram lay beyond the hills at the edge of the flat grassy plain that was ecologically the vestibule of the great Kipchak steppe. Though a Genoese consul was sometimes in residence, al-Qiram was a decidedly Muslim town in its economy and culture (a mosque carrying Ozbeg Khan's inscription on it still stands).[5] Ibn Battuta met several scholars, including the Hanafi and Shafi'i judges, and stayed in a Sufi hospice.

Though Tuluktemur, the Muslim Turkish governor of the town, was not feeling well, he received the visitors anyway and presented the

Moroccan with a horse. It was soon learned that this *amir* was preparing to set out for New Saray to see the khan. In Persia Ibn Battuta had been given the unexpected privilege of traveling in the *mahalla* of the Mongol king, and now once again the chance of his itinerary had brought him to al-Qiram just in time to make a 700-mile journey to the Volga under imperial escort with no worries about personal amenities, highwaymen, or malevolent guides. To this purpose he bought three wagons and animals to pull them: one cart for himself and a slave girl (probably one of the young Greek women he acquired in Asia Minor), a second smaller one for al-Tuzari, and a third large one for the rest of his companions.

Up to that point Ibn Battuta had had almost no experience with wagons, for they were largely unknown in the Arab world where, since Roman times, the backs of camels and other beasts had replaced wheeled conveyances as the means of transporting people and goods. This was not, however, the case in Central Asia. Over the next year Ibn Battuta would find himself bumping and swaying over the steppe in the Turkish version of the prairie schooner. Both two and four wheeled carts were used, pulled by teams of horses, camels, or oxen. Mongol and Turkish nomads customarily followed their herds in wagons over which they erected round lath and felt tents (*yurts*). Whenever they halted for a period of time they disassembled these residences, or removed them in one piece, and set them up on the ground. When William of Rubruck, the Flemish Franciscan who compiled a precious description of the steppe peoples during the early Mongol Age, left Sudak in 1253 on his way to the court of the Great Khan, he was advised by Greek merchants to carry his possessions by wagon rather than pack horse. That way he could leave his belongings on board throughout the trip, and if he wanted to ride his own horse he could go along at the relaxed pace of the oxen.[6] The felt sides of the wagon covering, Ibn Battuta notes, were fitted with little grilled windows: "The person who is inside the tent can see [other] persons without their seeing him, and he can employ himself in it as he likes, sleeping or eating or reading or writing, while he is still journeying." A prosperous steppe-dweller might own one or two hundred wagons.

The *ordu* of a rich Moal [Mongol] seems like a large town, though there will be very few men in it. One girl will lead twenty or thirty carts, for the country is flat, and they tie the ox or camel carts the one after the other, and a girl will sit on the front one driving the ox, and all the others follow after with the same gait.[7]

Ibn Battuta traveled as an honored member of the wagon train, whose privileged company included not only the *amir* Tuluktemur but also his brother, two sons, the wives of all these men, and a small bureaucracy of Muslim functionaries. He reckons that the first long stage of the journey from al-Qiram to Azak (Tana, now Azov) on the southern side of the delta of the Don took 23 days. He does not mention any known stopping places, so the route is a puzzle. Very likely the caravan crossed the peninsula separating the Crimea from the mainland, then turned eastward over the grassland north of the Sea of Azov and across the esturaries of the Miuss and the Don.[8]

Since driving the wagons through the shallow fords of the rivers was a muddy, bothersome operation, Tuluktemur had the solicitude to send Ibn Battuta on ahead with one of his officers and a letter of introduction to the governor of Azak. Since European ships could sail directly to the mouth of the Don but no further, this town had become the most distant of the important Frankish establishments, competing actively with Kaffa for the sale of Italian and Flemish textiles.

Ibn Battuta and his party camped in their wagons outside the town, though they were welcomed by the governor and the local religious personalities. In two days' time Tuluktemur arrived and amid the requisite displays of obeisance and hospitality on the part of the citizenry erected three huge tents, one of silk and two of linen and around them a cloth enclosure with an antechamber in the shape of a tower.

Here the *amir* entertained his retinue and Azak's dignitaries with titanic quantities of the rude cuisine the upper classes of Inner Asia normally consumed — millet gruel, macaroni, boiled meat of horse and sheep, and fermented mare's milk, called *qumizz*. Carried in hide bags on the wagons, *qumizz* was the nutritious staple of the Turko–Mongol diet. William of Rubruck, tasting it for the first time, "broke out in a sweat with horror and surprise," though later he decided it was "very palatable . . ., makes the inner man most joyful and . . . intoxicates weak heads."[9] He also liked the millet beer which flowed freely at Mongol banquets. The House of Genghis was notorious for its bibulousness, a family attribute scarcely affected by conversion to Islam, since the Hanafi doctors conveniently took the position that this particular potation was not expressly prohibited by the Qur'an. Ibn Battuta found *qumizz* "disagreeable" and, being a strait-laced Maliki, would have nothing to do with liquor. But he had no other cause to complain about Tuluktemur's hospitality. He got the usual robe and horse and indeed reports somewhat smugly that as they entered the audience tent the *amir* "made me precede him, in order that the governor of Azak should see the high esteem he had for me."

At this time Ozbeg Khan was not in residence at New Saray but camped about 280 miles southeast of Azak in the region known in modern times as the Stavropol Plateau, a rugged upland jutting northward from the main mass of the Caucasus Mountains. Since the founding of the Ilkhanate of Persia, these mountains had been the de facto frontier between the two states, but the grazing land was too good and the trade routes running between the Black Sea and the Caspian too important to allow the region any peace. In 1262 Berke and Hulegu, first cousins though they were, had gone to war for control of the Caucasus, and in the ensuing century the two dynasties hurled armies at one another time and time again. It is conceivable that Ozbeg perhaps led his *ordu* south in 1332 to see to frontier defenses or plan an operation against Abu Sa'id.[10] But the *Rihla* says nothing of such a purpose. Possibly, the khan went south to take the waters, for he was camped at Bish Dagh (Pyatigorsk), celebrated than as now for its mineral spas.

Tuluktemur soon left Azak to join the khan, but Ibn Battuta and his associates stayed behind for three days waiting for the governor to provide him with new equipment for the next leg of his journey. Perhaps attaching himself to a military column, he then set out southeasterly across the Kuban–Azov lowland. Arriving at Bish Dagh, he found that the khan had already decamped. Traveling eight more days, he finally caught up with the *ordu* in the vicinity of al-Machar (Burgomadzhary). It was the early days of Ramadan, May 1332 (1334).[11]

> I set up my tent on a low hill thereabouts, fixed my flat in front of the tent, and drew up my horses and wagons behind, then the *mahalla* came up . . . and we saw a vast city on the move with its inhabitants, with mosques and bazaars in it, the smoke of the kitchens rising in the air (for they cook while on the march), and horse-drawn wagons transporting the people.

On the morrow of his arrival in the camp he presented himself before the khan on recommendation of two of the sovereign's religious dignitaries. He found Ozbeg seated upon a silver gilded throne in the midst of an enormous tent whose exterior was covered, after the fashion of all the Kipchak rulers, with a layer of bright golden tiles. The Khan's daughter, his two sons, other royal kinsmen, and the chief *amirs* and officers were assembled below the throne, but his four *khatuns*, or wives, sat on either side of him. Ibn Battuta has a good deal to say in the *Rihla* about the freedom, respect, and near equality enjoyed by Mongol and Turkish women in startling contrast to the custom in his own land and the other Arab countries. (When a well-dressed and unveiled Turkish woman comes into the bazaar in the company of her husband, he remarks derisively, "anyone seeing him would take him to be one of her servants.") If wives and mothers often influenced politics in the palaces of the Moroccan Marinids, as we may assume they did, counsel was given in the confines of the *harim*. But in the Mongol states the women of the court shared openly and energetically in the governing of the realm. Princesses of the blood, like their brothers, were awarded apanages, or landed properties, which they ruled and taxed as private fiefs quite apart from the state domain. The *khatuns* sometimes signed decrees and made major administrative decisions independently of the khan. The prim Moroccan *faqih*, in whose own country the notion of a wife of the sultan appearing publicly at his side would have seemed unimaginable, could only grimace in amazement at the Kipchak ceremonial. He relates that when the senior *khatun* and queen of the khanate enters the golden tent, the ruler "advances to the entrance of the pavilion to meet her, salutes her, takes her by the hand, and only after she has mounted to the couch and taken her seat does the sultan himself sit down. All this is done in full view of those present, and without any use of veils."

In the following days Ibn Battuta went round to visit the *khatuns*, each of whom occupied her own *mahalla*.

The horses that draw her wagon are caparisoned with cloths of silk gilt . . . In front of [the wagon of] the *khatun* are ten or fifteen pages, Greeks and Indians, who are dressed in robes of silk gilt, encrusted with jewels, and each of whom carries in his hand a mace of gold or silver, or maybe of wood veneered with them. Behind the *khatun*'s wagon there are about a hundred wagons, in each of which there are four slave girls full-grown and young . . . Behind these wagons [again] are about three hundred wagons, drawn by camels and oxen, carrying the *khatun*'s chests, moneys, robes, furnishings, and food.

Ibn Battuta had to sleep in his own wagon because the ruling class of Central Asia had the exasperating habit of not giving lodging to their distinguished visitors. But he dined a number of times in the presence of the khan and thankfully accepted horses, sheep, foodstuffs, and robes from the *khatuns* after regaling them (through interpreters) with his earlier adventures. He probably stayed in the camp throughout Ramadan.[12] He was there to celebrate the 'Id al-Fitr, the Breaking of the Fast, an occasion of public feasting during which Ozbeg Khan, notwithstanding his contribution to the enduring triumph of Islam in the western steppe, made himself helplessly drunk and arrived late and staggering at the afternoon prayer.

A short time after this festival the khan and his retinue set out for the city of Astrakhan, which lay about 80 miles across the North Caspian lowlands on the left bank of the Volga.

When Ibn Battuta visited Princess Bayalun, Ozbeg's third ranking wife, and told her of the great distance he had journeyed from his native land, he reports that "she wept in pity and compassion and wiped her face with a handkerchief that lay before her." She knew how it felt to live in an alien country far from the familiar society of her childhood, for she was a daughter of Andronicus III, Emperor of Byzantium.[13] Several times in the thirteenth and fourteenth centuries dynastic marriages took place between daughters of Greek emperors and Mongol or Turkish rulers. These alliances were ultimately of small help in checking the expansion of the Ottomans (Orkhan married a Byzantine princess in 1346), but relations between Constantinople and the court of the Golden Horde were generally good. The emperors knew that Kipchak power was an effective counterweight to their Balkan rivals, the Christian kingdoms of Serbia and Bulgaria; they also endeavored to defend the interests of the Byzantine church in the Mongol protectorates of Christian Russia. The khans, for their part, wanted the Bosphorus (which ran under the walls of Constantinople) open to the trade and diplomatic exchanges on which the vitality of their alliance with the Mamluks of Cairo depended.

When the royal *ordu* reached Astrakhan, it was learned that Princess Bayalun had received permission from her husband to return temporarily to Constantinople to give birth to a child in the palace of her father. As we should not be surprised to learn, Ibn Battuta immediately applied to the khan for authorization to go along. Here was an unexpected opportunity to venture beyond the Dar al-Islam for the first time in his career and to see one of the great cities of the world, renowned among Muslims for its spectacular setting, its fabulous bazaars, its splendid buildings, and the fact that it had held out against the relentless expansion of Islam over the previous 700 years. There was nothing extraordinary about a Muslim visiting Constantinople in the fourteenth century. Merchants and envoys from Turkish or Arab lands went there when business required it, and in the previous century the Emperor Michael VIII had sponsored reconstruction of a mosque in the heart of the city.[14] A Muslim gentleman would not have been advised to wander overland through Christian territory as a purely private adventure, but he might do so in the train of an embassy from one ruler to another. At first Ozbeg refused the Moroccan's request, fearing the risk.

> But I solicited him tactfully and said to him "it is under your protection and patronage that I shall visit it, so I shall have nothing to fear from anyone." He then gave me permission, and when we took leave of him he presented me with 1,500 dinars, a robe, and a large number of horses, and each of the *khatuns* gave me ingots of silver . . . The sultan's daughter gave me more than they did, along with a robe and a horse, and altogether I had a large collection of horses, robes, and furs of miniver and sable.

On 10 Shawwal (5 July 1332 or 14 June 1334) the cavalcade set out westward across the hot flat prairie, crossing the Don and the Dnieper, then turning southward toward the delta of the Danube.[15] Ibn Battuta was attended by a small following of companions and slaves, the Princess Bayalun by 5,000 horsemen under the command of an *amir*, 500 of her own troops and servants, 200 slave girls, 20 Greek and Indian pages, 400 wagons, 2,000 horses, and about 500 oxen and camels. The peasants and herdsmen who had the misfortune to live along the route were obliged (as such folk were in all the Mongol states) to supply this monstrous caravan with food, often to their destitution and ruin. After traveling some 52 days the company arrived at the fortress of Mahtuli on the frontier between Byzantium and the Christian kingdom of Bulgaria. The place is probably to be identified with the town of Jamboli (Yambol) in the southeastern interior of modern Bulgaria.[16] Here the steppe wagons were exchanged for horses and mules, the Turkish *amir* and his troops turned back to the Volga, and the *khatun* continued on into the mountains of Thrace with her personal retinue. Ibn Battuta soon had plenty of evidence that he was entering an alien world:

> She left her mosque behind at this castle and the prescription of the call to prayer was discontinued. Wines were brought to her as part of her hospitality-gift, and she would drink them, and [not only so but even] swine . . . No one was left with her who observed the [Muslim] prayers except a certain Turk, who used to pray with us. Inner sentiments concealed [hitherto] suffered a change through our entry into the land of infidelity, but the *khatun* charged the amir Kifali to treat me honorably, and on one occasion he beat one of his *mamluks* when he laughed at our prayer.

About three weeks after leaving Mahtuli the procession reached the landward walls of Constantinople.

Ibn Battuta stayed in the city for more than a month. As a guest of the daughter of Andronicus III, he was given a robe of honor and awarded an interview with the emperor (who employed a Syrian Jewish interpreter and questioned him about the Christian shrines of Palestine). He wanted to see as much of the city as he could, and for this the emperor assigned him a Greek guide, who mounted him on a royal steed and paraded him through the streets in a noisy fanfare of trumpets and drums. He visited markets, monasteries, and the great church of Hagia Sophia (though he did not go inside because he would have had to prostrate himself before the cross). He traversed the Golden Horn, that is, the arm of the Bosphorus protecting the northern side of the city, in order to see the busy Genoese colony of Galata.

He also had a brief promenade and conversation with a monk named George, whom he identifies as the ex-emperor Andronicus II. This little episode has confounded Byzantinists and scholars of the *Rihla*. Ibn Battuta reports accurately enough that in 1328 in the climax of a seven-year civil war Andronicus III forced his predecessor and grandfather to abdicate at the point of a sword. The hapless old man retired to a monastery. He died, however, in February 1332, and by no plausible rearranging of the *Rihla*'s itinerary could Ibn Battuta have visited Constantinople in time to see him alive. But since the story of his encounter with *someone* in the streets of the city has the ring of truth about it, we may fairly suppose that the palace guide failed to clarify the identity of the mysterious cleric or, worse yet, was having a bit of fun with his credulous Arab guest.[17]

Ibn Battuta's recollection of Constantinople is offered in a spirit of tolerance, objectivity, and indeed wonder. But taken by itself it would mislead us. The Byzantines thought of themselves as the heirs of Rome and the guardians of Hellenic culture, but by the fourteenth century all the ponderous grandeur of nobles and prelates amounted to a vast pretension, kept up behind the walls of the bastion-city while all around the empire was slowly crumbling to bits. Though Andronicus stayed the territorial shrinkage on the European side and presided over a time of considerable artistic and literary vitality (as is often the case in civilizations on the brink of destruction), Byzantium in the 1330s was a minor Greek state of southeastern Europe and little more. Its international trade had been abandoned to the Italians, its currency was almost worthless, its landlords were grinding the peasantry unmercifully, its army was an assemblage of alien mercenaries, and its Asian territories had been all but lost to the triumphant Turks. It was a state living on borrowed time and past glory. Ibn Battuta either senses little of this or, to his credit, refrains from twisting the knife. Could he have believed that 121 years after his visit the descendants of Orkhan would storm the massive walls and transform Hagia Sophia into a mosque?

Though the historical record suggests that Bayalun eventually returned to her husband's *ordu*,[18] she made known to the Turks in her suite that she still professed Christianity and wished to remain with her father for an indefinite period. She granted her escorts permission to return home, and thus Ibn Battuta left with them, probably sometime in the autumn of 1332 (1334).[19] After journeying back through Thrace and recovering his wagons at the Greek frontier, he rode north into the steppe just as the bitter Asian winter was setting in. He was soon barricading himself inside three fur coats, two pairs of trousers, two layers of heavy socks, and horseleather boots lined with bearskin.

I used to perform my ablutions with hot water close to the fire, but not a drop of water fell without being frozen on the instant. When I washed my face, the water would run down my beard and freeze, then I would shake it and there would fall from it a kind a snow . . . I was unable to mount a horse because of the quantity of clothes I had on, so that my associates had to help me into the saddle.

Reaching Astrakhan and finding that Ozbeg had returned to New Saray 225 miles up the Volga, the company turned northward in pursuit, riding along the frozen river as if it were a highway. They reached the capital probably in late November.[20]

New Saray was a creation of the Pax Mongolica. Ozbeg may have undertaken its construction only about 1330, but Ibn Battuta found it "of boundless size" and "choked with its inhabitants." He claims that he spent half a day walking across the breadth of the town and back again, "this too through a continuous line of houses, among which there were no ruins and no gardens."[21] It was a city of wood more than of stone, but he counted 13 congregational mosques and numerous smaller ones. Its complex of craft shops exported metal ware, leather, and woven silk and woolens. Its bazaars handled the Volga traffic in grain, furs, timber, and slaves, crisscrossed with the flow of the trans-Asian luxury caravans linking Persia and China with the Italian colonies on the Black Sea.

Along with the silks, the decorated pottery, the mosaic tiles, and all the other goods by which civilized taste might be expressed on the Islamic frontier, there also arrived the little bands of scholars, mystics, and hopeful bureaucrats. Some of them came from Egypt, Bulghar, or Anatolia, most from the Irano–Turkish regions of northern Persia and Khwarizm. During his brief stay in the icy town, Ibn Battuta entered their circle and accepted their hospitality. One of the most eminent of the immigrants, an authority on medicine and former head of a hospital in Khwarizm, even gave him a Turkish slave boy as a gift.[22] The Moroccan also presented himself at the royal residence to give a full report on his trip to Byzantium. We may wonder what Ozbeg's reaction may have been to his wife's decision to remain in Constantinople, but on this the *Rihla* is silent.

Having proudly reached the northerly limit of his traveling career, Ibn Battuta left the Volga about mid December, determined, it would seem, to progress in the general direction of India. Over the ensuing eight months he made his way by an erratic and, to students of the *Rihla*, perplexing course to the valley of the Indus. For about the first five of those months he traveled in parts of Khwarizm, Transoxiana (Mawarannahr), and possibly Khurasan. Politically these regions fell among the Mongol realms of Kipchak, Persia, and Chagatay. Together, they embraced the immense arid zone extending from the northern Iranian plateau to the Altai Mountains and the Kazakh steppe, a land of sand deserts and barren, echoing plains. Not until his journey through the western Sahara 19 years later would he confront such menacing, indomitable territory.

Yet Muslim civilization had pushed into this unsparing country much before his time. The two river systems of the Amu Darya and the Syr Darya (Jaxartes) bisected the desert and, like the Nile, supported dense agricultural populations and big towns along discontinuous ribbons of irrigated land. In the previous century the armies of Genghis had perfected their instruments of terror on the unfortunate peoples of Transoxiana and in the aftermath of the conquest civilization for a time nearly vanished. It is a tribute to the human spirit that the desert bloomed with markets and mosques so quickly again, and this despite the later invasion of Hulegu and a succession of mass destructions perpetrated in wars between the Persian Mongols and their cousins, the khans of Chagatay.

Ibn Battuta passed through the region during a period of relative peace and prosperity. He found some of the towns he visited populous and flourishing. In Urgench (Urganj), provincial capital of the Golden Horde in Khwarizm and chief emporium of the fertile Amu Darya delta, he remembers that the bazaar was so crowded he could not get his horse through it and had to save his visit for a Friday, when most of the shops were closed. And this in a town which Genghis Khan had submerged entirely under water by opening a dam in the river. Bukhara, by contrast, once the most sophisticated city of all Transoxiana, was still struggling to revive after having been sacked, burned, and depopulated by Tatar armies in 1220, 1273, and 1316. "Its mosques, colleges, and bazaars are in ruins," the *Rihla* reports, and "there is not one person in it today who possesses any religious learning or who

Map 8: Ibn Battuta's Itinerary in Central Asia and Afghanistan, 1332–33 (1334–35)

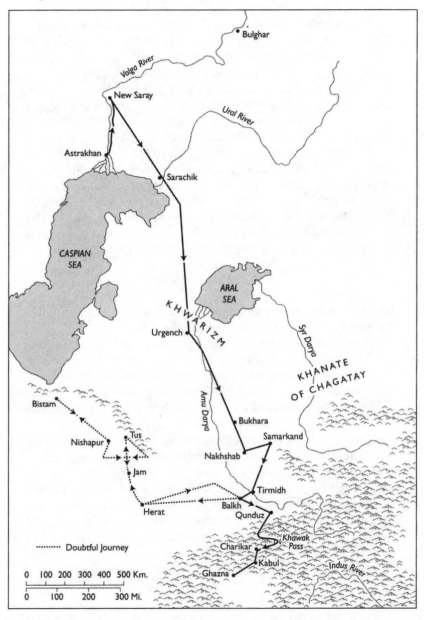

shows any concern for acquiring it." Balkh, oldest city of the Amu Darya valley and capital of the ancient Greco–Bactrian empire, Ibn Battuta found "completely delapidated and uninhabited." Mongol holocausts or no, Khurasan–Transoxiana remained to the landward commerce of Afro–Eurasia what the Arabian Sea was to the monsoon trade: the complex crossroads of trails connecting all the major agrarian regions of the hemisphere with one another. Most of the time, Ibn Battuta and his party kept to the main roads linking the principal cities, sometimes, perhaps almost always, in the company of commercial caravans. The wagons he had traveled with in the northern steppe were no longer suitable further south. Crossing the Ustyurt plateau between the Volga and Khwarizm, he accompanied a caravan of camel-drawn carts, but in Urgench he reverted to horses and to camels mounted with litters. When he left Khwarizm he was sharing a double litter with al-Tuzari. He also had 50 horses given to him by Princess Bayalun during the trip to Constantinople. These animals had been meant to supplement his food supply, but he preferred simply to add them to his growing store of personal wealth. He admits that after he arrived in Khwarizm he began to accumulate a greater number of horses than he dared mention. He even bought an unusually beautiful black steed with part of a gift of a thousand dinars that the Kipchak governor of the region gave him.

Aside from horses, the traveler's property included a retinue of slaves, though we can never be sure how many he had with him, male or female, at any particular time. When he left the Volga he was sharing his wagon with no fewer than three young women. While traveling near Bukhara, one of them gave birth to a baby girl. The new father believed that the child was born "under a lucky star" and that his fortunes improved from the moment of her birth. But, sadly, she died two months after he reached India.

He scarcely mentions his male companions other than the ubiquitous and shadowy al-Tuzari. Travelers always banded together on the open road, especially in such dangerous and waterless parts of the earth as this, so we may suppose that the composition of the party changed from one town to the next. In New Saray he was joined by one 'Ali ibn Mansur, a *sharif* and merchant of Iraq who planned to go all the way to India. But in Urgench this gentleman met up with a party of traders from his native town, changed his mind, and went off with them in the direction of China. At Tirmidh on the upper Amu Darya, Ibn

Battuta linked up with a Persian *sharif* and his two sons who were also on their way to look for employment in Delhi.

He and this kaleidoscope of associates visited about 21 important towns on his zigzag course through Khwarizm, Transoxiana, Khurasan, and Afghanistan. Or so he claims. If he visited all the cities of Ilkhanid Khurasan that he mentions (Herat, Jam, Tus, Nishapur, Bistam, and others), his tour was rushed and distracted, evidenced in the *Rihla* in cursory descriptions and perfunctory recollections of experiences and encounters.[23]

The most memorable event of these months was his meeting with 'Ala al-Din Tarmashirin, Khan of Chagatay (1326–3?). Ibn Battuta names him as one of the seven mighty kings of the world, though in most respects he was the least of the lot. Alughu, a grandson of Chagatay (the second son of Genghis), founded the khanate in the 1260s in the aftermath of the border wars and dynastic quarrels that split the conqueror's world empire into four kingdoms. The realm of the House of Chagatay encompassed an enormous region of desert, steppe, and mountain extending from the Amu Darya and Afghanistan to beyond the Irtisch River deep in the recesses of nomadic Asia. This was the geographic heart of the Mongol empire, but it was also the region where agrarian resources were most limited, where towns were most widely scattered, and where Turko–Mongol captains perpetuated the harsh ways of their ancestors long after their kinsmen in China and Persia were living in palaces and dining with lawyers and sycophantic poets.

Ibn Battuta celebrates Tarmashirin as "a man of great distinction" and "just in his government" because, like Ozbeg, he was the first of his dynasty to make Islam the official religion of state and only the second who would have paid much attention to an itinerant jurist from North Africa. Ibn Battuta stayed with the khan in his camp on the road southwest of Samarkand for 54 days in the cold late winter of 1333 (1335). When he left he was given 700 silver dinars, two camels, and a warm sable coat. Only later in India did he learn that perhaps within a few months of his departure from the *ordu* this khan "of vast kingdom and immense power" had been rudely overthrown by a treacherous nephew and a league of anti-Muslim commanders. The Moroccan had been lucky to see this tempestuous kingdom in a brief moment of unity under Islam, for in the aftermath of the rebellion civil war broke out and the realm was sheared in half, not to be reunited again.

Ibn Battuta crossed the towering Hindu Kush, the great divide separating Inner Asia from the watershed of the Indus, in the late spring of 1333 (1335).[24] He might have chosen any of several high passes through the mountains. Merchants running caravans from Transoxiana to Afghanistan routed themselves through one pass or another depending on the reports of snow, rock slides, or bandits. After camping for a few weeks at Qunduz not far south of the upper Amu Darya in order to graze his horses and camels and await the warm weather, the *faqih*, his slaves, and his learned associates ascended the northern slope through the gorges of the Andarab River valley. He crossed the divide at the 13,000-foot Khawak Pass. "We crossed the mountain," Ibn Battuta recalls, "setting out about the end of the night and traveling on it all day long until sunset. We kept spreading felt cloths in front of the camels for them to tread on, so that they should not sink in the snow."

Descending along the spectacular Panjshir Valley, the caravan passed through Charikar and onto the Kabul plain, where all the main mountain trails converged. At Ghazna Ibn Battuta and his friends were entertained by the Chagatay governor. Then, moving southwestward in the company of merchants driving 4,000 horses to market in India, they crossed the Sulayman Mountains by the main route through the Khyber Pass, or possibly by a more southerly road.[25] Traversing a narrow gorge, they had a skirmish with a band of Afghan highwaymen, and later Ibn Battuta and some of his party became separated for a time from the main caravan. But these were minor adventures, and after a three- to four-month journey from the far side of the Hindu Kush, they rode into the Indus plain. Ibn Battuta tells us that he reached the great river on the first day of 734 A.H., or 12 September 1333.[26]

With this event, the first part of the *Rihla* comes to an end, signifying an important transition in Ibn Battuta's career. During the three years between his departure from Mecca and his arrival at the banks of the Indus, he had become, with his slaves, his horses, and his pack train of expensive accoutrements, a traveler of considerable private means — but a traveler nonetheless. Except for his service as caravan *qadi* on the road between Tunis and Alexandria, he had never had any sustained employment in legal scholarship. Now, however, he was about to seek an official career. Word had gone round the mosques and *madrasas* of Islamdom that fortune and power were to be had in service to Muhammad Tughluq and the court of Delhi. The *Rihla* explains:

The king of India . . . makes a practice of honoring strangers and showing affection to them and singling them out for governorships or high dignities of state. The majority of his courtiers, palace officials, ministers of state, judges, and relatives by marriage are foreigners, and he has issued a decree that foreigners are to be called in his country by the title of 'Aziz (Honorable), so that this has become a proper name for them.

Gentleman, pilgrim, jurist, raconteur, world traveler, and guest of *amirs* and khans, Ibn Battuta had good reason to think he was just the sort of public servant Muhammad Tughluq was looking for.

Notes

1. William Woodville Rockhill (trans. and ed.), *The Journey of William of Rubruck to the Eastern Parts of the World* (London, 1900), p. 94.

2. "Rumi" is usually to be translated as "Greeks," but at other points in the narrative IB uses the term when he means Genoese. See Gb, vol. 2, p. 467n.

3. W. Heyd, *Histoire du commerce du Levant au moyen-âge*, 2 vols. (Leipzig, 1936), vol. 2, pp. 172–74.

3. IB associates a visit to Sudak with his later trip from Astrakhan to Constantinople. Other than inserting Sudak into the itinerary, he says nothing about a detour into the Crimea. More plausibly, IB passed through Sudak on his way from Kaffa to al-Qiram. See Gb, vol. 2, p. 499n and Hr, pp. 470, 478–79.

5. B. D. Grekov and A. J. Iakubovskij, *La Horde d'Or*, trans. F. Thuret (Paris, 1939), p. 91.

6. Rockhill, *William of Rubruck*, p. 49.

7. Ibid., p. 57. Marco Polo also describes the wagons. *The Book of Ser Marco Polo*, trans. and ed. Henry Yule, 2 vols., 3rd edn, rev. Henri Cordier (London, 1929), vol. 1, pp. 252–55.

8. The caravan might conceivably have crossed the Kerch Strait east of al-Qiram, then approached Azaq from the south. Some topographical hints in the *Rihla*, however, argue for the northern route. Hr, pp. 470–71.

9. Rockhill, *William of Rubruck*, pp. 67, 85.

10. Ozbeg led unsuccessful invasions of Ilkhanid territory in 1319, 1325, and 1335. J. A. Boyle, "Dynastic and Political History of the Ilkhans" in *The Cambridge History of Iran* (Cambridge, England, 1968), vol. 5, pp. 408, 412–13; Bertold Spuler, *Die Goldene Horde* (Leipzig, 1943), pp. 93–96.

11. IB states that he arrived at Bish Dagh on 1 Ramadan, which was 27 May 1332 or 6 May 1334.

12. At this point in the narrative IB claims to have made a journey, all within the month of Ramadan, from Ozbeg's camp to the middle Volga city of Bulghar and back again, a total distance of more than 800 miles. Stephen Janicsek has argued convincingly that this trip never took place. "Ibn Battuta's Journey to Bulghar: Is it a Fabrication?" *Journal of the Royal Asiatic Society* (October 1929), pp. 791–800. Janicsek shows that IB's cursory description of both Bulghar and the Land of Darkness beyond (to which he does not claim to have gone but only heard about) are based on earlier geographical writings in Arabic. He also points out that

IB could not possibly have made the journey in anywhere near the time he allots to it and that he says virtually nothing about his route, his companions, his personal experiences, or the sights he would have seen along the way. The Bulghar trip is the only section of the *Rihla* whose falsity has been proven beyond almost any doubt, though the veracity of some other journeys may be suspected, such as the trip to San'a in the Yemen. We must remember, however, that the *Rihla* was composed as a literary survey of the Islamic world in the fourteenth century. It was well known among literate Muslims that Bulghar was the most northerly of Muslim communities. Moreover, several medieval geographers wrote in fascination about the frigid Land of Darkness, that is, Siberia. If IB did not go to Bulghar, he might nonetheless satisfy his readers' expectations of a book about travels through the Dar al-Islam by saying that he did. Scholars of the *Rihla* are generally in agreement that the Bulghar detour is a fiction. Gb, vol. 2, p. 491n and Hr, pp. 471–73. Also, because of IB's rich and detailed description of life in Ozbeg's *ordu,* we may suppose that he remained there throughout Ramadan 1332 (1334).

13. A letter addressed from one Byzantine monk to another and dated 1341 has confirmed that at that time a daughter of Andronicus III was married to Ozbeg Khan. R. J. Loenertz, "Dix huit lettres de Gregoire Acindyne, analysées et datées." *Orientalia Christiana Periodica* 23 (1957): 123–24; also Hr, pp. 474–76. "Bayalun" is a Mongol name, not a Greek one. Paul Pelliot, *Notes sur l'histoire de la Horde d'Or* (Paris, 1949), pp. 83–84.

14. Mehmed Izzeddin, "Ibn Battouta et la topographie byzantine," *Actes du VI Congrès Internationale des Études Byzantines,* 2 vols. (Paris, 1951), vol. 2, p. 194.

15. IB's reporting of his itinerary from Astrakhan to Constantinople is blurry and confused. There is, however, no reason to doubt that he and the princess traveled by way of the northern and western shores of the Black Sea. See Gb, vol, pp. 498–503n; and Hr, pp. 476–79.

16. Gb, vol. 2, p. 500n. The complexities of IB's itinerary along the western rim of the Black Sea are analyzed in H.T. Norris, "Fact or Fantasy in Ibn Battuta's Journey along the Northern Shores of the Black Sea," in *Ibn Battuta: Actes du Colloque international organizé par l'Ecole Supérieure Roi Fahd de Traduction à Tanger les 27, 27, 29 octobre 1993* (Tangier, 1996), pp. 11–24; and "Ibn Battuta's journey in the north-eastern Balkans," *Journal of Islamic Studies* 5, 2 (1994): 209–220.

17. IB presents detailed vivid, and generally accurate descriptions of the Byzantine court and the city's important buildings. The account, however, is also muddled by errors, puzzling observations, and impossible stories. He informs us, for example, that the Latin Pope made an annual visit to Constantinople! The supposed meeting with the ex-emperor Andronicus II (whom IB calls George, when his monastic name was Antonius) is only the most egregious of his misunderstandings. Hrbek (Hr, p. 481) believes that IB had a meeting with someone important but fabricated his identity in order "to add a further item to his collection of personal acquaintances with sovereigns." Neither Gibb nor Hrbek believe that the itinerary can be rearranged to place IB in Constantinople before February 1332.

18. According to the letter of Gregoire Acindyne, she was with Ozbeg in 1341. See note 13.

19. Hr, p. 477.

20. Ibid., p. 482.

21. Scholars formerly believed that both Old and New Saray were founded in the thirteenth century, the one by Batu, the other by his brother Berke. But recent numismatic evidence suggests that Ozbeg not only made his capital at New Saray but founded the city as well.

22. On this scholar, Grekov and Iakubovskij. *La Horde d'Or,* pp. 157–58.

23. IB's journey through Khurasan is doubtful. His itinerary is confusing and his description almost devoid of personal details. He mentions only one stopover between Bistam in the western part of Khurasan and Qunduz in northern

Afghanistan, the straight line distance between them being more than 700 miles. He would also have had to undertake this excursion at top speed in order to sandwich it into his own chronological scheme. Gibb (Gb, vol. 2, p. 534) believes that this section of the narrative is "highly suspect" but offers no case. Most of the descriptive material is taken up with an account of the popular rebellion that gave rise to the Sarbadar state, one of the kingdoms that seized a share of greater Persia following the collapse of the Ilkhanate in 1335. The revolt began in 1336. IB was in India by that time and does not claim to have witnessed any of the events he describes. See J. M. Smith, Jr., *The History of the Sarbadar Dynasty 1336–1381 A.D.* (The Hague, 1970).

24. Gibb (Gb, vol. 2, p. 531) proposes that IB crossed the Hindu Kush at the Khawak Pass about the end of June. IB's reference to snow and cold weather in the pass, however, suggests a month no later than May. See J. Humlum, *La géographie de l'Afghanistan* (Copenhagen, 1959). The Arabic passage of the *Rihla* Gibb translates "we stayed on the northern side of the Hindu Kush until the warm weather had definitely set in" may be rendered "until the warm weather had begun to set in." D&S, vol. 3, p. 84.

25. IB's route from Kabul to the Indus is a puzzle owing to the uncertain identity of several place names as well as his failure to say precisely where he reached the river. Gibb, Mahdi Husain, and Peter Jackson have analyzed the problem and each arrives at a different conclusion. The issue pivots on the identity of "Shashnagar," which IB claims to have passed through on his road from Kabul to the river. If this locality is Hashtnagar, a district near Peshawar (in northern Pakistan), IB is likely to have crossed the Sulayman Mountains through the Khyber Pass. MH, pp. 1–2. If, however, it is to be identified with Naghar, a place south of Kabul, he probably entered the Indus plain in the Bannu (Banian) district about 100 miles south of Peshawar. Peter Jackson, "The Mongols and India (1221–1351)", Ph.D. diss., Cambridge University, 1977, p. 224. To complicate the problem further IB tells us that he spent 15 nights crossing a "great desert." Gibb (Gb, vol.3, p. 591n) believes that he probably traveled through the desert south of Ghazna and reached the Indus in the Larkana district of Sind, that is, less than 300 miles from the mouth of the river.

26. IB's statement that he arrived at the Indus River on 1 Muharram 734 (12 September 1333) is probably more or less accurate. The date is open to question, however, since he claims to have left Mecca at the end of 732 A.H. (12 September 1332), yet he took about three years traveling from there to India. Therefore, one date or the other must be wrong, and if the Mecca departure date is correct he would not have reached India until the autumn of 1335. (See Chapter 6, note 2 for a fuller discussion of this issue.) On the whole, the indications that he crossed the Indus by the autumn of 1333 are more compelling than the arguments supporting his departure from Arabia in 1332. The evidence for the 1333 arrival may be summarized as follows:

(a) IB reports events surrounding the departure of Sultan Muhammad Tughluq from Delhi in order to suppress a rebellion in Ma'bar in the far south of India (see Chapter 9). The revolt broke out in 1334. IB states that the sultan left the capital on 9 Jumada I, which was 5 January in 1335 (see Chapter 9, note 21). IB had clearly been living in the capital for some time when this event occurred. If the dating here is correct, he must have entered India in 1333, or at least many months before the fall of 1335.

(b) Muslim medieval sources date the deposition and death of Tarmashirin, Khan of Chagatay, in 1334–35 (735 A.H.). IB states that he heard about the khan's being overthrown "two years" after his arrival in India (Gb, vol. 3, p. 560). This would accord with IB's having visited the ruler's camp in the late winter of 1333. If he had been there in 1335, that is, very shortly before Tarmashirin was overthrown, he would likely have heard the news within a short time of reaching India, not two years.

(c) Passing through Ajodhan (Ajudahan) on his way from the Indus to Delhi, IB recounts that he met the holy man Farid al-Din al-Badhawuni. Mahdi Husain (MH, p. 20) explains that no *shaykh* of that name existed at that time and that IB must have been referring to his grandson 'Alam al-Din Mawj-Darya. Mahdi Husain also notes that this latter personage died in 734 A.H. Assuming Mahdi Husain is right on the question of the saint's identity, then IB must have crossed the Indus no later than that year. Gibb (Gb, vol. 2, p. 529n and vol. 3, p. 613n) also argues this point.

9 Delhi

Many genuine descendants of the Prophet arrived there
from Arabia, many traders from Khurasan, many painters
from China . . . many learned men from every part. In
that auspicious city they gathered, they came like moths
around a candle.[1]

Isami

Arriving at the western edge of the Indo–Gangetic plain, Ibn
Battuta was entering a world region where his co-believers made
up only a small minority of the population. They were, however,
the minority that ruled the greater part of the subcontinent of
India. Over the very long term the fundamental patterns of Indian
society and culture had been defined by the repeated invasions of
barbarian charioteers or cavalrymen from Afghanistan or the
steppe lands beyond. In the eleventh century, about the same time
that the Seljuks were radically changing the political map of the
Middle East, the Muslim Turkish rulers of Afghanistan began
dispatching great bands of holy warriors against the Hindu
cultivators of the Indus and Ganges valleys. These *ghazis* seized
the main towns of the Punjab, or upper Indus region. Lahore
became a capital of two Turko–Afghan dynasties, first the
Ghaznavids and later the Ghurids.

In 1193 Qutb al-Din Aybek, a Ghurid slave commander,
captured Delhi, then a small Hindu capital strategically located on
the Yamuna River at the eastern end of the natural military route
through the Punjab plain to the fertile Ganges basin. In 1206 he
seized power in his own right, proclaiming Delhi the capital of a
new Muslim military state. During the ensuing century the sultans
of the Slave Dynasty, as it was called after the *mamluk* origins of
its rulers, defeated one after another the Hindu kingdoms into
which North India was fragmented and founded an empire extending from the Indus to the Bay of Bengal.

The first phase of the Muslim conquest of North India was a
splendid *ghazi* adventure of looting, shooting, and smashing up

Map 9: Ibn Battuta's Itinerary in India, Ceylon, and the Maldive Islands, 1333–45

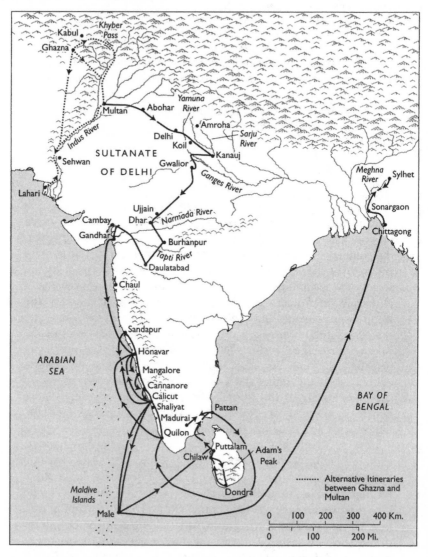

the gods of Hindu idolators. The new kings of Dehli, however, imposed civil order on the conquered areas and created a structure of despotism designed to tax rather than slaughter the native peasantry. In the rich plains around the capital, the Muslim military elite secured its authority as a kind of ruling caste atop the stratified social system of the Hindus. A pyramid of administration was erected linking the sultan, from whom all power derived by right of conquest, with several levels of officialdom down to the petty Hindu functionaries who supervised tax collections in thousands of farming villages. Like the Turkish rulers of the Middle East and Anatolia, the sultans learned proper Muslim statecraft from the Abbasid tradition, though adding here and there colorful bits of Hindu ceremonial. Within several decades of the founding of the sultanate, these erstwhile tribal chieftains were transforming themselves into Indo–Persian monarchs, secluded from the populace at the center of a maze of intimidating ritual and an ever-growing army of officials, courtiers, and bodyguards.

Delhi grew rapidly in the thirteenth century, not because it was an important center of industry or a key intersection of trade, but because it was the imperial residence. As Ibn Battuta had witnessed in other leading capitals, the operation of the army, the bureaucracy, and the royal household required an immense supporting staff of clerks, servants, soldiers, construction workers, merchants, artisans, transporters, shopkeepers, tailors, and barbers. Delhi was typical of parasitic medieval capitals, its royal establishment feeding magnificently off the labor of the lower orders and the revenues of hundreds of thousands of Hindu farmers.

In 1290 the Slave dynasty expired and was succeeded by two lines of Turkish sultans. The first were the Khaljis (1290–1320), men sprung from an Afghan tribe of that name. The second were the Tughluqids (1320–1414), called after the founding ruler, Ghiyas al-Din Tughluq. During the first four decades of these kings, the empire expanded spectacularly. 'Ala al-Din Khalji (1296–1316), a brilliant administrator, created a new standing army of cavalry, war-elephants, and Hindu infantry. Advancing to the Deccan plateau of Central India, he conquered one important Hindu state and raided nearly to the tip of the subcontinent. Areas of South India that 'Ala al-Din merely plundered, Ghiyath al-Din Tughluq (1320–25) and his son Muhammad Tughluq (1325–51) invaded again, then annexed to the empire, replacing Hindu tributaries with Turkish or Afghan governors appointed from Delhi. By 1333 Muhammad Tughluq ruled over most of India. Thus the congeries of ethnic groups, languages, and castes that comprised the civilization of the subcontinent were politically united, however precariously, for the first time since the Gupta empire of the fifth century A.D.

The great danger of dispatching armies as much as 1,300 miles south of Delhi was that the northwest frontier might be inadequately defended against new disturbances emanating from Inner Asia. In 1221–22, just 18 years after the founding of the sultanate, Chinggis Khan advanced across the Hindu Kush and penetrated as far east as the Indus. In the reign of the Great Khan Ogedei, the Tatars invaded again, seizing Lahore in 1241. Later in the century the Khans of Chagatay, hemmed into the steppe by the other three Mongol kingdoms, looked upon India as the most promising outlet for their combative energies. Chagatay armies and raiding parties crossed the Sulayman mountain passes in the 1290s and continued to do so repeatedly for three more decades. About 1329 Tarmashirin, the Chagatay khan whom Ibn Battuta visited a few years later, invaded India and even threatened Delhi. But Muhammad Tughluq chased him back across the Indus, putting an end to further Mongol incursions of any moment (at least until the catastrophic invasion of Tamerlane at the end of the century).

By successfully defending North India against the Tatars over the course of more than a century, the sultans earned well-deserved reputations in the wider world as champions of Muslim civilization, a status akin to their contemporaries, the Mamluks of Egypt. Thus Delhi, along with Cairo and the Turkish-ruled towns of Anatolia, became a refuge for skilled and literate men who had fled Transoxiana or Persia before the Mongols killed or enslaved them. The silver lining around the devastations of the Islamic heartland was the consequent flowering of civilized life in cities just beyond the reach of Mongol cavalry. In the time of the early Slave dynasty, Delhi had been an armed camp, an outpost of hardy faith fighting for its survival against Hindu idolators on three sides and Mongol devils on the fourth. But once the sultans showed they could defend the community of believers against such powers of darkness, Delhi rose quickly as the central urban base for the advance of Islam into the subcontinent. The rulers basked in their hard-won prestige by opening up their court and administration to all Muslims of talent, skill, or spiritual repute and patronizing them with stipends and gifts, as well as grand public edifices in which to pursue their vocations.

From Khurasan and Transoxiana came theologians and legists who introduced the universalist standards of the Sacred Law. The sultan appointed immigrant scholars as *qadis* and legal advisers and generally deferred to them to enforce the *shari'a* in matters of religious practice and civil disputes involving believers. Since the Hanafi *madhhab* was dominant in Khurasan and Central Asia, it became the basis of juridical practice in the sultanate. As the Muslim population grew, so did the demand for qualified jurists, requiring the construction of colleges offering studies in Hanafi *fiqh* and the other religious sciences. According to the Egyptian scholar al-Umari, who wrote from plainly exaggerated information supplied by travelers returned from India, there were "one thousand *madrasas* in Delhi, one of which is for the Shafi'ites and the rest for the Hanafites."[2]

Also from central Islamdom came belle-lettrists, historians, poets, and musicians to entertain the imperial court, chronicle its achievements, and extol the virtues of the king. Though Hindi, Turkish, Gujarati, and numerous other Indian tongues could be heard in the streets and bazaars of Delhi, Persian was used in polite circles, thus extending its range as the language of literate prestige all the way from Anatolia to Bengal. Speaking and writing in Persian, the Muslim elite of India reaffirmed in effect their cultural and historical connections to the central lands and at the same time created a linguistic barrier of exclusivity and privilege between themselves and the Hindu masses.

Craftsmen migrating from the west imported Arabo-Persian architectural and decorative traditions. Delhi, like other rising Muslim cities of that period, grew outward from a hub of grand public buildings — mosques, palaces, Sufi *khanqas*, colleges, and mausolea — that incorporated the domes, arches, and calligraphic inscriptions characteristic of Middle Period architecture in Persia. Since the immigrant community was small, however, Hindu artisans and laborers had to be hired in large numbers to carry out most of the work. Thus all sorts of native structural and decorative elements found their way into these buildings, some of them built with the sandstone blocks of demolished Hindu temples.

The earliest Muslim Delhi was established within the refortified walls of the old Hindu town, Kil'a Ray Pithora. Here Sultan Qutb al-Din Aybek (and several of his successors) built the con-

gregational mosque and mausolea complex called the Quwwat al-
Islam. Near it rose the Qutb Minar, the great tapering sandstone
tower whose bands of Arabic inscriptions proclaimed Koranic
truths and the military triumphs of the first Slave sultans. By Ibn
Battuta's time three additional urban aggregations — three more
cities of Delhi — had been founded, all on the west bank of the
Yamuna River within about five miles of one another. One was Siri,
built by 'Ala al-Din Khalji as a military camp and later walled in.
The second was Tughluqabad, a walled complex and fortress
founded by Ghiyas al-Din Tughluq. The third was Jahanpanah,
where Muhammad Tughluq built a magnificent residence, the
Palace of a Thousand Pillars.

The prospering of Muslim life in Delhi and numerous other
Hindustani towns in the thirteenth and early fourteenth centuries
was evidence of a continuous stream of native conversion. India's
immigrant population of Turks, Afghans, Persians, and Arabs
never represented more than a small minority of the total. By the
time Ibn Battuta visited the country, the great majority of Muslims
there were Indian-born. Most of India's rural population remained
true to the Hindu tradition. Though the sultanate required
Hindus, at least in theory, to pay special taxes (as Christians and
Jews under Muslim authority were required to do), the government for the most part left them alone to live and worship as
they wished. Nevertheless, Indo–Muslims were by the late
thirteenth century working their way into the intelligentsia and the
elite circles of the sultanate. Ministers and provincial governors of
Indo–Muslim origin were being appointed. Indian-born scholars,
poets, and religious doctors were appearing in the royal court. As
Islam in the Indian context matured, the most conspicuous social
tensions within the upper strata were occurring, not between
Muslim and Hindu, but between the rising Indo–Muslim elite and
the still dominant notables who traced their lineages to the older
Islamic lands.

In fact the cultural ties between India and the rest of the Dar al-
Islam were becoming stronger in the early fourteenth century.
Under the Muslim Ilkhans Persia was restored to its old position as
the hub of circulation throughout the Islamic world. As a result,
merchants, Sufis, and envoys were moving in greater numbers
between there and India over the high roads through Afghanistan.
Both the Khalji and Tughluq sultans cultivated diplomatic ties not
only with the Ilkhans but also with the Mamluks and, later, the

The Qutb Minar, Delhi
Ray Smith

rulers of Kipchak and Chagatay. These connections in turn helped broadcast information about the sultanate among international professional and scholarly circles. Ibn Battuta may have first heard in Cairo about attractive opportunities for official service at the brilliant court of Delhi.

It was sometime between 1327 and 1330 that Sultan Muhammad Tughluq decided on the policy of systematically filling the highest posts of his administration and judiciary with foreigners and re-warding them with fabulous gifts and stipends. This plan was but one of several peculiarities of his reign. Ibn Battuta was himself one of the prominent chroniclers of that period and shared with other contemporary writers certain norms and expectations as to the behavior of a proper Sunni ruler.[3] Most of the sultans and *amirs* who starred in the drama of the later Mongol Age complied outwardly with the standards of orthodoxy well enough that their historians applied the conventional panegyrics to them and their regimes. If the ruler upheld the *shari'a* in religious and civil affairs, patronized the scholars and spiritual luminaries, gave generously to the prominent and the poor, attended feasts and Friday prayers, condemned pagans and Shi'ites, and refrained from indulging publicly in things forbidden, then learned opinion normally gave its stamp of approval.

Muhammad Tughluq, however, was the odd duck of fourteenth-century rulers — eccentric, anomalous, baffling. In the eyes of the educated men who served him (and later wrote books about him), he repeatedly deviated from the norms of tradition and advocated policies that were visionary, extreme, and unfathomable. Though he presided over his court in the grand style of the Abbasid Caliphs, cultivated relations with the major states of Islam, and doubled, in God's name, the size of the Indian empire, the official establishment could not adjust themselves to his quixotic schemes and contradictions. They ultimately deserted him wholesale.

Muhammad was a religious scholar of greater attainments than any of the other more or less polished rulers of his time. He insisted that his Muslim subjects perform the ritual prayers and abstain from wine. He took a lively interest in legal studies and memorized large sections of the corpus of Hanafi law. He mastered the art of calligraphy and wrote elegant Persian verse. He learned Arabic in order to read religious texts. He showered patronage on scholars and divines. Yet he also pushed his inquiries well beyond the boundaries of orthodox propriety. He invited Hindu and Jain sages to court and engaged them in theological discussion. He consorted with yogis. He even took up the study of Greek philosophical rationalism, a subject anathema to fourteenth-century Sunni doctors.[4]

Muhammad was also a man of action in the best tradition of the Turkish war captain. Rather than confining himself to the usual policy of merely seizing chunks of Hindu territory and squeezing them for taxes, he pursued in a spirit of relentless logic a series of ingenious, sweeping, and unprecedented projects to reorganize government and society. Most of these schemes were initiated during the first ten years of his reign, that is, prior to Ibn Battuta's arrival. All of them ended in disaster. The sultan developed a plan to rationalize and improve agricultural production and tax-gathering in the fertile Doab region between the Ganges and Yamuna Rivers southeast of Delhi. The result was a serious decline of productivity and a protracted peasant revolt. He conceived a grand strategy to take the offensive in the northwest and invade the Chagatay Khanate. He raised a huge mounted force, kept them on the muster role for a year at great expense, then abandoned the entire plan — except for dispatching an army into Kashmir, where Hindu mountain folk annihilated it.[5] He issued copper coins backed by gold in the treasury in order to compensate for a shortage of silver, probably getting the idea from China. If the Chinese were amenable to token money, however, Indians were not. Counterfeiting became rampant, the coins dropped precipitously in value, and the sultan finally had to redeem them for gold at immense cost to the government.

In 1326, he decided to found a new capital at Deogir, renamed Daulatabad, a city located in the barren Deccan plateau more than 400 miles south of Delhi. His aim was apparently to better assimilate newly conquered areas by shifting the center of government to South India. If the scheme was politically logical and reasonably planned, it was from a human standpoint grievously unrealistic. The official classes comfortably ensconced in Delhi resisted the move, wanting nothing to do with life in that remote province. The sultan responded to such recalcitrance by ordering a mass exodus of the royal household and almost the entire governing corps. Modern historians are divided on the question of the extent to which Delhi was depopulated and ruined in consequence of the migration. In any case the experiment failed. If Muhammad briefly achieved a tighter grip on the south, conspiracies and revolts were soon erupting in the north, forcing him to return. Moreover, about 1329 he was obliged to defend Delhi against the invading army of Tarmashirin Khan. Within but a few years of his decision to move his government to Daulatabad, his officials and their retinues were being given authorization to desert the city and trek back to Delhi.

The sultan appears to have decided early in his reign, perhaps following the resistance of his officials to resettling in Daulatabad, that he could best put his innovative policies into action by entrusting them to foreign political servants on whose personal loyalty he could count in return for salaries and perquisites. Since educated men were constantly circulating from one Muslim court to another in that age, it was easy enough to attract them to India. But once again the plan backfired. The more respectable Sunni gentlemen recoiled at the sultan's queer orthodoxy. The less honorable tried to get rich on Muhammad's naive generosity, then sneak out of the country at the first opportunity.

All of the sultan's murky, fruitless dreams for a model Muslim state reveal both an impressive vision and a deplorable inability to accommodate his will to social and political realities. He was a bull in the china shop of Indian society, insensitive to the delicate compromises among social groups and power cliques that had held the sultanate together for more than a century. The intricate regional and caste divisions within Hindu society, the primitive communications system, and the dogged rivalries within the Muslim elite itself all put far greater limits on central authority than Muhammad could bring himself to admit.

As the criticisms of his *'ulama* and the leading divines became known to him, he reacted with petulant brutality. Rather than compromise with opinion, he chose to ferret out and punish those who failed by their disloyalty or incompetence to make his reforms succeed. In any Muslim state of that age the ruling warrior class was expected to be arbitrary, capricious, and nasty up to a certain limit in the interest of public order. But Muhammad Tughluq went too far. It was one thing to chastise rebels and thieves by having them cut in half, skinned alive, or tossed about by elephants with swords attached to their tusks. It was quite another thing to inflict such humiliations on distinguished scholars and clerics for merely questioning public policy or happening to be a friend of someone who did. "Not a day or week passed," reports the contemporary chronicler Barani, "without the spilling of much Musulman blood and the running of streams of gore before the entrance of his palace."[6]

At the same time that he repressed and terrorized his own boon companions and officers of state, Muhammad continued to bestow stupendous prizes and salaries on those he happened to favor at the moment. Barani relates:

> His indiscriminate liberality did not stop to differentiate between the deserving and the undeserving, between an acquaintance and a stranger, between a new and an old friend, between a citizen and a foreigner, or between the rich and the poor. All of them appeared to him just the same. Nay more, the gift of the monarch preceded the request and the amount or value of the donation exceeded the wildest expectations of the receiver; so that the latter was literally confounded.[7]

The political message such actions carried was that the sultan, the Shadow of God, was the temporal source of all power, whether for good or evil, and that the people must understand their utter subordination to his will. Thus to take service with Muhammad Tughluq was to live a life of reckless insecurity, to spin the wheel of chance with every word or action on which the sultan might choose to have an opinion.

As Muhammad's schemes went awry and the empire began to crack, the atmosphere of the imperial court became increasingly paranoid and brooding. By 1334 the constructive energies of the government were exhausted, a seven-year drought was about to begin, and the sultan was facing the earliest of the 22 major rebellions that would consume the last decade and a half of his reign. The Sultanate of Delhi had reached its peak of power and was about to founder. It was in these conditions of imminent disaster that the Moroccan traveler chose to arrive in Hindustan.

Ibn Battuta reached the valley of the Indus River at an uncharacteristically tranquil moment in the history of that tumultuous frontier. After more than a century of chronic hostilities between the sultanate and the Mongols, Muhammad Tughluq had accomplished something of a truce with his Tatar neighbor. The routes from Persia and Central Asia were busy with trade, and distinguished visitors were arriving regularly at the government immigration and customs posts set up at the main crossing points along the river.

At the Indus, intelligence officers charged with controlling the movements of persons in and out of the empire subjected the Moroccan and his friends to meticulous observation. Who is this individual? What does he look like? Where has he come from? How does he dress and behave? How many servants and animals does he have with him? The answers to these and numerous other questions were immediately written up and dispatched by rapid courier relay to the governor of the northwest frontier at Multan, a city east of the river in the Punjab region, and to the sultan in Delhi (or wherever in the kingdom he happened to be). The visitors were then instructed to proceed to Multan to await the sultan's orders regarding their fitness to continue to Delhi and the degree of honor to be accorded them.

Ibn Battuta relates that he did not in fact go directly to Multan but set off on a side trip to visit Sind, the arid valley of the lower Indus and its delta. The region was of special historic interest to educated travelers — and to readers of the *Rihla* — since it had first been conquered for Islam by an Arab army early in the eighth century. The highlights of Ibn Battuta's detour included a five-day boat trip down the great river to the delta port of Lahari in the company of its governor, meetings with various Sufi divines, and an unpleasant brush with a rhinoceros. The itinerary of the trip is ambiguous because Ibn Battuta fails to make clear where along the Indus, within a range of about 550 miles, he had first arrived from Afghanistan.[8] Moreover, a study of chronological matters in the narrative suggests that the events he describes in connection with Sind may well have taken place at a later time, probably in 1341 when he traveled there from Delhi at the summons of the sultan.[9] It seems plausible that he and his company did in fact go directly to Multan in order to secure official clearance before traveling further into the empire.

Located at that time near the Ravi River, one of the tributaries of the Indus, Multan was the military capital of the western borderlands. Multan was also known as the headquarters of the Suhrawardiya, one of the two important Sufi orders represented in India. Upon arriving in the city, Ibn Battuta presented himself before the governor, then took lodgings in a Suhrawardi *khanqa* just outside the town. He was even introduced to Rukn al-Din Abu l'Fath, the Grand Shaykh of the brotherhood, thus fulfilling the astonishing prediction that the old Egyptian mystic had made to him in Alexandria seven years earlier. (On the road from Multan to Delhi a short time later he would visit Ala al-Din Mawj-i Darya, master of the Chishti order. This man was not quite the second of the three divines the Egyptian told Ibn Battuta he would meet in India. Rather it was his grandson.)

Ibn Battuta remained in Multan at least two months and perhaps throughout much of the winter of 1333–34.[10] There he had the company of traveling notables from Bukhara, Samarkand, and other cities to the west. Most prominent among them was Khudhawand-Zada Qiwam al-Din, *qadi* of the Chagatay city of Tirmidh. Ibn Battuta had been traveling off and on with this judge, two of his brothers, and a nephew on the journey through Afghanistan. When the intelligence reports on the new visitors reached Muhammad Tughluq, he replied that Qiwam al-Din was to be given special honors. Consequently, there arrived in Multan from Delhi one of the sultan's chamberlains with instructions to accompany the *qadi* and other foreign gentlemen to the capital. Al-Makhdumah Jahan, the sultan's mother, also sent along three eunuchs to escort Qiwam al-Din's wife and children.

No one, however, was to be permitted to proceed to Delhi on pretense of seeking official employment unless he planned to stay permanently. Ibn Battuta was interviewed again: was he serious in his intentions to serve the sultanate? He answered with conviction, and we have no reason to doubt that at this point in his career he was expecting a long residence in India. Nonetheless, his intentions had to be put in writing. "When I told them that I had come to stay they summoned the *qadi* and notaries and drew up a contract binding me and those of my company who wished to remain in India, but," he adds, "some of them refused this engagement."

As another sign of his commitment, he had taken the trouble either in Afghanistan or the Punjab to buy a selection of suitable gifts to present to the emperor at the critical moment of his first audience. His purchases included a load of arrows, several camels, more than thirty horses, and, he recalls vaguely, "white slaves and other goods." The financing of these expensive presents reflected rather ominously on the climate of brash opportunism prevailing in Delhi. It was customary, everyone knew, for Muhammad Tughluq to respond to honorable visitors with gratuities of far larger value, making the symbolic point that he, and no one else, was the wellspring of all good things. Speculating on the likelihood of such unequal exchanges, men with capital advanced funds to newcomers to buy gifts with the promise of a handsome return out of the value of the sultan's reciprocation. Always quick to grasp the local custom, Ibn Battuta took a loan from a Multani entrepreneur to buy part of what he needed. He notes in the *Rihla* that when he later paid the man back, "he made an enormous profit through me and became one of the principal merchants."

Leaving Multan probably some time in the late winter of 1334, Ibn Battuta and the other foreign gentlemen followed the chamberlain and his government retinue along the main military and commercial road leading eastward from the Indus watershed to the valley of the upper Ganges. The route ran the breadth of the high Punjab plain, where dense rice-growing settlements lay along the tributary system that spread like the fingers of many hands to the northeast of the Indus.[11] Ibn Battuta was leading a group of about 40 companions, servants, and slaves. They were, we may assume, mainly the same people who had accompanied him through Afghanistan, including the Egyptian friend al-Tuzari and the young slave woman with the infant daughter she had borne her master in the camp of Tarmashirin Khan.[12] Qadi Qiwam al-Din and his entourage, however, were all the center of official attention. Twenty cooks were even hired to go ahead of the main party each day, set up the evening camp, and greet the judge with a hot meal as soon as he arrived.

The chamberlain might have been advised to take on fewer cooks and a larger body of soldiers to protect his guests. On the morning the caravan left the town of Abohar, Ibn Battuta and 21 others lagged behind in the place for several hours. Finally setting out about midday to catch up with the main group, they were suddenly attacked by 82 Hindu bandits. Only two of the assailants had the advantage of being on horseback, but it was a close call nonetheless.

My companions were men of courage and vigor and we fought stoutly with them, killing one of their horsemen and about twelve of the footsoldiers, and capturing the horse of the former. I was hit by an arrow and my horse by another, but God in His grace preserved me from them, for there is no force in their arrows.

Apparently no force at all, for Ibn Battuta and his friends were certainly not dressed in armor plate. The bandits were soon driven off, and to celebrate victory in the fashion of the time the heads of the 13 slain were cut off, carried to that evening's stopping place, and suspended from the walls of a government fort. The incident was the young visitor's first experience with the limits of imperial power among the rural Hindu population, even near the trunk roads of the sultanate. In his next brush with native insurgents some seven and a half years later, he would not be so lucky.

Ibn Battuta's first impression of Delhi might be clearer to us if he did not describe it in one part of the *Rihla* as "a vast and magnificent city . . . the largest city in India, nay rather the largest of all the cities of Islam in the East" and in another part as "empty and unpopulated save for a few inhabitants." The contradiction probably reflects the *'ulama's* disapproval, which Ibn Battuta shared, of Sultan Muhammad's decision in 1327 to move them to Daulatabad, his new capital in the dreary Deccan. Over about two years large numbers of officials, courtiers, and artisans did relocate. When Ibn Battuta arrived some time in the spring of 1334, part of the intelligentsia was still in Daulatabad. When he tells us the city was "empty and unpopulated", he was probably thinking only of the people that mattered, like a bored social climber at a crowded cocktail party who recalls that "nobody was there." In fact the large lower-class Hindu population of Delhi likely never went anywhere, excepting servants and employees of the state. Indeed about the same time that the sultan imposed his Daulatabad policy he also started building Jahanpanah, his new walled urban complex and palace a few miles northeast of old Delhi. Moreover, by the early 1330s he was giving up his dream of a capital in the center of his empire and permitting groups of unhappy exiles to return north if they wished. There seems little doubt that the city Ibn Battuta saw was in fact the largest in India and growing rapidly to serve the insatiable needs of the governing class.[13]

When he arrived there, the sultan was absent in the Doab region southeast of Delhi. A tax revolt had erupted among the much-burdened peasantry, and Muhammad had been obliged to lead an army out from the capital to crush it. Nevertheless Ibn Battuta and his party went immediately to the new palace in Jahanpanah. There, in the huge wooden-roofed audience chamber called the Hall of a Thousand Pillars (Hazar Sutun), they paid their respects to Khwaja Jahan, the sultan's vizier. They also presented gifts at the palace residence of al-Makhdumah Jahan (the sultan's blind mother), ate a ceremonial meal, and accepted silk robes and other token gratuities befitting their status. At a second audience on the following day the vizier gave Ibn Battuta 2,000 silver dinars to "wash his head," a symbolic gift of welcome proportioned in amount to the visitor's importance. A comfortably furnished house awaited him and his personal retinue in Kil'a Ray Pithora, the ancient Delhi of sandstone buildings and narrow streets clustered around the Quwwat al-Islam and its lofty minaret. In this house he would live during the next several years, passing many hours, we may presume, in the courts and domed arcades of the great mosque.

Until Muhammad Tughluq returned to Delhi, Ibn Battuta had no official appointment. However, the sultan was receiving regular reports on all the foreigners arriving in the capital in his absence. He sent orders to the vizier to give the new man, who had not yet lifted a finger in service to the state, an annual stipend of 5,000 silver dinars to be paid from the revenue of two and a half villages located about 16 miles north of the city.[14] It was customary for state officials, army officers, and special honorees of the sultan to be paid regular allowances from taxes on crops produced in peasant villages rather than directly from the royal treasury. In the areas of North India where the authority of the sultanate was firm, the thousands of rural hamlets were registered, grouped in units of one hundred, and administered at the local level by petty Hindu or Muslim functionaries under the authority of the provincial governors. Grants of revenue from these villages could be awarded, withdrawn, or transferred at the pleasure of the sultan, and they carried no hereditary rights. The grantee did not have to live on his estate (and normally did not) nor take responsibility for the governing of its inhabitants, a task the state assumed directly. The poor farmers who toiled to produce this income had, of course, nothing to say about these arrangements.

Unknown *faqih* that he was, Ibn Battuta's initial emolument did not amount to much by comparison with the revenue estates of the established elite. Nonetheless, while awaiting the emperor's return during the late spring of 1334, he took the trouble to ride out to the North Indian plain to inspect his two and a half villages. The Hindu country folk inhabiting these wretched clusters of mud wall and thatch held no fascination for him. He says nothing in the *Rihla* about the look of the hamlets or their residents, and he probably never bothered to visit them more than once.

Then on 8 June word came that Muhammad Tughluq was camped at a castle just seven miles from the city. On the vizier's orders, Ibn Battuta and the other newcomers went immediately out to the fort to greet the ruler with their gifts of obeisance. In order of their professional eminence each suppliant entered the audience room and was presented to the Master of the World, a tall, robust, white-skinned man seated, his legs tucked beneath him, on a gold-plated throne.[15] This was the critical moment, for the emperor's first reaction to a man could mean the difference between future riches and total, immediate ostracism from the royal court.

> I approached the sultan, who took my hand and shook it, and continuing to hold it addressed me most affably, saying in Persian "This is a blessing; your arrival is blessed; be at ease, I shall be compassionate to you and give you such favors that your fellow-countrymen will hear of it and come to join you." Then he asked me where I came from and I said to him "From the land of the Maghrib" . . . Every time he said any encouraging word to me I kissed his hand, until I had kissed it seven times, and after he had given me a robe of honor I withdrew.

Thus Ibn Battuta jumped the first hurdle into the circle of privilege. The next day he joined the triumphal entry into Delhi, a spectacular cavalcade of festooned elephants and cavalry, Hindu infantry columns, and singing girls. Muhammad Tughluq, the crusher of insurgent peasants, was now the benefactor to his people in the most extravagant tradition of a Hindu king:

> On some of the elephants there were mounted small military catapults, and when the sultan came near the city parcels of gold and silver coins mixed together were thrown from these machines. The men on foot in front of the sultan and the other persons present scrambled for the money, and they kept on scattering it until the procession reached the palace.

Shortly after these events two court officials paid a visit to Ibn Battuta and some of his associates to tell them the emperor was ready to make appointments to various government and religious posts: ministers, secretaries, commanders, judges, and *madrasa* teachers. "Everyone was silent at first," Ibn Battuta remembers, "for what they were wanting was to gain riches and return to their countries." He for one was ready to come forward, declaring that he was descended from a long line of legal scholars and that he would be pleased to serve in some juridical capacity.

Forthwith he and several other notables were led to the Hall of a Thousand Pillars, where Sultan Muhammad awarded him the important office of *qadi* of Delhi. The emperor controlled all appointments to the judiciary, which constituted a branch of government separate from the political administration. Ibn Battuta would serve under the *qadi al-qudat*, or Chief Judge of the realm. Moreover, in a city as large as Delhi he was probably only one of several judges holding comparable positions.[16] His compensation was to be two villages in addition to the ones he already had, carrying a total annual salary of 12,000 silver dinars. He also received 12,000 dinars in cash as an advance bonus, a horse with saddle and bridle, and yet another robe of honor. Such an income was not nearly as large as that of other, more prominent appointees. The average Hindu family, however, lived on about 5 dinars a month; a solider in the royal army was paid 19½.[17] Compared to ordinary folk of Hindustan, the obscure Moroccan *faqih* was about to become a very rich man.

After several years of enjoying the favor of numerous kings and princes purely on the strength of his social status, earnest piety, and bright personality, Ibn Battuta was now walking into circumstances far more promising than anything he had known before. Muhammad Tughluq's policy was to pack his government with foreign professionals on whose personal loyalty he thought he could rely. Alien origin had become a more important criterion for office than distinction and experience. Only such circumstances can explain this stranger from the Far West of Islam being handed a magistracy whose responsibilities should have put him way out of his depth. Since leaving Morocco, he had spent hardly any time in sustained study of the law, excepting his brief sojourn in Damascus and his months in Mecca. He had had virtually no experience as a jurisconsult or sitting judge. Persian was the language of administrative and legal affairs in the sultanate, yet he did not, as he pointed out to his new master, speak it well at all. He also admitted that, as a Maghribi, he was trained in the Maliki *madhhab*, whereas almost all *shari'a* decisions in India were founded on the Hanafi school. Very few people from Maliki countries lived in India, so there could hardly be much work to do. The sultan dismissed all these objections and appointed two Persian-speaking Hanafi scholars to serve as his "substitutes." Their job was presumably to do the day-to-day work of hearing cases of religious infraction or civil disputes among Muslims, the normal responsibilities of a *qadi*. "They will be guided by your advice," the emperor charged his new magistrate, "and you will be the one who signs all the documents."

Ibn Battuta's appointment to what can only be characterized as a sinecure[18] supports the complaint of contemporary critics that the official *'ulama* of the sultanate, comprising both the judiciary and the various state ministries, were on the whole a mediocre, self-interested, and acutely insecure group of men, more so than in other Muslim states of the time, and more so under Muhammad Tughluq than his predecessors. The emperor's method of governing was to mobilize the skills and energies of the learned classes in the interests of his personal despotism. He demanded that the *'ulama* endorse his every scheme. He even routed the most saintly, apolitical Sufis out of their lodges, dispersing them to the provinces to propagate the faith under his personal orders. Though publicly he showed respect for the *shari'a* and the legal scholars (on a few occasions submitting with symbolic humility to a *qadi*'s unfavorable judgment in a case against the state), he curtailed the independence of his judges and controlled their legal opinions more closely than did other Muslim rulers of the time.

Among officers of state, the sultan's energy, wilfulness, and fabulous generosity invited toadyism and corruption. On the other hand, the *'ulama*, though not as a group highly distinguished, leaned to rigidity and ultra-conservatism in their Sunni orthodoxy, an attitude brought on partly by Islam's precarious dominance in an overwhelmingly infidel land. Consequently, the sultan's continuing flirtations with unacceptable, even pagan, philosophies, his strange reform ideas, and finally his failure to hold on to all the territory won for the faith in South India produced a swell of outrage, private mutterings, and secret resistance. Muhammad was undeterred. "My remedy for rebels, opponents, disobedient persons and evil-wishers is the sword," he says in a hypothetical conversation with the chronicler Barani. "I will continue punishing and striking with my sword till it either cuts or misses. The more the people oppose me, the greater will be my punishments."[19] Ibn Battuta indeed bears witness to a desperate crescendo of brutality far worse than anything he had seen in other lands.

In spite of all that we have related of his humility, his sense of fairness, his compassion for the needy, and his extraordinary liberality, the sultan was far too free in shedding blood . . . [He] used to punish small faults and great, without respect of persons, whether men of learning or piety or noble descent. Every day there are brought to the audience-hall hundreds of people, chained, pinioned, and fettered, and those who are for execution are executed, those for torture tortured, and those for beating beaten.

Open-hearted, eager to please, and far too gregarious for his own good, the young *qadi* soon found himself enmeshed in the morbid, dangerous politics of the imperial court. The sultan remained in Delhi only about seven months — from June 1334 to the following January. During this period neither Ibn Battuta nor his two "substitutes" got around to hearing any legal cases. Rather he occupied his time attending at court or accompanying his master on the great gaudy hunting expeditions for which all Turkish and Mongol warrior kings were known. These colossal promenades in the Delhi hinterland required the participation of almost the entire ruling establishment. Courtiers and high officials were expected to purchase their own outing equipment, as it were, in diminutive imitation of the sultan's splendid encampment. Like everyone worthy of esteem, Ibn Battuta felt obliged to buy a large tent with a white fabric enclosure, together with food, utensils, clothing, carpets, animals, and a corps of servants sufficient to haul and supervise all this matériel. A team of eight men had to be hired to carry the *dula*, or decorated palanquin, in which a notable rode when not preferring his horse or elephant. In the *Rihla* Ibn Battuta makes much of the "vigor and energy" he showed in always being ready to leave Delhi the same day the sultan did and how he was honored during these excursions with invitations to sit or ride in close proximity to the Shadow of God.

Keeping up with the ruling class of India, however, was frighteningly expensive. Like the Turko–Mongol states, the sultanate was an extremely personal system of power. Bonds of loyalty and respect between social groups were maintained through a chain of favor starting with the sultan and extending downward through the political ranks to the lowliest servant. What the ruler expended in gifts and stipends his officeholders were expected to give back in future presents to him or redistribute to their own servants, clients, and suppliers. This medieval version of "trickle down theory" kept the political system reasonably stable, but it also put tremendous pressure on men of position to spend freely. Spectacular donations and purchases strengthened a man's authority over those below him and his prestige among those above. Caution and frugality invited scorn. Any temptation to invest in long-term capital enterprise or save for a rainy day was easily resisted, for the state could part a man from his riches with devastating suddenness. Everyone in the elite circles, and especially the governors and senior military officers, were thus encouraged to compete feverishly with one another in stupendous, ceaseless spending. "If one of the nobles bestowed fifty horses in his wine party and gave robes to two hundred persons," says Barani, "another noble hearing this would feel jealous, and would try to give away a hundred horses and to bestow robes on five hundred persons."[20]

Ibn Battuta was not of course in the same league with the great commanders of the realm, but he lost no time piling up debts to finance his gifts to the sovereign and a properly luxurious household. He confesses frankly in the *Rihla* that he developed a reputation for extravagance and that the sultan was well aware of it. We should not conclude, however, that he was necessarily a bigger spender than other men of comparable status. He admits freely of his prodigality, not to confess humbly to a bad habit, but to show that he lived generously and expansively as befitting a *qadi* of Delhi. Nonetheless, he had to find a way to pay off the merchants who had staked him to his début in the capital because they were preparing to leave the country on a commercial venture. The amount in question was 55,000 silver dinars. The *Rihla* rather tires the reader with its lengthy description of his strategies for getting Muhammad Tughluq to pay his bills for him, suggesting that he spent a good part of his first half year in Delhi preoccupied with his personal finances. To broach the subject before his master he composed a praise poem to him in Arabic that ended, candidly enough, with the lines:

Make speed to aid the votary to thy shrine,
And pay his debt — the creditors are dunning.

The sultan was pleased with the ode and agreed to pay, but the disbursement from the treasury was held up. Ibn Battuta then got his creditors to make an appeal to Muhammad on his behalf. Success again, but payment was delayed a second time because of certain procedural improprieties involving another official. Ibn Battuta appealed once more, this time sending the sultan three camels, two gilded saddles, and plates of sweets. At long last the money was released, not only the 55,000 dinars for the debt but also the 12,000 the sultan had earlier agreed to give him.

By the time all this was settled Muhammad Tughluq was preparing to leave the capital once again. Sometime in 1334 rebellion had broken out in Ma'bar, the Tamil-speaking region in the far southeast of the subcontinent that had been annexed to the empire by Muhammad Tughluq's father only eleven years earlier. The leader of the rising was not a Hindu prince but Jalal al-Din Ahsan Shah, the sultan's own governor. Rallying the support of the Muslim *amirs* and soldiers under his authority, he proclaimed himself Sultan of Ma'bar. Despite the political perils of campaigning 1,300 miles from the capital, Muhammad mustered an army to march to Daulatabad, then on to Madurai, chief city of Ma'bar. Ibn Battuta expected to be ordered to go along on the expedition. To his surprise and relief, the sultan instructed him to remain in Delhi and, aside from his judgeship, appointed him administrator of the mausoleum of Qutb al-Din Mubarak, the Khalji sultan who reigned from 1316 to 1320 and under whom Muhammad Tughluq had entered military service as a young man. Just before the royal departure on 5 January 1335,[21] Ibn Battuta gained one more audience with his master, this time persuading him to allot extra funds for the upkeep of the tomb, not to mention money to repair his own residence.

During the next two and a half years, he resided in Delhi, refurbishing his house, building a little mosque next to it, and running up more debts. He even spent, much to his later embarrassment, 1,060 dinars a friend had left in his trust before leaving with the sultan. He and his substitutes may have heard legal cases in Delhi during this period, but he makes no mention of them. His principal interest seems to have been the mausoleum. The burial place of a sultan was often an important royal endowment. It was first of all a mosque but might also have associated with it a college, a Sufi retreat, and facilities to dispense food and lodging to wayfarers and the needy. Ibn Battuta had to supervise all these functions. He recalls that this complex employed 460 persons, including Qur'an reciters, teachers, theological students, Sufis, mosque officials, clerks, and various classes of cooks, servants, and guards. All of these people were supported from the revenue of 30 villages whose crops were assigned to the tomb and with funds allocated directly from the state treasury. He also busied himself overseeing construction of a dome over the sepulchre.[22]

His responsibilities were made even greater by the disastrous famine that hit North India in 1335 and lasted seven years. Barani reports that "thousands upon thousands of people perished of want,"[23] and Ibn Battuta speaks of Indians being reduced to eating animal skins, rotten meat, and even human flesh. As the famine became general and starving country folk poured into Delhi to find relief, Ibn Battuta distributed quantities of food from the stores allocated to the mausoleum. He presents a picture of himself in this work as an exemplary administrator, mentioning that the sultan sent him a robe of honor from Daulatabad after hearing from one of his officers about the fine job the Maghribi was doing dispensing welfare to the stricken.

Some time during this period, probably in the summer of 1335 or 1336, he left Delhi for two months to make an official inquiry in the region of Amroha, a town located across the Ganges about 85 miles east of Delhi.[24] He traveled with a proper retinue, including 30 companions and "two brothers, accomplished singers, who used to sing to me on the way." Charges had been made that 'Aziz al-Khammar, the district's tyrannical tax-collector, was holding back on grain shipments assigned from a number of villages to the mausoleum. Meeting first with the notables of Amroha, Ibn Battuta learned that al-Khammar was to be found in a village on the Sarju River, requiring a journey of another 190 miles or so eastward across the north Gangetic plain.[25] Finally catching up with his man, he succeeded in having him arrange for transport of a large quantity of grain to Delhi.

But more revealing of the young *qadi*'s authority was his official investigation of a violent feud that had broken out between al-Khammar and the *amir* of the military district. Al-Khammar presented a number of complaints against the officer, including the charge that one of the *amir*'s servants, a man named al-Rida, had broken into his house, stolen 5,000 dinars, and drunk some wine.

I interrogated al-Rida on this subject and he said to me "I have never drunk wine since I left Multan, which is eight years ago." I said to him "Then you did drink it in Multan?" and when he said "Yes" I ordered him to be given eighty lashes and imprisoned him on the charges preferred, because of the presumptive evidence against him.

Ibn Battuta was not behaving with arbitrary severity here. Rather he was imposing the precise *shari'a* punishment for imbibing wine — 80 lashes, no more, no less. It was a religious infraction falling within a *qadi*'s normal authority. On the charge of burglary, however, the man was to suffer the penalty of the sultan's law and thus sent off to Delhi in chains. If Ibn Battuta sentenced other malefactors to the lash while he served in Delhi, we have no way of knowing, for this is the only judgment he reports having made during his years in India.

Some time in 1337 or 1338 the sultan returned north. Because of the famine that still raged around Delhi, he apparently stopped there only briefly before moving to a temporary capital at a place on the west bank of the Ganges some distance north of the town of Kanauj (Qinnawj).[26] Intending to remain there several months, he ordered construction of a modest palace and called it Sargadwari, the Gate of Paradise. It was hardly so happy a residence, for the expedition against Ma'bar had ended in total failure. Muhammad had advanced as far as the central Deccan when an epidemic broke out among his troops, forcing him to return to Daulatabad and leaving the traitorous Ahsan Shah still on his throne in Madurai. Not only did the embattled sultan lose any hope of preventing the secession of Ma'bar, but between the time he left Delhi and returned to the north, several other defecting Turkish or Afghan commanders raised rebellions, effectively terminating imperial rule over much of South and Central India.

The empire disintegrating around him, the sultan summoned

many of his Delhi officials to join him at Sargadwari, Ibn Battuta among them. Some time after the *qadi* and his entourage arrived there, 'Ain al-Mulk, the Indo–Muslim governor of the province immediately east of the Ganges, revolted out of fear that the emperor wrongly suspected him of disloyalty. After boldly raiding the army's stocks of elephants and horses, 'Ain al-Mulk, four of his brothers, and a force of Hindu soldiers escaped eastward across the river to safety. At this point the sultan contemplated marching back to Delhi to reinforce his depleted army and deal with the rebels at some later time. Ibn Battuta, who was in the thick of the crisis and an eye witness to all that occurred, reports that Muhammad's commanders urged him to strike back at the rebels before they had time to consolidate their position. If Muhammad Tughluq was a disaster as a politician, he had proven himself a skillful soldier and tactician from the time of his father's reign. Taking his officers' advice, he advanced by forced march along the west bank of the Ganges to Kanauj to secure the town ahead of 'Ain al-Mulk. Ibn Battuta was traveling in the vanguard under the command of the vizier Khwaja Jahan. In the meantime 'Ain al-Mulk and his company crossed the river again. Foolishly overestimating his own military talents and the likelihood of defections from the sultan's ranks, 'Ain al-Mulk attacked the imperial vanguard near Kanauj in the early hours of the morning.

The troops, then, drawing their swords, advanced towards their adversaries and a hot battle ensued. The sultan gave orders that his army's password should be "Dilhi" [Delhi] and "Ghazna"; each one of them therefore on meeting a horseman said to him "Dilhi" and if he received the answer "Ghazna" he knew that he was one of his side and if not he engaged him. The aim of the rebel had been to attack only the place where the sultan was, but the guide led him astray and he attacked the place of the vizier instead . . . In the vizier's regiment there were Persians, Turks and Khurasanians; these, being enemies of the Indians, put up a vigorous fight and though the rebel's army contained about 50,000 men they were put to flight at the rising of the day.

Numerous rebel soldiers drowned trying to reach the east bank of the river; others were captured, including 'Ain al-Mulk himself, and brought before the sultan. "Muleteers, peddlars, slaves and persons of no importance" were released, but on the very afternoon of the battle 62 of the traitorous leaders were thrown to the elephants. "They started cutting them in pieces with the blades placed on their tusks and throwing some of them in the air and catching them," Ibn Battuta remembers, "and all the time the bugles and fifes and drums were being sounded." 'Ain al-Mulk must have expected a similar fate, or worse. But what Muhammad Tughluq could take away he could also give. Convinced that his governor had acted rashly "through mistake," as Barani has it,[27] the emperor pardoned him and gave him the modest post of supervising the royal gardens in Delhi.

Despite his total victory, Muhammad returned to his capital in a fury of despair.[28] The famine raged on, Bengal had broken away from the sultanate or was about to, other revolts were igniting here and there, and all his dreams of a tidy, productive empire were falling to ruin. Thus he lashed out at whatever enemies, real or imagined, happened to be at hand. In such a sinister environment as this, only the most circumspect, inconspicuous officeholder might expect to survive indefinitely. Eager, sociable young *qadis*, on the other hand, were likely to make a disastrous slip sooner or later.

It might well have happened earlier than it did. At some point during his residence in Delhi, Ibn Battuta married a woman named Hurnasab and had a daughter by her. As usual we learn almost nothing in the *Rihla* about his domestic affairs, except that this woman was a daughter of Ahsan Shah, leader of the Ma'bar rebellion, and a sister of Sharif Ibrahim, a court official and governor who had plotted a rebellion and was subsequently executed in the palace while Ibn Battuta was in attendance there. Although the *Rihla* gives no hint that his marriage to Hurnasab brought him under suspicion, having family ties with men guilty of high treason was hardly an advantage at the court of Muhammad Tughluq. Ibn Battuta would later in his travels be a guest of one of Ahsan Shah's successors in Ma'bar, suggesting that he may well have had some concealed sympathy for the rebellion there.[29]

The event that finally got him into trouble was his friendship with Shaykh Shihab al-Din, a venerable Sufi originally from Khurasan. It was a long-held tradition among the most pious and principled divines of Islam to shun relationships with secular rulers on the argument that such collaboration would taint them and detract from their total service to God. Nizam al-Din Awliya, the illustrious master of the Chishti brotherhood who died eight years before Ibn Battuta came to India, bluntly cold-shouldered both Khalji and Tughluq emperors at every opportunity. "The house of this humble one has two doors," Nizam al-Din is known to have said. "If the Sultan enters through one, I shall go out by the other."[30] Such aloofness as this was quite unacceptable to Muhammad Tughluq, whose political theory included the idea that Sufi ascetics and ivory-tower theologians should submit to his will as much as the official *'ulama*.

Whether Shihab al-Din was a Chishti or not is unclear, but twice he brashly refused to obey his sovereign's commands. In the first incident he spurned a government post offered to him. In retaliation Muhammad had the *shaykh*'s beard plucked out hair by hair, then banished him to Daulatabad. Some time later he had him restored to favor and appointed him to an office, which in that instance Shihab al-Din agreed to accept. When Muhammad went off on the Ma'bar expedition, Shihab al-Din established a farm near the Yamuna River a few miles from Delhi and there dug himself a large underground house complete, as Ibn Battuta describes it, with "chambers, storerooms, an oven and a bath." Returned to the capital, the sultan ordered Shihab al-Din to appear at court, but the troglodyte refused to emerge. When Muhammad had him summarily arrested, the *shaykh* retorted that the sultan was an oppressor and a tyrant. The court *'ulama* pleaded with him to recant. When he would not, he was tortured in the most heinous manner, then beheaded.

Ibn Battuta, by contrast, was hardly the sort to martyr himself for rigid principles. The odor of politics did not bother him at all, and official service and reward were his ambition. Unfortunately, he had made the mistake of going out one day to see Shihab al-Din and his marvelous cave. Following the *shaykh*'s arrest, the sultan demanded a list of all who had visited him, and the Maghribi's name was on it. "Thereupon," Ibn Battuta recalls, "the sultan gave orders that four of his slaves should remain constantly beside me in the audience-hall, and customarily when he takes this action with anyone it rarely happens that the person escapes." For nine days Ibn Battuta remained under guard, imagining in cold horror his short final journey to the main gate of the Jahanpanah palace where executions were carried out and the corpses left to lie three days in public view.

> The day on which they began to guard me was a Friday and God Most High inspired me to recite His words *Sufficient for us is God and excellent the Protector*. I recited them that day 33,000 times and

passed the night in the audience-hall. I fasted five days on end, reciting the Qur'an from cover to cover each day, and tasting nothing but water. After five days I broke my fast and then continued to fast for another four days on end.

Then, just after Shihab al-Din was executed, the terrified *qadi*, much to his surprise, was suddenly released and allowed to go home.

Shaken by this dreadful experience, he secured permission a short time later to withdraw from his official duties and seclude himself with Kamal al-Din 'Abdallah al-Ghari, a well-known Sufi who occupied a hermitage, indeed another cave, on the outskirts of Delhi. Kamal al-Din was a rigorous ascetic, living in extreme poverty and performing awesome feats of self-denial. Ibn Battuta had gone into brief periods of spiritual retreat previously in his career, but this time he threw himself into the abstinent life, ridding himself of his possessions, donning the clothes of a beggar, and fasting to the point of collapse. He remained in these penitent circumstances for five months, probably unsure of what he would do next. Apparently he had decided at least that life with Muhammad Tughluq was far too dangerous to continue.

Meanwhile, the sultan went on a military tour to Sind and from the town of Sehwan summoned his *qadi* to appear before him. Ibn Battuta presumably made the journey immediately, though the *Rihla* has no comment on it or the route.[31] When he arrived, Muhammad received him "with the greatest kindness and solicitude" and pressed him to return to his judgeship and rejoin the palace circle. Determined to avoid that fate at all costs, Ibn Battuta countered with a request to make the *hajj*, the most persuasive reason he could come up with for getting permission to leave the country. Much to his relief, the sultan agreed. For several weeks thereafter, beginning in June 1341, he resided in another Sufi *khanqa*, this time progressively extending his periods of self-denial until finally he could fast for 40 days at a stretch.

Then suddenly he was called into the royal presence again, this time to hear an astounding proposal. Knowing his "love of travel and sightseeing," the sultan wished to make his North African *qadi* ambassador to the Mongol court of China. His mission would be to accompany 15 Chinese envoys back to their homeland and to carry shiploads of gifts to the Yuan emperor. Ibn Battuta was preparing to leave for Mecca and until that moment probably had no thought of traveling eastwards of India. Now he was being handed an opportunity, not only to get away from Muhammad Tughluq and the gloom of Delhi, but to visit the further lands of Islam and beyond — and to do it in grander style than he had ever traveled before. It was an offer much too promising to refuse.

Notes

1. Quoted in P. Hardy, *Historians of Medieval India* (London, 1960), p. 98.

2. Ibn Fadl Allah al-'Umari, *A Fourteenth Century Arab Account of India under Sultan Muhammad bin Tughluq*, trans. and ed. Iqtidar Husain Siddiqi and Qazi Mohammad Ahmad (Aligarh, 1971), p. 36.

3. Since IB lived and traveled in India for about a decade and since he and his editor expected literate Moroccans to be particularly interested in facts about that distant land, he devotes nearly a fifth of the *Rihla* to a description of the history, political affairs, social customs, class relations, and Muslim religious life of the sultanate and other regions of the subcontinent. The *Rihla* is one of a very few contemporary literary sources on fourteenth-century India, especially the life and times of Muhammad Tughluq. IB is indeed the sole source of information on a number of historical events, including some of the rebellions against the sultan. He also gives a brief dynastic history of the kingdom, based, as he reveals, on information supplied to him mainly by Kamal al-Din ibn al-Burhan, the chief judge. Where IB's reporting has been checked against the other contemporary sources, he has been found reasonably accurate. For the modern historian, however, the value of the narrative has been restricted by the lack of a clear chronological framework and almost no references to either absolute or relative dates. The other chronicles of the time suffer from the same deficiency.

   Since the *Rihla* is a book for Muslims about Muslims, indeed literate Muslims, it is an inadequate source on Hindu society and civilization. Though IB does describe certain Hindu customs and gives some examples of the interpenetration of Hindu and Muslim culture, he is generally disinclined to examine the life of Muslim peasant folk, much less infidel peasant folk. Despite the thread of amiable tolerance that runs through the *Rihla*, IB's perspective is identical with that of the other Muslim writers of the time. "For them, indeed as for Muslim historians outside India," Peter Hardy writes, "the only significant history is the history of the Muslim community; they are historians of the *res gestae* of the politically prominent members of a group united by ties of common faith rather than historians of the whole people of the area controlled by the Delhi sultan." *Historians of Medieval India*, p. 114.

4. Muhammad Tughluq was also suspected of being under the pernicious influence of a disciple of Ibn Taymiyya (d. 1328), a famous theologian and exponent of the Hanbali *madhhab* who had lived in Damascus. Ibn Taymiyya incurred the opposition of the orthodox scholars by his critical rejection of Sufi mysticism and by his insistence on the right of *ijtihad*, that is, the freedom to inquire into the foundations of particular points of law even where an authoritative *madhhab* decision already existed. IB claims to have heard him preach in Damascus in 1326 and characterizes him as having, according to Gibb's translation, "some kink in his brain." Gb, vol. 1, p. 135. The validity of IB's remark is examined by D. P. Little, "Did Ibn Taymiyya Have a Screw Loose?" *Studia Islamica* 41 (1975): 39–111.

5. Peter Jackson links the plan for the conquest of Chagatay with an abortive invasion of Kashmir, called the Qarachil expedition. "The Mongols and the Delhi Sultanate in the Reign of Muhammad Tughluq (1325–51)," *Central Asiatic Journal* 19 (1975): 128–43.

6. Ziya al-Din Barani, *Tarikh-i-Firuz Shahi*, trans. and ed. H. M. Elliot and John Dowson, *The History of India as Told by its Own Historians*, vol. 3 (Allahabad, 1964), p. 236. Barani was a courtier at the court of Muhammad Tughluq and perhaps an acquaintance of IB. Under the patronage of Firuz Shah, Muhammad's successor, he wrote a history of the sultanate from 1266 to 1351. He interprets each reign in the light of his own orthodox morality and finds Muhammad Tughluq badly wanting. Barani does not mention IB.

7. Quoted in K. M. Ashraf, *Life and Conditions of the People of Hindustan*, 2nd edn (New Delhi, 1970), p. 150.

8. See Chapter 8, note 25.

9. IB states that his first visit to Sind took place shortly after the suppression of a local uprising, the Sumra revolt, by the military governor Imad al-Mulk Sartiz. This official was not appointed, however, until about 1337. Peter Jackson, "The Mongols and India (1221–1351)," Ph.D. diss., Cambridge University, 1977, pp. 225–26. IB may therefore be confusing this alleged tour of Sind with the trip he took there from Delhi shortly before July 1341. He also says that he visited Sind for the first time during the "hottest period of the summer." Such a remark fits poorly into the chronological scheme of his arrival in India, which he claims began on 12 September 1333. There is no evidence that he remained in the Punjab and Sind from then until the following summer. The 1341 visit, however, apparently did take place in early summer, which was indeed the time of the scorching southwesterly winds. Jackson develops a line of argument about IB's chronology to suggest that he did not visit China at all, that he stayed in India until 1346–47 (747–48 A.H.), and that he left there definitively by way of an overland route through Sind and Khurasan. Jackson admits, however, that if IB did pass through Sind as late as 1346–47, Sartiz was no longer governor there, having been transferred to the Deccan in 1345 (p. 226). Thus the Sumra rebellion, for which IB offers the only description, may well have taken place in 1341 rather than 1333. M. R. Haig discusses IB's itinerary in Sind and struggles unsuccessfully with the chronological difficulties. "Ibnu Batuta in Sindh," *Journal of the Royal Asiatic Society* 19 (1887): 393–412. C. F. Beckingham suggests the Sind visit may have taken place in 1341 rather than 1333–34. "Ibn Battuta in Sind" in Hamida Khuhro (ed.), *Sind through the Centuries: Proceedings of an International Seminar, Karachi 1975* (Karachi, 1981), pp. 139–42.

10. IB states that he had been in Multan for two months when the sultan's chamberlain arrived. Gb, vol. 3, p. 606. If he did not in fact visit Sind at this time, he may have stayed quite a bit more than two months in Multan.

11. A description of the route during the Sultanate period is found in A. M. Stow, "The Road between Delhi and Multan," *Panjab University Historical Society* 3 (1914–15): 26–37.

12. He mentions in connection with his arrival on the Indus that he had about 40 people with him. This company probably numbered more or less the same on the continuing trip to Delhi.

13. Mahdi Husain, *Tughluq Dynasty* (Calcutta, 1963), pp. 145–75. The author presents a lengthy analysis of the transfer of the capital and its consequences for Delhi. He suggests that the destruction of Delhi alleged by Barani and others has been greatly exaggerated. Other modern historians disagree.

14. IB names the villages, which have been identified by Gibb (Gb, vol. 3, p. 741) and Mahdi Husain (MH, p. 122).

15. Mahdi Husain (*Tughluq Dynasty*, p. 480) presents a description of the sultan compiled from various medieval sources.

16. On the general organization of the judicial system, S. M. Ikram, *Muslim Rule in India and Pakistan*, 2nd edn (Lahore, 1966), pp. 149–52; and A. B. M. Habibullah, *The Foundation of Muslim Rule in India*, 2nd edn. (Allahabad, 1961), pp. 271–79.

17. Ashraf, *Life and Conditions*, p. 291.

18. On sinecurism among the religious, judicial, and educational officeholders of fifteenth-century Egypt see Carl F. Petry, *The Civilian Elite of Cairo in the later Middle Ages* (Princeton, N.J., 1981), pp. 201, 319.

19. Quoted in Mohammad Habib and Afsar Umar Salim Khan, *The Political Theory of the Delhi Sultanate* (Allahabad, n.d.), p. 159.

20. Quoted in M. Mujeeb, *The Indian Muslims* (Montreal, 1967), p. 209.

21. IB gives the departure date as 9 Jumada I, or 5 January 1335. All recent authorities are agreed that the Ma'bar rebellion broke out in 1334, and Mahdi Husain (*Tughluq Dynasty*, p. 243) affirms that Muhammad Tughluq must have left Delhi the following year. Unfortunately, in a note in his translation of the narrative (MH, p. 140), he mistakenly converts 9 Jumada I to 21 October 1341. Gibb (Gb, vol. 3, p. 758) repeats the error.

22. The tomb of Qutb al-Din Mubarak no longer exists.

23. Barani, *Tarikh-i-Firuz Shahi*, p. 238.

24. IB states that he made this trip during "the period of the rains," that is, during the summer or early fall monsoon season. Although he says nothing in the context of his years in Delhi about excursions other than the trips to Kanauj (see below) and Sind, he mentions later in the *Rihla* of having visited Gwalior, a city about 150 miles south of the capital, sometime between 1334 and 1341.

25. IB's Saru River is the Sarju. MH, p. 145n.

26. Gibb (Gb, vol. 3, p. 698) and Mahdi Husain (*Tughluq Dynasty*, pp. 254, 658) agree that the sultan established his temporary capital on the Ganges in 1338. Jackson ("The Mongols and the Delhi Sultanate," p. 149) suggests 1337 or 1338. IB states that Muhammad was absent from Delhi on the Ma'bar expedition for two and a half years from January 1335.

27. Barani, *Tarikh-i-Firuz Shahi*, p. 249.

28. Mahdi Husain (*Tughluq Dynasty*, p. 254) asserts that Muhammad Tughluq stayed at Sargadwari from late 1338 until mid 1341, then returned to Delhi. IB also implies that the sultan remained there two and a half years (Gb, vol. 3, p. 698), but he does not make clear how much of that time he spent with the royal party. Mahdi Husain (*Tughluq Dynasty*, p. 256) dates the 'Ain al-Mulk rebellion to 1340. A date of mid 1341 for the sultan's return to Delhi, however, does not accord well with IB's statement that he visited him in Sind sometime before July of that year.

29. Mahdi Husain (*Tughluq Dynasty*, pp. ii, iii) speculates on this possibility.

30. Aziz Ahmad, "The Sufi and the Sultan in Pre-Mughal Muslim India," *Der Islam* 38 (1962): 147.

31. See note 9.

10 Malabar and the Maldives

> And in this land of Malabar there are Moors in great
> numbers . . . They are rich, and live well, they hold all the
> sea trade and navigation in such sort that if the King of
> Portugal had not discovered India, Malabar would already
> have been in the hands of the Moors, and would have had
> a Moorish King.[1]
>
> Duarte Barbosa

About 1340, 15 ambassadors representing Toghon Temur, the Mongol emperor of the Yuan Dynasty of China, arrived at the court of Delhi.[2] Commercial ties between China and the sultanate may have been the main business of the mission, since the Yuan emperors were pursuing a vigorous overseas trade policy. Ibn Battuta's explanation of the event is that the delegation came to seek permission of Muhammad Tughluq to have a Buddhist shrine constructed at a town about 80 miles east of Delhi.[3] The sultan declined to authorize the project, and this was the message he wished his special envoy to carry to Peking. Ibn Battuta claims that the sultan chose him for this honor because he knew his *qadi* loved "to travel and go abroad." This is hardly a convincing rationale for appointing an ambassador to the largest and most populous kingdom in the world. Perhaps Muhammad thought the peripatetic Moroccan would have the energy and motivation to persevere in the mission despite the hardships of a long sea voyage. And perhaps he wished to maximize the prestige of the embassy by selecting an Arab, a pious scholar of the Prophet's race, to represent him. (Ibn Battuta was an Arab in his literate culture, though Berber in ethnic origin.)

Whatever the reason, the ex-*qadi* was taking on a greater weight of official responsibility than he ever had before. Not only was he required to get himself to Peking and back, he also had to transport, and safeguard with his life, an entire caravan of royal presents for the Yuan emperor. The Chinese emissaries had earlier arrived in Delhi with 100 slaves and cartloads of fine clothing, brocade, musk, and swords, compliments of Toghon Temur. Muhammad Tughluq naturally felt obliged to reciprocate with an even more magnificent array of gifts. The list included 200 Hindu slaves, songstresses, and dancers, 15 pages, 100 horses, and wondrous quantities of choice textiles, robes, dishware, and swords. Ibn Battuta left Delhi at the head of his mission in late summer, probably 2 August 1341.[4] His companions included the 15 Chinese gentlemen, who were returning home, and two officials of the sultanate besides himself. One of them was Zahir al-Din al-Zanjani, a scholar of Persian origin. The other was a eunuch named Kafur, who held the title of *shurbdar*, or cupbearer, and had day-to-day responsibility for overseeing the slaves and the bullock carts laden with the imperial presents. Al-Tuzari was also along, as well as other unnamed individuals among Ibn Battuta's personal friends, old comrades, and concubines. Muhammad al-Harawi, one of the sultan's *amirs*, led a troop of 1,000 horse to escort the embassy from Delhi to the coast. The plan of travel was to march southward along the government trunk road to Daulatabad, then make for the western coast at Cambay (Kinbaya), the chief port of Gujarat. From there the mission would take ship for Calicut on the Malabar coast of South India. At Calicut they would board ocean-going junks to carry them across the Bay of Bengal to China. The landward itinerary from Delhi to Cambay was hardly the most direct route possible, as Daulatabad lay some 240 miles southeast of that port. Sultan Muhammad may have given his envoy official business in Daulatabad that the *Rihla* fails to mention, or perhaps he instructed the caravan to make an appearance there as a symbolic show of Delhi's continuing authority in the Deccan.

If Ibn Battuta had undertaken this mission eight or ten years earlier, that authority would have been relatively secure and the journey all the way to Gujarat accomplished in safety. By the 1340s, however, the conditions of travel, even under armed escort, had changed drastically. Seven years of famine, repeated rebellion, and disastrous government had left the rural areas of what remained of the empire more and more difficult to control. Hindu insurgency and brigandage had become endemic outside the walls of the garrison towns, even in the Ganges heartland. Traffic on the high roads connecting the major cities was even more susceptible to interference than when Ibn Battuta had his first encounter with Hindu dacoits on his way to Delhi in 1334.

The embassy had left the capital only a few days when it ran into trouble and came near to losing its leader. Arriving at Koil (modern Aligarh), a city in the Doab plain about 75 miles southeast of Delhi, a report reached the company that a force of Hindu insurgents was laying siege to the nearby town of Jalali. Riding immediately to the rescue, al-Harawi's cavalry escort caught the rebels by surprise. Although outnumbered four to one, the troops made short bloody work of the assailants, killing, according to Ibn Battuta, all 4,000 of them and capturing their horses and weapons. The imperial force lost 78 men, including Kafur, the cupbearer. At this point Ibn Battuta decided that he should send a messenger to inform the sultan about what happened and ask him to dispatch a replacement for the unfortunate Kafur. In the meantime the mission would wait in Koil for a reply from Delhi. Since the district was apparently in a state of alarm and Hindu bands continued to raid the outskirts of Jalali, al-Harawi and his men joined forces with the local commander to undertake counter-insurgency sweeps through the local countryside.

Riding into the Doab one morning in the heat of August, Ibn Battuta and a party of his comrades intercepted a rebel band that was just then retreating after an attack on one of the villages near Jalali. The Muslims gave chase but in the confusion of the pursuit Ibn Battuta and five of his men became separated from their companions. Suddenly a force of Hindus on foot and horse sprang from a wood. The six men scattered and Ibn Battuta found himself alone. Ten of the assailants pursued him at full gallop across the fields, then all but three fell away. Twice he was forced to stop and dismount, first to pick a stone from his horse's hoof, then to recover one of his swords, which had bounced out of its scabbard. His pursuers closing in, he eluded them by driving away his mount and hiding at the bottom of a deep ditch.

When his enemies had finally given up trying to find him, he started off on foot to find his way back to safety. Going only a short distance, he was confronted again, this time by 40 bowmen, who promptly robbed him of his remaining sword and everything else he had with him except his shirt, pants, and cloak. The brigands then led him to their camp and put him under guard. Ibn Battuta did not speak any Hindi, but he succeeded in communicating with two Indo–Muslims in the camp who knew some Persian, telling them a little about himself but wisely concealing his status as an officer of Delhi. The two men let him know that, whoever he was, he was certainly to be killed, and it soon became apparent that his three guards, one of them an old man, had been instructed to do the job whenever they were so disposed. The assassins, however, seemed to lack resolve. After keeping their prisoner in a cave throughout the night, they returned in the morning to the robber camp, which was by this time deserted. Here they sat throughout the day, the captors working up the nerve to do their deed, Ibn Battuta sweating in mortal fear that each breath was to be his last. Then at nightfall three of the bandits suddenly returned and demanded to know why the prisoner had not been dispatched. The guards had no satisfactory answer, but one of the young brigands, perhaps admitting the pointlessness of executing a man who had already given up his possessions, suggested that as far as he was concerned the foreigner could go free. Jumping at this change of events, Ibn Battuta offered the man his expensive tunic in thanks, accepted an old blue loincloth in return, and bolted into a nearby bamboo forest.

Alive but alone again and completely lost in a fairly heavily populated district whose hostility toward representatives of Muhammad Tughluq was all too apparent, he wandered the countryside for six days, avoiding villages, sleeping under trees or in abandoned houses, and subsisting on well water and herbs. At one point he eluded a band of 50 armed Hindus by hiding all day in a cotton field. On the seventh day, exhausted and starving, he entered a village in desperation, but when he begged for something to eat, one of the locals threatened him with a sword, searched him, and stole his shirt.

Then on the eighth day salvation came. After having escaped from the Hindu village with nothing but his trousers, the fugitive found himself beside a deserted well. He was just cutting one of his boots into two pieces, after having lost its mate down the well while trying to draw water with it, when a dark complexioned man suddenly appeared, offered him some beans and rice, and revealed that he too was a Muslim. The man invited Ibn Battuta to accompany him and even insisted on carrying him on his back when the exhausted wanderer's legs gave out. Reciting a verse from the Qur'an over and over as they plodded along, Ibn Battuta finally fell asleep. When he awoke, his mysterious benefactor had disappeared, but he found himself in a village with a government officer in residence who warmly took him in, fed him, and gave him a bath and a suit of clothes.

Learning from his Muslim host that the village they were in was only six or seven miles from Koil, Ibn Battuta immediately sent a message to his comrades. In a day or two a party of them arrived to collect their foot-weary ambassador, astonished and jubilant that he was still alive. He then learned that during his absence the sultan had sent an official named Sumbul to replace the dead Kafur and that the mission was to proceed on its way.

I also learned that my companions had written to the sultan informing him what had befallen me and that they had regarded the journey as ill-omened on account of the fate which I and Kafur had met in the course of it and that they intended to return. But when I saw the sultan's injunctions ordering us to prosecute the journey I pressed them to prosecute it and my resolution was made firm.

Thus undaunted by his ordeal, he led his embassy on to Daulatabad without further incident. The caravan appears to have followed more or less the main government route to the erstwhile southern capital, a road fastidiously kept up to ensure rapid courier and military communication between Delhi and the Deccan. From the fortress city of Gwalior on the southern edge of the Ganges plain, the company trekked southwesterly across the Malwa plateau to Ujjain, the chief commercial entrepôt on the direct route from Delhi to Cambay. From there they crossed the Vindhya Hills, descending the steep southern scarp near Dhar to the Narmada River, the traditional historic dividing line between the cultural worlds of North India and the Deccan. South of the Narmada they crossed the wooded Satpura Range, probably by way of the Burhanpur Gap, the famous pass through which the armies of the Turks had repeatedly invaded South India. The last stretch of the journey took them from the Tapti River through the richly cultivated tableland of northern Maharashtra to Daulatabad.[5]

There the mission was the guest of Qutlugh Khan. He had been Muhammad Tughluq's governor of the Deccan provinces since 1335, commanding his territories from the spectacular citadel of Deogir set atop a granite, cone-shaped rock rising 800 feet above the surrounding plain. Defended by a perpendicular scarp 80 to 120 feet high on all sides, the castle could be reached only by passageways and staircases hewn out of the solid rock. An outer wall two and a half miles around enclosed the city of Daulatabad,

which lay to the south and east of the keep. Despite its aban-
donment as the capital of the empire, the town appears from the
Rihla's brief description to have been prospering from trade and
from the tax revenues of the densely populated Maharashtra
countryside. Yet not much more than two years after Ibn Battuta's
visit, a band of army officers would rise in rebellion, seize the great
fort, and in 1347 found another independent Muslim kingdom, the
Bahmani. And so, as the Maghribi traveler made his way out of
the Sultanate of Delhi, it progressively collapsed behind him.

The embassy probably stayed in Daulatabad only a few days,
then continued northwesterly through Maharashtra, across the
Tapti and Narmada rivers again, and thence along the eastern
lowland shore of the Gulf of Cambay into the region of Gujarat.

The fair city of Cambay stood on the northern shore of the Mahi
River estuary where it flows into the head of the gulf. Walking
among the bazaars and imposing stone houses of the port, Ibn
Battuta found himself for the first time in a decade in the familiar
cultural world of the Arabian Sea. The sultanate had ruled
Cambay since the early part of the century, but the soul of the city
was more kindred to Muscat, Aden, or Mogadishu than to
Daulatabad or Delhi. It was indeed one of the great emporia of the
Indian Ocean. "Cambay is one of the most beautiful cities as
regards the artistic architecture of its houses and the construction
of its mosques," Ibn Battuta recalls. "The reason is that the
majority of its inhabitants are foreign merchants, who continually
build there beautiful houses and wonderful mosques — an
achievement in which they endeavor to surpass each other." Many
of these "foreign merchants" were transient visitors, men of South
Arabian and Persian Gulf ports, who migrated in and out of
Cambay with the rhythm of the monsoons. But others were men
with Arab or Persian patronyms whose families had settled in the
town generations, even centuries, earlier, intermarrying with
Gujarati women and assimilating everyday customs of the Hindu
hinterland. Ibn Battuta visited Cambay just at a time when these
dark-skinned, white-shirted Gujarati traders were venturing
abroad in increasing numbers, founding mercantile colonies as far
away as Indonesia and creating a diaspora of commercial
association that would continue on the ascendancy in the Indian
Ocean until the time of the Portuguese.[6]

The ambassador spent a few days in the town as the guest of the
governor and some of the religious lights, then led his company

back along the eastern shore of the gulf to the port of Gandhar (Qandahar) at the mouth of the Narmada. Owing to the shallowness of the upper gulf, Cambay could not accommodate sea-going ships, so it was normal practice for them to put in either at Gandhar or at another port, which lay directly across the gulf.[7] Agents of the sultan had apparently made advance arrangements with the local ruler of Gandhar, a Hindu tributary, to provide the delegation with four ships for the voyage down the coast to Malabar. As usual Ibn Battuta has virtually nothing to tell us about the architecture of these vessels. Certainly they were all two-masted "dhows" with stitched hulls, the same general type of ships Ibn Battuta had sailed along the coasts of Africa and Arabia. Three of them were ordinary cargo ships, but large ones, since they had to have room for the Great Khan's presents, including the 100 horses and 215 slaves and pages. The fourth vessel was a type of war galley. Ibn Battuta's ship, one of the three merchantmen, carried a force of 100 soliders to defend the mission against the Hindu pirates who habitually lay in wait along the western coast. Fifty of the warriors were archers. The others were black spearmen and bowmen, representatives of a long tradition of African fighting men taking service on the larger trading ships of the Indian Ocean.[8]

Embarking from Gandhar, the four ships put in briefly at two other gulf ports. Then, turning due south, the little fleet made for the Arabian Sea. If the time was about December, they ran briskly before the northeast monsoon under clear skies and a placid sea.

When Ibn Battuta visited the East African coast more than a decade earlier, he had found a series of petty maritime principalities competing with one another for long-distance trade between the sea basin and the uplands of the interior. Along the west coast of India the political pattern was similar. From the southern frontier of Gujarat to Cape Comorin at the tip of the subcontinent, he counted twelve trading states strung out along the narrow coastal lowlands. The Turkish sultans may have claimed suzerainty over some of these little kingdoms, but the peaks and ridges of the Western Ghats, which ran the length of peninsular India 50 to 100 miles inland, effectively prevented Delhi from exerting direct authority on the coast south of Gujarat, excepting sporadic intervention in a few of the more northerly ports.[9] From Delhi or Daulatabad, imperial cavalry could reach the northerly coast, called the Konkan, only by squeezing their way through rugged woodland passes usually guarded by belligerent Hindu chieftains. The great ports of Malabar, on the southerly shore, were more easily accessible from the interior but much too far from the centers of Turkish power to make sustained military pressure feasible. No doubt Muhammad Tughluq pined to conquer the coastal territories, but in fact the commercial needs of the empire were better served by leaving the sea towns to carry on their business in peace.

The summer monsoons, blowing up against the Ghats, emptied heavy rains on the coastal lowlands, producing a lush tropical economy startlingly different from that of the interior plateaus. In medieval times the maritime towns exported rice, coconuts, gemstones, indigo and other dyes, and finished textiles. Among the spice exports, black pepper was king in the overseas trade. The forests of the steep western slopes of the Ghats, the only region of dense woodland anywhere around the rim of the Arabian Sea, produced the teakwood with which most of the oceanic trading ships were built. The major ports all had busy shipbuilding industries, and Indian teak was exported to the Persian Gulf, Arabia, and northeast Africa to meet the general needs of those wood-starved regions.

The natural landfall for ships making the long hauls across the Arabian Sea or the Bay of Bengal was southwest India. The largest and richest west coast towns were in Malabar, partly because of their relatively broad agricultural hinterland, their pepper crop, and their links to the populous interior of South India, but also because they served as the main transshipment centers for goods moving between the western and eastern halves of the Indian Ocean. Trade from the China Seas westward across the Bay of Bengal was carried mainly in Chinese junks. These great ships were structurally capable of sailing safely from one end of the Indian Ocean to the other, but the normal pattern, at least until the early fifteenth century, was for them to go only as far west as Malabar. There, goods in transshipment were carried in lateen-rigged vessels to all the countries of the Arabian Sea. Thus Malabar was the hinge on which turned the inter-regional seaborne trade of virtually the entire Eastern Hemisphere.

Almost all the transit trade of the west coast (as well as that of both Ceylon and the southeastern coast of India, called Coromandel) was in the hands of Muslims. The rulers of nearly all the maritime states, however, were Malayalam- or Tamil-speaking Hindus. The populations of the hinterlands were Hindu as well, or, in the case of Ceylon, Buddhist. Arab and Persian merchants had been settling on those shores since Abbasid times, but by the later medieval period most west coast Muslims were racially Indian, notwithstanding some cherished strain linking them to the prestigious Arabo–Persian center. Moreover, the culture of the towns, like the ports of East Africa, represented a complex, long-simmering synthesizing of native and alien elements, that is, traits and practices responsive to the requirements of the Sacred Law inter-penetrating with local Hindu customs, styles, dress, and cuisine. The Hindu *rajas* of the coastal states left their Muslim subjects to worship as they wished, indeed encouraged it, since the rulers' power and wealth depended almost entirely on customs revenues and the profits of their personal transactions in the maritime trade. We may suppose that the government of these cities was nothing less than a working partnership between the *rajas* and the leading Muslim merchants.

For three days out of the Gulf of Cambay Ibn Battuta's four ships made good speed along the Konkan coast, the dark green wall and sheared-off summits of the Western Ghats looming off the port beam. Bypassing Chaul, Sandapur (Goa), and other busy ports which lay on little bays or the estuaries of rivers flowing from the mountains, the fleet finally put in at Honavar (Hinawr), a town on the stretch of coast known as North Kanara.

In the fourteenth century Honavar was a thriving port with a typical Indo–Muslim coastal culture, its children, according to Ibn Battuta, dutifully attending a choice of 36 Qur'anic schools, its Muslim women wearing colorful saris and golden rings in their nostrils. Jamal al-Din Muhammad, the ruler of the town, was, exceptionally enough, a Muslim, though under vassalage to the Hindu king of the Hoysalas state, whose center was in the interior.[10] Ibn Battuta describes Jamal al-Din as one of "the best and most powerful rulers" on the coast, possessing a fleet of ships and a force of cavalry and infantry so impressive that he could command annual tribute from the ports of the West India coast as "protection" against seaborne attack. In the three short days the mission rested up in Honavar and restocked the ships, Jamal al-Din fêted his distinguished visitor in all the correct and predictable ways and introduced him to the local notables. But more than that, a friendship of sorts seems to have been sparked between the two men. At least it was a relationship Ibn Battuta would be eager to draw on a few months later when he returned to the town under drastically different circumstances.

South of Honavar along the Kanara and Malabar coasts, the towns became progressively larger and more affluent. This was black pepper country and the land where the commercial dominions of the dhow and the junk made their crucial connection. Perhaps because the sailing season to China was still a few months off and the urban scene along the south Kanara and Malabar shores notably worth investigating, the embassy cast anchor and enjoyed the local hospitality at eight different ports, including Mangalore (Manjurur) and Cannanore (Jurfattan).[11]

Then, about three weeks out of Honavar, the little convoy arrived off Calicut to a warm official reception. The dignitaries of the city, both Muslim and Hindu, came out to meet the mission, Ibn Battuta says, with "drums, trumpets, horns, and flags on their ships. We entered the harbor amid great ovation and pomp, the like of which I have not seen in these parts." The ambassador and his associates were given houses as guests of the *zamorin*, or prince, of Calicut and settled in for three months of leisure, since no ships would embark for East Asia until March, that is, near the end of the northeast monsoon season.[12] In the meantime the *zamorin* made advance arrangements for the delegation to travel to China on a large ocean-going junk and one smaller vessel (or possibly more) that would accompany it. The Chinese envoys, who had been travelling with Ibn Battuta up to this point, were to make plans to return home on a separate ship.

Ibn Battuta saw 13 junks wintering at Calicut, their corpulent hulls and multiple soaring masts dwarfing even the largest lateen-rigged vessels in the harbor. These were the ocean liners of the medieval age, artifacts of the great technological leap forward achieved in China between the eleventh and thirteenth centuries. Not only Ibn Battuta, but other travelers of the time, including Marco Polo, made clear their preference for sailing on junks over the creaky, sewn-together ships of the Arabian Sea. The shell of a junk was built of double-superimposed timbers attached with iron nails to several transverse bulkheads, dividing the hull into a series of watertight compartments that prevented the ship from sinking even if it were pierced below the water line in more than one place. A large junk might step five masts or more. The lug-type fore-and-aft sails were aerodynamically more efficient and far easier to maneuver than the lateen type. They were made of bamboo matting stiffened with battens, or laths, which gave them their characteristic ribbed appearance. Unlike lateen sails, they could be reefed and furled with ease by means of a complex arrangement of sheets. The tautness, variety, and adjustability of the sails permitted a junk to make headway under almost any wind condition. Medieval junks were all equipped with stern rudders, the efficient way of steering a ship that was becoming known in the Mediterranean world only near the end of the thirteenth century.

Ibn Battuta was so impressed with Chinese ships that he even rouses himself in the *Rihla* to offer a word or two about their nautical design. He was most interested, naturally, in the comforts they offered traveling notables like himself. The dhows of the western sea were only partially decked or not decked at all, and if some vessels had a rudimentary cabin or two, most of the passengers were expected to brave the elements the whole time they were at sea. Owing to bulkhead construction, which distributed weight evenly on the hull, ocean-going junks could support as many as five decks, as well as numerous enclosed cabins for the convenience of the more affluent passengers. Some of the rooms even had private lavatories, a convenience far superior to the little seat hooked over the side of a dhow. Fire-fighting equipment, steward service, lifeboats, and common rooms for the passengers added to the comfort and safety of a voyage across the eastern sea. Ibn Battuta, man of private pleasures that he was, informs us that

a good cabin has a door which can be bolted by the occupant, who may take with him his female slaves and women. Sometimes it so happens that a passenger is in the aforesaid residential quarters and nobody on board knows of him until he is met on arriving at a town.

He also claims that the crew of a sizable junk might number 1,000 men, counting both sailors and fighting marines. He may exaggerate, but within tolerable limits since Odoric of Pordenone, the Latin monk who traveled through South Asia earlier in the century, reports that he sailed out of Malabar on a junk with "seven hundred souls, what with sailors and merchants."[13] Ibn Battuta says that in his time junks were built exclusively in the southern Chinese ports of Guangzhou (Canton) or Quanzhou

(Zaitun). Owing to the Yuan policy of encouraging foreign participation in the sea trade, however, the owners and captains of the
ships, as well as the big merchants, were more often than not
Muslims of Indian, Arab, or Persian descent.

Astonishing as they were in cargo capacity and technical
efficiency, these "whales" of the sea, as the Chinese called them,
could be simply too big and too rigid for their own safety if they
chanced to blow into shallows or reef-infested waters. There was
some truth in Ibn Battuta's remark that "if a ship nailed together
with iron nails collides with rocks, it would surely be wrecked; but
a ship whose beams are sewn together with ropes is made wet and
is not shattered."

And so he discovered as his grand embassy to China was
suddenly aborted in tragedy off Calicut harbor. What exactly
happened the *Rihla* does not make entirely clear. As the day for
the mission to embark arrived, probably sometime in Feburary
1342,[14] a minor difficulty arose over accommodations. Chinese
merchants, it seems, had reserved in advance all the best cabins on
the large junk the embassy was to board, and the Sultan of India's
ambassador was going to have to settle for a more modest room,
one with no lavatory. Ibn Battuta had his luggage and entourage
put aboard but then decided the following morning that the cabin
was simply unsuitable and far too small. The ship's agent, a Syrian
gentleman, suggested that the best solution might be for the envoy
and his personal retinue to travel on the *kakam*. This was a
somewhat smaller junk-type vessel that would accompany the
larger ship, but it had good cabins available.[15] Ibn Battuta thought
this compromise was all right and so ordered his servants, concubines, personal friends, and belongings to be transferred. However, Zahir al-Din and Sumbul, the other officers of the mission,
remained on the larger vessel along with the slaves, horses, and
presents destined for Peking. Meanwhile Ibn Battuta spent the day
in Calicut attending Friday prayer.

Then that evening a storm came up. Calicut harbor was not a
deep, sheltered bay but a shallow roadstead. Recognizing the
danger of riding at anchor close to shore, the captains of the junk,
the *kakam*, and a third large vessel quickly put out to sea.
Throughout the night Ibn Battuta waited helplessly on the beach
and the next morning watched in horror as the two larger ships
went aground in the shallows, broke up, and sank. Some of the
passengers and crew on one of the junks were saved, but no one

survived on the vessel he himself was to have boarded the previous day. On Sunday morning the bodies of Zahir al-Din and Sumbul washed ashore, the one with his skull broken in, the other with an iron nail piercing his temples. The slaves, pages, and horses were all drowned, and the precious wares either sank or washed up on the beach, where the *zamorin*'s gendarmes struggled to prevent the townsfolk from making off with the loot. Meanwhile, the captain of the *kakam* steered his ship safely out to sea and, not wanting to risk entering the harbor again, sailed southward down the coast. On board were Ibn Battuta's baggage, servants, and concubines, one of these women carrying her master's child.

Alone on the Calicut shore, the lofty ambassador found himself suddenly reduced to the status of a penniless *faqih*. He had nothing to his name, save his prayer rug, the clothes on his back, and ten dinars an old yogi had given him. But for all that, he was fortunate to be alive. And it seems he still had the company of al-Tuzari and perhaps one or two other companions. Even more hopeful, there was still a chance of catching up with the *kakam*. The vessel, he was told, was almost certain to put in at the port of Quilon (Kawlam) 180 miles down the coast before sailing away from India altogether. So, hiring a Muslim porter to carry his carpet for him, he made his way to Quilon, traveling this time by riverine craft that plied the lagoons and interconnecting canals paralleling the southern Malabar shore.

After ten miserable days in the company of the porter, who turned out to be a quarrelsome drunkard, he arrived in the city, not to the applause of the local *raja*'s court, but to a modest reception in a Sufi hospice, the usual refuge of an anonymous wanderer. Much to his surprise his old associates, the Chinese envoys, turned up while he was there. They had left Calicut somewhat before the sea tragedy had occurred, but they had also barely escaped with their lives when their own ship ran aground. The Chinese merchants resident in Quilon helped them out with clothes and assistance and later sent them home on another junk. The forlorn ex-ambassador, however, waited in vain for his *kakam* to show up and after several hopeless days in the Sufi lodge decided to move on.

But where indeed was he to go? "I wanted to return from Quilon to the sultan," he remembers, "in order to tell him what had happened to the gifts. But I feared that he would condemn me, saying 'Why did you separate yourself from the presents?'"[16]

If the mission's two other officials, together with the slaves, horses, and magnificent wares all went to the bottom of the sea, why was the Maghribi so shiftless in his duty that he failed to go down with them? Knowing well that his wish to travel in private comfort with his slave girls was hardly a convincing explanation for not boarding the junk, and perhaps imagining his head affixed to a pole or his skin stuffed with straw hanging from the wall of Jahanpanah palace, he concluded easily enough that, no, he would not return to Delhi. He did, however, need a patron to restore him to a position of dignity and perhaps give him a job while he waited for news of the *kakam* or figured out some new plan. The closest and most likely seigneur was Jamal al-Din Muhammad, the pious Sultan of Honavar and the only Muslim ruler on the southwestern coast of India.

Returning to Calicut, he found there a fleet of ships belonging to Muhammad Tughluq himself. They were *en route* to the Persian Gulf to recruit more Arab notables for service in the sultanate. Ibn Battuta struck up an acquaintance with the chief of the expedition, a former chamberlain in the Delhi government, who advised him to stay away from the capital but invited him to accompany the fleet as far up the coast as Honavar. Ibn Battuta gladly accepted the offer and sailed northward out of Calicut sometime around 1 April 1342.[17]

If he expected Jamal al-Din of Honavar to elevate him at once to a high office on the strength of the imperial rank he had held the first time he visited the town, he was to be disappointed.

> He quartered me in a house where I had no servant and directed me to say prayers with him. So I sat mostly in his mosque and used to read the Qur'an from beginning to end every day. Later on, I recited the whole Qur'an twice daily . . . I did this without a break for three months, of which I spent forty consecutive days in devotional seclusion.

While the Moroccan *faqih* quietly passed a steaming summer on the Kanara coast in a bout of spiritual renewal, Sultan Jamal al-Din busied himself plotting the violent overthrow of his neighbor, the *raja* of Sandapur. Wars between the little maritime states of the west coast do not appear to have occurred very often in medieval times. Conflict was terrible for trade, and in any case none of the petty princes had armies or fleets large enough to sustain control over long stretches of the coast for indefinite periods of time. Yet a fortuitous opportunity to seize a neighboring port and milk its customs revenues might be too tempting to pass up. As the *Rihla* explains it, an internal struggle had broken out within the ruling family of Sandapur, a fine port located on an island in the estuary of a river about 90 miles north of Honavar. (In 1510 Sandapur would become Goa, capital of Portugal's seaborne empire in Asia.[18]) A son of the *raja* of Sandapur, scheming to wrest the throne from his father, wrote a letter to Jamal al-Din, promising to embrace Islam if the sultan would intervene on his side in the quarrel. Once victory was achieved, the new *raja* would marry the sultan's sister, sealing an alliance between the two towns. Forthwith, Jamal al-Din outfitted a war fleet of 52 ships, two of them built with open sterns to enable his cavalry to make a rapid amphibious assault on Sandapur beach.

Weary of inactivity and perhaps hoping to ingratiate himself with his patron by some more vigorous show of homage, Ibn Battuta had the idea of offering his services to the expedition. He claims that Jamal al-Din was so pleased with his proposal that he put him in charge of the campaign, though we may presume the office was more or less honorific. Preparations complete, the fleet set sail from Honavar on 12 October 1342.[19]

On Monday evening we reached Sandapur and entered its creek and found the inhabitants ready for the fight. They had already set up catapults. So we spent the night near the town and when morning came drums were beaten, trumpets sounded and horns were blown, and the ships went forward. The inhabitants shot at them with the catapults, and I saw a stone hit some people standing near the sultan. The crews of the ships sprang into the water, shield and sword in hand . . . I myself leapt with all the rest into the water . . . We rushed forward sword in hand. The greater part of the heathens took refuge in the castle of their ruler. We set fire to it, whereupon they came out and we took them prisoner. The sultan pardoned them and returned them their wives and children . . . And he gave me a young female prisoner named Lemki whom I called Mubaraka. Her husband wished to ransom her but I refused.

Having acquitted himself well in this day-long holy war and even acquired part of the living spoils, Ibn Battuta remained at

Sandapur for about three months in the company of Jamal al-Din, who seems to have been in no hurry to turn the town over to his Hindu ally, the *raja*'s son. Then about the middle of January 1343[20] Ibn Battuta decided to take leave of his patron and travel back down the coast in search of information on the fate of the *kakam*. On this trip he visited once again most of the ports he had seen the previous year, including Calicut, and spent "a long time," perhaps a few months, in Shaliyat (Shalia), a famous Malabar weaving town.

Then, returning to Calicut, he came upon two of his own servants who had been aboard the *kakam* and had somehow made their way back to Malabar. The news was bad. The ship had sailed to the Bay of Bengal, apparently without stopping at Quilon, and after reaching Indonesia had been seized by an infidel ruler of Sumatra. The concubine who was carrying Ibn Battuta's child had died, and the other slave girls, as well as his possessions, were in the hands of this king. The mystery of the *kakam* finally settled in more tragedy, he returned immediately to Sandapur, arriving there in June 1343.[21]

However, any expectation he had of taking up an official career in the service of Jamal al-Din soon ended in yet another disaster. Sometime in August the deposed *raja* of Sandapur, who had escaped at the time of the invasion, suddenly reappeared with a Hindu force, rallied the peasants of the hinterland, and laid siege to the town. Most of Jamal al-Din's troops, apparently unaware of an impending attack, were scattered in the surrounding villages and could not get back into the city to defend it. Having attached himself to Jamal al-Din in victory, Ibn Battuta saw no reason to stick by him in defeat, a point of view in the best tradition of Muslim public men, for whom loyalty to one sultan or another was of no great importance. In the thick of the assault, he somehow managed to get past the siege line and headed down the coast again, perhaps this time by land. In a few weeks he reached Calicut, entering that city now for the fifth time.[22]

Sometime during the months following the Calicut tragedy, he decided to try to visit China on his own. His prospects for a career on the west coast of India were no longer encouraging, he could not return to Delhi, and he had no immediate urge to make another pilgrimage to Mecca. Moreover, he knew that he could find hospitality among the Muslim maritime communities all along the sea routes to the South China coast. He even had a potential entrée to the Yuan government through the 15 Chinese diplomats, who were presumably then on their way home. His plan would be to make a brief tour of the Maldive Islands ("of which I had heard a lot"), continue to Ceylon to see the famous religious shrine of Adam's Peak, then cross over to the southeastern coast of India to visit the Sultanate of Ma'bar, whose ruler was married to a sister of Hurnasab, the ex-wife Ibn Battuta had left back in Delhi. From there he would go on to Bengal, Malaysia, and China.

After staying in Calicut for an unspecified time, perhaps some months, he met up with a sea captain from Honavar named Ibrahim and took passage on his ship bound for Ceylon and Ma'bar by way of the Maldives.[23] The idea of visiting this outlying tropical archipelago on his way to the Bay of Bengal was not such an erratic scheme as it might appear, even though the islands lay about 400 miles west and a bit south of Ceylon. Sea-going ships trading eastbound from the Arabian Sea could not sail through the Palk Strait that divided the subcontinent from Ceylon owing to the extremely shallow reef called Adam's Bridge that traversed the channel. Rather, they had to go around the southern tip of Ceylon. For traffic moving both east and west, the Maldive atolls were close enough to this route to be drawn into the international commerce between the western and the eastern seas. Shuttle trade between Malabar and the Maldives seems to have been very regular in medieval times. Moreover, the islands exported two commodities that were of major importance in the trans-hemispheric economy. One was coir, or coconut fiber rope, used to stitch together the hulls of the western ocean dhows. The other was the shells of the little marine gastropod called the cowrie, which were used as currency as far east as Malaysia and as far west as the African Sudan.

The people of the Maldives (Dhibat al-Mahal) were a brown-skinned fishing and sea-trading folk. They spoke Divehi, a language closely related to Sinhalese, evidence of ancient sea-borne migrations from Ceylon. About the middle of the twelfth century they had been converted from Buddhism to Islam. In the *Rihla* Ibn Battuta recounts the legend, told even today by old men of the islands, of Abu l'Barakat, a pious Berber from the Maghrib who rid the land of a terrible demon (*jinni*) and brought the people to the faith of the Prophet.[24] Each month the fiend had arisen from the sea and demanded a young virgin to ravish and kill. When Abu l'Barakat arrived in the islands and heard about the situation, he offered to go to the idol house where the sacrifice took place and substitute himself for the girl. He seated himself in the temple and recited the Qur'an through the night. As he expected, the demon refused to approach him out of fear of the Sacred Word. When Abu l'Barakat repeated this feat a second time a month later, the king of the islands razed the infidel shrines and ordered that the new faith be propagated among his subjects. Behind the veil of this heroic myth may be discerned the coming and going of Muslim merchants in the Maldives from as early as Abbasid times and the incorporation of the islands into the commercial network of the western ocean. Since North African and Andalusian Muslims seem to have been more active in the India trade in the eleventh and twelfth centuries than they were later on, there was nothing implausible about a Berber turning up to introduce the faith.[25]

Approaching the Maldives from Malabar, Ibn Battuta may have blinked in wonder at the sight of tall coconut palms apparently growing directly out of the sea. He was to discover that the islands rise barely a few feet above the surface of the ocean and that not a single hill is to be found on any of them. Stretching 475 miles north to south like a string of white gems, the Maldives are divided into about twenty ring-shaped coral atolls. Each of these clusters of islands and tiny islets is grouped more or less around a central lagoon. With the help of a Maldivian pilot who knew his way through the dangerous reefs that surrounded the islands, Captain Ibrahim put ashore at Kinalos Island in the northerly atoll of Malosmadulu.[26] As usual, the visiting *faqih* immediately found lodging with one of the literate men of the place.

For all the tropical charm of the Maldives and their people, Ibn Battuta had no other intention than to play the tourist for a few weeks and get on with his planned itinerary. As soon as he arrived, however, he got fair warning that a different fate lay ahead. The islands were politically united, and had been since pre-Islamic times, under a hereditary king who ruled in a reasonably benign spirit in collaboration with his extended royal family and a small class of titled noblemen. The Maldives had no real towns, but the center of government was on the mile-long island of Male located about midway in the chain of atolls. At the time Ibn Battuta arrived, the monarch happened to be a woman, Rehendi Kabadi Kilege, called Khadija, the nineteenth in the line of Muslim rulers. Female succession to the throne was unusual in Maldivian history, and in fact Sultana Khadija's administration was thoroughly dominated by her husband, the Grand Vizier Jamal al-Din (not the same man of course as the Sultan of Honavar). Aside from island governors and other secular officials, the queen appointed Muslim judges and mosque dignitaries and expected them to uphold the standards of the *shari'a*.

However, the man who held the position of chief *qadi* at that time was not given much credit for ability. No sooner had Ibn Battuta set foot on Kinalos and revealed himself to be a scholar of refinement and worldly experience than one of the educated men there told him he had better not go to Male if he did not want the grand vizier to appoint him as judge and oblige him to stay on indefinitely. Ibn Battuta was no doubt better qualified for this job than he had been for his magistracy in Delhi. Not only was Arabic, rather than Persian, the language of jurisprudence and literate prestige in the islands, but the Maliki *madhhab*, Ibn Battuta's own legal school, was practiced. The existence of a Maliki community in the Indian Ocean is odd, but if the men who introduced Islam to the Maldives were North Africans, they would have brought their Maliki learning with them. (In the sixteenth century the islanders would shift to the Shafi'i *madhhab*, which made more sense in the context of sustained maritime connections with Malabar and the other Muslim lands around the Arabian Sea.[27])

Anchoring his ship off Kinalos Island probably some time in December 1343,[28] Captain Ibrahim hired a small lateen-rigged boat of the sort the Maldivians used in inter-island trade and set off for Male with Ibn Battuta and several unnamed companions aboard. As soon as they arrived, they went the short walk to the wooden, thatched-roof palace to be introduced to Queen Khadija and Grand Vizier Jamal al-Din. Captain Ibrahim, who had been in the islands before, guided the other visitors in the peculiarities of Maldivian ceremonial:

> When we arrived in the council-hall — that is, the *dar* — we sat down in the lobbies near the third entrance . . . Then came Captain Ibrahim. He brought ten garments, bowed in the direction of the queen and threw one of the garments down. Then he bowed to the grand vizier and likewise threw another garment down; subsequently he threw the rest . . . Then they brought us betel and rose-water, which is a mark of honor with them. The grand vizier lodged us in a house and sent us a repast consisting

of a large bowl of rice surrounded by dishes of salted meat, fowl, quail, and fish.

Ibn Battuta had learned by experience that Muslim rulers whose kingdoms lay in the outer periphery of the Dar al-Islam were always avid to attract the services of *'ulama* with previous links to the great cities and colleges of the central lands. He had also learned that once a scholar developed a public reputation for pious learning, his royal benefactor might use more than simple persuasion to prevent him from moving somewhere else. In order to forestall any complications over his own timely departure, Ibn Battuta decided to say nothing to the Maldivians about his legal background and enlisted Captain Ibrahim to honor the secret. The sultans of Delhi had never had the slightest authority, symbolic or otherwise, in the Maldives, but the small-time nobility of the islands nevertheless looked upon the empire with fear and awe. Any former high official of the sultanate who turned up in the atolls would have to carry a heavy load of distinction and might even stir up a certain apprehension.

For about the first ten days of his visit Ibn Battuta managed to preserve his secret, as he and his companions explored the coconut groves of the island and enjoyed the hospitality of the government. But then a ship arrived from Ceylon carrying a group of Arab and Persian Sufis. Some of them happened to know Ibn Battuta from his Delhi years and immediately let the cat out of the bag. The Moroccan visitor, the queen and her court were told, had been an important *qadi* in the service of the mighty Muhammad Tughluq. The grand vizier was delighted at the news. Here was a celebrity who should be specially honored and must not be allowed to escape the islands too easily or too soon!

To his dismay, but also, the tone of the *Rihla* makes clear, to his vain satisfaction, Ibn Battuta was suddenly the center of attention. At first Jamal al-Din tried to flatter him into staying on Male with gifts and preferments. He invited him to the nightly feasts of Ramadan in the queen's palace. He gave him a piece of land and offered to build him a house on it. He sent him slave girls, pearls, and golden jewelry. Ibn Battuta accepted all this fuss with grim courtesy, but he was in no mood to revise his travel plans, even less so when he fell seriously ill for some weeks, possibly with the malaria that was endemic in the islands.[29] As soon as he recovered sufficiently to move about, he tried to hire passage on an outbound ship, but Jamal al-Din made it impossible for him by obstructing the financial arrangements. Finally he had to conclude that the grand vizier was going to keep him on Male whether he liked it or not. Under such circumstances as these, it was better to negotiate his fate voluntarily than to be coerced into service. Presenting himself before Jamal al-Din, he gave his word that he would remain in the islands indefinitely, making the condition, however, that he would not go about Male on foot and that the Maldivian custom of allowing only the vizier to appear publicly on horseback (the queen rode in a litter) would in his case have to be set aside.

The brashness of this demand was the first sign that Ibn Battuta's sojourn in the Maldives was to be unlike any of his other traveling adventures. His years in India reveal plainly that he had political ambition. But there he had been a relatively small fish in a large, shark-infested pond. Among the ingenuous Maldivians, however, his prestigious connections to the sultanate gave him a status of eminence out of all proportion to the power he had actually exercised in Delhi. Once he agreed to stay in the islands, he seems to have determined to capitalize on his reputation and throw himself into politics. To be sure, the upper-class factional quarrels of this remote equatorial paradise had something of a comic opera quality about them in contrast to the majestic affairs of the sultanate or the Mongol kingdoms. Nevertheless, Ibn Battuta became a very big man in the Maldives for a few fleeting months, and he is at pains to have the reader of the *Rihla* understand that this was the case. Even though the account of his involvement is disjointed, incomplete, and ambiguous, he reveals more about his personal social and political relations there than he does in connection with any of his other experiences, including his years in Delhi. There is no reason to doubt that he became deeply enmeshed in the rivalries of the Maldivian nobility, even to the point where, if things had gone his way, he might have ended his traveling career there in a position of lasting power.

In February 1344, probably less than two months after his arrival, he married a woman of noble status.[30] She was the widow of Sultan Jalal al-Din 'Umar, who was the father (by another marriage) and a predecessor of Queen Khadija. This noblewoman also had a daughter who was married to a son of the grand vizier. Marriage among the governing families of the Maldives was as much a political tool as it was in any other kingdom in that age. Ibn Battuta, like other scholars who circulated among the cities and princely courts of Islam, sought marriage as a way of gaining admission to local elite circles and securing a base of social and political support. By wedding this woman (whose name is never mentioned in the *Rihla*, though he says he found her society "delightful"), he allied himself to both the royal family and the household of the grand vizier.

Jamal al-Din had in fact urged the marriage on him and as soon as it was consummated invited his new cousin to fill the office of chief judge of the realm. Ibn Battuta pleads rather coyly in the *Rihla* that "Jamal al-Din compelled me against my will to accept the *qadi*'s post," but he hardly discouraged his own candidacy when he criticized the incumbent judge for being "absolutely no good at anything." Ibn Battuta makes it plain that once he got the job he used the office to wield considerably more power over other men than he ever had in his opulent sinecure in Delhi:

> All sentences proceed from the *qadi*, who is the most influential man with them, and his orders are carried out like those of the sultan or even more punctiliously. He sits on a carpet in the council-hall and has three islands, the income which he appropriates for his personal use according to an old custom.

In the absence of any independent observation, we cannot know how much he may have inflated his power in the islands for the benefit of admiring readers of the *Rihla*. He claims, in any case, to have gone about his judicial practice in the same spirit of orthodox zeal that had prompted him to expose the errant bath operators in that Nile town of Upper Egypt 18 years earlier. "When I became *qadi*," he reports triumphantly, "I strove with all my might to establish the rule of law," implying that the Maldivian bumpkins had much to learn about rigorous canonical standards and that he was just the man to rid the kingdom of "bad customs." Among his reforms, he ordered that any man who failed to attend Friday prayer was to be "whipped and publicly disgraced." He strove to abolish the local custom that required a divorced woman to stay in the house of her former husband until she married again; he had at least 25 men found guilty of this practice "whipped and paraded round the bazaars." At least once he sentenced a thief to have his right hand severed, a standard *shari'a* judgment that nonetheless caused several Maldivians present in the council hall to faint dead away. In one matter, however, the populace refused to conform to his idea of scriptural propriety. Most of the women, he relates, wear only a waist-wrapper which covers them from their waist to the lowest part, but the remainder of their body remains uncovered. Thus they walk about in the bazaars and elsewhere. When I was appointed *qadi* there, I strove to put an end to this practice and commanded the women to wear clothes; but I could not get it done. I would not let a woman enter my court to make a plaint unless her body were covered; beyond this, however, I was unable to do anything.

When the zealous magistrate was not hearing cases in the council chamber or ferreting out derelictions of Koranic duty, he was busy building up his network of political alliances with the chief families and making a high place for himself in the pecking order of power. Within a short time of his first marriage, he wed three more women, four being the most wives a man could have according to Islamic law. His second wife was the daughter of an important minister and great granddaughter of a previous sultan. His third was a widow of Queen Khadija's brother and immediate predecessor. His fourth was a step-daughter of 'Abdallah ibn Muhammad al-Hadrami, a nobleman who had just been restored to a ministerial position after having spent a period of time in exile on one of the outer islands for some unnamed transgression against the state. "After I had become connected by marriage with the above-mentioned people," Ibn Battuta tells us bluntly, "the vizier and the islanders feared me, for they felt themselves to be weak."

Despite the unity of Maldivian government, the political claustrophobia of tiny Male coupled with the fragmented geography of the kingdom encouraged both factional intrigues and dissidence.[31] The *Rihla* makes it apparent that the grand vizier, the de facto ruler, did not have the whip hand over his nobility and could not fully control the actions of political cliques. Ibn Battuta's recounting of the events that led to his precipitous departure from the islands is subjective and episodic and leaves the reader of the narrative straining to discern the deeper currents of the political drama. He leaves no doubt, however, that he had not been a figure in the royal court for very long before he began to make enemies. Vizier 'Abdallah, the minister who had returned from temporary exile, seems to have regarded him as an *arriviste* and a threat to his own position of power. The two men got on badly from the start, clashing over symbolic matters of precedence and protocol that concealed a far more serious rivalry for influence in the kingdom. As Ibn Battuta explains it, and we will never know anyone else's side of the story, 'Abdallah and certain of his kinsmen and allies plotted to turn the grand vizier against his new *qadi*, and they finally succeeded. A nasty row broke out between Ibn Battuta and Jamal al-Din over a legal judgment involving a sordid affair between a slave and a royal concubine. The grand vizier accused Ibn Battuta of insubordination and called him before the ministers and military officers assembled in the palace.

> Usually I showed him the respect due to a ruler, but this time I did not. I said simply "*salamu 'alaikum.*" Then I said to the bystanders, "You are my witnesses that I herewith renounce my post as *qadi* as I am not in a position to fulfill its duties." The grand vizier then said something addressing me, and I rose up moving to a seat opposite him, and I retorted in sharp tones . . . Thereupon the grand vizier entered his house saying, "They say I am a ruler. But look! I summoned this man with a view to making him feel my wrath; far from this, he wreaks his own ire on me."

On the heels of this stormy confrontation, Ibn Battuta paid off his debts, packed up his luggage, divorced one of his wives (probably 'Abdallah's step-daughter), and hired a boat to take him to Captain Ibrahim's ship, which was at that moment in the southern region of the atolls. Yet far from washing his hands of the Maldive government and sailing off in an offended huff, he reveals, tantalizingly and obscurely, that he was playing for bigger stakes than merely the independence of his authority as *qadi*. Describing his departure from Male, he writes in the *Rihla*, as if adding a forgotten detail,

> I made a compact with the vizier 'Umar, the army commander, and with the vizier Hasan, the admiral, that I should go to Ma'bar, the king of which was the husband of my wife's [that is, Hurnasab's] sister and return thence with troops so as to bring the Maldive islands under his sway, and that I should then exercise the power in his name.[32] Also I arranged that the hoisting of the white flags on the ships should be the signal and that as soon as they saw them they should revolt on the shore.

Then he adds rather disingenuously, "Never had such an idea occurred to me until the said estrangement had broken out between the vizier and myself." He also hints that Jamal al-Din had at least a suspicion of this astonishing plot, but the vizier's own political position had apparently weakened so much that he could not risk arresting his *qadi*. Whatever Jamal al-Din's fears may have been, the threat of an invasion was not entirely far-fetched, for the Chola empire of South India had conquered the islands in early medieval times.[33]

As it turned out, Ibn Battuta left Male without further incident and sailed in several days' time to Fua Mulak (Muluk) island, which lay near the southern end of the archipelago just across the equator.[34] Here Captain Ibrahim's ship awaited him. Ibn Battuta had sailed out of Male with three wives in his company, but he divorced them all in a short time. One of these women, the wife of his first Maldive marriage, fell seriously ill on the way to Fua Mulak, so he sent her back to Male. Another he restored to her father, who lived on Fua Mulak. He offers no explanation for his divorcing the third woman, though she was pregnant. He stayed on Fua Mulak for more than two months, and there he married, and presumably divorced, two more women. Quite apart from his political motives in taking a total of six wives during his sojourn in the islands, such transitory alliances reflected the custom of the country:

> It is easy to marry in these islands because of the smallness of the dowries and the pleasures of society which the women offer . . . When the ships put in, the crew marry; when they intend to leave they divorce their wives. This is a kind of temporary marriage. The women of these islands never leave their country.[35]

Ibn Battuta made a brief trip back to Male in the company of Ibrahim in order to help the captain iron out a dispute he had with the inhabitants of Fua Mulak. He did not, however, leave the ship while it was anchored in Male harbor. Then, after touching briefly at Fua Mulak once again, they set sail northeastward for the coast of Ceylon. The time was late August 1344.[36]

Notes

1. *The Book of Duarte Barbosa*, trans, and ed. Mansel Longworth Dames, 2 vols. (London, 1918–21), vol. 2, p. 74.

2. The *Rihla* is the sole record of this event. No evidence of the embassy has come to light in Chinese sources so far as I know, though Peter Jackson notes that a Yuan mission is known to have visited Egypt in 1342–43. "The Mongols and India (1221–1351)," Ph.D. diss., Cambridge University, 1977, p. 222. The envoys probably

arrived several months before IB left Delhi. On the dating of his departure see note 5.

3. Henry Yule identifies this town as Sambhal east of Delhi. *Cathay and the Way Thither*, 4 vols. (London, 1913–16), vol. 4, p. 18. Also MH, p. 150.

4. IB states that he left Delhi on 17 Safar 743 A.H., that is, 22 July 1342. Evidence suggests that he did not remember the year correctly or that an error was made in copying the *Rihla*. A departure date of 17 Safar 742 (2 August 1341) makes more sense within the context of subsequent statements in the *Rihla* about chronology and itinerary. The fundamental problem with IB's chronology for the travels in India, the Maldive Islands, and Ceylon is that he claims to have left the Maldives (following the first and longer of two visits) in the middle part of Rabi' II 745 (late August 1344), that is, a little more than two years after leaving Delhi. His own statements about traveling times and lengths of sojourns in particular places, however, indicate that about *three* years elapsed between his leaving Delhi and his first departure from the Maldives. For the period of travels between these two events, the *Rihla* is not very helpful, since IB offers not one absolute year date. The Maldive departure date of 745, however, is probably accurate. In the space of a few months following that date, he arrived in the Sultanate of Ma'bar in the far southeastern corner of the subcontinent. There he witnessed and was involved in events surrounding the death of Sultan Ghiyath al-Din and the accession of Nasir al-Din. Numismatic evidence shows that this regnal change took place in 745 A.H. (The last coin of Ghiyath al-Din is dated 744; the first coin of Nasir al-Din is dated 745.) S. A. Q. Husaini, "Sultanate of Ma'bar" in H. K. Sherwani and P. M. Joshi (eds.), *History of Medieval Deccan*, 2 vols. (Hyderabad, 1973–74), vol. 1, pp. 65, 74. If IB's Maldive departure date is accurate, at least for the year, then we may hypothesize that the Delhi date should be pushed back a year to make room for three years of travel.

5. As it is set forth in the *Rihla*, IB's itinerary from Delhi to Daulatabad is erratic and illogical. Part of the explanation is probably that some of the stages have been placed in incorrect order. For example, he states that he visited Dhar before Ujjain, when it was almost certainly the reverse. Furthermore, he may have visited some of the places mentioned during earlier excursions out of Delhi which he does not report and whose descriptive information is woven into the account of the trip to Daulatabad. He indicates, for example, that he had visited Gwalior at some earlier time, though nothing is said about the circumstances of such a trip (D&S, vol. 4, p. 33). IB offers almost no help in deducing the chronology of his journey through the interior of India. Mahdi Husain calculates that he arrived in Daulatabad on 3 November. A general estimate of late autumn seems reasonable, but this author's precise town-to-town chronology for the entire range of IB's travels in India, the Maldives, and Ceylon is delusive, for it is based almost entirely on informed guessing and inferential evidence such as "normal" traveling times from one place to another. MH, pp. lxiv–lxvi.

6. Gujaratis were well established in the East Indies in the fifteenth century and were probably arriving there in the fourteenth. M. A. P. Meilink-Roelofsz, "Trade and Islam in the Malay–Indonesian Archipelago Prior to the Arrival of the Europeans" in D. S. Richards (ed.), *Islam and the Trade of Asia* (Oxford, 1970), pp. 144–45.

7. *Duarte Barbosa*, vol. 1, pp. 134, 136, 138.

8. Simon Digby, "The Maritime Trade of India" in Tapan Raychaudhuri and Irfan Habib (eds.), *The Cambridge Economic History of India*, 2 vols (Cambridge, England, 1982), vol. 1, p. 152.

9. P. M. Joshi, "Historical Geography of Medieval Deccan" in Sherwani and Joshi, *Medieval Deccan*, vol. 1, pp. 18, 20.

10. IB states that the suzerain of Jamal al-Din was a ruler named Haryab, but historians have disagreed as to whether this individual is Ballala III of the Hoysalas

or Harihara I of the Kingdom of Vijayanagar. See R. N. Saletore, "Haryab of Ibn Battuta and Harihara Nrpala," *Quarterly Journal of the Mythic Society* 31 (1940–41): 384–406; also MH, p. 180n.

11. The location and identity of these ports, some of which no longer exist, are investigated in *Duarte Barbosa*, vol. 1, pp. 185–236, vol. 3, pp. 1–92; Yule, *Cathay*, vol. 4, pp. 72–79; and MH, pp. 178–88.

12. According to the fifteenth-century navigator Ibn Majid, the best time for sailing from the west coast of India to the Bay of Bengal was around 11 April, or from mid March through April. G. R. Tibbetts, *Arab Navigation in the Indian Ocean before the Coming of the Portuguese* (London, 1971), p. 377.

13. Yule, *Cathay*, vol. 2, p. 131.

14. Junks normally left the Malabar coast for China after mid March (see note 12). However, it seems likely that IB's vessels were planning to stop over at Quilon, a major port further down the coast, before departing for the Bay of Bengal. Moreover, the subsequent chronological clues IB gives suggest that his departure from Calicut was not scheduled for any later than about 1 March (see note 19).

15. IB does not describe this vessel. Joseph Needham suggests the name may be related to *cocca, coque*, or cog, which was a medieval ship of the Mediterranean and North Atlantic. *Science and Civilization in China*, vol. 4, part 3, *Civil Engineering and Nautics* (Cambridge, 1971), p. 469n.

16. My translation. D&S, vol. 4, pp. 103–4.

17. IB says that his second departure from Calicut took place "at the end of the season for traveling on the sea," meaning the weeks before the southwest monsoon came up in full force. Although the Malabar ports did not close down altogether until June, IB almost certainly left Calicut no later than about 1 April, since vessels bound for Arabia or the Persian Gulf had to reach their destinations before the monsoon reached full strength in those latitudes. Tibbetts, *Arab Navigation*, p. 375. Therefore, the sinking of IB's junk off Calicut must have taken place no later than about 1 March to make room for his trip to Quilon and back, which probably consumed at least 25 days. (He says it took him ten days to travel from Calicut to Quilon.)

18. Yule (*Cathay*, vol. 4, pp. 64–66) identifies Sandapur with Goa. *Duarte Barbosa*, vol. 1, pp. 170–72. IB presents the only account of Jamal al-Din's conquest of the city and its subsequent recovery by the *raja*.

19. IB states that the ships left Honavar on Saturday and attacked Sandapur on the following Monday, or 13 Jumada I 743 A.H. (14 October 1342).

20. IB declares that he stayed in Sandapur from 13 Jumada I until the middle part of Sha'ban, that is, about three months. 15 Sha'ban 743 corresponds to 13 January 1343. In connection with his first visit to Honavar, IB mentions that at some subsequent time he stayed with Jamal al-Din for eleven months (D&S, vol. 4, p. 70), but a sojourn of this length fits badly with the other meager chronological information IB provides concerning his India travels.

21. He says he arrived there in late Muharram, which is the first month of the Muslim year; 28 Muharram, that is, one of the last days of the month, calculates as 22 June 1343.

22. IB's date for his flight from Sandapur when it was under seige is 2 Rabi' II. That date in 744 A.H. corresponds to 24 August 1343. In his initial description of the west coast in the *Rihla*, he implies that at some point he traveled along the road that paralleled the Kanara and Malabar coasts. This may have been the time, since escape from Sandapur by sea would likely have been more difficult than by land.

23. IB says that he left Sandapur on 2 Rabi' II, and he implies that he arrived in the Maldives shortly before the following Ramadan. The intervening time was four to five months, presumably divided between his journey from Sandapur to Calicut, his stay in the latter place, and his ten-day sea voyage (as he recalls it) to the Maldives.

24. Clarence Maloney collected a version of the legend, very similar to IB's story, in the mid-1970s. *People of the Maldives* (Madras, 1980), pp. 98–99.

25. S. D. Goitein, "From Aden to India: Specimens of the Correspondence of India

Traders of the Twelfth Century," *Journal of the Economic and Social History of the Orient* 23 (1980): 43–66; "Letters and Documents on the India Trade in Medieval Times," *Islamic Culture* 37 (1963): 188–205; "From the Mediterranean to India: Documents on the Trade to India, South Arabia and East Africa from the Eleventh and Twelfth Centuries," *Speculum* 29 (1954): 181–97.

26. IB's Kannalus may be identified with Kinalos Island. *The Voyage of François Pyrard of Laval to the East Indies, the Maldives, the Moluccas and Brazil*, trans. and ed. Albert Gray, 2 vols. (London, n.d.; reprint edn., New York, 1963?), vol. 2, p. 438. François Pyrard was a French sailor who spent five and a half years in the Maldives in the early seventeenth century and subsequently wrote a lively and detailed description of the customs and manners of their inhabitants. The edition cited here also includes edited translations of earlier reports on the Maldives, including IB's narrative.

27. Maloney, *People of the Maldives*, pp. 219, 233.

28. IB implies that he reached the islands some weeks before Ramadan 744. That month began on 17 January 1344 (see note 23).

29. IB and subsequent travelers to the islands speak of the "Maldivian fever," which was almost certainly malaria. Maloney, *People of the Maldives*, p. 398. If IB became infected with malaria, he would probably have been seriously ill for a few weeks.

30. He dates his first marriage in the Maldives to the month of Shawwal, which began on 16 February 1344.

31. Maloney, *People of the Maldives*, pp. 191–96.

32. Mahdi Husain's translation reads "so as to bring back the Maldive islands under his sway" (MH, p. 214). "Bring back" is an accurate translation of the verbal noun *tarajju'i*, but the islands had not previously been invaded or ruled by the Sultanate of Ma'bar. See D&S, vol. 4, p. 160.

33. In the seventeenth century the King of Bengal would send a fleet of galleys to raid and sack the Maldives. Gray, *François Pyrard*, vol. 1, pp. 310–20.

34. Ibid., vol. 2, p. 465.

35. Pyrard also remarks on the high frequency of marriage and divorce in the islands. Ibid., vol. 1, pp. 150–55.

36. IB gives the date of his departure from the islands as mid Rabi' II 745 A.H.; 15 Rabi' II calculates as 26 August 1344. That would have been the late summer monsoon period and a plausible time to be sailing northeastward from the Maldives. Here my revised chronology, placing his departure from Delhi in 742 rather than 743, falls back into line with IB's own dating. His departure from the Maldives in 745 accords well with the dating of the subsequent visit to Ma'bar (see note 4). IB mentions that he lived in the Maldives for a year and a half (D&S, vol. 4, p. 114), but this statement does not seem compatible with the other chronological data he provides. A stay of about eight months, from mid Sha'ban 744 to mid Rabi' II 745, makes more sense.

11 China

> I assure you that for one spice ship that goes to Alexandria
> or elsewhere to pick up pepper for export to Christendom,
> Zaiton is visited by a hundred . . . I can tell you further
> that the revenue accruing to the Great Khan from this city
> and port is something colossal.[1]
>
> Marco Polo

Ibn Battuta visited Ceylon (Sri Lanka) on his way to Ma'bar so
that he might go on pilgrimage to the top of Adam's Peak, the
spectacular conical mountain that loomed over the southwestern
interior of the island. "That exceeding high mountain hath a
pinnacle of surpassing height, which, on account of the clouds, can
rarely be seen," wrote John de Marignolli, the Christian monk
who passed through Ceylon just a few years after Ibn Battuta.
"But God, pitying our tears, lighted it up one morning just before
the sun rose, so that we beheld it glowing with the brightest
flame"[2] Ibn Battuta recalls that he first saw the peak from far out
to sea, "rising up into the sky like a column of smoke." The
mountain was sacred to Muslims, Hindus, and Buddhists alike,
and pilgrims of all three faiths climbed together to the summit to
behold a depression in the surface of the rock vaguely resembling
the shape of an enormous foot. For Buddhists it is the footprint of
Siddhartha Gautama, the Buddha. For Hindus it is a trace of the
Great God Shiva, and for some Christians it belongs to St.
Thomas. In Muslim tradition God cast Adam and Eve from the
seventh heaven in disgrace, and when they tumbled to earth the
man landed hard on the peak of the mountain, leaving an impress
of his foot in the solid rock. He remained there for a thousand
years atoning for his sins, until the Archangel Gabriel led him to
Arabia, where Eve had fallen. The man and the woman met on
the plain of 'Arafat and later returned to Ceylon to propagate the
human race. Adam was not only the first man but the first prophet
of Islam as well, and it was to reverence him that Muslim pilgrims
trekked to the Foot, as they still do today.

Arriving from the Maldives in the company of Captain Ibrahim, Ibn Battuta put ashore at a place he calls Battala, probably modern Puttalam on the west central coast.[3] In the pattern of Muslim maritime settlement, Ceylon's western coast was an extension of Malabar. Merchants of the Arabian Sea had operated from ports like Puttalam since Abbasid times, exporting rubies, pearls, areca nuts, and from about the fourteenth century large quantities of cinnamon. Puttalam lay within the domain of the Hindu kingdom of Jaffna, which at that time dominated the northern half of the island, prospering from the Indo–Ceylonese trade and the wealth of the pearl fisheries in the Gulf of Mannar.

Ibn Battuta arrived in Puttalam to find the King of Jaffna, the Arya Chakravarti, temporarily in residence. Announcing himself a kinsman by marriage of the Sultan of Ma'bar (with whom Jaffna had good relations), he had no trouble getting himself introduced into the royal court. Since the Arya Chakravarti understood some Persian, Ibn Battuta regaled him for three days with stories of "kings and countries," then politely requested patronage to secure guides and provisions for the long walk to Adam's Peak. The king not only gave him all the supplies he needed but also a palanquin for his personal comfort plus the fellowship of 10 Brahmin priests, 15 porters, 10 courtiers of the royal household, and 4 yogis. At this point Ibn Battuta's personal suite appears to have consisted of al-Tuzari, a second Egyptian gentleman, and two slave girls.

The party made the round trip up the mountain and back to Puttalam by a circular route through the southwestern quarter of the island, a journey facilitated by Ceylon's superior network of high roads, stone bridges, and rest houses.[4] They first traveled due south along the palm-lined coast to the port of Chilaw (Bandar Salawat). There they turned southeastward into the interior, passed briefly through the territory of the Buddhist Sinhalese kingdom of Gampola, then climbed gradually upwards through the lush montane forests of the central highlands.[5] There were two tracks to the summit of the mountain, but custom instructed that a pilgrim would acquire divine merit only if he ascended by the more difficult route and came down by the easy one. The final ascent up the rocky cone was itself an act of religious faith, for the pilgrim had to haul himself grunting and sweating up a series of nearly vertical cliffs by means of little stirrups affixed to chains suspended from iron pegs.

Making it to the top in one piece, Ibn Battuta and his comrades

Adam's Peak, Ceylon
Sally and Richard Greenhill

camped for three days at a cave near the summit. Following tradition, he walked each morning and evening to the site of the Foot and joined the cluster of Hindus, Buddhists, and fellow Muslims, each group possessing its own notion of what holy event the imprint represented but sharing nonetheless a rare moment of transcendent brotherhood. He also beheld one of the most breathtaking scenic views anywhere in the world, a panorama of wooded hills rippling away from the base of the Peak to the golden band of the sea in the far distance.

The party returned to the coast by a roundabout route southward to the port of Dondra (Dinawar), then up along the western shore. When they reached Puttalam again, Ibn Battuta found the faithful Captain Ibrahim waiting to ferry him and his companions across the Gulf of Mannar to the shore of the subcontinent and the kingdom of Ma'bar. The stages of the trip to Adam's Peak and back suggest that he may have put out from Puttalam in October.[6]

This was the transitional period between the two monsoons, a season when heavy squalls might come up in the gulf without warning. More than that, Ibn Battuta mentions twice in the *Rihla* that despite his long acquaintanceship with Ibrahim, he never really had much confidence in him as a sailor. Setting a course northeastward from Puttalam, the vessel had almost made it to the South Indian coast, when suddenly

> the wind became violent and the water rose so high that it was about to enter the ship, while we had no able captain with us. We then got near a rock, where the ship was on the point of being wrecked; afterwards we came into shallow water wherein the ship began to sink. Death stared us in the face and the passengers jettisoned all that they possessed and bade adieu to one another.

Racing against the wind and waves, the crew managed to cut down the main mast and throw it overboard, then lash together a crude raft and lower it to the sea. Ibn Battuta got his two companions and his concubines down onto it, but there was no room left for him. Too poor a swimmer to jump into the water and hang onto the raft with a rope, he could only stick with the ship and hope for the best. The sailors who stayed behind tried vainly to tie together more floats, but darkness fell and the work had to be given up.

Throughout the night Ibn Battuta huddled terrified in the stern as the water rose around him. In the meantime his companions made it safely to shore and sought help from Tamil villagers, for in the morning a rescue party of boatmen suddenly appeared alongside the rapidly sinking dhow. The crew and remaining passengers were all taken to shore, apparently including Captain Ibrahim, though of him we hear no more.

Reunited with his friends and slave women on a rural stretch of the southeastern coast, Ibn Battuta gladly accepted food and shelter from the Tamil country folk who had plucked him from the sea. He seems to have saved some of his personal belongings from the shipwreck, including mementos from various Sufi divines and a bag of pearls, rubies, and other gems given to him by the King of Jaffna. The party remained with the local Tamils while word was sent to Ghiyath al-Din, the Sultan of Ma'bar, that a brother-in-law of his, late of Delhi, had arrived on the coast in distressing circumstances. The sultan happened to be on a military tour not far away, and in three days' time a company of horse and infantry arrived to conduct the visitors across the dry coastal lowlands to the royal camp.

Ibn Battuta spent altogether about two months in Ma'bar, but it was not a period of his travels he recalls with any joy. More than a decade had passed since Jalal al-Din Ahsan Shah, the father of Ibn Battuta's ex-wife, Hurnasab, had revolted against Muhammad Tughluq and founded an independent Muslim state held precariously together by a small, turbulent minority of Turko–Afghan fighting men. Jalal al-Din had died in 1338 or 1339 while Ibn Battuta was still in Delhi. His successor ruled less than two years before taking a Hindu arrow in the head. The third sultan was assassinated by his own commanders after only a few months in power. The fourth was Ghiyath al-Din. A former cavalryman under Muhammad Tughluq and husband of Hurnasab's sister, he had fought his way to the throne in 1340 or 1341.

Since the entire Muslim population of Ma'bar was small, limited to the military aristocracy, coastal merchants, and a modest bureaucratic and religious corps, Ghiyath al-Din would likely have welcomed the former *qadi* of Delhi to his court whether the marriage connection existed or not. Beyond that, Ibn Battuta arrived with a fascinating proposal that Ghiyath al-Din was only too happy to entertain:

> I had an interview with the sultan in the course of which I broached the Maldive affair and proposed that he should send an expedition to those islands. He set about with determination to do so and specified the warships for that purpose.

The plan the two men devised was to have Ibn Battuta lead a naval invasion of the atolls and intimidate Queen Khadija into accepting an unequal alliance with the sultanate. Ghiyath al-Din would marry one of the queen's sisters while men loyal to him, Ibn Battuta among them, would run the kingdom as a satellite of Ma'bar. The plot had only to await preparation of an attack fleet, which, the sultan's naval chief reported, would take at least three months.[7]

Presumably the admiral set to work fitting out the warships, but the plan began to go awry almost as soon as it was hatched. From the outset, Ibn Battuta took a dislike to Ghiyath al-Din, whose troops went about the land rounding up Tamil villagers and indiscriminately impaling them on sharpened stakes, the sort of political atrocity absolutely forbidden to Muslim rulers by Qur'anic injunction. Ibn Battuta and his retinue spent some time in Pattan (Fattan), the main port of Ma'bar,[8] then traveled upcountry to Madurai, the capital of the sultanate and one of the major towns of southeastern India. There he found the population in the throes of an epidemic so lethal that "whoever caught infection died on the morrow, or the day after, and if not on the third day, then on the fourth." He purchased a healthy slave girl in the city, but she died the following day. Ghiyath al-Din, who was already ill from taking a love potion containing iron filings, witnessed the loss of his mother and son to the epidemic. A week later he himself died.[9] Nasir al-Din, a nephew of the dead sultan and a soldier of apparently low origins, quickly seized the throne and got to the business of dismissing or murdering various political enemies.

The new ruler was happy enough to retain the services of his predecessor's brother-in-law and pressed him to carry on with the expedition. Ibn Battuta might at that point have been willing to move ahead, but he suddenly fell seriously ill himself, probably not with the disease that had killed so many in Madurai but from the malaria he had contracted in the Maldives. By the time he recovered he had lost all interest in the conspiracy, disliked Madurai intensely, and wanted only to get out of Ma'bar. He never explains why he had such a drastic change of heart, but he gives the impression that he had little confidence in Nasir al-Din and liked him even less than Ghiyath al-Din. Whatever the reason, he refused the sultan's urgings to launch the war fleet and finally got permission to leave Ma'bar with his little entourage. His original plan of travel — before he got involved in Maldivian politics — was to visit Ceylon and Ma'bar, then go directly on to Bengal. But if he was leaving from Pattan about December 1344, he would not have found any vessels sailing into the Bay of Bengal until the start of the summer winds in May.[10] Ships were going in the other direction, however — westward around Ceylon to Malabar and Aden. If his immediate object was to flee the Sultanate of Ma'bar as fast as possible, then he and his companions would go wherever the monsoon blew.[11] And so he returned once again to Quilon on the Malabar coast.

His career at sixes and sevens, he stayed in Quilon for three months, still recovering from his illness. Then he decided to try his luck with his old patron Jamal al-Din of Honavar. The sultan might well have been less than delighted to see the man who had abandoned him so abruptly during the siege of Sandapur two and a half years earlier, but in any case the reunion was not to be. Ibn Battuta and his group took passage on a ship bound for Honavar, well enough aware that storms and shallows were not the only perils on the west Indian coast. Marco Polo had passed through the region about a half century earlier and described the danger well:

> You must know that from this kingdom of Melibar, and from another near it called Gozurat, there go forth every year more than a hundred corsair vessels on cruise . . . Their method is to join in fleets of 20 or 30 of these pirate vessels together, and then they form what they call a sea cordon, that is, they drop off till there is an interval of 5 or 6 miles between ship and ship, so that they cover something like a hundred miles of sea, and no merchant ship can escape them. For when any one corsair sights a vessel a signal is made by fire or smoke, and then the whole of them make for this, and seize the merchants and plunder them. After they have plundered them they let them go, saying: "Go along with you and get more gain, and that mayhap will fall to us also!" But now the merchants are aware of this, and go so well manned and armed, and with such great ships, that they don't fear the corsairs. Still mishaps do befall them at times.[12]

For Ibn Battuta and his luckless friends, the "mishap" occurred near a small island just south of Honavar.[13] Caught in the corsair's net, twelve ships suddenly converged on the lonely vessel and attacked at once. Clambering over the gunwales from all directions, the pirates quickly overpowered the hapless crew, and stripped the passengers of everything they had. "They seized the jewels and rubies which the king of Ceylon had given me," Ibn Battuta remembers, "and robbed me of my clothes and provisions with which pious men and saints had favored me. They left nothing on my body except my trousers."[14] Then, with an encouraging word to their terrified victims to pass that way again sometime, the brigands politely dropped them all off on the nearby shore unharmed.

Dispossessed and humiliated once again, Ibn Battuta did not walk the short distance up the Kanara coast to Honavar, probably concluding that it would be impolitic, if not thoroughly boorish, to appear before Jamal al-Din a second time in a state of destitution. Somehow he and his party managed to make their way back down the coast to Calicut — no details are given — where "one of the jurists sent me a garment, the qadi sent me a turban, and a certain merchant sent me another garment."

While recuperating in Calicut he learned through the port gossip that the other Jamal al-Din, the grand vizier of the Maldives, had died and that the pregnant woman Ibn Battuta had divorced had given birth to a son shortly after his departure the previous year.[15] He also learned that his old nemesis, the vizier 'Abdallah, had married Queen Khadija and assumed the office of chief minister. By this time Ibn Battuta had given up any idea of returning to the islands at the head of the Ma'bar navy, but he did have an urge to claim his son, a right he had in Muslim law. Well knowing that 'Abdallah could make considerable trouble for him if he turned up on Male again, especially if the Ma'bar conspiracy had become known, he decided nonetheless to chance a visit. Sailing from Calicut, presumably no later than May 1345, he reached the atolls in ten days.[16]

Landing first on Kinalos Island then sailing southward to Male, he found 'Abdallah reasonably well disposed toward him, though a bit suspicious. He dined with the vizier and was given lodgings near the royal palace, but he says nothing in the *Rihla* of renewing his political contacts. When his ex-wife learned that she was about to lose her son, probably for all time, she complained bitterly to 'Abdallah, who was nevertheless disinclined to stand in the father's way. The father, however, was a man with a long history of abandoning we may only guess how many sons and daughters in various parts of the Muslim world. After seeing the little boy and, we might hope, responding to the pleas of his wretched mother, he "deemed it fit for him to continue with the islanders." And so, after staying in the Maldives only five days, he boarded a junk bound for Bengal. He was not to return again, much to the relief, we may suppose, of all concerned.

Sailing round the southern tip of Ceylon into the Bay of Bengal, Ibn Battuta was joining a surge of Muslim migration into the maritime lands of greater southeastern Asia. The fourteenth was a century of bright opportunities for any believer seeking career, fortune, or spiritual self-mastery out beyond the frontier of the Dar al-Islam, where the Sacred Law and the rightly guided society it embodied had yet to be introduced to benighted millions. It was the century when Islamic urban culture secured itself firmly in Bengal, when Muslim mercantile settlements took charge of the international trade through the Strait of Malacca, and when cosmopolitan Islam reached its zenith of influence and prosperity in China.

Arab and Iranian seamen of the eighth century had first introduced Islam in the Far East during bold, year-and-a-half trading voyages from the Persian Gulf to the South China coast and back again. Yet these missions were given up by the tenth century as the Abbasid state and the T'ang empire of China deteriorated simultaneously. The Arabo–Persian settlement at Guangzhou virtually disappeared, and the voyages left hardly any Islamic impress on eastern Asia. Historians used to suppose that the cessation of these direct, long-distance links between the Middle East and China was evidence of a protracted "decline" of Muslim trade with the farther East. On the contrary, the long run of commercial developments between the eleventh and fifteenth centuries involved a more or less steady increase in the variety, and no doubt volume, of goods exchanged along the chain of southern seas, as well as proliferation of ports and local hinterlands incorporated into the inter-regional system. By the eleventh or twelfth centuries a Muslim network of trust, friendship, and social expectation ruled the commerce of the western Indian Ocean. Since the sea routes from there through the Bay of Bengal to the China Seas had since ancient times constituted a continuum of commercial exchange, it was almost inevitable that the network should push out along the shores north and east of Ceylon in search of new bases of operation. Sharing as they did an unusual *esprit de corps* and monopolizing the routes leading to the markets of Africa, Persia, and the Mediterranean basin, upstart Muslim merchants had powerful advantages over Indian, Malay, or Chinese trading groups, who found themselves gradually superseded by or, more likely, coopted into the Muslim club.

During the era of the two Sung dynasties (960–1279), China experienced spectacular economic growth. Agricultural and industrial output shot up, population soared, cities multiplied, and the internal network of roads and canals was vastly improved. A remarkable expansion of overseas trade accompanied these trends. Chinese nautical and naval technology was well in advance of the Arabian Sea tradition and could conceivably have been wielded to enforce a monopoly over the eastern sea routes. In fact, the Sung emperors embraced a dual policy. They encouraged Chinese merchants to trade directly to India (or in some isolated instances as far west as the Red Sea). But at the same time they invited foreign traders, notably Muslims, to establish, or in the case of Canton re-establish, settlements in the cities of South China.

Moreover, Chinese overseas mercantile operations tended to be hampered by the Sung government's insistence on close regulation and control. By contrast, the alien Muslim trading groups were fluid, versatile, and unimpeded by any central bureaucratic authority. They could therefore move goods across the Bay of Bengal and the South China Sea more speedily, more efficiently, and probably at lower cost than could the Chinese junk masters. Thus, the "commercial revolution" of Sung China stimulated the expansion of Muslim shipping east of Malabar and the growth of busy, multinational settlements in Quanzhou (Zaitun), Guangzhou (Canton), and other south coast ports. Muslim mercantile communities even sprang up in Hangzhou, the capital of the Southern Sung Dynasty (1127–1279), and other major towns along the interior land and water routes. Indeed, a significant proportion of Chinese merchants in the international trade appear to have converted to Islam, improving, as it were, their credit rating.

The Mongol invasion of China and overthrow of the Sung only reinforced these trends. The Yuan dynasty was the only one of the four great Mongol khanates whose rulers never converted to Islam. Nevertheless, the khans of the early Yuan period, distrusting, as well they might have, the loyalty and commitment of the sullen, hyper-civilized class of Chinese scholar-bureaucrats, brought in numerous foreigners of diverse origins and religions and placed them in responsible, even powerful, positions of state. These men depended completely on their Mongol masters to protect them and promote their careers and were expected to give unquestioning loyalty in return. The influence of foreign cadres reached its peak in the reign of Khubilai Khan (1260–94), when hundreds of Muslims of Central Asian or Middle Eastern origin (not to mention a few European adventurers such as Niccolo Polo and his son Marco) held jobs as tax-collectors, finance officers, craftsmen, and architects.

The Yuan "open door" policy on foreign recruitment, combined with their enthusiastic promotion of pan-Eurasian trade, attracted Muslim merchants into China's vast, largely unexploited market as never before. They came not only to the China Sea ports and the cities of the populous south, but also across Inner Asia and through the gates of the Great Wall to found settlements in the northern towns, including even Korea. The largest communities were in Quanzhou and Guangzhou on the southern coast. These groups largely governed the internal affairs of their own city quarters, and Muslim merchant associations, called *ortakh*, even took loans from the Yuan government to capitalize their foreign trade enterprises. Mosques, hospitals, *khanqas,* and bazaars rose up in the Muslim neighborhoods of Ch'üan-chou and Canton, and *qadis* were appointed to adjudicate the Sacred Law in civil and business affairs.[17]

Following Khubilai's death in 1294, the appointment of foreigners to official posts trailed off as the Yuan emperors lost touch with the stout ways of the steppe, took up the habits of traditional Chinese potentates, and gradually brought the Confucian scholar-gentry back into government. The Sinicization of the dynasty, which was especially pronounced after 1328, does not seem to have much affected Muslim trading enterprise in the cities, which continued to thrive until the collapse of the Mongol regime in 1368. Until that time, a Muslim might travel the main roads and canals of China, finding in the major towns little clusters of co-believers always eager to offer hospitality and to hear news from the west. After 1368, however, the alien Muslim settlements along the south Chinese coast shrank or disappeared, perhaps partly because local Chinese Muslim merchants took over this commercial sector.

The growth of Muslim commercial settlements in China in the Mongol Age was mirrored in similar developments along the coasts of Southeast Asia. The strategic link in the trade between India and China was the Strait of Malacca, connecting the Bay of Bengal with the South China Sea. Like the Malabar coast, the strait was a hinge in the monsoonal sailing system. Vessels crossing the Bay of Bengal eastbound on the summer monsoon could not normally reach China before the opposing northeast wind set in. Therefore they would winter in a port along the strait before continuing around the Malay Peninsula and across the South China Sea in April or May. Climatic reality encouraged India-based merchants to sell their goods in the strait towns, then return directly to Malabar on the winter wind. China shippers followed the same seasonal pattern of travel, only in reverse.

By the thirteenth century local Malay rulers of the strait, men who practiced Hinduism or a combination of Hindu–Buddhist devotions, were avidly encouraging Muslim traders to settle in their ports owing to the obvious fiscal advantages of tying themselves securely into the southern seas' commercial network. Wherever such communities sprouted, their members felt impelled to order their collective lives in accord with the demands of the *shari'a* to the extent the authorities permitted. Thus a call went out for the scribes, judges, Qur'anic teachers, mosque officials, craftsmen, and, since business was good, more merchants. In time, the Muslim population, with its universalist claims and its cosmopolitan connections, became large, rich, and prestigious enough to win over members of the Malay elite and ultimately to impress, intimidate, or manipulate the princely court into official conversion. This event in turn set off a new round of immigration from abroad, as enterprising, footloose men responded to what Marshal Hodgson calls the "drawing power" of new Muslim communities.[18]

This process was only just beginning in Southeast Asia when Ibn Battuta came through. A Malay prince, ruler of the port of Samudra on the northwestern coast of Sumatra, converted to Islam sometime in the late thirteenth century, and his is the earliest Islamicized state in the region historians have been able to discover.[19] Elsewhere in the Eastern Archipelago, that is, in the countries bordering the Java Sea and the "spice islands" further off to the east, Islam was still largely unknown in the first half of the fourteenth century. The subsequent three hundred years would be

the crucial period of quiet, persistent conversion, ultimately transforming Indonesia into an overwhelmingly Muslim country.

From the eleventh century, when the high age of Arab
geographical writing had almost run its course, down to the end of
the Islamic Middle Period, the *Rihla* stands alone as an eye-
witness Muslim travel account of Eastern Asia. Yet the story of
Ibn Battuta's journey to China must be told briefly and in a spirit
of uneasy skepticism. If we take his word for the itinerary he
followed, insofar as we can make sense of it, this was the longest
more or less uninterrupted trip of his career, spanning somewhere
between 11,000 and 12,000 miles of travel by land and sea. Yet his
narrative of the entire tour from the Maldives to Bengal, Sumatra,
China as far north as Beijing, and back to Malabar occupies less
than 6 percent of the *Rihla* text. And as both a descriptive account
and a record of personal experience of what alleges to be a bold,
arduous journey far beyond the frontiers of the Dar al-Islam, it is
the least satisfying and most problematic section of the entire
book.

The itinerary is vague, possibly disordered, and sometimes
baffling. Chronological information, except for what can be inferred here and there, is almost altogether lacking. Descriptions of
places, events, and things observed are often muddled or patently
inaccurate. The sort of precise personal witnessing that lends
credibility to so much of the narrative, while not altogether
lacking, is suspiciously spare. The fuzziness and obscurity of the
story stands out uneasily against the rich, vivid, even introspective
accounts of the years in India and the Maldives. Indeed, the
deficiencies of this part of the book give the impression that Ibn
Battuta remembered the details of his much earlier travels in
Persia, Africa, or Anatolia better than he did the Far Eastern trip,
which occurred less than a decade before the *Rihla* was composed.
Moreover, an estimation of the probable starting date of the
journey (that is, his second departure from the Maldives) and his
own recollection of the month when he returned to Malabar
suggest that he made the entire journey from the Maldives to
Peking in the far north of China and all the way back to South
India again in the space of about twenty months, including several
leisurely rest stops. Since we can safely eliminate the possibility of
his traveling by jet plane or speedboat, such a pace seems incon-
ceivable, and if not that, then at least pointless. All of these

difficulties have led some scholars to doubt that Ibn Battuta really traveled to China or even anywhere east of Ceylon, contending that this part of the *Rihla* may be a fabrication and the descriptive information it contains based entirely on hearsay.[20]

No one, however, has made a completely convincing case that Ibn Battuta did *not* go to East Asia, at least as far as the ports of South China. The riddle of the journey probably defies solution since the *Rihla*, we must remind ourselves, is a work of literature, a survey of the Muslim world of the fourteenth century in narrative form, not a travel diary composed along the road. We have no way of knowing the precise relationship between Ibn Battuta's real life experience and the account of it contained in the fragile manuscripts that have come down to us from his time. Moreover, the narrative of the China trip is by no means a collection of abstract reports or improbable tales. For all its sketchiness and ambiguity, it is still a story of countries and cities visited, events experienced, people talked to, and aspects of everyday life observed. And so, honoring Ibn Battuta with the benefit of the doubt, we follow him, albeit warily, to Bengal and beyond.

Instead of sailing directly from the Maldives to the Strait of Malacca on some pepper ship out of Malabar, Ibn Battuta decided first to visit Bengal. He probably had no trouble finding a vessel to take him there since the islanders carried on regular trade with that region, importing quantities of rice from the Ganges Delta, paid for in cowrie shells.[21]

Like the Deccan, Bengal in the thirteenth and early fourteenth centuries was a frontier of Turkish arms and Persian-style Islamic culture emanating from the Indo–Gangetic plain. But much unlike the central plateau, Bengal was a heavily populated, water-soaked garden of immense fertility. In the early thirteenth century the region was annexed to the Sultanate of Delhi. As Muslim governors and garrisons occupied the important delta towns, immigrants streamed in from the northwest, making Bengal the eastward overland terminus for the class of skilled and literate refugees and their descendants who had introduced Arabo–Persian civilization to India. By Ibn Battuta's time, a number of Bengali cities had *madrasas* and important Sufi lodges, and the conversion of Hindu or Buddhist peasant folk that would prove so successful in subsequent centuries was already getting under way.

The sultans of Delhi, however, found it exasperatingly difficult to hold the mastery of their eastern frontier. Unlike the northern plains, Bengal was extremely unaccommodating to the operations of cavalry. Jungles and mountains obstructed the routes in from the capital, and rivers were numerous and unfordable. Consequently, the local Turkish lords, who built up riverine navies to ensure their own purely regional power, repeatedly rebelled against Delhi. Muhammad Tughluq succeeded in placing governors over his delta provinces early in his reign, but when the pretense of his vast subcontinental empire became exposed, Bengal was one of the first provinces to bolt. In 1338, the eastern half of the region broke away when Muhammad's governor died, prompting an obscure Turkish officer named Fakhr al-Din Mubarak Shah to seize the main chance and proclaim a kingdom of his own. Two years later West Bengal seceded under similar circumstances.

Ibn Battuta seems to have wanted to visit the delta in the summer of 1345 mainly to seek the blessing of Shah Jalal. He was a celebrated holy warrior who, in the year our traveler was born, participated in the Muslim takeover of Sylhet, a town and district in the northeastern corner of the delta.[22] Under normal circumstances, Ibn Battuta would also have had himself presented at the princely court of Fakhr al-Din, whose capital was at Sonargaon, a city about half way along the route from the coast to Sylhet. In this case, however, Fakhr al-Din's dissidence was too recent and his own identification with Muhammad Tughluq too well known to make such an introduction advisable. Consequently, he decided to steer clear of royal interviews and make a quick trip up to Sylhet as anonymously as possible.

He probably disembarked at the busy eastern port of Chittagong, a city overflowing with agricultural goods transported by river craft down through the maze of delta channels to the coast.[23] He notes in the *Rihla* that foreigners liked to call Bengal "a hell crammed with good things." The noxious, humid vapours exuded from the delta's marshes and riverbanks made for an oppressive climate, but food was abundant and remarkably cheap. To prove his point, he even offers in the *Rihla* a list of prices for rice, meat, fowl, sugar, oil, cotton, and slaves. Not to pass up a bargain himself, he purchased an "extremely beautiful" slave girl in Chittagong. One of his comrades acquired a young boy for "a couple of gold dinars."

He tells us nothing very lucid about the itinerary or time schedule of his trip from Chittagong to Sylhet, but he very likely traveled by boat northward along the Meghna River valley, a lush, watery, rice-growing country leading to the Assam Plateau and the Tibetan Himalayas beyond.[24] He seems to have had a party of companions, but they are more phantom-like than ever. Al-Tuzari was apparently with him when he visited Ma'bar, but he is never mentioned after that and indeed we learn parenthetically in an earlier part of the *Rihla* that the man died in India.[25]

Shah Jalal of Sylhet, whose tomb is still a local pilgrimage center, was renowned in medieval India for awesome miracles, prognostications, and the feat of dying at the age of 150.[26] One day, the *Rihla* reports, the old *shaykh*, who had no previous knowledge of Ibn Battuta, told his disciples that a traveler from the Maghrib was about to arrive and that they should go out to meet him. This they did, intercepting the visitor two days' distance from the *khanqah*. The story gives Ibn Battuta a convenient entrée to remind his readers of his own singular accomplishments as a globetrotter:

> When I visited him he rose to receive me and embraced me. He enquired of me about my country and journeys, of which I gave him an account. He said to me, "You are a traveler of Arabia." His disciples who were then present said, "O lord, he is also a traveler of the non-Arab countries." "Traveler of the non-Arab countries!" rejoined the *shaykh*, "Treat him, then, with favor." Therefore they took me to the hospice and entertained me for three days.

Returning southward along the Meghna River past "water wheels, gardens, and villages such as those along the banks of the Nile in Egypt," he reached Sonargaon (not far from modern Dacca), the capital of Sultan Fakr al-Din. Without dallying long or identifying himself at the royal residence, he bought passage on a commercial junk departing down the river and went directly on to Sumatra.

The route of his voyage to the Strait of Malacca, which would probably have taken place in the fall or winter of 1345–46, is an annoying puzzle since this part of the *Rihla* is murky and possibly disarranged. The ship made one stop at a place he calls Barah Nagar, which may have been a small Indo–Chinese tribal state along the western coast of Burma.[27] The ship's company presented gifts to the local chief (who appeared dressed in a goatskin and

Map 10: Ibn Battuta's Itinerary in Southeast Asia and China, 1345–46

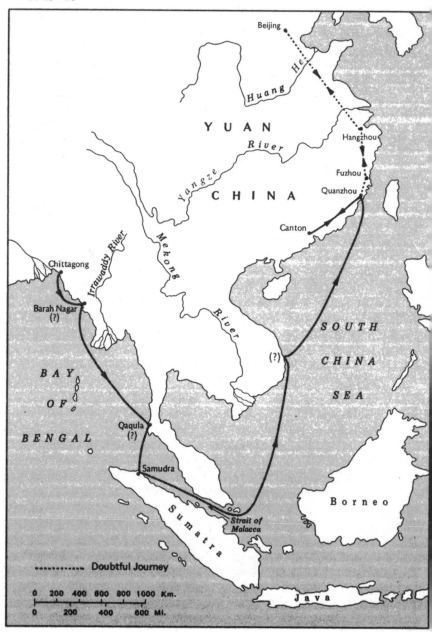

riding an elephant), then did a bit of trading and sailed away. A second stop was made at a port called Qaqula (Kakula, or Qaqulla), a lair of pirates. It may have been located somewhere along the Tenasserim coast on the western side of the Malay Peninsula.[28] Here Ibn Battuta visited the walled town, accepted the hospitality of the infidel Malay ruler for three days, and had the grisly treat of watching one of the prince's subjects decapitate himself as a show of affection for his sovereign!

Continuing south along the Malay coast and into the mouth of the strait, the junk put in at the Sumatran port of Samudra, a transshipping town located on one of the rivers flowing down from the wild mountains of the northwestern interior.[29] In a political sense Samudra was the last outpost of the Dar al-Islam. Though other towns down along the Sumatran coast had thriving commercial settlements, no sovereign Muslim states are known to have existed anywhere east of Samudra before the mid fourteenth century.

Al-Malik al-Zahir Ahmad, the prince of the place and third in a line of Muslim rulers extending back some years before 1297,[30] warmly entertained Ibn Battuta and his companions in his wooden-walled town, which was a few miles upriver from the port settlement. Except for the mosque, the Friday prayer ritual, the foreign Muslims attending at court, and the fact that the sultan enjoyed lively discussion on points of Islamic law with a small cadre of legal scholars, the palace of Samudra followed custom and ritual not much different from any of the Hindu–Buddhist states of Malaya or the Archipelago.[31] Getting into the spirit of things, Ibn Battuta exchanged his under-breeches for a loincloth, and before appearing at court, donned a rich set of garments in the local fashion. His first official host was a ranking military officer, whom, it turned out, he already knew. The man had traveled to Delhi some years earlier on a diplomatic mission for Samudra. Later, the newcomer was presented to al-Malik al-Zahir, who invited him to sit on his left at royal meals and plied him with questions about his travels and the affairs of Delhi.

Ibn Battuta recalls that he spent only two weeks in Samudra, but it may have been longer than that since he did not leave for China until about April 1346, that is, when the southwest monsoon started and ships bound for Quanzhou or Guangzhou normally left the strait.[32] In any event, he departed in style. Al-Malik al-Zahir honored his learned guest by outfitting and provisioning a junk for him and even sending along one of his courtiers to provide good company at shipboard meals.

The normal sailing time from Sumatra to the South China coast was about 40 days,[33] but Ibn Battuta remembers that the trip took something short of four months. He accounts for the longer time by describing two stops at ports along the way, possibly on the coasts of eastern Malaya, Champa, or Tonkin. Unfortunately, the *Rihla*'s description of these places is so murky and, in the case of one of them, of such doubtful authenticity that their location remains a puzzle.[34]

Ibn Battuta arrived on the coast of China during the last peaceful years of Mongol rule. Signs were growing of the violent popular uprisings against the Yuan that would begin in a few years, but in 1346 the country was still unified and prosperous. On the throne was Toghon Temur. He had come to power in 1333 after an unsettling period of murderous succession fights within the royal family. Turning his back on the Mongolian steppe, he ruled in the style of a traditional Confucian emperor and cultivated reasonably amiable relations with the Chinese elite.

Ibn Battuta praises China as vast and bounteous, noting the quality of its silk and porcelain, the excellence of its plums and watermelons, the enormous size of its chickens, and the advantages of its paper money. He says that "China is the safest and most agreeable country in the world for the traveler. You can travel all alone across the land for nine months without fear, even if you are carrying much wealth."[35] On the other hand, he admits to experiencing the worst culture shock of his traveling career, unable to accept or understand much of what he witnessed, like a member of some American tour group, hopping through Asia from one Hilton and air-conditioned bus to another.

> China was beautiful, but it did not please me. On the contrary, I was greatly troubled thinking about the way paganism dominated this country. Whenever I went out of my lodging, I saw many blameworthy things. That disturbed me so much that I stayed indoors most of the time and only went out when necessary. During my stay in China, whenever I saw any Muslims I always felt as though I were meeting my own family and close kinsmen.[36]

Through the cultural lens of a Maliki schoolman, he saw the Chinese as heathens, worse indeed than the Christians in their ignorance of the One God and every single one of the prophets. More disturbing than that, the Confucian scholars were supremely confident that the Moroccan traveler's own ideas of God and the universe were not worthy of serious discussion. If we accept the assumption that he did in fact visit China, we should be tolerant of his failure to learn much about Chinese culture or to report much of what he had learned in the *Rihla*. It was, after all, a book about the triumphant expansion of the Dar al-Islam, not about civilizations still befogged in idolatry.

Even his account of his own itinerary through China is vague, brief, and uncharacteristically superficial. Although he claims to have traveled something close to 3,500 miles, mostly along China's extensive river and canal system, he mentions visiting only six different cities and what he says about them is mostly either conventional or inaccurate.[37] Only his encounters with acquaintances old or new seem to ring true. After landing at the great port city of Quanzhou on the coast of Fujian province, he had the good fortune, as he certainly hoped he would, to meet up with one of the Chinese envoys who had accompanied him from Delhi to Calicut and who had made it back to China ahead of him. This gentleman willingly introduced him to the Yuan chief of customs in Quanzhou, who assigned him a comfortable house. Ibn Battuta told this official that he had come to China as the ambassador of the sultan of India, and a letter to this effect was duly sent off to the emperor in Beijing. Since Muhammad Tughluq's gifts to Toghon Temur were lying at the bottom of the sea off Calicut, one wonders just how Ibn Battuta, suddenly wandering in with none of the retinue or accoutrements of an official diplomat, established his credibility. In any case, the emperor was to decide whether the man should be told to proceed to the capital.

In the meantime the visitor met the Muslim worthies of Ch'üan-chou and even ran into a man named Sharif al-Din al-Tabrizi, one of the merchants who had loaned him money when he was first setting himself up in Delhi. He also made a brief trip 300 miles down the coast to the port of Canton (Guangzhou), where he lodged for two weeks with one of the rich traders.

Soon after he returned to Quanzhou, he received word that he was indeed to go on to Beijing as the guest of the emperor. He relates that he traveled by river boat, but he mentions only two place names between Quanzhou and Hangzhou (Khansa), cities almost 400 miles apart as the crow flies. It would have been logical for him to travel northward along the canal system, but we can only guess at the route he took. He made one stop at a city he calls Qanjanfu, which may have been the port of Fuzhou.[38] Here he had the remarkable pleasure of meeting a fellow Moroccan. The man was a young scholar named al-Bushri who had come originally from Ceuta, a city only 40 miles from Tangier. He had left home to travel to the eastern lands in the company of an uncle. Ibn Battuta in fact had already made a slight acquaintance with him in Delhi.

> I had spoken of him to the sultan of India, who gave him three thousand dinars and invited him to stay at his court, but he refused, as he was set on going to China, where he prospered exceedingly and acquired enormous wealth. He told me that he had about fifty white slaves and as many slave-girls, and presented me with two of each, along with many other gifts.[39]

Al-Bushri accompanied his compatriot for four days out of Qanjanfu, then sent him on his way north to Hangzhou.

Former capital of the Southern Sung empire, Hangzhou may well have been the largest city in the world in the fourteenth century.[40] Ibn Battuta declares that it was indeed the biggest place he had ever seen and that its foreign Muslim population was large and thriving. He speaks of residing in the Muslim quarter with a family of Egyptian origin, then later meeting the Yuan governor in the palace and enjoying banquets, canal rides, and performances of magic. Yet his description of Hang-chou is cursory, blurred, and defective, as though he *had been told* it was the greatest city on earth but could not convey in the *Rihla* any concrete or convincing images of what such a place was like.[41]

He claims to have continued on from Hangzhou to Beijing (a distance of about 700 miles) by way of the Grand Canal, which the Mongol rulers had extended as far as Beijing earlier in the century. This section of the *Rihla,* however, is so strange and so deficient in historical accuracy that it seems highly unlikely he traveled anywhere north of Hangzhou, if that far, or that he ever completed his checkered diplomatic mission to Toghon Temur.[42] Indeed, his own dating clues lead us to infer that his entire tour of China was jammed into the summer and early autumn of 1346. Unless a full year has mysteriously dropped out of the chronology, the journey to Beijing must be apocryphal. However deep into China he actually went, he recounts that he returned to Quanzhou by retracing his route through Hangzhou and Qanjanfu and that he arrived on the south coast to find a junk belonging to the Sultan of Samudra ready to embark for the Strait of Malacca.

Setting sail from the port on the first rush of the fall monsoon of 1346, he was, if he did not quite know it at the time, on his way home again. Within a little over three years he would be walking the steep streets of Tangier and telling his wondrous tales among the learned men of Fez.

Notes

1. *The Travels of Marco Polo*, trans. and with an introduction by Ronald Latham (New York, 1958), p. 237.
2. Henry Yule, *Cathay and the Way Thither*, 4 vols. (London, 1913–16), vol. 3, p. 232.
3. S. Pathmanathan, *The Kingdom of Jaffna* (Colombo, 1978), p. 235; MH, p. 217n.
4. William Geiger, *Culture of Ceylon in Mediaeval Times* (Wiesbaden, 1960), pp. 105–08.
5. IB states that he visited a place he identifies as Kunakar, capital of the king called Kunwar. He does not say that he met this ruler and indeed reveals that, about the time he passed through, the lords of the realm rose against the man and installed his son on the throne in his place. Mahdi Husain (MH, p. 219n) identifies Kunakar with Kurunegala, but more recent studies suggest it was either the city of Ratnapura, which lay south of Adam's Peak, or Gampola, the Sinhalese capital, which was more or less on the way from Puttalam to the mountain. C. W. Nicholas and S. Paranavitana, *A Concise History of Ceylon* (Colombo, 1961), p. 296; Pathmanathan, *Kingdom of Jaffna*, p. 240. IB's Kunwar was probably not the Sinhalese king but a well-known chief minister who was exercising power in the ruler's name. Nicholas and Paranavitana, *History of Ceylon*, p. 296; Pathmanathan, *Kingdom of Jaffna*, p. 238. The Sinhalese state had been a large and powerful one in earlier medieval times, but by the fourteenth century it had declined precipitously and would be invaded by Jaffna about 1359.
6. IB offers no chronological information on his journey through Ceylon. By his own reckoning he left the Maldives in August. Mahdi Husain (MH, pp. lxviii–lxix) estimates a stay on the island of about two months, which seems reasonable.
7. IB says the admiral reported that no voyage could be made to the islands for three months. This might be taken to mean that the summer monsoon was in full strength, making the expedition risky from a navigational point of view. But unless our chronological scheme is hopelessly off track, IB arrived in Ma'bar in the fall, that is, near the start of the northeast monsoon and the best time to sail for the Maldives.
8. IB's Pattan has not been identified, but Yule (*Cathay*, vol. 4, p. 35) suggests that it stood somewhere on the Palk Strait leading into the Bay of Bengal. H. A. R. Gibb suggests Kaveripattanam or Negapatam in the Kaveri River delta. *Ibn Battuta: Travels in Asia and Africa* (London, 1929), pp. 365–66n. Large vessels leaving this port for the Maldives would have had to circumnavigate Ceylon owing to the blocking reefs of Adam's Bridge.
9. IB gives no clue about the pathology of this epidemic, but he does not link it specifically to plague, which he witnessed later in Syria. The assertion of some

historians that the Black Death passed through India on its way to the Middle East and Europe on the grounds that IB witnessed it in Madurai is not justified. Michael W. Dols, *The Black Death in the Middle East* (Princeton, N.J., 1977), p. 377.

10. G. R. Tibbetts, *Arab Navigation in the Indian Ocean before the Coming of the Portuguese* (London, 1971), p. 377.

11. Ships would very likely have been leaving the Ma'bar coast in December for voyages to Malabar and on to South Arabia. *The West Coast of India Pilot*, 11th edn. (London, 1975), p. 24; Tibbetts, *Arab Navigation*, p. 375. Such a departure time fits in well with my suggested reconstruction of the chronology.

12. *The Book of Ser Marco Polo*, trans. and ed. Henry Yule, 2 vols., 3rd edn., rev. Henri Cordier (London, 1929), vol. 2, p. 389.

13. Yule (*Cathay*, vol. 4, p. 35) identifies this place with Pigeon Island.

14. At several other places in the *Rihla* IB refers to gifts and souvenirs he lost in this holdup, including a set of tomb inscriptions he had copied when he passed through Bukhara in Central Asia.

15. IB states that his son was about two years old when he saw him in the Maldives. But if the boy was born shortly after his father left the islands the first time (in August 1344), he would have been less than a year old at the time of the second visit. See note 16. Perhaps a lapse of memory is the explanation here.

16. Following the monsoon pattern, IB must have left Calicut no later than May. Calicut harbor would have been closed in June and July, and if he waited until the end of the summer to go to the Maldives, he would not have found ships at that season sailing from there to Bengal.

17. Morris Rossabi, "The Muslims in the Early Yuan Dynasty" in John D. Langlois, Jr., *China under Mongol Rule* (Princeton, N.J., 1981), pp. 274–77; Howard D. Smith, "Zaitun's Five Centuries of Sino-Foreign Trade," *Journal of the Royal Asiatic Society*, pts. 3 and 4 (1958): 165–77.

18. Marshall G. S. Hodgson, *The Venture of Islam*, 3 vols. (Chicago, 1974), vol. 2, p. 541.

19. A. H. Hill, "The Coming of Islam to North Sumatra," *Journal of Southeast Asian History* 4 (1963): 6–21.

20. The most adamant skeptic is Gabriel Ferrand, *Relations de voyages et textes géographiques arabes, persans et turks relatifs à l'Extrême Orient du VIII au XVIII siècles*, 2 vols. (Paris, 1913–14). He finds IB's itinerary through Southeast Asia and China "absurd or unrealizable" (vol. 2, p. 429) and concludes that IB "never went to Indochina and invented the journey out of whole cloth; or else either Ibn Juzayy or copyists of manuscripts of the narrative modified the text to the point where it is devoid of any exactitude" (vol. 2, pp. 432–33). Yule, who had published the most detailed annotation of the China trip, accepts IB's veracity in general but points out numerous flaws and puzzles in this section of the *Rihla* that must raise genuine doubts. *Cathay*, vol. 4, pp. 50–51 and *passim*. Gibb believes IB went to China, observing that to reject its veracity raises more problems with the text than otherwise. *Travels in Asia and Africa*, pp. 13–14. More recently, Peter Jackson has argued that IB's sojourn in China is "highly suspect," emphasizing Yule's observations that (1) the mosque IB claims to have seen at Guangzhou in 1346 burned down in 1343 and was not rebuilt until 1349–51, and (2) his account of political events in Beijing and North China during his visit there in 1347 bears almost no resemblance to what we know from numerous other sources. "The Mongols and India (1221–1351)," Ph.D. diss., Cambridge University, 1977, p. 221.

21. *The Voyage of François Pyrard of Laval to the East Indies, the Maldives, and Moluccas and Brazil,* trans. and ed. Albert Gray, 2 vols. (London, n.d. [Hakluyt Society]; reprint edn., New York, 1963?), vol. 1, pp. 237–42; MH, p. 201.

22. N. K. Bhattasali, *Coins and Chronology of the Early Independent Sultans of Bengal* (Cambridge, England, 1922; reprint edn., New Delhi, 1976), pp. 150–54.

23. IB identifies the place of his debarkation as Sudkawan. Several historians have taken sides on the issue of whether this toponym corresponds to Chittagong, today an

important city in southeastern Bangladesh, or Satgaon, a medieval commercial center in the western delta region north of modern Calcutta. The proponents of Chittagong are Muhammad Abdur Rahim, *Social and Cultural History of Bengal* (Karachi, 1963), pp. 12–14; Bhattasali, *Coins and Chronology*, pp. 145–49; Gibb, *Travels in Asia and Africa*, p. 366n; MH, p. 235n; and Yule, *Cathay*, vol. 4, p. 82n. The advocates of Satgaon are Jadunath Sarkar (ed.), *The History of Bengal*, 2 vols. (Dacca, 1948), vol. 2, p. 100; *Ibn Batutah's Account of Bengal*, trans. Harinath De, and ed. P. N. Ghosh (Calcutta, 1978), app. I, pp. 1–4; Ferrand, *Relations de voyages*, pp. 434–35; and Henri Cordier, editor of 3rd edn. of Yule's *Cathay*, vol. 4, p. 82n. Without laying out the several semantic and geographical arguments advanced on both sides, I find the case for Chittagong the more convincing, especially in the context of IB's subsequent movements through Bengal.

24. IB states that he went to see Shah Jalal in the mountains of Kamaru, that is, Kamrup in Assam. Sylhet, however, is on the edge of the delta region just south of the hills of Assam. IB does not mention Sylhet by name, but Shah Jalal is known to have resided there. Yule, *Cathay*, vol. 4, pp. 151–52. Mahdi Husain (MH, p. 237n) suggests that IB made a long looping tour up the Brahmaputra River through central Assam, then southward to Sylhet. But there is nothing in IB's account of his personal experiences indicating he went any further north than Sylhet.

25. In connection with his befriending al-Tuzari in Cairo, IB states that the man "continued to accompany me for many years, until we quitted the land of India, when he died at Sandabur." Gb, vol. 2, p. 415. However, IB says nothing of al-Tuzari in the account of his experiences at Sandapur, and the man was apparently still in his suite later in Ma'bar. It is conceivable that IB made a subsequent visit to Sandapur that he never mentions in the *Rihla* and left al-Tuzari there; or else al-Tuzari went there on his own when IB left India on his way to China.

26. IB calls the man he visited Shaykh Jalal al-Din al-Tabrizi, but he appears to have confused the saint of this name, a divine of the Suhrawardi order who died about 1225, with Shah Jalal, the Muslim conqueror of Sylhet. Abdul Karim, *Social History of the Muslims of Bengal* (Dacca, 1959), pp. 91–101; Abdur Rahim, *Social and Cultural History of Bengal*, pp. 85–103; Bhattasali, *Coins and Chronology*, pp. 149–54. This mistake might raise questions about the authenticity of IB's journey into the interior of Bengal, except that Bengalis themselves commonly confuse these two holy men and even use "Shah Jalal" as a generic term for any powerful saint. Personal communication from Richard Eaton, University of Arizona.

27. G. R. Tibbetts, *A Study of the Arabic Texts Containing Material on South-East Asia* (Leiden, 1979), p. 97; Yule, *Cathay*, vol. 4, pp. 93–94n.

28. The identification of Qaqula is a puzzle. IB places his visit there *after* his stopover in Sumatra and identifies the place with Mul-Java, which in some Arabic texts means the island of Java. None of the principal commentators, however, are convinced that IB actually visited Java. Cordier (Yule, *Cathay*, vol. 4, p. 157n) believes Qaqula to be located on the east coast of the Malay Peninsula, that is, along IB's route from the Strait of Malacca to China. Tibbetts (*Arabic Texts*, pp. 97–98) makes an interesting case for placing Qaqula on the western, or Tenasserim, coast of Malaya. He suggests that the description of it may be displaced in the *Rihla* and that IB probably stopped there on his way from Burma to Samudra (northwest Sumatra).

29. IB calls the island of Sumatra "Java," which was common medieval usage. Marco Polo calls Sumatra "Java the Less." Paul Pelliot, *Notes on Marco Polo*, 2 vols. (reprint edn, Paris, 1959–63), vol. 2, pp. 757–58; Yule, *Cathay*, pp. 94–95. The commercial center, known as Samudra, whose exact medieval site is not certain, later gave its name to the entire island. Kenneth R. Hall, "Trade and Statecraft in the Western Archipelago at the Dawn of the European Age," *Journal of the Malaysian Branch of the Royal Asiatic Society* 54 (1981): 30–31; Hill, "North Sumatra," pp. 7–12.

30. Hill, "North Sumatra," pp. 13–15.
31. Kenneth R. Hall, "The Coming of Islam to the Archipelago: A Re-Assessment" in Karl L. Hutterer (ed.), *Economic Exchange and Social Interaction in Southeast Asia* (Ann Arbor, Mich., 1977), p. 226.
32. IB implies in the *Rihla* that he left at the start of the southwest monsoon, as Défrémery and Sanguinetti (D&S, vol. 4, p. 239) note parenthetically.
33. Teobaldo Filesi, *China and Africa in the Middle Ages*, trans. D. L. Morisen (London, 1972), p. 15.
34. One of the stops mentioned is Qaqula. See note 28. The other is a port called Kaylukari (Cailoucary) in the country of Tawalisi. IB's description of his visit to the female governor of the city (and daughter of the king) reads as though it were a pastiche of legends, misplaced anecdotes, and garbled geography. The people of this realm look like Turks, IB says, and the king is the equal of the emperor of China, against whom he conducts successful naval campaigns. The governor-princess, who happens to have the same name as one of the wives of Ozbeg, Khan of Kipchak, speaks Turkish, writes Arabic characters skillfully, but is not a Muslim! She also commands a force of female mounted archers! Yule (*Cathay*, vol. 4, pp. 157–60) develops a lengthy, unconvincing argument to suggest that Tawalisi is a kingdom in the Sulu Archipelago, the most southerly island group of the Philippines. Défrémery and Sanguinetti (D&S, vol. 4, p. 248) put forward Tonkin or the Celebes without explanation. Yamamato Tatsuro argues for Champa, i.e., southeastern Indochina. "Tawalisi Described by Ibn Battuta," *Memoirs of the Research Department of the Toyo Bunko*, no. 8 (1936), pp. 93–133. Tibbetts (*Arabic Texts*, p. 98) favors Indochina. Assuming that IB traveled the normal route from the Strait of Malacca to South China and did not visit Java, then intermediary stops along the Malayan or Indochinese coast would not have been out of the ordinary. The description of Tawalisi, however, does seem embellished with information pulled from other contexts. Legends and tales about a mysterious "kingdom of women" or "island of women" appear in Arabic, as well as European and Chinese, medieval literature. Pelliot, *Notes on Marco Polo*, vol. 2, pp. 671–725.
35. D&S, vol. 4, p. 267.
36. D&S, vol. 4, pp. 282–83.
37. Because of the language barrier, IB would certainly have had difficulty remembering, or even recording in notes, numerous Chinese place names. When he and Ibn Juzayy composed the *Rihla*, we may suppose they had at hand a library of standard Arab geographical and travel works and used them to help IB refresh his memory about particular places, including the spelling of toponyms. Such reference works, however, had little to say about China, obliging him to rely on his own recollections or notes (if there were any) when mentioning strange Chinese place names to his collaborator.
38. Gibb (*Travels in Asia and Africa*, p. 371n) makes a tentative case for Qanjanfu being Fuzhou. Yule (*Cathy*, vol. 4, pp. 126–27n) argues that the place may be identified with Kien Ch'ang Fu in the interior province of Jiangxi. But, as Gibb points out, a route from Quanzhou to Hangzhou by way of Jiangxi would have been roundabout and very unlikely.
39. Gibb, *Travels in Asia and Africa*, p. 292. Gibb notes (p. 14) that IB would never have told of such an encounter if he had not really traveled to China, since the citizens of Ceuta might well have confirmed the story through the family of al-Bushri at some later time. Also see Chapter 13 on IB's meeting al-Bushri's brother in southern Morocco in 1353.
40. Jacques Gernet, *Daily Life in China on the Eve of the Mongol Invasion 1250–1276*, trans. H. M. Wright (Stanford, Calif., 1970), pp. 27–31.
41. Yule (*Cathay*, vol. 4, p. 130) notes that "there are several very questionable statements in Ibn Batuta's account of the great city."
42. Aside from some descriptive incongruities, IB's account of his visit to Beijing

is made barely credible by his assertion that he witnessed the funeral of the Yuan emperor, who, he says, had died in battle attempting to quell a revolt led by a rival member of the royal house. There is no doubt at all, however, that Toghon Temur reigned straight through from 1333 to 1368. Yule (*Cathay*, vol. 4, p. 142) can find no "indication of any circumstance occurring about this time that could have made the foundation of such a story," though IB's description of Mongol funereal ritual is generally accurate (p. 143). Jackson ("Mongols and India", p. 221) thinks the story may be "a very garbled version" of a succession conflict that had taken place in China in 1328–29, when IB was far away in Arabia and Africa.

12 Home

Civilization both in the East and the West was visited by a destructive plague which devastated nations and caused populations to vanish. It swallowed up many of the good things of civilization and wiped them out . . . Civilization decreased with the decrease of mankind. Cities and buildings were laid waste, roads and way signs were obliterated, settlements and mansions became empty, dynasties and tribes grew weak. The entire inhabited world changed.[1]

Ibn Khaldun

Sometime in Ramadan 747 A.H. (December 1346 or January 1347) Ibn Battuta arrived back in Quilon on the south Malabar coast. He had sailed all the way through from Quanzhou to India on a single winter's monsoon, changing ships at Samudra in the Malacca Strait and making a return visit of a few weeks to the court of Sultan al-Malik al-Zahir. Once in Quilon he lodged with the qadi until the Breaking of the Fast, then traveled on up the coast to Calicut.[2]

Here he had another argument with himself over the advisability of returning to North India, throwing himself on the mercy of Muhammad Tughluq, and perhaps recovering his judicial sinecure. Such a plan might be brash enough to work in the short run. Yet quite apart from the possibility that his appearance before the royal Person would be swiftly followed by his execution, anyone in Malabar could have warned him that the Tughluq empire was in a more advanced state of deterioration than when he had left India and that Delhi in 1346 was hardly an auspicious place to rebuild a career in public service. And so, repudiating once and for all the attractions of that extraordinary city, he decided not to travel north. (Muhammad Tughluq had in fact left Delhi the previous year on one of his frantic campaigns. He would never return again, perishing of an illness on the banks of the Indus in 1351 while obsessively chasing down his last rebel.

266

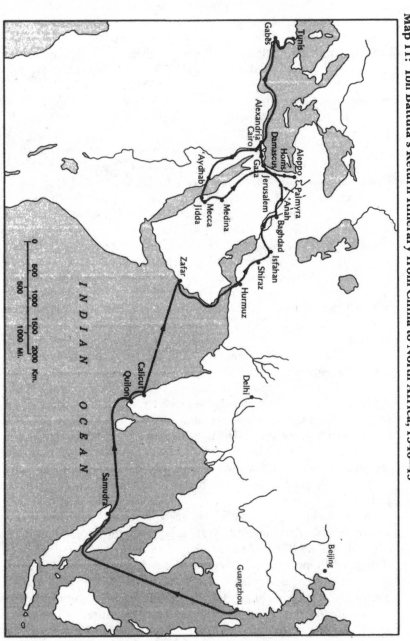

Map 11: Ibn Battuta's Return Itinerary from China to North Africa, 1346–49

His successor, Firuz Tughluq, would inherit only a modest North Indian state and be obliged to share the subcontinent with a patchwork of upstart Muslim and Hindu kingdoms.)

When Ibn Battuta had first angered Muhammad Tughluq back in 1340 over the Shihab al-Din affair, he had thought then of making the *hajj* again, if only as a credible excuse for getting out of the sultanate. Now, in the absence of any further prospects for a career in India, Mecca seemed more than ever a sensible destination.

The season for westbound voyages from Malabar was coming to an end, but he managed to secure passage on a ship embarking for Zafar (Dhofar), the South Arabian port he had visited 18 years earlier in connection with his trip to East Africa. He has nothing to say about his spring voyage across the open expanse of the Arabian Sea except that the trip took a normal 28 days and that he reached Zafar in Muharram 748, that is, sometime after 13 April 1347. Possibly because the next *hajj* season was almost a year away or because he would have had to wait in tedious Zafar until September to get a westbound ship to Aden, he decided to make a grand looping tour through Persia, Iraq, Syria, and Egypt, violating once again his quixotic oath never to travel by the same road twice.

From Zafar he sailed on a coasting vessel that was running before the early summer monsoon up to the Gulf of Oman and the Strait of Hurmuz. Arrived at Hurmuz city, he found the elderly Arab ruler of that great emporium locked in a naval war with two of his nephews for control of the family domain, which included all the key ports of the strait. The fighting had severely disrupted the India trade, and the country was gripped by famine. Ibn Battuta stayed there for about two weeks but had only one brief meeting with the old sultan, who was preoccupied fitting out his war galleys.[3]

The political and economic troubles Ibn Battuta found at the mouth of the Persian Gulf were echoes of the violent disintegration of the Ilkhanid state, which had occurred twelve years earlier when he was just beginning his career in Delhi. For three-quarters of a century the successors of the Mongol conqueror Hulegu had held greater Persia precariously together, but the finances of the Ilkhanate rested on an agricultural and urban recovery that was too limp to ensure firm, confident central rule over the long term. When the young king Abu Sa'id died suddenly in 1335 while on campaign in the Caucasus against the Golden Horde, he left a government debilitated by chronic frontier wars and a throne with no obvious successor groomed to mount it. On the instant, an omnivorous mix of Mongol and Turkish commanders leapt into the political void, violently challenging one another for control of the land. By the time Ibn Battuta returned to the region, the great kingdom had been superseded by a cluster of states, ruled by parvenu military dynasties. Thus the Khanate of the Ilkhans was the first of the four Tatar empires to run its course, heralding the last days of the Mongol Age.

Apparently having little urge to discover what any of these petty regimes might offer him, Ibn Battuta hurried through Persia, making his only important stopover at Shiraz. Traveling north to Isfahan, then westward over the Zagros Mountain passes to Basra, he retraced his journey of 1327 up the valley of the Euphrates. In January 1348 (Shawwal 748) he made a brief stop in Baghdad. From there he continued along the valley beyond 'Anah, then crossed the Syrian desert on the camel route through Palmyra (Tadmor). He reached Damascus, second capital of the Mamluk Sultanate, some time in the late winter of 1348.

The first time he had visited Damascus in 1326, he had married a woman of Moroccan origin. But he divorced her when he set out for Mecca, terminating a union that lasted hardly more than a few weeks. Much later in India he learned that after the separation the woman had given birth to a son. Feeling some responsibility for the boy, if not for the mother, he had sent his ex-wife's father, who lived not in Syria but in Morocco, a gift of 40 gold dinars, presumably through the good offices of a westbound merchant. Now arrived in Damascus again, he soon learned that the son he had never seen had died about 1336 at the age of ten.

More unhappy news followed. A Moroccan jurist who was affiliated with one of the Damascene colleges informed him that his father had passed away in Tangier some 15 years earlier. His mother, as far as the man knew, was still alive and well.

After resting in Damascus for several weeks, he decided about the end of March to make a trip up to Aleppo (Haleb), the second ranking city of industry and commerce in Syria and the seat of Mamluk administration on the northern frontier. This journey was to be one of his leisurely diversions, an itinerary to occupy a few months before it was time to travel toward Mecca. Yet even as he rode north, the catastrophe of the fourteenth century descended on Syria behind him.[4]

While Ibn Battuta was enjoying the company of the *'ulama* of Aleppo in June 1348, travelers reaching the city from the south reported that a virulent disease had been raging at Gaza on the Egyptian frontier and that more than a thousand people had been dying from it every day. Buboes, or inflamed swellings, appeared in the groin, armpits, or neck of the afflicted, and this irruption was typically accompanied by nausea, pain in the head, stomach, and limbs, insomnia, and delirium. If a victim began to spit blood and experience pneumonic symptoms, he usually died within hours.

Amid rumors of this lethal darkness advancing into Syria, Ibn Battuta decided to return south. He got as far as the town of Homs when he suddenly found himself engulfed in the epidemic, 300 people dying the day he arrived there. Continuing on to Damacus, he reached the great oasis in July to find that the plague had already struck. The death toll had risen to 2,000 a day, the population was reeling in shock, and the mundane routines of the city had come to a halt.

The people fasted for three successive days, the last of which was a Thursday. At the end of this period the *amirs, sharifs, qadis*, doctors of the Law, and other classes of the people in their several degrees, assembled in the great mosque, until it was filled to overflowing with them, and spent Thursday night there in prayers and liturgies and supplications. Then, after performing the dawn prayer . . ., they all went out together on foot carrying Qur'ans in their hands – the *amirs* too barefooted. The entire population of the city joined in the exodus, male and female, small and large, the Jews went out with their book of the law and the Christians with their Gospel, their women and children with them; the whole concourse of them in tears and humble supplications, imploring the favor of God through His Books and His Prophets.[5]

At the same time that Ibn Battuta had been sailing westward from China to his expectant reunion with the Islamic heartland, so the Black Death, the greatest pandemic disaster since the sixth century, was making its terrible way across the Central Asian grasslands to the shores of the Black Sea. Plague was endemic among ground-burrowing rodent populations of the Inner Asian steppe. It was transmitted from animals to humans by the bite of a common species of flea. Hatching and living in the fur of plague-afflicted rats, infected fleas found their way to sacks of grain and other foodstuffs or to clothing. The plague appears to have started among pastoral folk of East Central Asia, spreading outward from there along the trade routes both southwest and west, beginning about 1331. Lurking among the merchandise in commercial wagon trains or the storerooms of caravansaries, fleas carried the bacillus *Yersinia pestis* to the bloodstream of humans. The bubonic type of plague, which produced buboes on the body, could be spread only by infected fleas and their rodent hosts. However, pneumonic plague, the deadlier form of the disease, was transmitted directly from one human to another. As the pestilence broke out in one oasis or *khan* after another, survivors hurried onto the next place along the trail, thereby unwittingly carrying the disease throughout the commercial network of the steppe. The same Mongol law and order that made possible a century of intense human interchange between China and the Atlantic coast now quickened the progress of the plague bacillus across Eurasia. The Black Death was the grimly ironic price the world paid for the trans-hemispheric unity of the Pax Mongolica.

In China, where frontier fortifications were no defense whatsoever against the advance of the invader, major outbreaks of plague occurred in 1353 and 1354, producing massive mortality and economic disruption and probably contributing to the collapse of the Yuan dynasty 14 years later. In the west the disease advanced through the Kipchak Khanate to the Black Sea, where it struck the Genoese colony at Kaffa in 1346. From there Italian ships carried infected rats and fleas amongst cargoes of grain, timber, and furs southward to Constantinople, then on to Venice and Genoa. The epidemic appeared about simultaneously in Sicily and Egypt in the autumn of 1347. The Egyptian historian al-Maqrizi tells the ghastly tale of a trading ship, probably from the Black Sea, arriving one day in Alexandria harbor. Out of a total company of 332, all but 40 sailors, 4 merchants, and 1 slave had succumbed to the plague at sea. And all who had survived the voyage presently died in the port.[6]

In the calamitous year of 1348 ships of death coursed westward throughout the Mediterranean basin, inflicting their grim lading on one port after another. From the ports, mule trains and camel caravans transmitted the disease to the interior regions of Europe, northern Africa, and the Middle East. Paris and Bordeaux,

Barcelona and Valencia, Tunis and Cairo, Damascus and Aleppo all suffered massive plague mortality in the spring and summer of 1348. By the following year the contagion was moving up the valley of the Nile and crossing the English Channel to the British Isles. By the end of 1350, when the first assault of the disease was playing itself out, Europe may have lost as much as one-third of its population. Mortality rates in the Islamic lands were probably comparable. Cairo's pre-plague population of perhaps half a million may have been reduced by 200,000. The population of Damascus may have diminished from 80,000 to less than 50,000.[7]

The Black Death struck the cities and towns of Islam with the suddenness and surprise of a Mongol attack. The usual patterns of quotidian life were abandoned, and communities gave themselves to prayers of supplication and to the overwhelming task of washing, shrouding, and burying the proliferating dead. Funeral processions moved through the streets in a never-ending parade of grief. Stocks of burial garments ran out, and gravediggers who managed to survive commanded exorbitant fees for their work. Mosques closed when all the officials and caretakers died. Many who fled the plague in vain hope of evading it fell dead along the road with their horses and camels. A scholar witnessing the scene in Egypt writes of "these dead who are laid out on the highway like an ambush for others."[8]

Both Muslims and Christians struggled to fit this unprecedented disaster into a framework of spiritual meaning. Christian doctrine invited the conclusion that the sins of mankind had accumulated to the point where God was obliged to teach his creation a lesson it would never forget. Amid the horrors of the plague, many believed this lesson was to be the final one, the end of the world. A mood of impending apocalypse seized Europe, producing obsessive preoccupation with images of death, furious self-flagellating movements to expiate sins, and massacres of Jews, the traditional target of hostility and fear. In Islam, by contrast, no doctrine of original sin pervaded theology. All events affecting the community of believers were to be understood as the continuing revealing of God's will. Despite social trauma in the midst of the plague, Muslims mostly accepted it as a manifestation of God's unknowable plan for His creation. Mass public supplications to God to lift the scourge probably occurred in most cities and towns of the Middle East, but expiation crusades, messianism, or persecution of minorities were not in evidence.

Neither Muslims nor Christians in that age had the faintest notion of the medical pathology of the disease, which was not discovered until the late nineteenth century. In both Europe and the Islamic world the epidemic was generally attributed to a miasma, that is, a corruption of the air. Some authorities linked it to a polluted wind, a mysterious "impoisoned blast" blowing out of Central Asia or from the open sea.[9] Prophylactic advice abounded. Muslims were recommended to live in fresh air, sprinkle one's house with rose water and vinegar, sit as motionless as possible, and eat plenty of pickled onions and fresh fruit. Those who fell victim to the disease were advised to have their blood drawn, apply egg yolk to the plague buboes, wear magical amulets, or have their sick bed strewn with fresh flowers. Above all, God's creatures were urged to spend their nights in the mosque and beg divine mercy.

Ibn Battuta says nothing of any personal measures he may have taken to keep from falling ill, but he left Damascus sometime after July 1348 in good health, even as the pestilence raged around him. He does not seem to have taken to the road to escape the plague but only to continue on his way to Mecca by way of Egypt, where the sickness was as bad as it was in Syria, if not worse. Traveling southward into Palestine through one depopulated village after another, their water wheels idle and their fields abandoned, he arrived at Jerusalem to find that the contagion had abated there. In fact, the preacher of the grand mosque invited him to a feast in fulfillment of an oath to give special thanks to God as soon as a day passed on which no one perished.

Joining up with two gentlemen of North African origin, Ibn Battuta continued on in their company through Judaea to Gaza, which he found mostly deserted in the wake of the Death. Indeed the population of the entire Nile Delta region was declining drastically in the fall months of 1348, when the plague was at its worst.[10] The travelers passed through Alexandria, where the epidemic may have first entered Egypt in the fall of 1347, to learn that there the daily mortality rate was finally subsiding.

In Cairo, however, the toll was still rising. Urban land and property were being abandoned precipitately, commerce and industry became paralyzed, and, in the words of one chronicler, "the deaths had increased until it had emptied the streets."[11] The Mamluk Sultan al-Hasan fled from Cairo to a country estate in

September and stayed away from his capital for three months.[12] The royal officer corps, living in close quarters in the Citadel and refusing to leave Cairo for fear of losing their power and rank to rival Mamluks, sustained such a high rate of die-off that the army and administration of the sultanate fell into a state of disorder and diminished capacity lasting several decades.[13]

Ibn Battuta probably stayed in the ravaged city no more than a few days, then continued on up the Nile. Now, happily, he moved ahead of the plague, which did not strike Upper Egypt until about February 1349.[14] Crossing the Red Sea from 'Aydhab to Jidda as he had done in the reverse direction 18 years earlier, he performed the ceremony of the *tawaf* around the Holy Ka'ba on 16 November 1348 (22 Sha'ban 749), praising God that he had so far been spared. He remained in Mecca for more than four months as the guest of the Maliki *imam*, awaiting the *hajj* of 749. He relates nothing about plague in the city, though other historical sources report that it raged there during the pilgrimage season, introduced by the caravans from Egypt or Syria.[15]

Since returning from India, Ibn Battuta's wish had been to stand before the Holy House one more time. Now that he had done it, he may have had no further plans in particular. For the time being at least, he decided to go back to Cairo (by a route through Medina, Jerusalem, and the Sinai). The Mamluk capital was hardly the city he had known in 1326. Aside from the ruin and wastage of the plague (which abated only after January 1349), the quality of leadership over the Mamluk state had badly deteriorated since the death of al-Nasir Muhammad ibn Qala'un in 1341. Over the ensuing decade that great builder was succeeded by four different sons and grandsons, all of whom were lusterless or infantile pawns of one quarreling military faction or another.

Perhaps the bleak scene in Cairo quickened the journeyer's resolve to return at last to his native land. He was 45 years old, he had been abroad for 24 years, and, so far as he knew, his aged mother was alive and still living in Tangier. In his absence Fez, the capital of the Marinid dynasty, had blossomed into the premier city of Maliki religious and legal studies in western Islam. As a former *qadi* of the Sultanate of Delhi, he should, if he wished, have no trouble securing a government post either in Fez or some other Moroccan town. And, ironically enough, Morocco was one of the few corners of the Islamic world he had not yet explored. In the end, however, sentiment and nothing else may have impelled him to head for that beautiful land of the Far West: "I was moved [to go back] by memories of my homeland, affection for my family and dear friends, who drew me toward my land, which, in my opinion, was better than any other country."[16]

Leaving Egypt for the last time on a small vessel belonging to a mariner from Tunis, Ibn Battuta sailed along the Cyrenaican and Tripolitanian coasts to the port of Gabès (Kabis) on the south Ifriqiyan mainland where he passed the feast of the Prophet's birthday on 31 May 1349 (12 Rabi' I 750) in the company of the local notables. Continuing up the coast by sea, he joined a party of bedouin traveling overland to Tunis, a city then under the command of the Amir of the Muslims and Defender of the Faith Abu l'Hasan, Sultan of Morocco.

A quarter of a century earlier Ibn Battuta had traveled across the Eastern Maghrib in conditions of military turmoil. Now it might have appeared to him that little had changed. The Arab tribes of the Ifriqiyan plains were up in arms, and Tunis lay under siege. Yet the pattern of North African power politics had altered drastically in his absence. By going abroad for so long he had missed most of the reign of Abu l'Hasan (1331–51), the most illustrious of the Marinid kings. Called the Black Sultan because of the dark visage he inherited from his Ethiopian slave mother, Abu l'Hasan was more than any of his predecessors impassioned by the old Almohad vision of a vast Islamic state embracing the entire western Mediterranean basin. In 1333 he recaptured Gibraltar from King Alfonso XI of Castile and during the ensuing four years seized most of the important towns of the 'Abd al-Wadid kingdom of the central Maghrib, including Tlemcen, the capital. In 1340 he sent 44 war galleys into the Strait of Gibraltar to inflict a calamitous defeat on the Castilian fleet. Six months later he launched an invasion of Spain in alliance with the Sultanate of Granada. This time, however, a combined army of heavily armored knights from Castile, Aragon, and Portugal routed his forces near the Rio Salado.

The Battle of Rio Salado ended once and for all any serious Muslim hopes of reversing the Christian *reconquista*. Indeed, Abu l'Hasan may have been so fearful that the Spanish crusade would now advance on Africa that he redoubled his efforts to bring the entire Maghrib and its resources in commerce and manpower under his control. Taking advantage of a succession crisis within the ruling Hafsid family, he invaded Ifriqiya by land and sea in September 1347 and drove the Hasfids from Tunis.

The Marinid seizure of Tunis was a remarkable feat of military leadership. Yet Abu l'Hasan's army was now operating almost 900 miles from Fez, and the Ifriqiyan population remained implacably hostile to his occupation. In the spring of 1348 he ventured to firm up his authority over the plains south of the capital, but an alliance of bedouin tribes met his forces near Kairouan and beat them so badly that he was forced to retreat to Tunis by sea in utter humiliation. As if his human detractors were not troublesome enough, his Ifriqiyan campaign coincided with the arrival of the Black Death. According to the historian Ibn Khaldun, the plague so debilitated his army in the field that it "settled the affair" at the Battle of Kairouan.[17] When he fell back on Tunis, he found the contagion ravaging the city and killing off his courtiers and officials. Abu 'Inan, the sultan's son and governor of the central Maghrib, heard reports that his father had died at Kairouan. Fearing rebellion in Morocco, he had himself proclaimed sultan at Tlemcen in June 1348 and quickly marched on Fez.

When Ibn Battuta arrived in Tunis just one year later, the Marinid dream of Mediterranean empire was for the time being dead. Abu l'Hasan was still there, but bottled up within the Hafsid palace and doing nothing to repel the bedouin forces which commanded the countryside beyond the city walls. A large number of Moroccan scholars had accompanied the sultan to Ifriqiya, and Ibn Battuta found lodging with one of them, apparently a cousin of his. He had at least two audiences with his hapless sovereign, giving him the usual information about the countries he had visited.

Ibn Battuta stayed in Tunis for about a month, then decided to continue on to Morocco despite the agitated state of political affairs all across the Maghrib. He left Ifriqiya on a Catalan vessel, hardly a surprising choice since in the mid fourteenth century the merchants and ship masters of Barcelona dominated trade on the sea routes between Spain and the Sicilian Channel. The ship was bound for Tenès on the Algerian coast but on the way put in at Cagliari at the southern end of the island of Sardinia.[18]

The Kingdom of Aragon–Catalonia ruled the coastal regions of Sardinia, giving Ibn Battuta an opportunity to set foot on Latin Christian soil, the only time he would do so in his traveling career. The visit, however, was brief and disagreeable. He left the ship to

Map 12: Ibn Battuta's Itinerary in North Africa, Spain, and West Africa, 1349–54

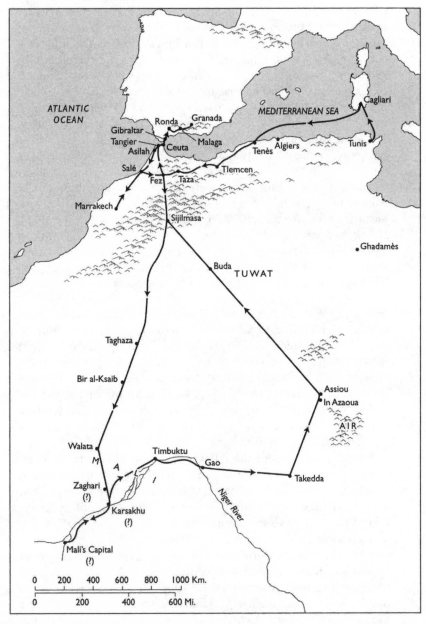

visit a marketplace inside a chateau-fort in the vicinity of the port. But then he was informed that some piratical residents of the island had in mind to pursue his vessel after it embarked in order to seize the Muslim passengers and presumably hold them for ransom. Swearing that he would fast for two consecutive months if the Almighty saved him from these sea rovers, he reboarded his ship, which, as it happened, continued on its way without incident. After ten days at sea, he reached Tenès.

From here he traveled overland to Tlemcen, which was then under the authority of the rebellious Abu 'Inan. Here he joined two men of Tangierian origin and continued westward in their company. In the wild hills near the modern day Algero–Moroccan border the little party had a close brush with a band of highwaymen, but they passed on safely to Taza, the little hillside city commanding the high road to Fez. Apparently meeting up with more travelers from Tangier, Ibn Battuta learned that the Black Death had carried off his elderly mother only several months earlier. Had she heard in her last days, perhaps from pilgrims returning from the *hajj* of 749, that her long-departed son had been seen in Mecca and might finally be coming home?

When Ibn Battuta left Morocco in 1325, he may well have intended at the time to return in two or three years to pursue advanced legal studies in Fez. Under the patronage of the Marinid sultans, the city had come to rival Tunis as the premier North African center of Maliki jurisprudence and Arab letters. The war captains of the Banu Marin had rudely seized power in Morocco in 1248 without possessing any religious ideology to justify their authority. Consequently, they moved quickly to assert their distinctive legitimacy by distancing themselves from the idiosyncratic theological doctrines of the Almohads. They moved the dynastic capital from Marrakech to Fez and invited learned exponents of Malikism, whose views had been suppressed during the Almohad century, to take up residence in the city, revitalize orthodox Maliki education, and serve the administrative and judicial needs of the new government.

When the Banu Marin came to power, Fez was already an important Almohad military center and a busy commercial junction linking the trans-Maghrib road with the caravan routes that brought West African gold and ivory to the ports of the Mediterranean. Nestled saucer-like in a lovely valley between the southern spurs of the Rif and the central plain, Fez had an abundant water supply and a rich agricultural hinterland which animated a profusion of craft industries.

Physically, ancient Fez occupied a remarkably small territory, its growing population of merchants, artisans, civil officials, scholars, laborers, and transients crammed within the circular walls that enclosed the valley. Then in 1276 Abu Yusuf Ya'qub, the second Marinid sultan, built a new urban foundation, called Fez Jdid, or New Fez, to serve as the military and administrative center of the dynasty. Set on a plateau above the old city and enclosed within high double walls, Fez Jdid, like the Mamluk citadel of Cairo, rose up as a conspicuous, fear-inspiring symbol of Marinid power and permanence. It was the exclusive sanctuary of the sultan, his high officials, his accountants and secretaries, and selected units of the royal army.

Fez Jdid nonetheless remained dependent on the teeming, labyrinthine city in the valley below, not only for its food and luxuries, but also for many of the literate men who managed the bureaus of state. As champions of Maliki orthodoxy, the early Marinids sponsored the founding of *madrasas* on the organizational and curricular pattern of the great colleges of the Middle East. Abu Yusuf built the first college sometime before 1285. Sultans Abu Sa'id and Abu l'Hasan founded five more, employing the most talented Moroccan and Andalusian craftsmen to produce buildings of exquisite decorative beauty. Abu l'Hasan also founded *madrasas* in several other Moroccan cities, including Tangier. The colleges of Fez soon attracted the flower of erudition from all across the Maghrib, as well as from Muslim Granada. Some of these luminaries divided their time between the *madrasas* in the depths of the old city and the ministries of Fez Jdid. Others came mainly to teach, thereby attracting to the colleges increasing numbers of bright young people, several hundred of them by the mid fourteenth century, to undertake advanced studies in the religious sciences.

Sufi ideas were only just beginning to penetrate higher education in Fez at the mid point of the fourteenth century. The more rigorous leaders of the Maliki elite opposed any teachings not firmly grounded in scriptural orthodoxy. The Marinids displayed respect for the most celebrated saints of western Islam, but they distrusted the potential political influence of the Sufi holy men who were becoming so popular among the Berber folk of the countryside. Yet despite the resistance of both the government and the conservative religious establishment to the teachings of a movement they could not satisfactorily control, the Sufi precepts of love, divine grace, and spiritual fulfillment were already by the middle of the century warming the chill corridors of Maliki formalism. An unknown Tangierian scholar just back from the East could expect at least the more liberal-minded within the learned circles of Fez to take a keen interest in his stories of personal meetings with the great mystics of the age.

Ibn Battuta arrived in Fez on 8 November 1349 to find the city in a state of uncertainty and suspense over the fate of the empire.[19] The usurper Abu 'Inan was the son of a Christian slave woman and as slender and fair as his father was corpulent and black. He had occupied Fez for more than a year and had made himself master of Morocco. Like his father, he was a pious, cultivated man, given to holding regular study sessions with the leading divines and jurists and to writing belles-lettres and poetry. The elite of Old Fez accommodated to his regime readily enough, but the fact remained that for the moment there were two sultans and no one knew when or if Abu l'Hasan might appear before the walls of Fez at the head of his army. The usual course for the cosmopolitan professional man in such circumstances was to submit to whomever happened to be occupying the royal audience chamber at the time.

Ibn Battuta, having just come from making obeisance to Abu l'Hasan in Tunis, now presented himself at the great palace of Fez Jdid to stand before his "illustrious master" Abu 'Inan. He apparently did not get an opportunity to address the sultan, but a vizier named Abu Ziyan ibn Wadrar offered him gifts and questioned him about Egypt, a country the minister had visited. Ibn Battuta decided not to stay in Fez for very long, however, since he was anxious to return to Tangier. Given the precarious political situation in the capital, it was probably prudent, in any case, to go elsewhere.

Arrived in his natal town some time during the fasting month of Ramadan, he tells us only that he visited his mother's grave.[20] He does not mention his deceased father, suggesting that the man may have died in some other place. Nor does he describe joyous reunions with brothers, sisters, cousins, or old friends. Indeed, the fourteenth-century reader of the *Rihla* would find too much of that sort of information tedious and irrelevant. Yet we can imagine a homecoming of warm recognition and nights spent in the central mosque or the houses of kinsmen, sharing tales of Muhammad Tughluq and Ozbeg Khan and of those glorious days in the precinct of the Holy House.

Restless again after only a few days among the haunts of his childhood, Ibn Battuta decided to make the short trip overland to Ceuta (Sabta), which in that age was the queen city of the Strait of Gibraltar. Endowed with a fine sheltered harbor and superb natural defenses, Ceuta was the headquarters of the Marinid navy and the chief Moroccan terminus of the West African gold trade. The town was set on a tongue of land jutting eastward into the Mediterranean. The eastern half of this little peninsula was dominated by the heights of Mount Hacho (Jabal al-Musa). From its summit lookouts had a commanding view of the strait and the Iberian shore beyond.[21]

When Ibn Battuta walked through Ceuta's western gate, he was in a sense already arriving in Muslim Spain. Located a mere 14 miles from Europe but separated from its own Moroccan hinterland by a chain of mountains, the city was culturally a prolongation of Andalusia. Its leading official and scholarly families had centuries-old ties to the great Muslim intellectual centers of Spain, and as the Christian *reconquista* progressed in the thirteenth and fourteenth centuries, it was the chief port of entry for skilled and educated refugees fleeing into Africa. From the point of view of a lettered man, Ceuta's mellow Andalusian sophistication made it a much more interesting place than Tangier. So it is not surprising that Ibn Battuta spent "several months" there, undoubtedly frequenting the new college Abu l'Hasan had built and perhaps making acquaintance with the al-Bushri family, whose scholar kinsman he had met a few years earlier in China. He was, unfortunately, ill during much of his visit. The plague was still raging in the region of the strait, but he says nothing about contracting the bubonic type (from which some did recover). More likely he was suffering from yet another bout of malaria.

At the time he arrived in Ceuta, the city was intently following reports from Gibraltar, 22 miles across the strait. In the previous July Alfonso XI of Castile, taking advantage of the Marinid civil crisis and Abu l'Hasan's absence in Ifriqiya, had laid siege to the Rock and its mighty fortifications. Since the loss of Algeciras to Castile in 1344, Gibraltar remained the only port on the northern shore of the strait still in Muslim hands. If Alfonso breached its walls, the immediate consequence would be to cut the main military supply route, not only to the few towns the Moroccans still held in Iberia, but also to their ally, the Nasrid Sultan of Granada. More than that, the loss of Gibraltar would give Castile and its Christian allies such a naval advantage in the strait that both Tangier and Ceuta would be under a greater danger of invasion than ever before.

Either in Tangier or Ceuta, Ibn Battuta learned that volunteers were urgently wanted to aid the Moroccan army in the defense of Gibraltar. Recovering from his illness in Ceuta and thanking God for it, he decided to respond to the call. He had taken up arms a time or two in his career, and he was certainly susceptible to the high esteem Islam paid to those who served spontaneously in the *jihad*. He set sail for the Rock on a small Moroccan vessel in March or April 1350.[22] By this time, however, the immediate military crisis had completely dissipated. During the months of the Castilian siege, the Black Death had made war on both armies with scrupulous impartiality. On 26 March 1350, it took the life of King Alfonso, distinguishing him as the only monarch of Christian Europe to die in the epidemic of mid century.[23] The loss of their valiant warrior king obliged the Castilian forces to abandon the siege, leaving the promontory and the isthmus of Gibraltar under Muslim control, a state of affairs that would endure, as it turned out, for another 112 years.

Whether to his disgruntlement or relief, Ibn Battuta was discharged of any military duty when he arrived in Gibraltar port and so was free to see the sights. He made a thorough inspection of the promontory and its ramparts, climbing up to the Calahorra, a massive stone tower Abu l'Hasan had constructed at the summit of the citadel to serve as the pivot of the town's defenses. The *qadi* of Gibraltar accompanied him on his tour and hosted him in his house on one of the streets of the town, which lay up against the western face of the Rock. "I desired to be, until the end of my life, among those who guarded and defended this place," Ibn Battuta recalls in the *Rihla* with perhaps a hint of bravado. But since at the moment there was no serious defending to be done, he was soon on the road again, crossing the sandy neck of land that linked Gibraltar to the highlands of Andalusia. He mentions no companions and may well have been traveling with only a servant or two.

With the withdrawal of the Christian siege, it was relatively safe for Muslim travelers to venture along the overland routes to Granada. This Ibn Battuta now proposed to do, probably with the hope of adding the Nasrid sultan Abu l'Hajjaj Yusuf ibn Isma'il to the list of Muslim rulers who had invited him to their table. The direct route from Gibraltar to Granada City ran along the Mediterranean coast to Malaga. Typically, he decided to go a different way, traveling northward through the rich vineyards and fruit orchards of the Rio Guadiaro valley, then up into the forests of the Sierra de Ronda. The city of Ronda, which occupied a spectacular site straddling the deep gorge of the Tajo River, was still a possession of the Marinids in 1350. Ibn Battuta may have gone there partly to see a paternal first cousin of his, who was the *qadi* of the town. After five days he returned to the coast again by the treacherous mountain road over the Sierra Bermeja to the little port of Marbella.

Here he made the acquaintance of twelve men who were just then setting out for Malaga along the coast road through Suhayl (Fuengirola), a fortress at the western frontier of the Nasrid kingdom. He intended to join up with them, but for some unexplained reason they left Marbella without him. He found another party of travelers, however, and was soon on his way.

Moving eastward along the narrow plain between the sea and the Sierra de Mijas, Ibn Battuta had a mind at one point to ride out ahead of his companions. All along this shore the Nasrid sultans, and other Muslim rulers before them, had constructed stone watchtowers at regular intervals to guard against coastal raiders and to survey the movements of foreign navies. As he was nearing one of these towers, he suddenly came upon a dead horse lying by the side of the road. Suspicious of trouble but moving along a little further, he came upon another horse recently slain. Then, hearing shouts behind him, he returned to his fellows to find them in the company of the Nasrid commander of Suhayl fort. The twelve horsemen who had left Ibn Battuta behind in Marbella, it seemed, had run into a band of Christian corsairs. The marauders had approached the coast in four galleys. Finding no one on guard at the watchtower to sound the alarm, a party of them had gone ashore and ambushed the first travelers who happened by. One of the horsemen had been murdered and one escaped. The remaining ten had been taken prisoner to be held for ransom. Thanking God for delivering him from infidel pirates for the second time in his life, Ibn Battuta accepted the invitation of the commander of

Suhayl to spend the night in the castle. The next day the officer escorted the travelers safely on to Malaga, chief port of the Nasrid realm.

Entering the city's central mosque, a magnificent building whose interior court bloomed with orange trees, Ibn Battuta found the *'ulama* and other notables of the town gathered to collect ransom money for the captured men, who were no doubt citizens of Malaga. He told the assembled group his story of having barely escaped death or capture himself. They were all astonished at his good fortune, and the *qadi* and preacher both gave him hospitality. If he ever learned how the negotiations with the pirates turned out, he does not report it.

From Malaga he continued eastward to Velez Malaga (Ballish), then turned into the mountains. He passed through Alhama, a town famous for its hot spring baths, then continued on northeastward to the Vega, the upper valley of the Genil River, whose fertile highland plain sustained Granada City's 50,000 inhabitants.[24]

Two decades earlier Ibn Battuta had visited Christian Byzantium at a time of military retreat before the triumphant Turks. Yet in the same period Constantinople was the scene of brilliant erudition in Greek science and philosophy, as if to make a final, defiant statement of a thousand years of creativity before surrendering to an ineluctable fate. At the opposite end of the Mediterranean the Sultanate of Granada was displaying a similar contradiction of trends. Like the three kingdoms of the Maghrib, the Nasrid state had been founded in the aftermath of the Almohad collapse. By 1348 it was, with the exception of the enclaves the Marinids held on the coast, the only remaining stronghold of Muslim power in Iberia. Pressed into its mountainous corner of the peninsula by Castile and Aragon—Catalonia, Granada struggled to survive by building up its frontier defenses and pursuing a policy of pragmatic diplomacy with Christian and Muslim neighbours alike.

The Sultanate had a population of perhaps a million people in the fourteenth century,[25] a fervently Muslim population ready to defend valley by valley what remained of its Iberian patrimony. Inescapably, time was on the side of the Christian states. But while Granada endured, its people dedicated themselves, perhaps consciously so, to the mission of summing up six centuries of

Outer walls of the Alhambra, Granada, Spain
Photo by the Author

A view of Old Fez.
Photo by the Author.

Andalusian civilization. The Nasrid cultural achievement was not intellectually or aesthetically innovative. Rather it was a final exquisite reaffirmation of the literary and artistic heritage of Islamic Spain.

Demonstrating once again his remarkable ability to visit Muslim kingdoms at their efflorescent best, Ibn Battuta saw Granada in the reign of Abu l'Hajjaj Yusuf, or Yusuf I (1333–54). Together with his successor Muhammad V (1354–59, 1369–91), Yusuf was the most successful ruler in a dynastic line of 23 largely undistinguished men. Following the débâcle of the Battle of Rio Salado, in which Granada had fought on the side of the Marinids, Yusuf succeeded in arranging what proved to be long-term military truces with both Castile and Aragon. Free for the time being from the threat of invasion, he and his circle of brilliant ministers and secretaries devoted themselves to perpetuating Andalusia's legendary tradition of urbane learning and taste. It was Yusuf (and later Muhammad) who constructed the most beautiful courtyards and portals of the Alhambra, "the red fort" which stands on a spur of the Sierra Nevada overlooking the city of Granada and the fertile valley of the Genil River beyond. The Alhambra was the seat of Nasrid government and court life. From the outside it was a forbidding, mysterious complex of stone ramparts, but within a buoyant, gossamer composition of exquisitely decorated halls and courts, juxtaposed one to another in a symphony of light, shadow, and flowing water. "The peculiar charm of this old dreamy palace," Washington Irving wrote in the nineteenth century, "is its power of calling up vague reveries and picturings of the past, and thus clothing naked realities with the illusions of the memory and the imagination."[26]

Ibn Battuta may have presented himself at the palace as soon as he arrived in Granada. But he had no audience with Yusuf I. The sultan, it seemed, was ill and not disposed to receive learned visitors from Morocco. The visitor, to his consternation, never did get to meet Yusuf during his brief sojourn in the city. He does not say in the *Rihla* whether he ever went inside the Alhambra and in fact omits any mention of it. The twentieth-century tourist is so amazed by those splendorous rooms and courts that Ibn Battuta's failure to take the slightest note of them seems puzzling. Yet the Alhambra is the only Islamic palace of that age to survive down to our own time in all its ornamental delicacy. Ibn Battuta had seen the royal mansions of far bigger and richer kingdoms than the Nasrid state, and to his eyes and his world the Alhambra may not have seemed so special as it does to us.

He was not on the other hand totally ignored by the royal family. When his arrival in Granada was made known to the authorities, as it routinely would be, the sultan's mother sent him a purse of gold coins, which he found "very useful" for meeting his expenses. He spent part of his time as the guest of various Maliki notables and the rest visiting a number of Sufi lodges in the Granadine suburbs or the nearby countryside. He even notes that little bands of mendicant Sufis from as far away as Anatolia, Persia, India, and Samarkand were settled in the town.

It was in the home of Abu l'Kasim ibn 'Asim, one of Granada's eminent jurists, that he made what later proved to be the most fateful acquaintance of his life. Over a period of two days and a night he sat amongst a group of Andalusian gentlemen in Abu l'Kasim's lovely garden, recounting scenes and episodes of his travels abroad. One of the men present was Abu 'Abdallah Muhammad ibn Juzayy, a 28- or 29-year-old *'alim* who held a secretarial post in the Nasrid government. He was one of three sons of a noted Granadine jurist and poet who had been killed at the Battle of Rio Salado. The young Ibn Juzayy carried on the family's distinguished literary tradition, writing poetry and composing respectable works in philology, history, and law.[27]

Absorbed by Ibn Battuta's stories and the sheer breadth of his travels, Ibn Juzayy meticulously copied down the names of famous doctors and *shaykhs* the journeyer had met over the previous quarter of a century. Since Ibn Battuta did not stay in Granada very long, his acquaintance with Ibn Juzayy was probably fleeting. But in another two and a half years the young secretary, in the pattern of roving Andalusian scholars, would leave Granada to take up service with Sultan Abu 'Inan in Fez. He would be there when Ibn Battuta returned from the far side of the Sahara Desert, ready to accept the sultan's assignment to set down in proper literary form the complete record of the Tangierian's remarkable career.

Sometime around the end of 1350 Ibn Battuta returned to Ceuta.[28] For the next several months he journeyed about his homeland, spending a few months in the Atlantic port of Asilah, visiting Salé briefly, then riding south across the coastal plains to Marrakech, late capital of the Almohads. The shift of political power to Fez, and probably the havoc of the Black Death, had caused Marrakech to fall into a dilapidated state, worse, he recalls, than Baghdad. Finding no reason to remain in those surroundings for long, he returned north to the coast and from there to Fez.

In the meantime the drama of the Marinid kings had come to its denouement in the triumph of Abu 'Inan. Late in 1349 Abu l'Hasan had abandoned Tunis and returned to Morocco, determined to reckon with his mutinous son. Reaching Marrakech with a small force of exhausted followers, he had attempted to erect a rival government. But in May 1350 Abu 'Inan defeated his forces outside the city, then pursued him southward into a valley of the High Atlas. Trapped and powerless, the old sultan held out through the ensuing winter, then made formal abdication in favor of his son. When he died of illness and despair in his mountain refuge later in the spring of 1351, Abu 'Inan carried his body to the city of Rabat and had it buried with all the honors of state in the royal necropolis of the dynasty.

These events occurred while Ibn Battuta was traveling about Spain and northern Morocco. When he arrived in Fez the second time, probably in the early fall of 1351, Abu 'Inan was ruling unrivaled a tranquil Morocco, plotting a new invasion of the eastern Maghrib, and busily constructing the grandest *madrasa* Fez had yet seen. It was an auspicious moment for Ibn Battuta to settle down, enter the Maliki judiciary, and reflect on his years abroad. Yet there were a few Muslim kings he still had not seen, among them Mansa Sulayman, Emperor of Mali, whose capital lay due south 1,500 miles across the most fearsome wilderness on earth.

Notes

1. Ibn Khaldun, *The Muqaddimah*, 2nd edn., trans. F. Rosenthal, 3 vols. (Princeton, N.J., 1967), vol. 1, p. 64.

2. IB's reckoning of time spent between Quanzhou and Quilon either at sea or in the port of Samudra adds up to 222 days, or almost seven and a half months. Yet if he left China at the start of the fall monsoon in September and arrived at Quilon, as he states in Ramadan 747 (the month began on 16 December 1346), the trip took no longer than about four and a half months. It was indeed feasible, as Arab seamen had demonstrated in Abbasid times, to sail from the South China coast to Malabar in a single monsoon season. George Hourani, *Arab Seafaring in the Indian Ocean in Ancient and Early Medieval Times* (Princeton, N.J., 1951), p. 75. We must assume either that IB failed accurately to remember time spent

between stages of the journey or possibly that part of the text is a later addition. IB's description of his voyage from Quanzhou to Samudra includes an oddly vague report of his ship being lost at sea for 42 days and an uncharacteristically credulous account of a close call with a *rukhkh*, a creature described in legend as a giant, predatory bird. Henry Yule, *Cathay and the Way Thither,* 4 vols. (London, 1913–16). vol. 4, p. 146.

3. In the *Rihla* IB links the civil war in Hurmuz and his meeting there with Sultan Qutb al-Din Tahamtan with his brief visit there in 1329 (1331). These events clearly occurred, however, in 1347. Jean Aubin, "Les Princes d'Ormuz du XIIIe au XVe siècle," *Journal Asiatique* 241 (1953): 102–08; Hr, pp. 447–48; Gb, vol. 2, pp. 402–03. See also Chapter 6, note 41.

4. He says that he stayed in Damascus until the end of 748 A.H. The last day of that year was 31 March 1348. The precise itinerary of IB's travels through greater Syria at this time is uncertain. Altogether, he traveled through some parts of Syria, Lebanon, and Palestine at least four different times during his career, in 1326, 1330 (1332), 1348, and 1350. The descriptions of numerous cities, towns, and castles he claims to have visited, however, are largely grouped into the account of his 1326 journey, whose chronology does not admit of such an extended, complicated tour. See Chapter 3, note 26. Therefore, a confident sorting out of the several itineraries through this region is hardly possible. The several dates he gives for his travels in Syria, Egypt, and Arabia in 1348 (748–749 A.H.), however, are generally corroborated by independent contemporary reports on the spatial transmission of the Black Death.

5. Gb, vol. 1, pp. 143–44.

6. Michael W. Dols, *The Black Death in the Middle East* (Princeton, N.J., 1977), p. 69.

7. Ibid., pp. 215, 219.

8. Ibid., pp. 238 and 236–54 *passim*.

9. Ibid., p. 96.

10. Ibid., pp. 154, 155, 160, 161.

11. Ibn al-Furat quoted in ibid., p. 277.

12. Ibid., p. 173.

13. David Ayalon, "The Plague and its Effects upon the Mamluk Army," *Journal of the Royal Asiatic Society* (1946): 67–73; and Dols, *Black Death*, pp. 185–92.

14. Dols, *Black Death*, p. 161.

15. Ibid., p. 63.

16. D&S, vol. 4, p. 326.

17. Quoted in Dols, *Black Death*, p. 64.

18. IB does not mention the name of the port he visited, but there is no real doubt that it was Cagliari. Monteil shares this opinion. D&S, vol. 4, p. 481.

19. IB says that he reached Fez on a Friday near the end of Sha'ban 750. D&S calculate this date as 8 November 1349. The last Friday in Sha'ban of that year, however, was 6 November.

20. Chronological clues regarding the length of his subsequent visit to Ceuta and the date of his departure for Spain suggest that if he was in Fez in Sha'ban 750, as he says, he probably went on to Tangier early in the following month of Ramadan.

21. Derek Latham, "The Strategic Position and Defence of Ceuta in the Later Muslim Period," *Islamic Quarterly* 15 (1971): 195.

22. IB states that he reached Gibraltar shortly after the death of Alfonso XI. That event occurred on 26 March 1350.

23. Robert S. Gottfried, *The Black Death* (New York, 1983), p. 51.

24. Rachel Arié, *L'Espagne musulmane au temps des Nasrides, 1232–1492* (Paris, 1973), p. 339.

25. Derek W. Lomax, *The Reconquest of Spain* (London, 1978), p. 162.

26. Washington Irving, *The Alhambra* (New York, 1926), p. 71.

27. "Ibn Djuzayy," EI_2, vol. 3, p. 756.

28. IB offers no specific dates for the period between his arrival in Fez in November 1349 and his departure from southern Morocco to West Africa on 18 February 1352. Therefore, the chronology of his movements from city to city in Andalusia and Morocco during that period is indeterminate.

13 Mali

> The people of Mali outnumbered the peoples of the Sudan
> in their neighborhood and dominated the whole
> region . . . Their authority became mighty and all the
> peoples of the Sudan stood in awe of them.[1]
>
> Ibn Khaldun

When Ibn Battuta visited Cairo in 1326 on his way to his first *hajj*, the population was undoubtedly still talking about the extraordinary pilgrim who had passed through the city two years earlier. Mansa Musa, ruler of the West African empire of Mali, had arrived at the Nile in the summer of 1324 after having crossed the Sahara Desert with a retinue of officials, wives, soldiers, and slaves numbering in the thousands and a train of one hundred camels loaded with unworked gold. A handsome young king of piety and noble bearing, he had created a minor sensation among Cairo's protocol-conscious officials by refusing to kiss the ground before the Mamluk sultan, al-Nasir Muhammad. Yet he "flooded Cairo with his benefactions," writes the historian al-Umari, and "performed many acts of charity and kindness."[2]

Having come so far from their distant grassland kingdom, the emperor and his gold-heavy entourage spent freely and indiscriminately in the Cairo bazaars, like prosperous and naive tourists from some American prairie state. "The Cairenes," says al-Umari, "made incalculable profits out of him and his suite in buying and selling and giving and taking. They exchanged gold until they depressed its value in Egypt and caused its price to fall."[3]

Musa was not the first *mansa* (king, sultan) of Mali to go on pilgrimage to Mecca, but none before had made such a dazzling display of pomp and riches. Well into the next century Egyptian chroniclers wrote about the event and its disturbing short-term effects on the Cairene gold market. In the history of medieval West Africa no single incident has been more celebrated. Indeed the *hajj* of Mansa Musa sums up Mali's important place among the kingdoms of Africa and Asia in Ibn Battuta's time.

The unworked gold which the *mansa* showered on Cairo came from three major alluvial deposits in West Africa. The mines of the *bilad al-sudan*, or simply the Sudan, as the Arab geographers called the steppe and savanna region south of the Sahara, had been known to the Mediterranean world since Phoenician times. But it was only the introduction of the dromedary to North Africa about the second century A.D. that made feasible in terms of costs and risks regular caravan trade from one rim of the Western Sahara to the other. The one-humped camel is a difficult and disagreeable animal, but he could carry a load of 125–150 kilograms, go without water ten days or more, and travel faster than any other available beast of burden. When Islam reached the Western Maghrib in the seventh century, Berber-speaking merchants were already running camel caravans to commercial settlements on the far side of the desert.

The founding of the Arab Empire and later the High Caliphate created an ever-growing demand in the Islamic heartland for West African gold to make coins and finery. This demand impelled Muslim merchants and cameliers of the Maghrib and the North Sahara to organize trans-desert business and transport operations to an unprecedented level of sophistication. About the same time, the Kingdom of Ghana emerged in the steppe region of West Africa known as the Sahel (Sahal), the transitional climatic zone between the southern desert and the savanna lands. The appearance of Ghana as an imperial state was undoubtedly linked to the gold trade, which encouraged the rise of military leaders aggressive enough to seize monopolistic authority over the commercial routes and settlements leading from the gold fields deep in the Sudan to the "ports" at the edge of the desert where the North African caravans arrived. The empire declined in the eleventh century, perhaps in connection with a prolonged drought, and eventually withered away.

Yet the pattern of imperial state-building in the Sudan continued with the rise of Mali early in the thirteenth century. The founders of this kingdom were Malinke-speaking people whose homeland was the region between the upper valleys of the Senegal and the Niger Rivers. This region was in the heart of the savanna and much nearer to the two gold-bearing areas, known as Bambuk and Bure, than the center of Ghana had been. The early kings of Mali, members of a chiefly clan of the Malinke known as the Keita, succeeded in taking control of territory between the gold fields and the Sahel, thereby positioning themselves to exact tribute in gold from the producing populations. In this way the cycle of expansion began. The gold revenues of the *mansas* permitted heavier expenditures on the army, which was comprised mainly of infantry bowmen and armored cavalry. As the royal forces were deployed across the fertile grasslands both east and west, greater numbers of farming and herding folk were subdued and taxed, expanding the wealth and military energies of the state even more.

In the course of the thirteenth and early fourteenth centuries, the *mansas* extended their domains westward to the Atlantic coast, eastward past the great bend of the Niger, and northward to the commercial towns scattered along the Saharan fringe, building an empire that incorporated many non-Malinke peoples. By achieving political domination over a band of steppe and savanna some 1,200 miles long at the peak of the empire, they effectively controlled and taxed the north–south flow of commerce across the Western Sudan.

Indeed, Mali's high age from the mid thirteenth to the mid fourteenth century corresponded to the period when Europe was exchanging silver for gold as its principal currency, prompting Italian and Catalan merchants to offer higher and higher prices for the little bags of dust and nuggets that were transported across the Sahara and over the Atlas Mountains to Ceuta and other North African ports. The rising European demand for gold, added to the perennial market in the Islamic states, stimulated more gold production in the Sudan, to the enormous fiscal advantage of Mali. In the later medieval period overall, West Africa may have been producing almost two-thirds of the world's gold supply.[4]

In addition to gold, north-bound caravans carried numerous products originating either in the grasslands or the tropical forests — ivory, ostrich feathers, kola nuts, gum resins, hides, and slaves. In return for these goods the southbound trade brought many products from North Africa and the Mediterranean basin: textiles, copper, silver, books, paper, swords, iron ware, perfumes, jewelry, spices, wheat, and dried fruits. Horses, which did not prosper in the deep savanna country owing to the lethal bite of the tsetse fly, were imported from the Maghrib to meet the needs of the Malian cavalry. Cowrie shells were used as a form of currency in the Sudan, as they were in India. As Ibn Battuta attests, they were harvested exclusively in the Maldive Islands, then exported to West Africa by way of Egypt and the Maghrib ports. The single most precious commodity imported to the Sudan was salt, a food essential to the human body that West Africa was unable to produce in sufficient quantity to meet demand. Salt came from mines in the Sahara and was transported southward in the form of giant slabs, two to a camel.

In the fourteenth century that section of the West Africa-to-Europe commercial exchange system extending from the northern edge of the rain forest to the Mediterranean coast was entirely in the hands of Muslims. Indeed from a global perspective the trans-Saharan trade routes were north–south branch lines of the hemispheric Muslim network that extended right across northern Africa and Asia to the ports of the South China Sea. As early as the ninth century, Berber-speaking merchants settled in commercial centers in the Sahel belt, where they acted as hosts and business agents for fellow Muslims who organized caravans in the corresponding entrepôts along the northern rim of the desert. In the time of Ghana, Muslim towns rose up alongside older Sahelian centers. In these new towns merchants of North African Berber or Arab origin were permitted by royal authority to govern their internal affairs according to the standards of the Sacred Law, just as they were beginning to do among non-Muslim peoples in the Indian Ocean basin.

These expatriate merchants did not organize the trade directly to the gold fields or to the towns deep in the savanna. That stretch of the network remained under the control of professional Sudanese traders. Most of them were of the Soninke and, later, Malinke culture groups. These men were among the first West Africans to convert to Islam, thereby linking themselves into the brotherhood of shared norms and trust that encouraged order and routine along the trans-Saharan system.

As in India and Southeast Asia, the founding of new Muslim trading communities created an immediate demand for literate cadres to organize and superintend Islamic worship, education, and law. From the beginning of Islamic expansion into West Africa, Maghribi men of learning were accompanying the merchant caravans across the desert to settle in the towns of the Sahel. These centers supported Islamic education south of the Sahara, and over the course of time gave rise to a class of Muslims grounded in the "normative" traditions of piety and scholarship as preached and practiced in North Africa. In the period of the Mali empire the communities of *'ulama* in the Sahelian towns included families of both Arabo-Berber and Sudanese origin, the latter mainly Malinke or Soninke. Deeper in the Sudan, learned families of purely West African origin predominated.

Sudanese chiefs and petty kings are known to have converted to Islam as early as the tenth or eleventh centuries. Whatever purely religious feelings may have motivated such men individually, conversion enhanced their esteem among Muslim merchants, the economically most powerful group in the land, and potentially tied them into a much wider commercial and diplomatic world than they had known before. The origins of Islam among the Malinke are obscure. In their tradition the founder of the empire was Sunjata (or Mari-Jaata), a larger-than-life homeric figure of the early thirteenth century who rose from physical adversity and exile to rid his homeland of an alien tyrant, then rebuilt the Malinke capital and ruled from it for 25 years. The reign of Sunjata is only vaguely associated with Islam, but at some point in the thirteenth century his successors made it the official religion of state, an act certainly linked to the growing importance of the Muslim mercantile communities which inhabited the main towns along the trans-savanna routes.

Yet the military and political success of the *mansas* also depended on the continuing allegiance and cooperation of the mass of their subjects — farming, fishing, and herding people who for the most part adhered to ancient animistic beliefs and rituals, not Islam. Unlike the sultans of Delhi, the *mansas* had not come to power as foreign invaders, prepared to organize a state as formally Islamic as they pleased. The legitimacy of their authority rested to a large extent on satisfying traditional Malinke expectations in their public conventions and ceremonies. Consequently, they were obliged to walk a narrow line between their urban Muslim subjects, who wanted them to behave up to the public standards of their Marinid or Mamluk counterparts, and the vast majority of the tax- and tribute-paying population, which took no notice of Maliki law or proper procedures at Friday prayer.

The character of official ritual and administration as more or less Islamic probably depended on the ruler's perception of the relative importance of his Muslim and non-Muslim subjects from one period to the next. Mansa Musa was naturally a great favorite of Muslim opinion, both in Mali and the wider Islamic world. His prestige resulted not only from his sensational pilgrimage, but also, writes al-Umari, because

> he built ordinary and cathedral mosques and minarets, and established the Friday observances, and prayers in congregation, and the muezzin's call. He brought jurists of the Malikite school to his country and there continued as sultan of the Muslims and became a student of religious sciences.[5]

Yet Mansa Musa also reigned during a period when relations with the Muslim merchants and with the states of North Africa were particularly important owing to the strong market for gold.

This expansive period in the trans-Saharan trade continued into the reign of Musa's brother Sulayman, who came to the throne about 1341. Sulayman came close to matching his brother's reputation for Islamic leadership and piety. Moreover, he ruled Mali in prosperity and peace. He was the sort of king from whom Ibn Battuta had come to expect an honorable and large-hearted reception.

In the autumn of 1351 the relentless traveler set out from Fez to visit Mali. He says nothing in the *Rihla* to explain why he felt impelled to cross the Sahara Desert. We may suppose he had the usual private plans to seek favor from yet another Muslim court. Obsessive traveler that he was, he may even have been urged on by the knowledge that the Sudan was the one important corner of the Dar al-Islam he had not yet seen.[6]

Some modern historians have suggested that Sultan Abu 'Inan appointed him as a state envoy to the emperor. Both Mansa Musa and Mansa Sulayman had initiated diplomatic exchanges with Abu l'Hasan, Abu 'Inan's father. Because of the Marinid campaign to conquer all of North Africa and thereby control the northern termini of the trans-Saharan trade from the Atlantic to Ifriqiya, the rulers of Mali had abundant reason to cultivate good relations with their northern neighbor. Abu 'Inan certainly knew that Ibn Battuta was making the journey and expected him to report in detail upon his return to Fez. Yet there is no convincing evidence that this Tangierian *faqih*, who was little known in Morocco's official circles, had anything like the ambassadorial status he had enjoyed (with such disastrous results) under Muhammad Tughluq.[7]

Traveling due south from Fez across the ranges of the Middle and High Atlas Mountains, he arrived in Sijilmasa, the pre-eminent desert port of the Western Maghrib, after a journey of eight or nine days. Sijilmasa lay in the midst of an immense oasis called Tafilalt, the last important outpost of sedentary life at the northern edge of the void. Today nothing remains of the city except an agglomeration of unremarkable ruins strewn among the palm groves. In the fourteenth century it was, according to al-Umari, a place "of imposing palaces, high buildings, and tall gates."[8] Tafilalt's rich agriculture, fed by a river flowing down out of the Atlas 50 miles to the north, supported the urban population, including a large resident community of Berber and Arab merchants. From the perspective of Mali, Sijilmasa was the chief northern terminus of the trans-Saharan gold caravans. Here the products of the savanna and forest were off-loaded, stored in warehouses, and finally carried by camel, mule and donkey trains over the mountains to Fez, Marrakesh, Tlemcen, and the Mediterranean ports.

Ibn Battuta spent about four months in Sijilmasa, waiting for the winter season, when the big caravans set out for Walata, their destination at the far side of the desert. During this time he purchased camels of his own and fattened them up. When he was in Ceuta some months earlier, he may have become acquainted with the al-Bushri family, whose kinsman he had met in China. For he lodged during his entire stay in Sijilmasa with one Muhammad al-Bushri, a legal scholar and brother of the al-Bushri of Qanjanfu. "How far apart they are," he remarks blandly in the *Rihla*.

In February 1352 (beginning of Muharram 753) he set out from Tafilalt with a caravan of "merchants of Sijilmasa and others." The leader was a fellow of the Masufa Berbers, a herding people of the Western Sahara who appear to have had something close to a monopoly on the supply of guards, guides, and drivers on the entire route between Tafilalt and the Sahel. The twelfth-century geographer al-Idrisi describes the normal routines for traveling safely across "the empty waste" that yawned for a thousand miles south of Sijilmasa:

They load their camels at late dawn, and march until the sun has risen, its light has become bright in the air, and the heat on the ground has become severe. Then they put their loads down, hobble their camels, unfasten their baggage and stretch awnings

A market in Tafilalt near the site of Old Sijilmasa.
Photo by the Author.

Ruins of Old Sijilmasa in the Tafilalt oasis.
Photo by the Author.

By tradition, the tomb of Ibn Battuta in Tangier.
Photo by the Author.

to give some shade from the scorching heat and the hot winds of midday . . . When the sun begins to decline and sink in the west, they set off. They march for the rest of the day, and keep going until nightfall, when they encamp at whatever place they have reached . . . Thus the traveling of the merchants who enter the country of the Sudan is according to this pattern. They do not deviate from it, because the sun kills with its heat those who run the risk of marching at midday.[9]

Twenty-five days out of Sijilmasa the caravan reached the settlement of Taghaza, the main salt-mining center of the Western Sahara. The paradox of Taghaza was the grim, treeless desolation of the place set against its extreme importance to the entire inter-regional commercial system. All the southbound caravans took on loads of slab salt, since no product was in greater demand in the Sudan. "This is a village with nothing good about it," Ibn Battuta complains. "It is the most fly-ridden of places." Then he goes on to speak of the enormous amounts of gold that changed hands there.

The caravan stayed in the village for ten days, giving him an opportunity to watch wretched slaves belonging to Masufa pro-prietors dig slabs out of the open mine and tie them against the sides of the dromedaries. He also had the curious experience of sleeping in a house and praying in a mosque made entirely of salt blocks, except for the camel-skin roofs. The water of Taghaza was brackish, and every bit of food for the laborers, except for camel meat, had to be brought in from either Morocco or Mali. More than a century and a half later the Granada-born traveler Leo Africanus would visit Taghaza and find conditions little changed:

Neither have the said diggers of salt any victuals but such as the merchants bring unto them: for they are distant from all inhabited places, almost twenty days journey, insomuch that oftentimes they perish for lack of food, whenas the merchants come not in due time unto them: Moreover the southeast wind doth so often blind them, that they cannot live here without great peril.[10]

Between Taghaza and Walata lay the most dangerous stretch of the journey, almost 500 miles of sand desert where the average annual rainfall is a scant five to ten millimeters and where only one watering point exists, a place called Bir al-Ksaib (Tasarahla).[11] If rain fell at all in the region, it usually came in late winter.[12] Ibn Battuta and his fellows were, according to his chronology, traveling south from Taghaza sometime in March. Fortunately, the rain had come that year, leaving pools of water here and there along the track, enough in fact for the caravaners to wash out their clothes. Yet there was danger enough in this wilderness for all that:

> In those days we used to go on ahead of the caravan and whenever we found a place suitable for grazing we pastured the beasts there. This we continued to do till a man named Ibn Ziri became lost in the desert. After that we neither went on ahead nor lagged behind. Strife and the exchange of insults had taken place between Ibn Ziri and his maternal cousin, named Ibn 'Adi, so that he fell behind the caravan and lost the way, and when the people encamped there was no news of him.

Arriving safely at Bir al-Ksaib minus Ibn Ziri, the caravan stopped for three days to rest and to repair and fill the water skins before navigating the trek across the vast sand desert called Mreyye, the final and most dangerous stage of the trip. Keeping to the usual procedure, the company hired a Masufa scout called the *takshif*, whose job it was to go on ahead of the caravan to Walata. If he did not lose his way among the dunes, or run out of water, or fall prey to the demons which Ibn Battuta tells us haunted those wastes, he would alert the people of the town to the caravan's approach. A group of Walatans would then be sent four days' journey north to meet the caravan with fresh water.

The Masufa *takshif* earned the 100 mithqals of gold the caravaners paid him, for on the seventh night out of Bir al-Ksaib they saw the lights of the Walata relief party. A few days later, sometime in the latter part of April 1352 (beginning of Rabi' I 753), they reached the sweltering little town. Its mud brick houses lay along the slope of a barren hill, a scattering of palm trees in a little wadi below. The site was bleak, but as the main southern terminus of the camel trains the town nonetheless supported a population of two or three thousand.[13] It ranked as a provincial capital of Mali and had an important community of educated men of Berber and Sudanese origin.

By a letter entrusted to the *takshif* Ibn Battuta had arranged to rent a house through the good offices of a "respectable" Moroccan trader named Ibn Badda', who resided in the town. Yet as soon as he arrived, he found cause to regret having come at all. Walata was the most northerly center under the jurisdiction of the *mansa*. Following custom, the members of the caravan went immediately to pay their respects to the *farba*, or governor. They found him seated on a carpet under a portico, surrounded by lancers, bowmen, and warriors of the Masufa. Though he sat very close to the visitors, he addressed them not directly but through a spokesman. In Mali this was proper ceremonial procedure symbolizing the sacred character of the *mansa*, in whose name the *farba* held his authority. Ibn Battuta, however, thought the governor's behavior a shocking display of bad manners, misinterpreting it as a show of contempt for the visiting "white men."[14] Later, the newcomers all went to receive hospitality from one of the governor's officials. The welcome turned out to be a bowl of millet with a little honey and yogurt.

> I said to them: "Was it to this that the black man invited us?" They said: "Yes, for them this is a great banquet." Then I knew for certain that no good was to be expected from them and I wished to depart.

He soon got the better of his urge to retreat back to Morocco, but the inclination of the Sudanese to combine Islamic practice with regional custom was no end of irritation to him. His prejudice, if he were to try to explain it, had nothing directly to do with race. It was a matter of the failure of the Malians to conduct themselves according to the normative standards that pious Muslims from North African cities might expect of virtuous officers of state. Such standards did not include rulers speaking to fellow believers through ritual heralds or entertaining visiting *'ulama* with small dishes of porridge.

The incident, unfortunately, was to be only the first of many occasions when Ibn Battuta, the sophisticated Maliki jurist, would find the Sudanese coming up short in their attention to moral and legal niceties. He admits that the scholars of Walata treated him warmly during his sojourn in the town, but he found their failure to subscribe to what he regarded as the civilized rules of sexual segregation even worse than the practices of the Central Asian Turks. On one occasion he appeared at the house of the *qadi* to find him seated in casual conversation with a young and beautiful woman. That a woman should be present in the reception room of a Muslim's house when a male guest arrived was bad enough. But the judge's explanation, that it was all right to come in because the woman was his "friend," made the visitor recoil in shock. On another occasion Ibn Battuta paid a call to a Masufa scholar and found this worthy's wife chatting with a strange man in the courtyard. When he expressed profound disapproval of such goings-on, the scholar replied insouciantly that "the association of women with men is agreeable to us and a part of good conduct, to which no suspicion attaches. They are not like the women of your country." Unpersuaded, Ibn Battuta left the house at once and never came back. "He invited me several times," he tells us, "but I did not accept."

He stayed in Walata several weeks, then started out for the capital of Mali in the company of three companions and a Masufa guide. He remarks that he did not need to travel in a caravan because "neither traveler there nor dweller has anything to fear from thief or usurper" owing to Mansa Sulayman's firm government. Nor did he have to carry a large stock of supplies. As he moved southward from the Sahelian steppe into the grassy plains, giant baobab trees rising stalk-like on the horizon, he encountered village after village of Sudanese farming folk. In them he and his comrades offered glass beads and pieces of Taghaza salt in return for millet, rice, milk, chickens, and other local staples. After two weeks or more on the road by way of Zaghari (which may be identified with the Sokolo area in modern Mali), he reached the left bank of the Niger River at a place he names Karsakhu.[15] He calls the river the Nile (Nil), following the mistaken notion of medieval Muslim geographers that that great river was a branch of the Egyptian Nile. Whatever his error, the crocodiles here were as dangerous as the ones he had seen in Egypt:

> One day I had gone to the Nil to accomplish a need when one of the Sudan came and stood between me and the river. I was amazed at his ill manners and lack of modesty and mentioned this to somebody, who said: "He did that only because he feared for you on account of the crocodile, so he placed himself between you and it."

The traveler's precise route from Walata to the Malian capital is a puzzle because we do not know for certain where the town was.

The *Rihla* gives neither a name to the place nor a very useful topographical description of it. The chief seat of royal power may have changed location from one period to another, indeed more than one "capital" may have existed at the same time. Some modern scholars identify the site, at least at that time in Mali's history, with the village of Niani, located south of the Niger in the modern Republic of Guinea. But the town may also have lain north of the river somewhere east of Bamako.[16] About ten miles from his destination Ibn Battuta crossed what he calls the Sansara River on a ferry (he never mentions crossing the Niger). If the capital is to be identified with Niani, that river would have been the Sankarani, a southern tributary of the Niger.

The seat of Mansa Sulayman was a sprawling, unwalled town set in a "verdant and hilly" country.[17] The sultan had several enclosed palaces there. Mansa Musa had built one under the direction of Abu Ishaq al-Sahili, an Andalusian architect and poet who had accompanied him home from the *hajj*. Al-Sahili surfaced the building with plaster, an innovation in the Sudan, and "covered it with colored patterns so that it turned out to be the most elegant of buildings."[18] Surrounding the palaces and mosques were the residences of the citizenry, mud-walled houses roofed with domes of timber and reed.[19]

Ibn Battuta arrived in the town on 28 July 1352 (14 Jumada I 753) and went immediately to the quarter where the resident merchants and scholars of Maghribi origin lived. He had written to the community in advance of his arrival, probably from Walata, and was relieved to learn that his letter had been received and a house made ready for him to occupy. Within a day, he made the acquaintance of the *qadi*, a Sudanese, as well as the other members of the Muslim notability. He was also introduced to the *mansa*'s "interpreter," or *griot*, a man named Dugha. This official was a Sudanese of special social caste who performed a multiplicity of important state functions: master of state ceremonies, royal bard and praise singer, herald, confidant, counsellor, and keeper of the oral traditions of the Keita dynasty.

Ibn Battuta no doubt expected to see the king promptly, but ten days after his arrival he fell grievously sick after eating some yams or similar root that may not have been cooked long enough to remove the poison from its skin.[20] He fainted away during the dawn prayer, and one of the five men who had shared the meal with him subsequently died. Ibn Battuta drank a purgative concoction to induce vomiting, but he remained so ill for two months that he could not rouse himself to make an appearance at court.

He finally recovered just in time to attend a public memorial feast for the deposed and deceased Moroccan sultan Abu l'Hasan, with whom Mali had had amicable diplomatic relations. The ceremonies of the *mansa*'s public sitting were not unlike the pageants the traveler had witnessed in dozens of Muslim courts, but elements of traditional Malinke chieftaincy were in evidence to be sure:

> [The sultan] has a lofty pavilion, of which the door is inside his house, where he sits for most of the time . . . There came forth from the gate of the palace about 300 slaves, some carrying in their hands bows and others having in their hands short lances and shields . . . Then two saddled and bridled horses are brought, with two rams which, they say, are effective against the evil eye . . . Dugha the interpreter stands at the gate of the council-place wearing fine garments of silk brocade and other materials, and on his head a turban with fringes which they have a novel way of winding . . . The troops, governors, young men, slaves, the Masufa, and others sit outside the council-place in a broad street where there are trees . . . Inside the council-place beneath the arches a man is standing. Anyone who wishes to address the sultan addresses Dugha and Dugha addresses that man standing and that man standing addresses the sultan.
>
> If one of them addresses the sultan and the latter replies he uncovers the clothes from his back and sprinkles dust on his head and back, like one washing himself with water. I used to marvel how their eyes did not become blinded.

The *qadi* and other scholars brought Ibn Battuta forward and presented him to the gold-turbaned monarch seated on his dais under a silken dome. There was nothing particularly special about a Moroccan *faqih* passing through the kingdom and this first meeting was perfunctory. Later, when Ibn Battuta had returned to his house, one of the scholars called to tell him that the sultan had sent along the requisite welcoming gift.

> I got up, thinking that it would be robes of honor and money, but behold! it was three loaves of bread and a piece of beef fried in *gharti* [shea butter] and a gourd containing yoghurt. When I

saw it I laughed, and was long astonished at their feeble intellect and their respect for mean things.

To make matters worse he spent almost another two months attending court before the sultan paid any further attention to him. Finally, on the advice of Dugha, he made an appeal to Sulayman, brashly raising the issue of the *mansa*'s prestige among the Muslim rulers of the world:

> I have journeyed to the countries of the world and met their kings. I have been four months in your country without your giving me a reception gift or anything else. What shall I say of you in the presence of other sultans?

In all probability Sulayman could not have cared less what this wandering jurist said of him. At first he sublimely disavowed having even known that Ibn Battuta was in the town. But when his notables reminded him that he had received the Moroccan a few months earlier and "sent him some food," the *mansa* offered him a house and an allowance in gold. Notwithstanding the sultan's desultory effort to put things right, Ibn Battuta never got over the indifferent treatment he received, concluding in the *Rihla* that Sulayman "is a miserly king from whom no great donation is to be expected" and that Mansa Musa by contrast had been "generous and virtuous."

Ibn Battuta ended a sojourn of a little more than eight months in the capital in a state of ambivalence over the qualities of Malian culture. On the one hand he respected Sulayman's just and stable government and the earnest devotion of the Muslim population to their mosque prayers and Qur'anic studies. "They place fetters on their children if there appears on their part a failure to memorize the Qur'an," he reports approvingly, "and they are not undone until they memorize it." On the other hand he reproached the Sudanese severely for practices obviously based in Malinke tradition but, from his point of view, either profane or ridiculous when set against the model of the rightly guided Islamic state: female slaves and servants who went stark naked into the court for all to see; subjects who groveled before the sultan, beating the ground with their elbows and throwing dust and ashes over their heads; royal poets who romped about in feathers and bird masks. Ibn Battuta seems indeed to be harsher on the Malians than he does on other societies of the Islamic periphery where behavior rooted in local tradition, but contrary to his scriptural and legal standards, colored religious and social practice. We may sense in his reportage a certain embarrassment that a kingdom whose Islam was so profoundly influenced by his own homeland and its Maliki doctors was not doing a better job keeping to the straight and narrow.

Ibn Battuta left Sulayman's court on 27 February 1353 (22 Muharram 754), traveling by camel in the company of a merchant. Since the location of the capital is uncertain, his itinerary away from it is equally problematic. If he had a general plan of travel, it seems to have been to explore the provinces of Mali further down the Niger. He mentions that in the ensuing days he crossed, not the great river itself, but a tributary channel, which might be identified with the "canal du Sahel," a northerly flood branch located east of the modern Malian town of Ségou.[21] From there he followed a northeasterly route, keeping well to the west of the river, then rejoining it again somewhere not far upstream from Timbuktu.

In the *Rihla* Ibn Battuta expresses no particular wonder at that legendary "city of gold." In fact the rise of Timbuktu as a trans-Saharan terminus and capital of Islamic learning came mainly in the fifteenth and sixteenth centuries. In the mid fourteenth century, when Ibn Battuta passed through, the town was only beginning to flower. It had a population of about 10,000 and a Malian governor, who had been installed when Mansa Musa visited the town on his return from the Hijaz.[22] It almost certainly had a sizable community of Maghribi and Sudanese scholars. According to tradition, Mansa Musa had commissioned an impressive grand mosque.[23] Yet until later in the century Timbuktu was junior to Walata as a trade and intellectual center. Ibn Battuta found nothing there to detain him for long and was soon on his way down the Niger.

At Kabara, Timbuktu's "port" on the river four miles south of the city, he abandoned his dromedary and boarded a small boat, a type of canoe ("carved out of a single piece of wood") that is still used in the region today.[24] From Kabara the Niger flows due eastward for about 180 miles through the flat Sahelian steppe. "Each night," he reports, "we stayed in a village and bought what we were in need of in the way of wheat and butter for salt, spices and glass trinkets." At one village he celebrated the Prophet's Birthday (12 Rabi' I 754 or 17 April 1353) in the company of the local commander, whose generosity the *Rihla* praises so effusively that the tacit negative comparison to Mansa Sulayman is not lost on the reader. The officer not only entertained his visitor warmly but even gave him a slave boy as a gift. The lad accompanied Ibn Battuta back across the Sahara and remained with him for some years.

Continuing down river, the traveler spent about a month in Gao (Kawkaw), a thriving commercial city at the eastern extremity of Mali's political orbit. Then, having by this time crossed a large part of the empire from west to east and visited most of the towns with important Muslim populations, he decided to make for home. Gao paralleled Walata and Timbuktu as a terminus of trans-Saharan trade, but with relatively more important route connections to Ifriqiya and Egypt. Ibn Battuta found "a big caravan" departing from Gao for Ghadamès (Ghadamis), a major stop in the northern desert about 450 miles due south of Tunis. He had no plans to go to Ghadamès, but it made sense for him to accompany the convoy as far east as the oasis of Takedda (Azelik), which lay to the southwest of the Saharan highland region called Air.[25] From there he could expect to intercept a caravan *en route* to Sijilmasa from the central Sudan (the region corresponding to the northern part of modern Nigeria).

His journey to Takedda was disagreeable. In Gao he purchased a riding camel, as well as a she-camel to carry his provisions. But the sweltering desert summer was approaching, and after only one stage on the trail the she-camel collapsed. Other travelers among the company agreed to help transport Ibn Battuta's belongings, but further on he fell sick, this time "because of the extreme heat and a surplus of bile." Stumbling on to Takedda, he found a house in which to recuperate as well as a welcoming community of resident Moroccans.

Like Taghaza, Takedda was a grim spot in the desert important for its mine, in this case copper. Unlike Taghaza, the town was also a junction of trade routes and consequently a place of some slight urbanity. Ibn Battuta reports:

> The people of Takedda have no occupation but trade. They travel each year to Egypt and import some of everything which is there in the way of fine cloth and other things. Its people are

comfortable and well off and are proud of the number of male and female slaves which they have.

Recovering from his illness, he thought of buying "an educated slave girl" for himself. The effort brought nothing but trouble, not least for the unfortunate young women involved. First, the *qadi* of the town got one of the other notables to sell the traveler a girl of his own for a quantity of gold. Then the man decided he had made a mistake and asked to buy her back. Ibn Battuta agreed on condition that a replacement be found. Another Moroccan in the caravan, a man named 'Ali 'Aghyul, had a woman he was ready to sell. But Ibn Battuta and this fellow had already had a personal row. On the journey to Takedda, 'Ali 'Aghyul had not only refused to help carry the load from Ibn Battuta's dead camel but even denied a drink of water to his countryman's slave boy. Nevertheless Ibn Battuta went through with the deal, this girl "being better than the first one." But then

> this Moroccan regretted having sold the slave and wished to revoke the bargain. He importuned me to do so, but I declined to do anything but reward him for his evil acts. He almost went mad and died of grief. But I let him off afterwards.

Some time following this shabby incident, a slave messenger arrived in a caravan from Sijilmasa carrying an order from Sultan Abu 'Inan that the *faqih* should return immediately to Fez. Ibn Battuta offers no explanation why the sultan should have kept such close track of his movements south of the Sahara. It seems likely that Abu 'Inan was anxious to have a report from him on political and commercial conditions in Mali, matters so important to the health of the Marinid state.[26]

Ibn Battuta left Takadda on 11 September 1353 (11 Sha'ban 754) in the company of a large caravan transporting 600 black female slaves to Morocco. These unfortunates had probably started out from the savanna lands southeast of Takedda, regions which, in the absence of gold deposits, engaged more extensively in slave commerce than did Mali.[27] Once arrived in Sijilmasa or Fez, the women would be sold into service as domestics, concubines, or servants of the royal court.

The caravan trekked northward through 18 days of "wilderness without habitation" to a point north of Air (possibly Assiou or In

Azaoua,[28] where the route leading to Ghadamès forked off from the road to Sijilmasa. From there the convoy skirted the western side of the Ahaggar (Hoggar, or Hukkar) Mountains of the central desert. Here they passed through the territory of veiled Berber nomads who, Ibn Battuta informs us, were "good for nothing . . . We encountered one of their chief men who held up the caravan until he was paid an impost of cloth and other things."

Now veering gradually to the northwest, the company eventually reached the great north Saharan oasis complex of Tuwat (Touat). Ibn Battuta mentions only one stopping place in this region (Buda), then tells us simply that they continued on to Sijilmasa. He stayed there no more than about two weeks, then continued on over the High Atlas in the dead of winter. "I have seen difficult roads and much snow in Bukhara, Samarkand, Khurasan and the land of the Turks, but I never saw a road more difficult than that." Somewhere along that frigid highway he halted to celebrate the Feast of Sacrifice, 6 January 1354.

> Then I departed and reached the capital Fez, capital of our Lord the Commander of the Faithful, may God support him, and kissed his noble hand, and deemed myself fortunate to see his blessed face. I remained in the shelter of his beneficence after my long travels, may God . . . thank him for the great benefits which he bestowed on me and his ample benignity.

Indeed Abu 'Inan could afford to be amply benign, for his reign had just about reached its high point when Ibn Battuta returned to the capital. Morocco was generally at peace, and the sultan was even planning for the day when he would best his father at conquering Ifriqiya and unifying North Africa once and for all. If the Black Death had temporarily deflated Fez's productiveness in craft and industry, the city was still the center of the intellectual universe west of Cairo. Among the stars of saintliness and erudition gathered there, Ibn Battuta might expect to shine for a moment or two on the strength of the stories he had to tell.

Notes

1. Abu Zayd 'Abd al-Rahman Ibn Khaldun, *Kitab al-'Ibar*, in L&H, pp. 333–34.
2. Ibn Fadl Allah al-Umari, *Masalik al-absar fi mamalik al-amsar*, in L&H, pp. 269–70.

3. Al-Umari, L&H, pp. 270–71.

4. Andrew M. Watson, "Back to Gold and Silver," *Economic History Review* 20 (1967): 30–31; Nehemia Levtzion, *Ancient Ghana and Mali* (London, 1973), pp. 131–33.

5. Al-Umari, L&H, p. 261.

6. The *Rihla* is the only existing eye-witness testimony on the Mali empire and therefore a precious historical source.

7. The commentaries are divided on the question of IB's purpose in going to the Sudan. The issue hinges on the translation of the phrase *bi-rasm al-safar* in the Arabic text. One version has it: "I took leave of our Master (may God uphold him). I departed *with orders to accomplish a journey* to the land of the Sudan." R. Mauny *et al.*, *Textes et documents relatifs à l'histoire de l'Afrique: extraits tirés des voyages d'Ibn Battuta* (Dakar, 1966), p. 35. Levtzion and Hopkins (L&H, p. 414), however, believe that this translation "seems to read too much into the text." They prefer "and set off *with the purpose of traveling* to the land of the Sudan." Both D&S (vol. 4, p. 376) and H&K (p. 22) give similar meaning to their translation of the phrase. Levtzion (*Ghana and Mali*, p. 216) states that IB was "on a private visit to the Sudan" but that Abu 'Inan knew of his movements. When IB was at Takadda in the southern Sahara, the sultan sent a messenger telling him to return to Fez. I agree with Levtzion. If IB were on an official mission to Mali, we might expect him to make a good deal of it in the *Rihla* or at least refer to it in connection with his appearance at the Mali court.

8. Al-Umari, L&H, p. 275.

9. Abu 'Abd Allah al-Idrisi, *Nuzhat al-mushtaq fi ikhtiraq al-afaq*, L&H, p. 118.

10. Leo Africanus, *The History and Description of Africa*, trans. Robert Pory, ed. Robert Brown, 3 vols. (New York, 1896), vol. 3, pp. 800–01. Modern spelling mine.

11. Mauny *et al.* (*Textes et Documents*, p. 38) identify IB's Tasarahla with Bir al-Ksaib.

12. Mauny *et al.*, *Textes et documents*, p. 37.

13. Raymond Mauny, *Tableau géographique de l'Ouest Africain au Moyen Âge d'après les sources écrites, la tradition et l'archéologie* (Amsterdam, 1967), p. 485.

14. H&K, p. 70n.

15. J. O. Hunwick identifies Zaghari with the Sokolo region and Karsakhu with a point on the Niger south of there. "The Mid-Fourteenth century capital of Mali," *Journal of African History* 14 (1973): 199–200. Other hypotheses on this stretch of IB's itinerary are offered by Claude Meillassoux, "L'itinéraire d'Ibn Battuta de Walata à Malli," *Journal of African History* 13 (1972): 389–95; and Mauny *et al.*, *Textes et documents*, pp. 46–47.

16. Textual, linguistic, and archaeological evidence have all been marshalled to find the fourteenth century capital of Mali. Recent discussions, which also review the earlier literature on the problem, are Wladyslaw Filipowiak, *Études archéologiques sur la capitale médiévale du Mali*, trans. Zofia Slawskaj (Szczecin, 1979); Hunwick, "Mid-Fourteenth Century Capital," pp. 195–206; and Meillassoux, "L'itinéraire d'Ibn Battuta,' pp. 389–95. Hunwick hypothesizes that IB did not visit Niani but a place north of the Niger, pointing out that the traveler never mentions crossing the river.

17. Al-Umari, L&H, p. 263.

18. Ibn Khaldun, L&H, p. 335.

19. Al-Umari, L&H, pp. 262–63.

20. H&K, p. 72n.

21. Hunwick, "Mid-Fourteenth Century Capital," p. 203.

22. Elias N. Saad, *Social History of Timbuktu: the Role of Muslim Scholars and Notables, 1400–1900* (Cambridge, England, 1983), pp. 11, 27.

23. Levtzion, *Ghana and Mali*, p. 201; Mauny, *Tableau géographique*, pp. 114–15; and Saad, *Social History of Timbuktu*, pp. 36–37.

24. Mauny *et al.*, *Textes et documents*, p. 71.

25. Mauny (*Tableau geógraphique*, pp. 139–40) identifies IB's Takadda with Azelik. Most other commentators agree.

26. Jean Devisse presumes that IB was on a mission for Abu 'Inan and speculates that the sultan wanted up-to-date intelligence out of fear that the gold trade was being increasingly diverted towards Egypt. "Routes de commerce et échanges en Afrique Occidentale en relation avec la Méditerranée," *Revue d'Histoire Économique et Sociale* 50 (1972): 373.

27. Levtzion, *Ghana and Mali*, pp. 174–76.

28. Mauny *et al.* (*Textes et documents*, p. 79) identify IB's watering place with one or the other of these points. L&H (p. 418n) are doubtful but offer no alternative.

14 The Rihla

I have indeed — praise be to God — attained my desire
in this world, which was to travel through the earth, and I
have attained in this respect what no other person has
attained to my knowledge.[1]

Ibn Battuta

We know only in a very general way what happened to Ibn Battuta
after he returned to Fez in 1354. Sultan Abu 'Inan certainly
listened to his report on Mali and no doubt wanted to hear about
his traveling career, the political highlights in particular. After the
interview Ibn Battuta might have expected to slip quietly out of
public notice, perhaps to seek a judicial appointment elsewhere in
Morocco. Yet the king was sufficiently impressed by this genial
and sharp-witted *faqih* that he ordered him to stay in Fez for the
time being and prepare a narrative of his experiences for the
pleasure of the royal court.

Since Ibn Battuta was no belle-lettrist, Ibn Juzayy, the young
secretary he had met briefly in Granada three years earlier, was
commissioned by the sultan to shape the Tangierian's story into a
proper oeuvre conforming to the literary standards of a *rihla*: an
account of travels centering upon a journey (or journeys) to
Mecca. Ibn Juzayy had fallen out of favor with his former
employer Yusuf I of Granada and left his service to accept a post
in Fez not long before Ibn Battuta's return there from Mali. He
already had a reputation for his poetry, his prose writings in
philology, history, and law, and his fine calligraphic style.[2] He
seems to have come to his assignment with enthusiasm and may
well have developed a warm friendship with the journeyer.

The two of them probably met together regularly for about two
years from shortly after Ibn Battuta's arrival in Fez until December 1355, when the redaction of the narrative was finished
under the florid formal title, "A Gift to the Observers Concerning
the Curiosities of the Cities and the Marvels Encountered in
Travels." The work sessions likely took place in different places: in

the older man's house or the younger's, in the gardens or halls of Fez Jdid, in the shady arcades of mosques. Ibn Juzayy admits that what he wrote was only an abridgment of all that his collaborator told him or had written out for him in notes. There is no direct evidence that Ibn Battuta ever read the completed manuscript or checked it for errors. Mistakes in the phonetic spelling of various foreign words suggest that he did not.[3] Ibn Juzayy may have continued to revise and refine the book after his interviews with the traveler were completed. In any case, the connection between the two men ended in 1356 or 1357 when Ibn Juzayy, not yet 37 years old, died of causes unknown.[4]

In his brief introduction to the *Rihla*, Ibn Juzayy explains precisely what the sultan had ordered Ibn Battuta to do:

> he should dictate an account of the cities which he had seen in his travel, and of the interesting events which had clung to his memory, and that he should speak of those whom he had met of the rulers of countries, of their distinguished men of learning, and of their pious saints. Accordingly, he dictated upon these subjects a narrative which gave entertainment to the mind and delight to the ears and eyes.

This is a concise statement of the general subject matter of Ibn Battuta's interviews with Ibn Juzayy, although he ranged over almost every conceivable aspect of fourteenth-century life from cuisine, botany, and marriage practices to dynastic history and the price of chickens. As he spoke or fed Ibn Juzayy notes, he wove his descriptive observations haphazardly into the account of his own experience. Ibn Juzayy, moreover, interjected rhetorical odds and ends into the manuscript here and there, including a bit of verse. But generally he stayed true to the structure of Ibn Battuta's verbal recounting. Consequently, the autobiography, the personal adventure, remains at the heart of the book, revealing the traveler's gregarious, high-spirited, pushy, impetuous, pious, ingratiating personality through the account of the life he lived. The plan of the *Rihla* was very different from the organization of that other famous travel narrative of the medieval age, the *Book of Marco Polo*. The Venetian's work is divided into two parts, the first a brief summary of his traveling career, the second, which makes up most of the account, a systematic, didactic presentation of information about China and other lands east of Europe. All in all, the book remains, in vivid contrast to the *Rihla*, "a treatise of empirical geography," revealing almost nothing about Marco's personality.[5]

There is no doubt, on the other hand, that in telling so much about himself, Ibn Battuta aimed to project a definite *persona*: the pious, erudite, Maliki gentleman, though one with a Sufi's sensitivity and reverence. It seems equally clear that as he told Ibn Juzayy his story, he tended, as perhaps most of us would in his place, to exaggerate his competence as a man of learning and his social status among the kings and princes who entertained him, as well as the importance of the judicial positions he held. Perhaps we can discern in the thread of puffery that runs through the *Rihla* a discomforting self-awareness of the limits of his education and commitment to the rigorous academic life. There is no evidence that he ever spent much time in serious study once he left Tangier at the age of 21. To the learned jurisconsults and *qadis* of the great cities of Islam, who toiled years on end reading and memorizing the important texts of their legal school, Ibn Battuta's deficiencies would have been plain to see. Ibn Juzayy introduces him with gusto as "the learned doctor of law." But another scholar, a celebrated Andalusian judge named Abu l'Barakat al-Balafiqi, had also met the traveler in Granada and duly sized him up. His observation, reported in the brief article on Ibn Battuta in Ibn al-Khatib's fourteenth-century compilation of notable biographies, was that the man may have traveled widely but he possessed only "a modest share of the sciences."[6] Or as another translator puts the passage, "He had not too much of what it takes."[7] He could never have landed a high judicial post in a city like Cairo or Damascus (except perhaps in the aftermath of the Black Death, when a large part of the civilian elite was dead). But he did thrive out on the peripheries of Islam where Muslim princes, badly needing experts in the *shari'a* and the prestige that came with enforcing it, were less particular about honoring and employing individuals with only "a modest share of the sciences." In that sense, Ibn Battuta belongs to a large class of lettered but not accomplished men who, for want of serious career possibilities in the central cities, gravitated out to the expanding Islamic frontiers, where a Muslim name, a reasonable education, and a large ambition could see a man to a respectable job, even to riches and power.[8]

If Ibn Battuta never became a master of his legal profession, he nonetheless possessed an extraordinary memory of the places he had visited and the things he had seen. It seems highly unlikely that when he got down to work with Ibn Juzayy he had extensive travel notes or journals at hand. He never mentions in the *Rihla* that he took notes, with the single exception of a remark that some tomb inscriptions he jotted down in Bukhara were one of the items he lost in the pirate attack off the coast of India.[9] If he had other notes with him at that time (1345), they would also have been lost. In any case, a reading of the *Rihla* does not suggest that he had a foggier memory of people, places, and events for the period of his career antedating 1345 than for the time after. On the other hand, he appears to have written out a rough version of his life and observations, perhaps after he returned to Fez, since near the end of the *Rihla* Ibn Juzayy refers to the work as his own "abridgment" of the "writing" or "notations" (*taqyid*) of the traveler.[10] From time to time in the narrative Ibn Battuta admits candidly that he simply cannot remember the name of a particular person or town. But he also misremembered numerous facts. He gets names and dates wrong occasionally, he reports certain contemporary or historical events inaccurately, he mixes up now and again the order of his itinerary. Yet too close attention to his errors can distract from the astonishing accuracy of the *Rihla* on the whole, as both a historical document and a record of experience.

To conclude that Ibn Battuta did not rely on notes during his interviews with Ibn Juzayy is not to say that the two of them had no "research" aids at all. In Muslim historical and geographical writing of that age, authors commonly drew upon the works of earlier authorities to flesh out their essays, sometimes explicitly crediting such authorities and sometimes not. Islamic literary theory regarded what we would call plagiarism with a wide latitude of tolerance. It was not considered improper to quote from or paraphrase other writers without citing them, even where the ideas or information such writers contributed might be partially or wholly disguised.[11] Ibn Juzayy may have had a substantial library of geographical and travel literature of his own. In any case, Fez had become such an important center of learning that the libraries of its leading intellectuals, as well as that of the Karawiyin mosque, which was founded about 1350, would have provided the two men with a wealth of source material if they needed it.[12]

It is perfectly plain that Ibn Juzayy copied outright numerous long passages from the *Rihla* of Ibn Jubayr, the twelfth-century

Andalusian traveler who wrote the most elegant of the medieval Muslim travel books. These passages pertain to Ibn Battuta's descriptions of Damascus, Mecca, Medina, and some other places in the Middle East. It seems likely that where Ibn Battuta could not remember very well certain places he visited, or where Ibn Jubayr's description was, from a literary point of view, as good as anything Ibn Juzayy could produce, then deference might be made to this learned predecessor.[13] Modern scholars have suggested, and in some cases proven, that Ibn Juzayy paraphrased from other earlier geographical books as well.[14]

In his introduction to the *Rihla*, Ibn Juzayy declares that his intention was to write down the story just as Ibn Battuta told it:

> I have rendered the sense of the narrative . . . in language which adequately expresses the purposes he had in mind and sets forth clearly the ends which he had in view. Frequently I have reported his words in his own phrasing, without omitting either root or branch.

Yet Ibn Juzayy had been commissioned not simply to transcribe mechanically Ibn Battuta's reminiscences but to undertake appropriate "pruning and polishing" of his associate's verbatim reports so as to produce a coherent, graceful work of literature in the high tradition of the *rihla* genre. In the interests of literary symmetry and taste, therefore, the raw record of the traveler's experience had to be reshaped to some extent. For one thing, the itinerary over the entire 29 years was exceedingly complicated. Ibn Battuta visited a number of cities or regions two or more times, and his routes crisscrossed, backtracked, and overlapped. Consequently, Ibn Juzayy found it desirable to group the descriptions of certain places within the context of Ibn Battuta's first visit there — and to do it without much heed to the precise details of his movements. The result is a more smoothly flowing narrative but a vexatious snarl of problems for any modern scholar trying to figure out exactly where Ibn Battuta went and when.[15]

Even more troublesome for the historian is Ibn Battuta's recounting of visits to at least a few places that in fact he probably never saw. Ibn Juzayy meant the *Rihla* to be at the broadest level a survey of the Muslim world of the fourteenth century. Ibn Battuta had not gone absolutely everywhere in that world. Yet Ibn Juzayy probably thought that for the sake of literary integrity almost every place in Eurasia and Africa having an important Muslim population should be mentioned within the framework of the traveler's first-person experience, even though in a few cases that experience might not be genuine. Ibn Battuta describes, albeit rather lamely and self-consciously, a trip up the Volga River to visit the Muslim community of Bulghar, a trip he almost certainly did not make.[16] Modern commentators have also cast doubts on the authenticity of his journeys to China and Byzantium, as well as to parts of Khurasan, Yemen, Anatolia, and East Africa, though scholarly opinion is very much divided on these questions.[17] Even if small parts of the *Rihla* are fabricated, we can never know for sure how to parcel out the blame. It is conceivable that Ibn Juzayy added certain passages without Ibn Battuta even knowing that he did. Nor can we discount the meddlings of later copyists.

If the authenticity of the *Rihla* has generally stood up well under modern scrutiny, Ibn Battuta was by no means let off easily in his own time. By an extraordinary piece of historical coincidence, 'Abd al-Rahman ibn Khaldun, the Tunisian historian and philosopher who came to tower over the Muslim intellectual world in the later medieval age, arrived in Fez in 1354 to join the circle of scholars around Sultan Abu 'Inan. Ibn Khaldun had been a young government officer in Tunis when Abu l'Hasan's army occupied that city. He was impressed by the erudition of the Moroccan scholars in the sultan's suite and, having lost both his parents in the Black Death, decided to leave home to pursue advanced studies in Fez. There is no evidence that he ever made Ibn Battuta's acquaintance. But in *The Muqaddimah,* his great work of historical sociology completed in 1377, he makes a brief and utterly incidental remark about a certain *"shaykh* from Tangier" who turned up in Fez after traveling widely in the Muslim world. "He used to tell about experiences he had had on his travels," Ibn Khaldun reports, "and about the remarkable things he had seen in the different realms. He spoke mostly about the ruler of India. He reported things about him that his listeners considered strange." Ibn Khaldun then repeats some of Ibn Battuta's stories about Muhammad Tughluq: his provisioning the famine-stricken people of Delhi out of his own income and his practice of having gold coins showered upon his subjects from the backs of elephants. Ibn Khaldun also notes that Ibn Battuta held a judgeship in the sultanate. But then he goes on to remark darkly that the Tangierian "told other similar stories, and people in the dynasty (in official positions) whispered to each other that he must be a liar."[18]

Abu l'Barakat al-Balafiqi, the Andalusian scholar who had met Ibn Battuta in Granada and was later to express a low opinion of his scholarship, also resided in Fez about this time and knew Ibn Khaldun.[19] According to Ibn al-Khatib, author of the fourteenth-century biographical notice on Ibn Battuta, al-Balafiqi said that people considered the traveler "purely and simply a liar."[20] Why such skepticism among the intelligentsia of Fez? Perhaps it was a reflection of their casual contempt for Ibn Battuta's pedestrian erudition. Or it might simply have been the incredulous parochialism of Far Western Muslims who had themselves never traveled very far from home.

Indeed Ibn Khaldun continues in *The Muqaddimah*:

> One day I met the Sultan's famous vizier, Faris ibn Wadrar. I talked to him about this matter and intimated to him that I did not believe that man's stories, because people in the dynasty were in general inclined to consider him a liar. Whereupon the vizier Faris said to me: "Be careful not to reject such information about the condition of dynasties, because you have not seen such things yourself."[21]

Moreover Muhammad ibn Marzuk, a famous scholar of Tlemcen who was occupying a government post in Fez when the *Rihla* was being composed, also expressed an opinion on Ibn Battuta, which found its way into Ibn Hajar's fifteenth-century biographical notice. According to Ibn Hajar, Ibn Marzuk cleared the traveler of al-Balafiqi's charge of lying and even declared, "I know of no person who has journeyed through so many lands as [he did] on his travels, and he was withal generous and welldoing."[22]

If Ibn Battuta stirred up courtly gossip for a few months with his exotic tales, he seems to have attracted no more attention in Fez after his work with Ibn Juzayy was completed. All that we know of his later life is that, according to Ibn Hajar's brief sketch, he held "the office of *qadi* in some town or other."[23] He probably lived in the modestly comfortable style of a provincial official, and, since he was not yet 50 years old when he ended his travels, he very likely married again and sired more children, little half brothers and sisters of the offspring growing up all across the Eastern Hemisphere.

As for the *Rihla*, very little is known of its history from the fourteenth to the nineteenth century. In contrast to Marco Polo's book, which was widely circulated and acclaimed in Europe in the later Middle Ages, the *Rihla* appears to have had a very modest impact on the Muslim world until modern times. There is no evidence of its being widely quoted or used as a source in Muslim historical or geographical works written after 1355. To be sure, copies of either the entire work or abridgments of it circulated among educated households in Morocco and the other North African countries. The *Rihla* was also known in the Western Sudan in the seventeenth century and in Egypt in the eighteenth, at least in the form of abridgments. It may also have turned up in libraries in Muslim regions east of the Nile.[24] Only in the mid nineteenth century, half a millennium after it was written, did the narrative begin to receive the international attention it so profoundly deserved. The credit for that achievement, ironically enough, fell to scholars of Christian Europe, the one populous region of Eurasia Ibn Battuta had never bothered to visit in his travels.

If the great journeyer attained no literary glory in his own time, he nevertheless had good reason to review his long career with satisfaction. He had seen and borne witness to the best that the fourteenth century had to offer, three decades of relative prosperity and political calm in the Afro-Eurasian world. The second half of the century was to be drastically different. It was in Barbara Tuchman's phrase the "calamitous" half of the century, a time of social disturbance and economic regression that seemed to afflict almost the entire hemisphere.[25] The troubles of the age were almost certainly associated with the great pandemic, not only the Black Death itself but the multiple recurrences of pestilence that followed decade after decade on into the fifteenth century. The Black Death killed untold millions, but the repeated outbreaks of plague prevented agrarian populations in Europe and the Middle East, and perhaps in India and China as well, from recovering to pre-plague levels.

The result was chronically depressed productivity, a condition that grievously affected many kingdoms of the hemisphere just about the time Ibn Battuta ended his travels. With the exception of a few regions where real political vigor was in evidence (the rising Ottoman Empire, Ming China after 1368, Vijayanagar in southern India), almost every state he had visited either disappeared (the Yuan dynasty in China, the Ilkhanids in Persia), rapidly deteriorated (the Delhi Sultanate, Byzantium), or experienced dynastic strife, rebellion, or social upheaval (the Khanates of Kipchak and Chagatay, the Mamluk Sultanate, Mali, Granada). Latin Europe, which he had not visited, experienced equally sorry times, with its deep economic recession, Hundred Years War, Papal Schism, and succession of peasant uprisings.

In his own homeland he lived out his last years amid the violent, anarchic disintegration of the Marinid state. Sultan Abu 'Inan invaded Ifriqiya and occupied Tunis in the fall of 1357, but he was forced to withdraw within two months. The following year he fell sick and was finally strangled by a rebellious vizier. No Marinid king succeeded in restoring order and unity to the country during the next century.

Perhaps safe in his remote judgeship from the turmoil of those times, the aging globetrotter could look back over a quarter century whose strong kingdoms, thriving hemispheric trade, and cosmopolitan cities had given him so many opportunities for adventure and fortune. And despite the spreading darkness of the later century, his confidence in the continuing triumph of Islam was doubtless undiminished. He would not have been specially impressed to know that, as the fifteenth century approached, Muslim merchants, preachers, soldiers, and peripatetic scholars like himself still carried on the work of implanting Islam and its treasury of values and institutions in Southeast Asia, East and West Africa, India, and Southeastern Europe. Even as the bellicose Portuguese prepared their attack on Ceuta and the age of European power began, Islam as both a living faith and a model of civilized life continued to spread into new regions of the earth.

Ibn Battuta died in 1368 or 1369 (700 A.H.).[26] Where his grave lies, no one knows for sure. The tourist guides of Tangier are pleased to take foreign visitors to see a modest tomb that allegedly houses the mortal remains of the traveler. But the site has no inscription and its genuineness is open to question.[27] A more vital memorial to him is the *Ibn Battouta,* the big ferry boat that shuttles people and their automobiles across the Strait of Gibraltar. From the kasba high above the city, you can see it steam out of the harbor, carrying young Moroccan scholars to their law schools in Paris and Bordeaux.

Notes

1. Gb, vol. 2, p. 282.

2. "Ibn Djuzayy," EI₂, vol. 3, p. 756; D&S, vol. 1, p. xxi.

3. H. A. R. Gibb, *Ibn Battuta: Travels in Asia and Africa* (London, 1929), p. 12.

4. "Ibn Djuzayy," EI₂. vol. 3, p. 756.

5. Leonardo Olschki, *Marco Polo's Asia: An Introduction to his Description of the World Called Il Milione* (Berkeley and Los Angeles, 1960) p. 12.

6. This is Gibb's translation (Gb, vol. 1, p. ix) of the passage as it appears in Ibn Hajar al-Ascalani's fifteenth-century biographical dictionary *Al-Durar al-Kamina*. The Arabic text and French translation of Ibn al-Khatib's notice, upon which Ibn Hajar's is partially based, is found in E. Levi-Provençal, "Le Voyage d'Ibn Battuta dans le royaume de Grenade (1350)" in *Mélanges offerts à William Marçais* (Paris, 1950), pp. 213, 223. Ibn al-Khatib quotes Abu l'Barakat as saying he met IB in Granada in the garden of Abu l'Kasim ibn Asim. IB confirms this meeting (D&S, vol. 4, p. 371). On Abu l-Barakat al-Balafiqi, see Soledad Gibert, "Abu-l-Barakat al-Balafiqi, Qadi, Historiador y Poeta," *Al-Andalus* 28 (1963): p. 381–424.

7. H&K, p. 5.

8. On the migration of Muslim literate cadres to the fringe areas of Islam, see Marshall G. S. Hodgson, *The Venture of Islam*, 3 vols. (Chicago, 1974), vol. 2, pp. 539–42.

9. D&S, vol. 3, p. 28.

10. D&S, vol. 4, p. 449. Major commentators are divided on the question of IB's notes. Gibb, Hrbek, and Défrémery and Sanguinetti believe he did not use travel notes when he worked with Ibn Juzayy. Gibb, *Travels in Asia and Africa*, p. 12; Hr, pp. 413–14; D&S, vol. 1, p. ix. Mahdi Husain thinks he did. MH, p. xviii.

11. See John Wansbrough, "Africa and the Arab Geographers" in D. Dalby (ed.), *Language and History in Africa* (London, 1970), pp. 89–101.

12. On the founding of the Karawiyin library, J. Berque, "Ville et université: aperçu sur l'histoire de l'école de Fès," *Revue Historique de Droit Français et Étranger* (1949): 72. On the practice of learned men making their libraries available to other scholars, George Makdisi, *The Rise of Colleges: Institutions of Learning in Islam and the West* (Edinburgh, 1981), pp. 24–27.

13. J. N. Mattock, "Ibn Battuta's Use of Ibn Jubayr's *Rihla*" in R. Peters (ed.), *Proceedings of the Ninth Congress of the Union Européene des Arabisants et Islamisants* (Leiden, 1981), pp. 209–18; and "The Travel Writings of Ibn Jubair and Ibn Batuta," *Glasgow Oriental Society Transactions* 21 (1965–66): 35–46.

14. On the *Rihla*'s possible debts to al-Bakri, Ibn Fadlan, al-'Umari, and other Muslim authors see Herman F. Janssens, *Ibn Batouta, "Le Voyageur de l'Islam"* (Brussels, 1948), pp. 108–09; Stephen Janicsek, "Ibn Battuta's Journey to Bulghar: Is it a Fabrication?" *Journal of the Royal Asiatic Society* (October 1929): 794; Mattock, "Ibn Battuta's Use of Ibn Jubayr's *Rihla*," pp. 210, 217; L&H, pp. 280–81.

15. See particularly Chapter 3, note 26.

16. See Chapter 8, note 12.

17. See various footnotes pertaining to the chronology and itinerary of trips to these areas.

18. Ibn Khaldun, *The Muqaddimah*, trans. and ed. Franz Rosenthal, 3 vols. (Princeton, N.J., 1958), vol. 1, pp. 369–70.

19. Ibn Khaldun, *The Muqaddimah*, vol. 1, p. xlii.

20. Ibn al-Khatib, quoted in Levi-Provençal, "Le Voyage d'Ibn Battuta," p. 213.

21. Ibn Khaldun, *The Muqaddimah*, vol. 1, pp. 370–71.

22. Ibn Hajar al-'Asqalani, *Al-Durar al-Kamina fi A'yan al-Mi'a al-Thamina*, 4 vols. (Hyderabad, 1929–31), 3: 480–81. Gb, vol. 1, pp. ix–x. On Ibn Marzuk see "Ibn Marzuk," EI₂, vol. 3, pp. 865–68.

23. Gb, vol. 1, p. x.

24. 'Abd al-Rahman ibn 'Abd Allah al-Sa'di, *Tarikh es-Soudan*, trans. O. Houdas (Paris, 1964), pp. 15–16; D&S, vol. 1, pp. xiii–xvi. H.T. Norris has pointed out a biographical entry on IB in a work written in 1799–1800 by a scholar from Walata in Mauritania. Review of Ross E. Dunn, *The Adventures of Ibn Battuta,* in *The Maghrib Review* 12, nos. 3–4 (1987), pp. 116–17. Tim Mackintosh-Smith (personal communication) informs me that the Moroccan Scholar Abdelhadi al-Tazi makes a case for IB's work being known in the Middle East from the end of the sixteenth century. Al-Tazi's Arabic edition of the *Rihla* has been unavailable to me in the United States. *Rihlat Ibn Battuta,* 5 vols. (Rabat: Royal Moroccan Academy, 1997).

25. Barbara W. Tuchman, *A Distant Mirror: The Calamitous Fourteenth Century* (New York, 1978).

26. Ibn Hajar's biography quoted in Gb, vol. 1, pp. ix–x.

27. According to Tim Mackintosh-Smith, Abdelhadi Tazi reports that the text of a letter by the fourteenth-century scholar Ibn al-Khatib indicates that IB served in his later years as a judge in the Moroccan region of Tamasna, whose principal city was Anfa. Therefore, IB may be buried there. Unfortunately, medieval Anfa lies underneath modern Casablanca! Tim Mackintosh-Smith, *Travels with a Tangerine: A Journey in the Footnotes of Ibn Battutah* (London, 2001), pp. 34–35.

Glossary

Akhi	Member or leader of an urban men's association, or *fityan*.
'alim (pl. *'ulama*)	A person learned in the Islamic sciences
amir	A military commander or ruler.
baraka	Quality of divine grace
faqih	A specialist in Islamic law; a jurist.
fiqh	Jurisprudence, the science of Islamic law.
fityan	Urban association of men devoted to Muslim religious and social ideals.
ghazi	A fighter in defense of Islam.
hadith	Traditions of the words or actions of the Prophet Muhammad; one of the major sources of Islamic law.
hajj	The pilgrimage to Mecca.
harim	The restricted women's quarters of a house or palace.
'Id al-Adha	Feast of the Sacrifice celebrated on the 10th of Dhu l-Hijja; part of the rites of the Muslim pilgrimage.
'Id al-Fitr	Feast of Breaking of the Fast celebrated on the 1st of Shawwal to mark the end of Ramadan, the Muslim month of fasting.
ihram	The state of ritual purity associated with the rites of the pilgrimage in Mecca; the simple white garments worn by males during the pilgrimage.
ijaza	Certificate authenticating the holder's mastery of an Islamic text; conveys the right to teach the text to others.
imam	Leader of prayer in mosques; for Shi'a Muslims the divinely ordained ruler of the Muslim community.
jihad	War in defense of Islam.
Ka'ba	The sacred, cube-shaped building in Mecca.

321

khan

A mercantile warehouse or hostel for merchants and other travelers; also in Turkish and Mongol usage a chief or ruler.

madhhab

A school of law in Sunni Islam. The four major schools are the Hanafi, the Hanbali, the Maliki, and the Shafi'i.

madrasa

A school or college teaching the Islamic sciences, especially law.

Maghrib

The lands of North Africa, corresponding to modern Morocco, Algeria, and Tunisia.

Maliki

One of the four *madhhabs*, or schools of law; predominant in North Africa.

mamluk

A military slave; a member of the Turkish-speaking cavalry elite that ruled Egypt and Syria under the Mamluk dynasty.

qadi

A Muslim judge.

Ramadan

The ninth month of the lunar year, which Muslims devote to fasting during daylight hours.

rihla

Travel; a type of Islamic literature concerned with travels, particularly for study and pilgrimage.

shari'a

Islamic law.

sharif

A descendant of the Prophet Muhammad.

shaykh

A title of respect, as for a tribal chief, learned man, or leader of a Sufi brotherhood.

Shi'a (Shi'ism)

Muslims who take the view that the Caliph 'Ali and his descendants are the rightful rulers of the Muslim community. The Shi'ia are divided into several minority sects within Islam. An adherent of one of these sects is a Shi'i.

Sufism

Islamic mysticism. A Sufi is a Muslim mystic and usually a member of a religious order.

Sunni

The majority sect in Islam whose members follow one of the four major

	madhhabs, or schools of law. Sunni Muslims are differentiated from followers of Shi'i Islam.
tawaf	The ritual of walking around the Ka'ba in Mecca seven times.
'ulama (sing. *'alim*)	Persons learned in the Islamic sciences.
zawiya	A Sufi religious center or hospice. In eastern Islam, *khanqa*

Bibliography

Works on Ibn Battuta and His Rihla

This list excludes a number of general works on the history of geography or travel that contain summary descriptions of Ibn Battuta's career. It also excludes partial translations of the *Rihla* that subsequently appeared as part of larger published works.

Abdur Rahim. "Six Hundred Years After — in the Footsteps of Ibn Battuta in Andalusia." *Peshawar University Review* 51 (1973): 1–21

Beckingham, Charles F. "From Tangier to China — 14th Century." *Hemisphere: An Asian-Australian Magazine*, 8 August 1978, pp. 26–31

—— "Ibn Battuta in Sind." In *Sind through the Centuries: Proceedings of an International Seminar, Karachi 1975*. Edited by Hamida Khuhro. Karachi, 1981, pp. 139–42.

—— "In Search of Ibn Battuta." *Asian Affairs* 8 (1977): 263–77.

Bhatnagar, R. "Madhyadesh in the Rehla of Ibn Battuta." *Saugar University Journal* 4 (1955–56): 97–109

Bousquet, G. H. "Ibn Battuta et les institutions musulmanes." *Studia Islamica* 24 (1966): 81–106

Carim, Fuad. *Maco Polo ve Ibn Batuta*. Istanbul, 1966

Chelhod, Joesph. "Ibn Battuta, Ethnologue." *Revue de l'Occident Musulman et de la Méditerranée* 25 (1978): 5–24

Chittick, H. Neville. "Ibn Battuta and East Africa." *Journal de la Société des Africanistes* 38 (1968): 239–41

Cuoq, J. M. *Recueil des sources arabes concernant l'Afrique occidentale du VIIIe au XVIe siècle*. Paris, 1975

De, Harinath (trans.), and Ghosh, P. N. (ed.). *Ibn Batutah's Account of Bengal*. Calcutta, 1978

Défrémery, C., and Sanguinetti, B. R. (trans. and eds.). *Voyages d'Ibn Battuta*. 4 vols. Paris, 1853–58; reprint edn., edited by Vincent Monteil. Paris, 1979

Dulaurier, Edouard. "Description de l'archipel d'Asie, par Ibn Bathoutha." *Journal Asiatique*, 4th ser., 9 (1874): 93–134, 218–59

Fanjul, Serafin. "Elementos folkloricos en la Rihla de Ibn Battuta." *Revista del Instituto Egipico de Estudios Islamicos en Madrid* 21 (1981–82): 153–79

—— and Arbós, Federico (trans. and eds.). *Ibn Battuta a través del Islam*. Madrid, 1981

Ferrand, Gabriel. *Relations de voyages et textes géographiques arabes, persans, et turks relatif à l'Extrême-Orient du VIII au XVIII siècles*. 2 vols. Paris, 1913–14. See vol. 2, pp. 426–58

Freeman-Grenville, G. S. P. "Ibn Batuta's Visit to East Africa, 1332 A.D.: A Translation." *Uganda Journal* 19 (1955): 1–6

Gabrieli, Francesco (trans. and ed.). *I viaggi di Ibn Battuta*. Florence, 1961

Gibb, H. A. R. (trans. and ed.). *Ibn Battuta: Travels in Asia and Africa*. London, 1929; reprint edn., 1983

—— "Notes sur les voyages d'Ibn Battuta en Asie Mineure et en Russie." *Etudes d'orientalisme dediées à la memoire de Lévi-Provençal.* 2 vols. Paris. 1962. vol. 1, pp. 125–33

—— *The Travels of Ibn Battuta A.D. 1325–1354, Translated with Revisions and Notes from the Arabic Text Edited by C. Défrémery and B. R. Sanguinetti.* 3 vols. Cambridge for the Hakluyt Society, 1958, 1961, 1971

Gies, Frances Carney. "To Travel the Earth." *Aramco World Magazine* (January–February 1978): 18–27

Haig, M. R. "Ibnu Batuta in Sindh." *Journal of the Royal Asiatic Society* 19 (1887): 393–412

Hamdun, Said, and King, Noel (trans. and eds.). *Ibn Battuta in Black Africa.* London, 1975

Hasan, Mehdi. "The Rihla of Ibn Battuta." *Proceedings of the Second Indian Historical Congress* 2 (1938): 278–85

Hrbek, Ivan. "The Chronology of Ibn Battuta's Travels." *Archiv Orientalni* 30 (1962): 409–86

Husain, Agha Mahdi. "Dates and Precis of Ibn Battuta's Travels with Observations." *Sind University Research Journal, Arts Series: Humanities and Social Sciences* 7 (1968): 95–108

—— "Ibn Battuta and His *Rehla* in New Light." *Sind University Research Journal, Arts Series: Humanities and Social Sciences* 6 (1967): 25–32

—— "Ibn Battuta, His Life and Work." *Indo-Iranica* 7 (1954): 6–13

—— "Manuscripts of Ibn Battuta's *Rehla* in Paris and Ibn Juzayy." *Journal and Proceedings of the Asiatic Society of Bengal* 20 (1954): 49–53

—— (trans. and ed.). *The Rehla of Ibn Battuta.* Baroda, India, 1976

—— "Studies in the *Tuhfatunnuzzar* of Ibn Battuta and Ibn Juzayy." *Journal of the Asiatic Society of Bangladesh* 23 (1978): 18–49

Ibn Battuta. *Rihla Ibn Batuta.* Beirut, 1964

—— *Rihla Ibn Battuta.* 2 vols. Cairo, 1964

Ibn Hajar al-'Asqalani. *Al-Durar al-Kamina fi A'yan al-Mi'a al-Thamina.* 4 vols. Hyderabad, 1929–31. See vol. 3, pp. 480–81 for biographical notice on Ibn Battuta.

Izzeddin, Mehmed. "Ibn Battouta et la topographie byzantine." *Actes du VI Congrès Internationale des Études Byzantines.* 2 vols. Paris, 1951, vol. 2, pp. 191–96

Janicsek, Stephen. "Ibn Battuta's Journey to Bulghar: Is it a Fabrication?" *Journal of the Royal Asiatic Society* (October, 1929): 791–800

Janssens, Herman F. *Ibn Batouta, "Le Voyageur de l'Islam."* Brussels, 1948

Khan, Abdul Majed. "The Historicity of Ibn Batuta Re. Sham-Suddin Firuz Shah, the So-Called Balbani King of Bengal." *Indian Historical Quarterly* 18 (1942): 65–70

King, Noel. "Reading between the Lines of Ibn Battuta for the History of Religion in Black Africa." *Milla wa-milla* 19 (1979): 26–33

Lee, Samuel (trans. and ed.). *The Travels of Ibn Battuta.* London, 1929

Leva, A. Enrico. "Ibn Batuta nell' Africa Nera." *Africa* 16: (1961): 169–77

Lévi-Provençal, E. "Le voyage d'Ibn Battuta dans le royaume de Grenade (1350)." *Mélanges offerts à William Marçais.* Paris, 1950, pp. 205–24

Markwart, J. "Ein arabischer Bericht über die arktischen (uralischen) Länder aus dem 10 Jahrhundert." *Ungaarische Jahrbücher* 4 (1924): 261–334

Mattock, J. N. "Ibn Battuta's Use of Ibn Jubayr's *Rihla.*" In *Proceedings of the Ninth Congress of the Union Européene des Arabisants et Islamisants.* Edited by R. Peters. Leiden, 1981, pp. 209–18

—— "The Travel Writings of Ibn Jubair and Ibn Batuta." *Glasgow Oriental Society Transactions* 21 (1965–66): 35–46

Mauny, R., Monteil, V., Djenidi, A., Robert, S., and Devisse, J. *Textes et documents relatifs à l'histoire d'Afrique: extraits tirés des voyages d'Ibn Battuta.* Dakar, 1966

Meillassoux, C. "L'itinéraire d'Ibn Battuta de Walata à Malli." *Journal of African History* 13 (1972): 389–95

Miquel, André. "Ibn Battuta, trente années de voyages de Pekin au Niger." *Les Africains* 1 (1977): 117–40

—— "L'Islam d'Ibn Battuta." *Bulletin d'Études Orientales* 30 (1978): 75–83

Mirza, M. Wahid. "Khusrau and Ibn Battuta, a Comparative Study." In *Professor Muhammad Shafi' Presentation Volume.* Lahore, 1955, pp. 171–80

Mollat, Michel. "Ibn Batoutah et la mer." *Travaux et Jours* 18 (1966): 53–70

Monteil, Vincent. "Introduction aux voyages d'Ibn Battuta (1325–53)." *Bulletin de l'IFAN*, ser. B, 30 (1968): 444–62

Moraes, G. M. "Haryab of Ibn Batuta." *Journal of the Bombay Branch of the Royal Asiatic Society* 15 (1938): 37–49

Morris, J. "Ibn Batuta: The Travels and the Man." *Ur* (1980): 23–27

N'Diaye, Aissatou. "Sur la transcription des vocables africains par Ibn Baththutah." *Notes Africaines* 38 (1948): 26–27; 41 (1949): 31

Netton, Ian Richard. "Myth, Miracle and Magic in the *Rihla* of Ibn Battuta." *Journal of Semitic Studies* 29 (1984): 131–40

Norris, H. T. "Ibn Battutah's Andalusian Journey." *Geographical Journal* 125 (1959): 185–96

Quiros Rodriquez, C. "B. Batuta: un viajero tangerino sel siglo XIV." *Archivos del Instituto de Estudios Aficanos* 6 (1952): 11–27

Rashid, Abdur. "India and Pakistan in the Fourteenth Century as Described by Arab Travellers." In *Congresso internacional de historia dos descobrimentos.* Lisbon, 1961

Rawlinson, H. G. "The Traveller of Islam." *Islamic Culture* 5 (1931): 29–37

Saletore, R. N. "Haryab of Ibn Battuta and Harihara Nrpala." *Quarterly Journal of the Mythic Society* 31 (1940–41): 384–406

Seco de Lucena, Luis. "De toponimia granadina: Sobre el vije de Ibn Battuta al reino de Granada." *Al-Andalus* 16 (1951): 49–85

Slane, M. G. (trans.). "Voyage dans le Soudan." *Journal Asiatique*, 4th ser., 1 (1843): 181–246

Sobret, J. "Les Frontières chez Ibn Battuta." In *Actes du 8ème Congrès de l'Union Européenne des Arabisants et Islamisants.* Aix-en-Provence, 1978, pp. 305–08

Stewig, R. "Versuch einer Auswertung der Reisebeschreibung von Ibn Battuta (nach der englischen Übersetzung von H. A. R. Gibb) zur Bedeutungsdifferenzierung westanatolischer Siedlungen." *Der Islam* 47 (1971): 43–58

Von Mzik, Hans (trans. and ed.). *Die Reise des Arabers Ibn Batuta durch Indien und China.* Hamburg, 1911

Yamamoto, T. "On Tawalisi as Described by Ibn Battuta." *Memoirs of the Research Department of the Toyo Bunko* 8 (1936): 93–133

Yule, Henry. *Cathay and the Way Thither.* 4 vols. London, 1913–16. See vol. 4, pp. 5–166.

General Works

Abun-Nasr, Jamil M. *A History of the Maghrib.* Cambridge, England, 1971

Adler, Elkan N. *Jewish Travelers.* London, 1930

Arberry, Arthur J. *The Koran Interpreted.* New York, 1955

Ashtor, E. *A Social and Economic History of the Near East in the Middle Ages.* Berkeley, 1976

Bel, Alfred. *La religion musulmane en Berbérie: esquisse d'histoire et de sociologie religieuses.* Paris, 1938

Boyle, John Andrew. *The Mongol World Empire 1206–1370.* London, 1977
Brice, William C. (ed.). *An Historical Atlas of Islam.* Leiden, 1981
Brignon, Jean; Amine, Abdelaziz; Boutaleb, Brahim; Martinet, Guy; and Rosenberger, Bernard. *Histoire du Maroc.* Paris, 1967
Chaunu, Pierre. *L'expansion européenne du XIIIe au XVe siècle.* Paris, 1969
Cook, M. A. (ed.). *Studies in the Economic History of the Middle East.* Oxford, 1970
Curtin, Philip D. *Cross-Cultural Trade in World History.* Cambridge, England, 1984
Dodge, Bayard. *Muslim Education in Medieval Times.* Washington, D.C., 1962
Encyclopaedia of Islam. 1st edn., 4 vols. Leiden, 1913–38
Encyclopaedia of Islam. 2nd edn., 5 vols. Leiden, 1954; London, 1956–
Goitein, S. D. *A Mediterranean Society.* 4 vols. Berkeley and Los Angeles, 1967–83
—— *Studies in Islamic History and Institutions.* Leiden, 1966
Grousset, René. *The Empire of the Steppes: A History of Central Asia.* New Brunswick, N.H., 1970
Hazard, Harry W., and Setton, Kenneth M. (eds.). *A History of the Crusades.* 5 vols. of which 3 are published. Madison, Wis., vols. 1 and 2, 2nd edn., 1969; vol. 3, 1975
Heyd, W. *Histoire du commerce du Levant au moyen-âge.* 2 vols. Leipzig, 1885–86; reprint edn., Leipzig, 1936
Hodgson, Marshall G. S. "Hemispheric Interregional History as an Approach to World History." *Journal of World History* 1 (1954): 715–23
—— "The Interrelations of Societies in History." *Comparative Studies in Society and History* 5 (1963): 227–50
—— "The Role of Islam in World History." *International Journal of Middle East Studies* 1 (1970): 99–123
—— "The Unity of Later Islamic History." *Journal of World History* 5 (1960): 879–914
—— *The Venture of Islam: Conscience and History in a World Civilization.* 3 vols. Chicago, 1974
Holt, P. M., Lambton, Ann K. S., and Lewis, Bernard. *The Cambridge History of Islam.* 2 vols. Cambridge, 1970
Hourani, A. H., and Stern, S. M. *The Islamic City.* Oxford, 1970
Howorth, Henry H. *History of the Mongols.* 3 vols. London, 1888
Ibn Jubayr, Muhammad ibn Ahmad. *The Travels of Ibn Jubayr.* Translated by R. J. C. Broadhurst. London, 1952
Ibn Khaldun. *Histoire des Berbères et des dynasties musulmanes de l'Afrique septentrionale.* Translated by Baron de Slane. 4 vols. Paris, 1925–56
—— *The Muqaddimah.* Translated and edited by Franz Rosenthal. 3 vols. Princeton, N.J., 1958; 2nd edn., 1967
Julien, Charles-André. *History of North Africa.* Translated by John Petrie and edited by C. C. Stewart. New York, 1970
Kwanten, Luc. *Imperial Nomads: A History of Central Asia.* Philadelphia, 1979
Lattimore, Owen. *Inner Asian Frontiers of China.* Boston, 1940
Levtzion, Nehemia. *Conversion to Islam.* New York, 1979
McNeill, William H. *The Rise of the West: A History of the Human Community.* Chicago, 1963
Makdisi, George. *The Rise of Colleges: Institutions of Learning in Islam and the West.* Edinburgh, 1981
Marçais, Georges. *La Berbérie musulmane et l'orient au Moyen Âge.* Paris, 1946
Miquel, André. *La géographie humaine du monde musulman jusqu'au milieu du IIe siècle.* 2 vols. Paris, 1975
Moule, A. C., and Pelliot, Paul. *Marco Polo: The Description of the World.* 2 vols. London, 1938; reprint edn., New York, 1976

Niane, D. T. (ed.). *General History of Africa. Vol. 4: Africa from the Twelfth to the Sixteenth Century*. Berkeley and Los Angeles, 1984

Oliver, Roland (ed.). *The Cambridge History of Africa*. Multivol. *Vol. 3: From c. 1050 to c. 1600*. Cambridge, 1977–

Olschki, Leonardo. *Marco Polo's Asia: An Introduction to his Description of the World Called Il Milione*. Berkeley and Los Angeles, 1960

Parry, J. H. *The Discovery of the Sea*. New York, 1974

Pelliot, Paul. *Notes on Marco Polo*. 2 vols. Reprint edn., Paris, 1959–63

Pipes, Daniel. *Slave Soldiers and Islam*. New Haven, Conn., 1981

Polo, Marco. *The Book of Ser Marco Polo*. Translated and edited by Henry Yule. 3rd edn., 2 vols. London, 1929

Richard, J. "European Voyages in the Indian Ocean and the Caspian Sea (12th–15th Centuries)." *Iran* 6 (1968): 45–52

Richards, D. S. (ed.). *Islam and the Trade of Asia*. Philadelphia, 1970

Richards, J. F. (ed.). *Precious Metals in the Later Medieval and Early Modern Worlds*. Durham, N.C., 1983

Saunders, J. J. *The History of the Mongol Conquests*. London, 1971

Schacht, Joseph. *An Introduction to Islamic Law*. Oxford, 1964

Seymour, M. C. *Mandeville's Travels*. Oxford, 1967

Spuler, Bertold. *History of the Mongols*. Berkeley and Los Angeles, 1972

——— *The Mongols in History*. Translated by G. Wheeler. New York, 1971

——— *The Muslim World. Vol. 2: The Mongol Period*. Translated by F. R. C. Bagley. Leiden, 1960

Terrasse, H. *Histoire du Maroc*. 2 vols. Casablanca, 1949–50

Trimingham, J. Spencer. *The Sufi Orders in Islam*. Oxford, 1971

Tritton, A. S. *Materials on Muslim Education in the Middle Ages*. London, 1957

Tuchman, Barbara W. *A Distant Mirror: The Calamitous Fourteenth Century*. New York, 1978

'Umari, Ibn Fadl Allah al-. *L'Afrique moins l'Égypte (Masalik al-absar fi mamalik al amsar)*. Translated and edited by Maruice Gaudfroy-Demombynes. Paris, 1927

Unger, Richard W. *The Ship in the Medieval Economy*. London, 1980

Westermarck, Edward. *Ritual and Belief in Morocco*. 2 vols. London, 1926

Chapter 1: Tangier

Brown, Kenneth L. *People of Salé: Tradition and Change in a Moroccan City, 1830–1930*. Cambridge, Mass., 1976

Caille, J. "Les Marseillais à Ceuta au XIIIe siècle." In *Mélanges d'histoire et d'archéologie de l'occident musulman. Vol. 2: Hommage a Georges Marçais*. Algiers, 1957, pp. 21–31

Dufourcq, Charles-Emmanuel. "Berbèrie et Iberie médiévales: un problème de rupture." *Revue Historique* 92 (1968): 293–324

——— 'La Question de Ceuta au XIIIe siècle." *Hespéris* 41 (1955): 67–127

——— *L'Espagne catalane et le Maghrib aux XIIIe et XIVe siècles*. Paris, 1966

——— "Méditerranée et Maghreb du XIIIe au XVIe siècles." *Revue d'histoire et du Civilization du Maghreb* 3 (1967): 75–87

Eickelman, Dale F. *Knowledge and Power in Morocco: The Education of a Twentieth Century Notable*. Princeton, N.J., 1985

Ibn Abi Zar. *Roudh el-Kartas: Histoire des souverains du Maghreb et annales de la ville de Fez*. Translated by Auguste Beaumier. Paris, 1860

Krueger, Hilmar C. "Genoese Trade with Northwest Africa in the Twelfth Century." *Speculum* 8 (1933): 377–95

Lane, Frederic C. *Venice, a Maritime Republic*. Baltimore, 1973

Latham, Derek. "Towns and Cities of Barbary — the Andalusian Influence." *Islamic Quarterly* 16 (1972): 189–204

Lévi-Provençal, E. "Un nouvel text d'histoire merinide: le Musnad d'Ibn Marzuk." *Hespéris* 5 (1925): 1–82

Lewis, Archibald R. "Northern European Sea Power and the Straits of Gibraltar, 1031–1350 A.D." In *Order and Innovation in the Middle Ages: Essays in Honor of Joseph R. Strayer*. Edited by William C. Jordan. Princeton, N.J., 1976, pp. 139–62

Mackeen, A. M. "The Early History of Sufism in the Maghrib Prior to al-Shadhili." *Journal of the American Oriental Society* 91 (1971): 398–408

Mascarello, Anna. "Quelques aspects des activités italiennes dans le Maghreb médiéval." *Revue d'histoire et de Civilisation du Maghreb* 5 (1968): 63–75

Mas Latrie, Louis de. *Traités de paix et de commerce et documents divers concernant les relations des Chrétiens avec les Arabes de l'Afrique septentrionale au moyen âge*. Paris, 1866

Michaux-Bellaire, Edouard. *Villes et tribus du Maroc: Tanger et sa zone*. Paris, 1921, vol. 7

Nasiri, al-Slawi al-. "Kitab al-Istiqsa li-Akhbar duwal al-Maghrib al-Aksa." Translated by Ismael Hamet. *Archives Marocaines* 23 (1934): 1–621

Robson, J. A. "The Catalan Fleet and Moorish Sea-power (1337–1344)." *English Historical Review* 74 (1959): 386–408

Salmon, George. "Essai sur l'histoire politique de Nord Marocain." *Archives Marocains* 2 (1904): 1–100

Thoden, Rudolf. *Abu l-Hasan Ali: Merinidenpolitik zwischen Nordafrika und Spanien in den Jahren 710–52 AH/1310–52*. Freiburg, 1973

Chapter 2: The Maghrib

Brunschvig, Robert. *La Berbérie orientale sous les Hafsides des origines à la fin du XVe siècle*. 2 vols. Paris, 1940 and 1947

—— "Quelques remarques historiques sur les Médersas de Tunisie." *Revue Tunisienne* 6 (1931): 261–85

Canard, M. "Les relations entre les Merinides et Les Mamlouks au XIVe siècle." *Annales de l'Institut d'Études Orientales* 5 (1939): 41–81

Cherbonneau, A. "Notice et extraits du voyage d'El-Abdary à travers l'Afrique septentrionale au VIIe de l'Hégire." *Journal Asiatique*, 5th ser., 4 (1854): 144–76

Daoulatli, A. *Tunis sous les Hafsides*. Tunis, 1976

Demeerseman, A. "Un type de lettré tunisien du XIVe siècle." *Revue de l'Institut des Belles Lettres Arabes* 22 (1959): 261–86

Dufourcq, Charles-Emannuel. "Les activités politiques et économiques des Catalans en Tunisie et en Algérie orientale du 1262 à 1377." *Bulletin de la real academia de buenas letras de Barcelona* 19 (1947): 1–96

Epalza, Miguel de, and Petit, Ramon. *Recueil d'études sur les Moriscos andalous en Tunisie*. Madrid, 1972

Idris, H. R. "De la realité de la catastrophe hilalienne." *Annales, E.S.C.* 23 (1968): 390–96

Lacoste, Yves. *Ibn Khaldoun: naissance de l'histoire passé du tiers-monde*. Paris, 1966

Latham, Derek. "Towards a Study of Andalusian Immigration and its Place in Tunisian History." *Les cahiers de Tunisie* 5 (1957): 203–52

Lawless, Richard I., and Blake, Gerald H. *Tlemcen: Continuity and Change in an Algerian Islamic Town*. London, 1976

Poncet, J. "Le mythe de la 'catastrophe' hilalienne." *Annales, E.S.C.* 22 (1967): 1099–120

Soyous, A. E. *Le Commerce des Européens à Tunis depuis le XIIe siècle jusqu'à la fin du XVIe siècle.* Paris, 1929

Talbi, Mohamed. "Les contacts culturels entre l'Ifriqiya hafside (1230–1569) et le sultanat nasride d'Espagne (1232–1492)." In *Actas del II Coloquis hispano-tunecino de estudios historicos,* pp. 63–90. Madrid, 1973

Thomassy, Raymond. "Des caravanes de l'Afrique septentrionale." *Bulletin de la Société de Géographie,* ser. 2, 20 (1843): 141–59

Tijani, 'Abdallah al-. "Voyage du Scheikh et-Tidjani dans la Regence de Tunis." Translated by A. Rousseau. *Journal Asiatique,* 4th ser., 20 (1852): 57–208; 5th ser., 1 (1853): 101–68

Chapter 3: The Mamluks

Abu-Lughod, Janet. *Cairo: 1001 Years of the City Victorious.* Princeton, N.J., 1971

Adams, William Y. *Nubia: Corridor to Africa.* Princeton, N.J., 1977

'Ankawi, 'Abdullah. "The Pilgrimage to Mecca in Mamluk Times." *Arabian Studies* 1 (1974): 146–70

Ayalon, David. "Aspects of the Mamluk Phenomenon." *Der Islam.* Part I, 53 (1976): 196–225; Part II, 54 (1977): 1–32

—— "The European-Asiatic Steppe: A Major Reservoir of Power for the Islamic World." *Acts of the 25th Congress of Orientalists* 2: 47–52. Moscow, 1960

—— *Gunpowder and Firearms in the Mamluk Kingdom.* London, 1956

—— *The Muslim City and the Mamluk Military Aristocracy.* Jerusalem, 1967

Clerget, Marcel. *La Caire: étude de géographie urbaine et d'histoire economique.* 2 vols. Cairo, 1934

Cougat, J. "Les routes d'Aidhab." *Bulletin de l'Institut Français d'Archéologie Orientale* 8 (1908): 135–43

Creswell, K. A. C. *The Muslim Architecture of Egypt,* 2 vols. Oxford, 1952, (1959)

Darrag, Ahmad. *L'Égypte sous le regne de Barsbay, 825–41/1422–38.* Damascus, 1961

Dodge, Bayard. *Al-Azhar: A Millennium of Muslim Learning.* Washington, D.C., 1961

Dopp, P. H. "Le Caire vu par les voyageurs occidentaux du Moyen Âge." *Bulletin de la Société Royale de Géographie d'Égypte* 23 (1950): 117–49

Dussaud, Rene. *Topographie historique de la Syrie antique et médiévale.* Paris, 1927

Gaudefroy-Demombynes, Maurice. *Le Syrie à l'époque des Mamelouks.* Paris, 1923

Gilbert, Joan E. "The 'Ulama of Medieval Damascus and the International World of Islamic Scholarship." Ph.D. dissertation, University of California, Berkeley, 1977

Grant, C. P. *The Syrian Desert: Caravans, Travel and Exploration.* London, 1937

Hasan, Yusuf Fadl. *The Arabs and the Sudan from the Seventh to the Early Sixteenth Centuries.* Edinburgh, 1967

Hitti, Philip K. *History of Syria.* 2nd edn. New York, 1957

Humphreys, R. S. "The Emergence of the Mamluk Army." *Studia Islamica* 45 (1977): 46 (1977): 147–82

Jomier, Jacques. *Le Mahmal et le caravane égyptienne des pélérins de la Mecque.* Cairo, 1953

Lane-Poole, Stanley. *The Story of Cairo.* London, 1902

Lapidus, I. M. *Muslim Cities in the Later Middle Ages.* Cambridge, Mass., 1967

Le Strange, Guy. *Palestine under the Moslems.* Beirut, 1965

Maqrizi, al-. *Histoire des Sultans Mamlouks de l'Égypte.* Translated by M. Quatremere. Paris, 1937

Marmardji, A. S. *Textes géographiques arabes sur la Palestine.* Paris, 1951

Muir, William. *The Mameluke or Slave Dynasty of Egypt, 1260–1517*. London, 1896
Murray, G. W. "'Aidhab." *The Geographical Journal* 68 (1926): 235–40
Paul, A. *A History of the Beja Tribes of the Sudan*. Cambridge, England, 1954
Petry, Carl F. *The Civilian Elite of Cairo in the Later Middle Ages*. Princeton, N.J., 1981
Popper, William. *Egypt and Syria under the Circassian Sultans, 1382–1486*. Berkeley, 1955 and 1957
Raymond, André, "La population du Caire de Maqrizi à la *Description de l'Égypt*." *Bulletin d'Études Orientales* 28 (1975): 201–15
Rogers, J. M. "Evidence for Mamluk–Mongol Relations, 1260–1360." In *Colloque international sur l'histoire du Caire*. 1969, pp. 385–403
Sauvaget, Jean. "Esquisse d'une histoire de la ville de Damas." *Revue des Études Islamiques* 4 (1934): 421–80
—— *La poste aux chevaux dans l'empire des Mamelouks*. Paris, 1941
Semeonis, Symon. *The Journey of Symon Semeonis from Ireland to the Holy Land*. Translated and edited by Mario Esposito. Dublin, 1960
Staffa, Susan Jane. *Conquest and Fusion: The Social Evolution of Cairo, A.D. 642–1850*. Leiden, 1977
Suchem, Ludolph von. *Ludolph von Suchem's Description of the Holy Land and of the Way Thither*. Translated by Aubrey Stewart. London, 1895
Trimingham, J. Spencer. *Islam in the Sudan*. London, 1965
Wiet, Gaston. *Cairo: City of Art and Commerce*. Norman, Okla., 1964
—— "Les communications en Égypte au Moyen Âge." *L'Égypte Contemporaine* 24 (1933): 241–64
Ziadeh, Nicloa A. *Damascus under the Mamluks*. Norman, Okla., 1964
—— *Urban Life in Syria under the Early Mamluks*. Beirut, 1953

Chapter 4: Mecca

Amin, Mohamed. *Pilgrimage to Mecca*. London, 1978
Bey, Ali. *The Travels of Ali Bey*. 2 vols. Philadelphia, 1816
Bidwell, Robin L. *Travellers in Arabia*. New York, 1976
Burckhardt, John Lewis. *Travels in Arabia*. 2 vols. London, 1829; reprint edn., London, 1968
Burton, Richard Francis. *Personal Narrative of a Pilgrimage to El-Medinah and Meccah*. 2 vols. Reprint edn., New York, 1964
Frescobaldi, Gucci and Sigoli. *Visit to the Holy Places of Egypt, Sinai, Palestine, and Syria in 1384*. Translated and edited by Theophilus Bellorini and Eugene Hoade. Jerusalem, 1948
Gaudefroy-Demombynes, M. *Le Pélérinage à la Mekke*. Paris, 1923
Gaury, Gerald de. *Rulers of Mecca*. London, 1951
Hogarth, D. C. *Arabia*. Oxford, 1922
Hurgronje, C. Snouck. *Mecca in the Latter Part of the Nineteenth Century*. Translated by J. H. Monahan. Leiden, 1931
Kamal, Ahmad. *The Sacred Journey*. London, 1961
Long, David Edwin. *The Hajj Today: A Survey of the Contemporary Pilgrimage to Mekkah*. Albany, New York.
Musil, Alois. *Arabia Deserta, a Topographical Itinerary*. New York, 1927
—— *The Northern Hegaz*. New York, 1926
Rutter, Eldon. *The Holy Cities of Arabia*. 2 vols. London, 1928
Varthema, Ludovico di. *The Travels of Ludovico di Varthema*. Translated by John W. Jones. London, 1863

Chapter 5: Persia and Iraq

Arberry, A. J. *Shiraz*. Norman, Okla., 1960

Barthold, W. *An Historical Geography of Iran*. Translated by Svat Soucek and edited with an introduction by C. E. Bosworth. Princeton, N.J., 1984

Boyle, J. A. (ed.). *Cambridge History of Iran. Vol. 5: The Saljuq and Mongol Periods*. Cambridge, England, 1968

Browne, Edward G. *A Literary History of Persia*. 4 vols. Cambridge, England, 1929–30

—— *A Year amongst the Persians*. London, 1893

Bulliet, Richard W. *The Patricians of Nishapur*. Cambridge, Mass., 1972

Dawson, Christopher. *The Mongol Missions*. London, 1955

Juvaini. *The History of the World Conqueror*. Translated by John Andrew Boyle. 2 vols. Cambridge, Mass., 1958

Lambton, A. K. S. *Islamic Society in Persia*. London, 1954

—— *Landlord and Peasant in Persia*. London, 1953

Le Strange, Guy. *Baghdad during the Abbasid Caliphate*. Oxford, 1924

—— *The Lands of the Eastern Caliphate*. Cambridge, England, 1905; 2nd edn., 1930; reprint edn., New York, 1966

—— *Mesopotamia and Persia under the Mongols in the Fourteenth Century A.D.: From the "Nuzhat al-Qulub" of Hamd Allah Mustaufi*. London, 1903

Lewis, Bernard. "The Mongols, the Turks and the Mulsim Polity." *Transactions of the Royal Historical Society*, 5th ser. (1968): 49–68

Minorsky, Vladimir. *The Turks, Iran and the Caucasus in the Middle Ages*. London, 1978

Morgan, D. O. "The Mongol Armies in Persia." *Der Islam* 56 (1979): 81–96

Mustawfi, Hamd-Allah. *The Geographical Part of the "Nuzhat al-Qulub."* Translated by G. Le Strange. Leiden, 1919

—— *Tarikh-i-Guzidah*. Translated by M. J. Gantin. Paris, 1903

Rashid al-Din. *The Successors of Genghis Khan*. Translated by John A. Boyle. New York, 1971

Smith, John Masson. "Mongol Manpower and Persian Population." *Journal of the Economic and Social History of the Orient* 18 (1975): 271–99

Spuler, B. *Die Mongolen in Iran*. 2nd edn. Berlin, 1955

Thesiger; Wilfred. *The Marsh Arabs*. London, 1964

Wiet, Gaston. *Baghdad: Metropolis of the Abbasid Caliphate*. Norman, Okla., 1971

Wilber, Donald N. *The Architecture of Islamic Iran: The Il Khanid Period*. Reprint edn., Leiden, 1980

Chapter 6: The Arabian Sea

Allen, James de Vere. "Swahili Culture and the Nature of East Coast Settlement." *International Journal of African Historical Studies* 14 (1981): 306–34

Ashtor, E. "The Karimi Merchants." *Journal of the Royal Asiatic Society* (1956): 45–56

Aubin, J. "Les Princes d'Ormuz du XIIIe au XVe siècle." *Journal Asiatique* 241 (1953): 77–138

Chelhod, J. "Introduction à l'histoire sociale et urbaine de Zabid." *Arabica* 25 (1978): 48–88

Chittick, Neville. *Kilwa: An Islamic Trading City on the East African Coast*. 2 vols. Nairobi, 1974

—— "Shirazi Colonization of East Africa." *Journal of African History* 6 (1965): 275–94

Faroughy, Abbas. *The Bahrein Islands, 750–1951*. New York, 1951

Fischel, Walter J. "The Spice Trade in Mamluk Egypt." *Journal of the Economic and Social History of the Orient* 1 (1958): 157–74

Freeman-Grenville, G. S. P. *The East African Coast: Select Documents from the First to the Earlier Nineteenth Century*. Oxford, 1962

—— *The Medieval History of the Tanganyika Coast*. Oxford, 1962

Garlake, Peter S. *The Early Islamic Architecture of the East African Coast*. London, 1966

Goitein, S. D. "From Aden to India: Specimens of the Correspondence of India Traders of the Twelfth Century." *Journal of the Economic and Social History of the Orient* 23 (1980): 43–66

—— "From the Mediterranean to India: Documents on the Trade to India, South Arabia, and East Africa from the Eleventh to the Twelfth Centuries." *Speculum* 29 (1954): 181–97

—— "Letters and Documents on the India Trade in Medieval Times." *Islamic Culture* 37 (1963): 188–205

—— "New Light on the Beginnings of the Karim Merchants." *Journal of the Economic and Social History of the Orient* 1 (1958): 175–84

Guest, R. "Zufar in the Middle Ages." *Islamic Culture* 9 (1935): 402–10

Hornell, J. "Classification of Arab Sea Craft." *Mariner's Mirror* 28 (1942): 11–40

Hourani, George. *Arab Seafaring in the Indian Ocean in Ancient and Early Medieval Times*. Princeton, N.J., 1951

Howarth, David. *Dhows*. London, 1977

Huntingford, G. W. B. (trans. and ed.). *The Periplus of the Erythraean Sea*. London, 1980

Ibn Rusta. *Kitab al-A'lak al Nafisa*. Edited by J. de Goeje. Leiden, 1892

Kammerer, A. *La Mer Rouge*. 4 vols. Cairo, 1929–35

Khazrejiyy, al-. *The Pearl Strings: A History of the Resuliyy Dynasty of Yemen*. 5 vols. Translated by J. W. Redhouse. Leiden, 1906–18

Kirk, William. "The NE Monsoon and Some Aspects of African History." *Journal of African History* 3 (1962): 263–67

Kirkman, J. S. *Monuments and Men on the East African Coast*. London, 1964

Labib, S. "Les marchands Karimis en Orient et sur l'Ocean Indien." In *Sociétés et compagnies de commerce en Orient et dans l'Océan Indien. Actes du 8ème colloque international d'histoire maritime*. Paris, 1970, pp. 209–14

Lewcock, R. B. "Islamic Towns and Buildings in East Africa." *Storia della Citta* 7 (1978): 49–53

—— and Smith, G. R. "Three Medieval Mosques in the Yemen." *Oriental Art* 20 (1974): 75–86, 192–203

Lewis, Archibald. "Maritime Skills in the Indian Ocean, 1368–1500." *Journal of the Economic and Social History of the Orient* 16 (1973): 238–64

Martin, B. G. "Arab Migration to East Africa in Medieval Times." *International Journal of African Historical Studies* 7 (1974): 367–90

Moreland, W. H. "The Ships of the Arabian Sea about A.D. 1500." *Journal of the Royal Asiatic Society* 1 (1939): 63–74, 173–92

Persian Gulf Pilot. 11th edn. London, 1967

Playfair, R. L. *A History of Arabia Felix or Yemen*. Bombay, 1859; reprint edn., London, 1970

Pouwels, Randall. L. "The Medieval Foundations of East African Islam." *International Journal of African Historical Studies* 11 (1978): 201–22, 393–409

Prins, A. H. J. "The Persian Gulf Dhows: New Notes on the Classification of Mid-Eastern Sea-Craft." *Persica* 6 (1972–74): 157–65

Razik. *History of the Imams and Seyyids of Oman*. Translated by George P. Badger. London, 1871

Red Sea and Gulf of Aden Pilot. 11th edn. London, 1967

Rubinacci, Roberto. "The Ibadis." In A. J. Arberry and C. F. Beckingham (eds.), *Religion in the Middle East*. 2 vols. Cambridge, England, 1969
Saad, Elias. "Kilwa Dynastic Historiography." *History in Africa* 6 (1979): 177–207
Serjeant, R. B. "The Dhows of Aden." *Geographical Journal* 14 (1942): 296–301
—— "Maritime Customary Law in the Indian Ocean." In *Sociétés et compagnies de commerce en Orient et dans l'Océan Indien*, Paris, 1970, pp. 195–207
—— "The Ports of Aden and Shihr (Medieval Period)." *Recueils de la Société Jean Bodin* 32 (1974): 207–24
—— *The Portuguese off the South Arabia Coast*. Oxford, 1963
Teixeira, Pedro. *Travels*. Translated by W. F. Sinclair. London, 1902
Tibbetts, G. R. *Arab Navigation in the Indian Ocean before the Coming of the Portuguese*. London, 1971
Toussaint, Auguste. *Histoire de l'Océan Indien*. Paris, 1961
Trimingham, J. Spencer. *Islam in East Africa*. Oxford, 1964
Tritton, A. S. *The Rise of the Imams of Sanaa*. Madras, 1925
Villiers, Alan. *Sons of Sinbad*. London, 1940
The West Coast of India Pilot. 11th edn. London, 1975
Wiet, Gaston. "Les marchands d'Épices sous les sultans mamelouks." *Cahiers d'Histoire Égyptienne* 7 (1952): 81–147
Wilkinson, J. C. "Oman and East Africa: New Light on Early Kilwan History from the Omani Sources." *International Journal of Afircan Historical Studies* 14 (1981): 272–305
—— "The Origins of the Omani State." In *The Arabian Peninsula: Society and Politics*. Edited by Derek Hopwood. London, 1972, pp. 67–88
Williamson, Andrew. "Hurmuz and the Trade of the Gulf in the 14th and 15th Centuries A.D." In *Proceedings of the Sixth Seminar for Arabian Studies*. London, 1973, pp. 52–68
Wilson, Arnold T. *The Persian Gulf: An Historical Sketch from the Earliest Times to the Beginning of the Twentieth Century*. Oxford, 1928; reprint edn., London, 1954

Chapter 7: Anatolia

Aflaki. *Manaqib al-'Arifin: les saints des derviches tourneurs*. 2 vols. Translated by C. Huart. Paris, 1918–22
Akurgal, Ekrem (ed.). *The Art and Architecture of Turkey*. Oxford, 1980
Beldiceanu-Steinherr, Irene. *Recherches sur les actes des règnes des Sultans Osman, Orkhan et Murad I*. Monachii, 1967
Bergeret, J. "Konya." *Archéologia* 96 (July, 1976): 30–37
Boase, T. S. R. (ed.). *The Cilician Kingdom of Armenia*. Edinburgh, 1978
Brown, John P. *The Dervishes, or Oriental Spiritualism*. London, 1868; reprint edn., 1927
Bryer, Anthony A. M. *The Empire of Trebizond and the Pontos*. London, 1980
Byrne, E. H. *Genoese Shipping in the Twelfth and Thirteenth Centuries*. Cambridge, Mass., 1930
Cahen, Claude. *Pre-Ottoman Turkey*. London, 1968
Cook, M. A. (ed.). *A History of the Ottoman Empire to 1730*. Cambridge, England, 1976
Gabriel, Albert. *Une capitale turque, Brousse*. 2 vols. Paris, 1958
Hasluck, F. W. *Christianity and Islam under the Sultans*. 2 vols. Oxford, 1929
Inalcik, Halil. *The Ottoman Empire: The Classical Age, 1300–1600*. Translated by Norman Itzkowitz and Colin Imber. London, 1973
Karpat, K. H. (ed.). *The Ottoman State and its Place in World History*. Leiden, 1974

Koprulu, M. F. *Les origines de l'empire ottoman.* Paris, 1935; reprint edn., Philadelphia, 1978

Lemerle, P. *L'Emirat d'Aydin, Byzance et l'Occident.* Paris, 1957

Lindner, Rudi Paul. *Nomads and Ottomans in Medieval Anatolia.* Indiana University Uralic and Altaic Series, vol. 144. Bloomington, Ind., 1983

Lloyd, Seton, and Rice, D. S. *Alanya (Ala'iyya).* London, 1958

Murray's Handbook: Constantinople, Brusa and the Troad. London, 1900

Murray's Handbook for Travellers in Asia Minor. Edited by Charles Wilson. London, 1895

Pitcher, Donald Edgar (ed.). *An Historical Geography of the Ottoman Empire.* Leiden, 1972

Shaw, Stanford J. *History of the Ottoman Empire and Modern Turkey.* 2 vols. *Vol. 1: Empire of the Gazis: The Rise of the Ottoman Empire, 1280–1808.* Cambridge, England, 1977

Vryonis, Speros, Jr. *The Decline of Medieval Hellenism in Asia Minor and the Process of Islamization from the Eleventh through the Fifteenth Century.* Berkeley and Los Angeles, 1971

Wittek, P. *Das Fürstentum Mentesche.* Reprint edn., Amsterdam, 1967

—— "Le Sultan of Rum." *Annuaire de l'Institut de Philologie et d'Histoire Orientales et Slaves* 6 (1938): 361–90

—— *The Rise of the Ottoman Empire.* London, 1938

Zachariadou, Elizabeth A. *Trade and Crusade: Venetian Crete and the Emirates of Menteshe and Aydin (1300–1415).* Venice, 1983

Chapter 8: The Steppe

Balard, M. "Notes sur l'activité maritime des Genois de Caffa à la fin du XIIIe siècle." In *Sociétés et compagnies de commerce en Orient et dans l'Océan Indien.* Paris, 1970, pp. 375–86

Barthold, W. *Histoire des Turcs d'Asie Centrale.* Paris, 1945

—— *Turkestan down to the Mongol Invasion.* 3rd edn. London, 1968

Bosworth, Clifford Edward. *The Medieval History of Iran, Afghanistan and Central Asia.* London, 1977

Bratianu, Gheorghe Ivan. *La Mer Noire des origines à la conquète ottomane.* Monachii, 1969

—— *Recherches sur le commerce genois dans la Mer Noire au XIIIe siècle.* Paris, 1929

Chambers, James. *The Devil's Horsemen: The Mongol Invasion of Europe.* Translated by Guy Le Strange. London, 1928

Clavijo, Ruy Gonzales de. *Clavijo: Embassy to Tamerlane, 1403–06.* London, 1979

Dupree, Louis. *Afghanistan.* Princeton, N.J., 1980

Ebersolt, J. *Constantinople byzantine et les voyageurs du Levant.* Paris, 1918

Fisher, Alan. *The Crimean Tatars.* Stanford, 1978

Gregkov, B. D. and Iakubovskij, A. J. *La Horde d'Or.* Translated by F. Thuret. Paris, 1939

Hambly, Gavin. *Central Asia.* London, 1969

Humlum, J. *La géographie de l'Afghanistan.* Copenhagen, 1959

Izzeddin, Mehmed. "Quelques voyageurs musulmans à Constantinople au Moyen Âge." *Orient* 9 (1965): 75–106

Jackson, Peter. "The Dissolution of the Mongol Empire." *Central Asiatic Journal* 22 (1978): 186–244

Krader, Lawrence. *Peoples of Central Asia.* 3rd edn. Indiana University Publications: Uralic and Altaic Series, vol. 26. Bloomington, Ind., 1971

Loenertz, R. J. "Dix-huit lettres de Gregoire Acindyne, analysées et datées." *Orientalia Christiana Periodica* 23 (1957): 114–44

Martin, Janet. "The Land of Darkness and the Golden Horde: The Fur Trade under the Mongols, XIII–XIVth Centuries." *Cahiers du Monde Russe et Sovietique* 19 (1978): 401–21

Meeker, Michael E. "The Black Sea Turks: Some Aspects of their Ethnic and Cultural Background." *International Journal of Middle East Studies* 2 (1971): 318–45

Nemtseva, N. B. "The Origins and Architectural Development of the Shah-i Zinde." Translated by J. M. Rogers and 'Adil Yasin. *Iran* 15 (1977): 51–73

Nicol, D. M. *The Last Centuries of Byzantium, 1261–1453*. London, 1972

Oliver, E. E. "The Chaghatai Mughals." *Journal of the Royal Asiatic Society* 20 (1888): 72–128

Ostrogorsky, George. *History of the Byzantine State*. 2nd edn. Translated by Joan Hussey. Oxford, 1968

Pelliot, Paul. *Notes sur l'histoire de la Horde d'Or*. Paris, 1949

Poliak, A. N. "Le caractère colonial de l'état mamlouk dans ses rapports avec la Horde d'Or." *Revue d'Études Islamiques* 9 (1935): 231–48

Riasanovsky, A. *A History of Russia*. 3rd edn. Oxford, 1977

Rockhill, William Woodville (trans. and ed.). *The Journey of William of Rubruck to the Eastern Parts of the World*. London, 1900

Rogers, J. M. "Summary of Soviet Research on the Khanate of the Golden Horde." Unpublished paper, 1980?

Sinor, Denis. *Inner Asia And its Contacts with Medieval Europe*. London, 1977

―― *Introduction à l'étude de l'Eurasie Centrale*. Wiesbaden, 1963

Smith, J. M., Jr. *The History of the Sarbadar Dynasty, 1336–1381 A.D.* The Hague, 1970

Spuler, B. *Die Goldene Horde*. Leipzig, 1943

Vernadsky, G. *The Mongols and Russia*. New Haven, Conn., 1953

Wilber, Donald N. *Afghanistan*. 2nd edn. New Haven, Conn., 1962

Chapter 9: Delhi

Ahmad, Aziz. *An Intellectual History of Islam in India*. Edinburgh, 1969

―― "Mongol Pressure in an Alien Land." *Central Asiatic Journal* 6 (1961): 182–93

―― *Studies in Islamic Culture in the Indian Environment*. Oxford, 1964

―― "The Sufi and the Sultan in Pre-Mughal Muslim India." *Der Islam* 38 (1962): 142–53

Ahmad, Maqbul. *Indo-Arab Relations*. Bombay, 1969

Ashraf, K. M. *Life and Conditions of the People of Hindustan*. 2nd edn., New Delhi, 1970

Ballhatchet, Kenneth, and Harrison, John. *The City in South Asia*. London, 1980

Barani, Ziya al-Din. *The Political Theory of the Delhi Sultanate*. Translated and edited by Mohammed Habib and Afsar Umar Salim Khan. Allahabad, n.d.

Basham, A. L. (ed.). *A Cultural History of India*. Oxford, 1975

Chand, Tara. *Influence of Islam on Indian Culture*. Allahabad, 1936

Day, U. N. *Some Aspects of Medieval Indian History*. New Delhi, 1971

Digby, Simon. "Muhammad bin Tughluq's Last Years in Kathiawar and his Invasions of Thattha." *Hamdard Islamicus* 2 (1979): 79–88

―― *War-horse and Elephant in the Delhi Sultanate: A Study of Military Supplies*. Oxford, 1971

Elliot, H. M. and Dowson, John. *The History of India as Told by its Own Historians*. 31 vols. *Vol. 3: The Muhammadan Period*. Allahabad, 1952–59

Habib, Irfan. "Economic History of the Delhi Sultanate, An Essay in Interpretation." *Indian Historical Review* 4 (1978): 287–303

Habibullah, A. B. M. *The Foundation of Muslim Rule in India*. 2nd edn., Allahabad, 1961

Haig, Wolseley (ed.). *The Cambridge History of India. Vol. 3: Turks and Afghans.* New York, 1928; reprint edn., Delhi, 1958

—— "Five Questions in the History of the Tughluq Dynasty of Dilhi." *Journal of the Royal Asiatic Society* (1922): 319–72

Hardy, Peter. *Historians of Medieval India.* London, 1960

Husain, Mahdi Agha. *Le gouvernement du sultanat de Delhi.* Paris, 1936

—— *Tughluq Dynasty.* Calcutta, 1963

Ikram, Sheikh Mohamad. *Muslim Rule in India and Pakistan.* 2nd edn., Lahore, 1966

Imperial Gazetteer of India. 26 vols. Oxford, 1907

Jackson, Peter. "The Mongols and the Delhi Sultanate in the Reign of Muhammad Tughluq (1325–51)." *Central Asiatic Journal* 19 (1975): 118–57

—— "The Mongols and India (1221–1351)." Ph.D. dissertation, Cambridge University, 1977

Khan, M. S. "An Undiscovered Arabic Source of the History of Sultan Muhammad bin Tughlaq." *Islamic Culture* 53 (1979): 187–205

Lal, K. S. *History of the Khaljis, A.D. 1290–1320.* 2nd edn. London, 1967

Lambrick, H. T. *Sind: A General Introduction.* Hyderabad, 1964

Lehmann, Fritz. "Architecture of the Early Sultanate Period and the Nature of the Muslim State in India." *Indica* 15 (1978): 13–31

Little, D. P. "Did Ibn Taymiyya Have a Screw Loose?" *Studia Islamica* 41 (1975): 39–111

Majumdar, R. C. (ed.). *The History and Culture of the Indian People. Vol. 6: The Delhi Sultanate.* Bombay, 1960

Mujeeb, Mohammad. *The Indian Muslims.* Montreal, 1967

—— *Islamic Influence on Indian Society.* Meerut, India, 1972

Nizami, K. A. *Some Aspects of Religion and Politics in India in the Thirteenth Century.* Aligarh, 1961

—— *Studies in Medieval Indian History and Culture.* Allahabad, 1966

Nath, R. *History of Sultanate Architecture,* New Delhi, 1978

Rothermund, Dietmar (ed.). *Islam in Southern Asia.* Wiesbaden, 1975

Schimmel, Annemarie. *Islam in India and Pakistan.* Leiden, 1982

Schwartzberg, J. E. *A Historical Atlas of South Asia.* Chicago, 1978

Singh, Attar (ed.). *Socio-Cultural Impact of Islam on India.* Chandigarh, 1976

Stow, A. M. "The Road between Delhi and Multan." *Journal of the Punjab Historical Society* 3 (1914–15): 26–37

'Umari, Ibn Fadl Allah al-. *A Fourteenth Century Arab Account of India under Sultan Muhammad bin Tughluq.* Translated and edited by Iqtidar Husain Siddiqi and Zazi Mohammad Ahmad. Aligarh, 1971

Chapter 10: Malabar and the Maldives

Barbosa, Duarte. *The Book of Duarte Barbosa.* 2 vols. Edited by Mansel Longworth Dames. London, 1918–21

Bell, H. C. P. *Maldive Islands.* Colombo, 1882

Carswell, J. "China and Islam in the Maldive Islands." *Transactions of the Oriental Ceramic Society* 41 (1975–77): 121–97

—— "Mosques and Tombs in the Maldive Islands." *Art and Archaeology Research Papers* 9 (1976): 26–30

Chaube, J. *History of the Gujarat Kingdom.* New Delhi, 1973

Cheriau, A. "The Genesis of Islam in Malabar." *Indica* 6 (1969): 13–20

Derrett, J., and Duncan, M. *The Hoysalas: A Medieval Indian Royal Family.* Oxford, 1957

Eaton, R. M. *Sufis of Bijapur, 1300–1700: Social Roles of Sufis in Medival India.* Princeton, N.J., 1978

Forbes, A., and Fanzia, Ali. "Republic of 100 Islands." *Geographical Magazine* 50 (1978): 264–68

Krishnaswanni Aiyangar, S. *South India and her Muhammadan Invaders*. London, 1921

Maloney, Clarence. *People of the Maldives*. Madras, 1980

Misra, S. C. *The Rise of Muslim Power in Gujarat*. New York, 1963

Moreland, W. H. "The Shahbandar in the Eastern Seas." *Journal of the Royal Asiatic Society* (1920): 517–33

Needham, Joseph. *Science and Civilization in China*. Multivol. *Vol. 4, Part 3: Civil Engineering and Nautics*. Cambridge, 1954–; this volume, 1971

Pyrard, François. *The Voyage of François Pyrard of Laval to the East Indies, the Maldives, the Moluccas and Brazil*. Translated and edited by Albert Gray. 2 vols. London, n.d. Reprint edn., New York, 1963?

Raychaudhuri, Tapan, and Habib, Irfan (eds.). *The Cambridge Economic History of India*. 2 vols. Cambridge, England, 1982

Sastri, Nilakanta K. A. *Foreign Notices of South India*. Madras, 1939

—— *A History of South India*. 3rd Edn., Madras, 1966

Sherwani, H. K. and Joshi, P. M. (eds.). *History of Medieval Deccan, 1295–1724*. 2 vols. Hyderabad, 1973–74

Venkata Ramanayya, N. *The Early Muslim Expansion in South India*. Madras, 1942

Chapter 11: China

Abdur Rahim, Muhammad. *Social and Cultural History of Bengal*. Karachi, 1963

Andaya, Barbara Watson and Leonard Y. *A History of Malaysia*. New York, 1982

Bhattasali, N. K. *Coins and Chronology of the Early Independent Sultans of Bengal. With Translation of "Ibn-Batuta's Travels in Bengal" from French by S. N. Bose*. Cambridge, England, 1922; reprint edn., New Delhi, 1976

Chang, Kuei-sheng. "The Maritime Scene in China at the Dawn of the Great European Discoveries." *Journal of the American Oriental Society* 94 (1974): 347–57

Coedes, G. *The Indianized States of Southeast Asia*. Translated by Susan Brown Cowing. Edited by Walter F. Vella. Honolulu, 1968

Cordier, Henri. *Histoire générale de la Chine*. 4 vols. Paris, 1920

Dardess, J. W. *Conquerors and Confucians: Aspects of Political Change in Late Yuan China*. New York, 1973

Elvin, Mark. *The Pattern of the Chinese Past*. Stanford, Calif., 1973

Filesi, Teobaido. *China and Africa in the Middle Ages*. Translated by David L. Morisen. London, 1972

Geiger, Wilhelm. *Culture of Ceylon in Mediaeval Times*. Wiesbaden, 1960

Gernet, Jacques. *Daily Life in China on the Eve of the Mongol Invasion 1250–1276*. Translated by H. M. Wright. Stanford, Calif., 1970

Hall, D. G. E. *A History of South-East Asia*. 4th edn. New York, 1981

Hall, Kenneth R. "Trade and Statecraft in the Western Archipelago at the Dawn of the European Age." *Journal of the Malaysian Branch of the Royal Asiatic Society* 54, part 1 (1981): 21–48

—— and Whitmore, John K. *The Origins of Southeast Asian Statecraft*. Ann Arbor, Mich., 1976

Hill, A. H. "The Coming of Islam to North Sumatra." *Journal of Southeast Asian History* 4 (1963): 6–21

Hutterer, Karl L. (ed.). *Economic Exchange and Social Interaction in Southeast Asia*. Ann Arbor, Mich., 1977

Jack-Hinton, Colin (ed.). *Papers on Early South-East Asian History*. Singapore, 1964

Johns, A. H. "From Coastal Settlement to Islamic School and City: Islamization in Sumatra, the Malay Peninsula and Java." *Hamdard Islamicus* 4 (1981): 3–28

—— "Islam in Southeast Asia: Reflections and New Directions." *Indonesia* 19 (1975): 33–55

Karim, Abdul. *Social History of the Muslims in Bengal.* Dacca, 1959

Langlois, John D. (ed.). *China under Mongol Rule.* Princeton, N.J., 1981

Lo, Jung-pang. "The Emergence of China as a Sea Power during the Late Sung and Early Yuan Periods." *Far Eastern Quarterley* 14 (1954–55): 489–503

—— "Maritime Commerce and its Relation to the Sung Navy." *Journal of the Economic and Social History of the Orient* 12 (1969): 57–101

Ma Huan. *Ying-yai Sheng-lan: The Over-all Survey of the Ocean's Shores.* Translated and edited by J. V. G. Mills. London, 1970

Nichols, C. W., and Paranavitana, S. *A Concise History of Ceylon.* Colombo, 1961

Pathmanathan, S. *The Kingdom of Jaffna.* Colombo, 1978

Raghavan, M. D. *India in Ceylonese History, Society and Culture.* 2nd edn. Bombay, 1969

Ray, H. C., and Paranavitana, S. *History of Ceylon.* Colombo, 1959

Ricklefs, M. C. *History of Indonesia.* Bloomington, Ind., 1981

Rossabi, Morris (ed.). *China among Equals: The Middle Kingdom and its Neighbors, 10th–14th Centuries.* Berkeley and Los Angeles, 1983

Sarkar, Jadunath (ed.). *The History of Bengal.* 2 vols. Vol. 2: *Muslim Period 1200–1757.* Dacca, 1948

Schurmann, Herbert Franz. *Economic Structure of the Yuan Dynasty.* Cambridge, Mass., 1956

Sirisena, W. M. *Sri Lanka and Southeast Asia: Political, Religious and Cultural Relations from A.D. 1000 to 1500.* Leiden, 1978

Smith, D. Howard. "Zaitun's Five Centuries of Sino-foreign Trade." *Journal of the Royal Asiatic Society*, 1958, parts 3 and 4, pp. 165–77

Tibbetts, G. R. *A Study of the Arabic Texts Containing Material on South-East Asia.* Leiden, 1979

Wheatley, P. *The Golden Khersonese: Studies in the Historical Geography of the Malay Peninsula before A.D. 1500* Kuala Lumpur, 1961

Chapter 12: Home

Arié, Rachel. *L'Espagne musulmane au temps des Nasrides (1232–1492).* Paris, 1973

Ayalon, David. "The Plague and its Effects upon the Mamluk Army." *Journal of the Royal Asiatic Society* (1946): 67–73

Benchekroun, M. B. A. *La vie intellectuelle marocaine sous les Merinides et les Wattasides.* Rabat, 1974

Berque, Jacques. "Ville et université: aperçu sur l'histoire de l'école de Fes." *Revue Historique de Droit Français et Étranger* (1949): 64–117

Blachère, R. "Quelques détails sur la vie privée du sultan merinide Abu l-'Hasan." In *Memorial Henri Basset.* Paris, 1928, pp. 83–89

Dols, Michael W. *The Black Death in the Middle East.* Princeton, N.J., 1977

Gibert, Soledad. "Abu-l-Barakat al-Balafiqi, Qadi, Historiador y Poeta." *Al-Andalus* 28 (1963): 381–424

Gottfried, Robert S. *The Black Death: Natural and Human Disaster in Medieval Europe.* New York, 1983

Grabar, Oleg. *The Alhambra.* Cambridge, Mass., 1978

Irving, Washington. *The Alhambra.* Edited by F. H. Law, New York, 1926

Ladero Quesada, Miguel Angel. *Granada: historia de un país islamico (1232–1571).* 2nd edn. Madrid, 1979

Latham, Derek. "The Later 'Azafids." *Revue de l'Occident Musulman et de la Méditerranée* 15–16 (1973): 109–25

—— "The Strategic Position and Defence of Ceuta in the Later Muslim Period." *Islamic Quarterly* 15 (1971): 189–204

Le Tourneau, Roger. *Fès avant le Protectorat.* Casablanca, 1949

—— *Fez in the Age of the Marinides.* Norman, Okla., 1961

Lévi-Provençal, E. *Histoire de l'Espagne musulman.* New edn., 3 vols. Paris, 1950

Lomax, Derek W. *The Reconquest of Spain.* London, 1978

Mackay, Angus. *Spain in the Middle Ages: From Frontier to Empire, 1000–1500.* London, 1977

McNeill, William H. *Plagues and Peoples.* Garden City, N.Y., 1976

Prémare, A. L. de. *Maghreb et Andalousie au XIVe siècle: notes de voyage d'un Andalou au Maroc, 1344–1345.* Lyon, 1981

Sauvaget, Jean. *Alep.* Paris, 1941

Shatzmiller, Maya. "Les premiers Merinides et le milieu religieux de Fès: l'introduction de médersas." *Studia Islamica* 34 (1976): 109–18

Terrasse, Charles. *Médersas du Maroc.* Paris, 1927

Terrasse, H. "Le royaume nasride dans la vie de l'Espagne du Moyen Âge: indications et problèmes." *Mélanges offerts à Marcel Bataillon.* Bordeaux, 1963, pp. 253–60

Torres Balbas, L. "Gibraltar: llave y guarda del reino de España." *Al-Andalus* 7 (1942): 168–216

Verlinden, Charles. "Le grande peste de 1348 en Espagne." *Revue Belge de Philologie et d'Histoire* 17 (1938): 103–46

Ziegler, Philip. *The Black Death.* New York, 1969

Chapter 13: Mali

Bovill, E. W. *The Golden Trade of the Moors.* London, 1968

Chapelle, F. de la. "Esquisse d'une histoire du Soudan Occidental." *Hespéris* 11 (1930): 35–95

Conrad, David, and Fisher, Humphrey. "The Conquest that Never Was: Ghana and the Almoravids, 1076." *History in Africa* 9 (1982): 21–59; 10 (1983): 53–78

Delafosse, Maurice. *Haut-Senegal–Niger.* 3 vols. Paris, 1919; reprint edn., 1972

—— "Le Gana et le Mali et l'emplacement de leurs capitales." *Bulletin du Comité d'Études Historiques et Scientifiques de l'A.O.F.* 9 (1924): 479–542

—— "Les relations du Maroc avec le Soudan à travers les âges." *Hespéris* (1924): 153–74

Devisse, J. "Routes de commerce et èchanges en Afrique Occidentale en relation avec la Méditerranée." *Revue d'Histoire Économique et Social* 50 (1972): 357–97

Filipowiak, Wladyslaw. "Contribution aux recherches sur la capitale du royaume de Mali à l'époque du haut Moyen-Âge." *Archaeologia Polona* 10 (1968): 217–32

—— Études archéologiques sur la capitale médiévale du Mali. Translated by Zofia Slawskaj. Szczecin, 1979

Hiskett, M. *The Development of Islam in West Africa.* London, 1982

Hopkins, A. G. *An Economic History of West Africa.* New York, 1973

Hunwick, J. O. "The Mid-Fourteenth Century Capital of Mali." *Journal of African History* 14 (1973): 195–208

Leo Africanus. *The History and Description of Africa.* Translated by Robert Pory and edited by Robert Brown. 3 vols. New York, 1896

Levtzion, Nehemia. *Ancient Ghana and Mali.* London, 1973

—— and Hopkins, J. F. P. (trans. and eds.). *Corpus of Early Arabic Sources for West African History.* New York, 1981

Lewis, I. M. *Islam in Tropical Africa.* 2nd edn. Bloomington, Ind., 1980

Lhote, H. "Recherches sur Takedda, ville décrite par le voyageur arabe Ibn Battouta et située en Aïr." *Bulletin d l'IFAN* 34 (1972): 429–70

McIntosh, Roderick J. and Susan Keech. "The Inland Niger Delta before the Empire of Mali: Evidence from Jenne-Jeno." *Journal of African History* 22 (1981): 1–22

McIntosh, Susan Keech. "A Reconsideration of Wangara/Palolus, Island of Gold." *Journal of African History* 22 (1981): 145–58

Malowist, M. "Sur l'or du Soudan: quelques observations sur le commerce de l'or dans le Soudan Occidental au Moyen Âge." *Annales E.S.C.* 25 (1970): 1630–36

Mauny, Raymond. *Tableau géographique de l'Ouest Africain au Moyen Âge d'après les sources écrites, la tradition et l'archéologie.* Amsterdam, 1967

Monteil, Charles. *Les Empires du Mali.* Paris, 1968

Niani, D. T. *Sundiata: An Epic of Old Mali.* Translated by G. D. Pickett, London, 1965

Peres, Henri. "Relations entre le Tafilelt et le Soudan à travers le Sahara du XIIe au XIVe siècle." In *Mélange de géographie et d'orientalisme offerts à E.-F. Gautier.* Tours, 1937, pp. 410–14

Saad, Elias N. *Social History of Timbuktu: The Role of Muslim Scholars and Notables, 1400–1900.* Cambridge, England, 1983

Sa'di, 'Abd al-Rahman ibn 'Abd Allah al-. *Tarikh es-Soudan.* Translated by O. Houdas. Paris, 1964

Terrasse, Henri. "Note sur les ruines de Sijilmasa." *Revue Africaine* 368–69 (1936): 581–89

Trimingham, J. Spencer. *A History of Islam in West Africa.* Oxford, 1962

Wansbrough, John. "Africa and the Arab Geographers." In *Language and History in Africa.* Edited by D. Dalby. London, 1970, pp. 89–101

Watson, Andrew M. "Back to Gold and Silver." *Economic History Review*, 2nd ser., 20 (1967): 1–34

Willis, John R. (ed.). *Studies in West African Islamic History.* 3 vols. *Vol. 1: The Cultivators of Islam.* London, 1979

Supplemental Bibliography

Abercrombie, Thomas J. "Ibn Battuta: Prince of Travelers." Photographs by James L. Stanfield. *National Geographic* 180 (Dec. 1991): 3–49

Arcas Campoy, M. "Ibn Battuta y las escuelas jurídicas en los países del Mediterráneo. In D. A. Agius and I. R. Netton. *Across the Mediterranean Frontiers: Trade, Politics and Religion, 650–1450. Selected Proceedings of the International Medieval Congress, University of Leeds, 10–13 July 1995, 8–11 July 1996,* Turnhout, Belgium, 1997

Arno, Joan, and Grady, Helen. "Ibn Battuta: A View of the Fourteenth-Century World, A Unit of Study for Grades 7–10," Los Angeles: National Center for History in the Schools, UCLA, 1998

Beckingham, C. F. "The *Rihla:* Fact or Fiction?" In I. R. Netton, ed. *Golden Roads: Migration, Pilgrimage and Travel in Mediaeval and Modern Islam,* Richmond, England, 1993, pp. 86–94

Benatti, L. "Ibn Battuta e i suoi viaggi." *Africa e Mediterraneo* 14–15 (1995): 78–81.

Bro, Thyge C. *Ibn Battuta: En arabisk rejsende fra det 14. århundrede,* Oslo, 2001. In Danish.

Bullis, Douglas. "The Longest Hajj: The Journeys of Ibn Battuta." *Saudi Aramco World* 51 (July/August 2000): 2–39

Dunn, Ross E. *Gli straordinari viaggi di Ibn Battuta: Le mille avventure del Marco Polo arabo,* Milan, 1993. Italian edition.

———. "Ibn Battuta and Muslim Cosmopolitanism in the 14th c." *Hadeeth ad-Dar,* Dar al-Athar al-Islamiyyah, Kuwait, 12 (2001): 10–13

———. "Migrations of Literate Muslims in the Middle Periods: The Case of Ibn Battuta." In I. R. Netton, ed. *Golden Roads: Migration, Pilgrimage and Travel in Mediaeval and Modern Islam,* Richmond, England, 1993, 75–85

————. *Petualangan Ibnu Battuta: Seorang Musafir Muslim Abad ke-14,* Jakarta, 1995. Indonesian edition.

Durkee, Noura. *The Amazing Adventures of Ibn Battuta,* Washington, D.C., 1995. For children.

El Moudden, Abderrahmane. "The Ambivalence of *Rihla:* Community Integration and Self-Definition in Moroccan Travel Accounts, 1300–1800." In Dale F. Eickelman and James Piscatori, eds. *Muslim Travelers: Pilgrimage, Migration, and the Religious Imagination,* Berkeley, 1990, pp. 69–84

Gibb, H. A. R., ed. *The Travels of Ibn Battuta A.D. 1325–1354, Translated with Notes from the Arabic Text Edited by C. Defremery and B. R. Sanguinetti.* 5 vols. Vols. 1–3: Cambridge University Press for the Hakluyt Society, 1958, 1961, and 1971. Vol. 4: Translation Completed with Annotations by C. F. Beckingham. London: Hakluyt Society, 1994. Vol. 5: Index, A. D. H. Bivar, Compiler, Aldershot, England: Ashgate Publishing, 2001

Guennoun, Abdallah. *Memoirs of Important Men of Morocco: Ibn Battuta.* Rabat: Islamic Eucational, Scientific and Cultural Organization, 1996

Hamdun, Said, and Noel King. (trans. and eds.). *Ibn Battuta in Black Africa.* Foreword by Ross E. Dunn, Princeton, N.J.: Markus Wiener, 1994

Ibn Battuta: Actes du Colloque international organizé par l'Ecole Supérieure Roi Fahd de Traduction à Tanger les 27, 27, 29 octobre 1993, Tangier, 1996

Ibn Battuta: Muslim Scholar and Traveler. Calliope 9 (April 1999). Entire issue.

Kruk, R. "Ibn Battuta: Travel, Family Life, and Chronology: How Seriously Do We Take a Father?" *Al-Qantara: Revista de Estudios Árabes* 16, 2 (1995): 369–84

Mackintosh-Smith, Tim, ed. *The Travels of Ibn Battutah,* London, 2003

————. *Travels with a Tangerine: A Journey in the Footnotes of Ibn Battutah,* London, 2001

Mapelli López, E. "Escolio sobre la Málaga de Ibn Battuta (1350)." *Boletín de la Real Academia de Córdoba* 65, 126 (1994): 221–9

Martínez Enamorado, V. "Granadinos en la Rihla de Ibn Battuta: Apuntes biográficos." *Al-Andalus* 2 (1994, 1996): 203–21

Mazzoli-Guintard, C. "Le Royaume de Grenade au milieu du XIVe siècle: Quelques données sur les formes de peuplement à travers le voyage d'Ibn Battûta." *Voyages et voyageurs au Moyen Age: XXVIe Congrès de la S.H.M.E.S. (Limoges-Aubazine, mai 1995),* Paris, 1996, pp.145–64

Morgan, David O. "Ibn Battuta and the Mongols." *Journal of the Royal Asiatic Society,* 3rd ser., vol. 2 (April 2001), pp. 1–11

Netton, Ian Richard, "Arabia and the Pilgrim Paradigm of Ibn Battuta: A Braudelian Approach." In Ian Richard Netton, ed. *Arabia and the Gulf: From Traditional Society to Modern States: Essays in Honour of M. A. Shaban's 60th Birthday,* London 1986, pp. 29–40

Norris, H. T. "Ibn Battuta's Journey in the North-eastern Balkans." *Journal of Islamic Studies* 5, 2 (1994): 209–20

Rumford, James. *Traveling Man: The Journey of Ibn Battuta, 1325–1354,* Boston, 2001. For children.

Tolmacheva, Marina A. "Ibn Battuta on Women's Travels in the Dar al-Islam." In Bonnie Frederick and Susan H. McLeod, eds. *Women and the Journey: The Female Travel Experience,* Pullman, Wash.: Washington State University Press, 1993, p. 119–40

INDEX

Page numbers in italics refer to maps.

Cover Design: Madeleine Ward
Compositor: Star Type, Berkeley
Printer and Binder: Maple-Vail